Pushkin in 1827

John Mersereau, Jr.
RUSSIAN
ROMANTIC
FICTION

Ardis, Ann Arbor

Y 10 5

Ardis Publishers
2901 Heatherway
Ann Arbor, Michigan 48104

Mersereau, John, 1925-
    Russian romantic fiction.

    1. Russian fiction—19th century—History and criticism. 2. Romanticism. I. Title.
PG3098.3.M47 1983   891.73'3'09   82-20758
                ISBN 0-88233-739-4 (cloth)

CONTENTS

Mikhail Lermontov

Introduction

Russian Realism has received an enormous amount of critical and scholarly attention at home and abroad, and rightly so, but Realism's very popularity has been at the expense of other movements. Romanticism, for one, has not only been particularly neglected but even pointedly ignored. Until recently Soviet scholars have operated as if Romanticism were the enemy of Critical Realism or Socialist Realism, and, notwithstanding their current efforts to rehabilitate Romanticism, they still tend to distinguish "progressive," "active," "revolutionary," and "Decembrist" Romanticism from the socially and politically negative "passive," "reactionary," and "esthetic" Romanticism. Further, what little attention has been focused upon Romantic authors has been directed at the poets of the movement, while the writers of fiction have continued to suffer from benign or deliberate neglect. Collected works of some Romantic prose writers have been published in Russian, but there have been almost no monographic studies devoted to individual authors. Outside the Soviet Union, the situation has been worse, even despite the absence of discrimination against Romanticism per se. Teachers of Russian literature, myself included, have little time and few texts to bridge the gap between the Sentimentalism of Karamzin and the Realism of the early Turgenev and Tolstoy, and so, in covering the nineteenth century, we hop from Pushkin to Gogol to Lermontov and then right on to the titans of psychological Realism, leaving unmentioned, and certainly unread, a whole body of sometimes fascinating fiction.

This study seeks to provide a comprehensive picture of Russian Romantic fiction in its evolution from Sentimentalism to Realism, a period embracing roughly 1815 to 1840. Pushkin, Gogol, and Lermontov will be seen in the midst of the movement to which they belonged, and we shall learn that this trio, though distinguishable from their contemporaries by the quality of their writing, were operating under the same dominant norms as their less talented comrades.

Readers are free to disagree with my definition of fiction, which for the purpose of this study includes travel notes, at least until 1830, and excludes most fairy tales. The travelogue was a vital school for prose writers, and in that genre one often finds elements of fiction. The fairy tale, if authentic, belongs to oral literature. Adaptations and stylizations of fairy tales are, admittedly, fiction, but works in that manner have quite special norms and are basically unlike the rest of imaginative prose.

9

My approach to the analysis of the texts of Romantic fiction is eclectic and based on personal interest. My main concern is with the texts and their literary components. Of course, one cannot help but bring in history, politics, sociology, and philosophy, or even authors' biographies. However, I do not believe in seeking to explain literature in terms of biography, because the correlation is often arbitrary and of little utility. So, the focus here is upon the texts and what is in them, not upon what the author supposedly intended or what some critics think was intended. In general, the texts must also be taken as a whole, and any interpretation must involve all of the whole, not just parts which conveniently suit one's analysis.

The best, the mediocre, and the downright poor rub shoulders here, original and innovative writers mingling with hacks and epigons. The story must be presented this way, for the hierarchy of values which we set today was not the same at the time of Romanticism's reign. Probably I have overlooked some authors of relative merit, and for that I beg their and the reader's pardon. I also apologize for those cases where I unjustly mock certain works, forgetting that my perspective of one hundred and fifty years is an advantage which should not be employed superciliously. Still, I have tried to be fair and to evaluate the works in the context of their period.

Some readers may wonder why there are so many long quotations and plot summaries. The quotations are there to provide some tangible examples in support of my descriptions of an author's style and typical features, and because, owing to the absence of translations of most of the works, it is unlikely that the average reader will have access to the works themselves. Even those who know Russian will find it difficult to obtain Russian texts, since many of the works discussed are out of print, available only at large libraries in Europe or America, or are locked in rare book sections of libraries in the Soviet Union. While realizing that plot summarization is not scholarship or criticism, I feel that the synopses will not only provide the reader with the general content of the works in question but also enable him to synthesize for himself something of contemporary Romantic attitudes and concerns, at least insofar as the writers of fiction reflected them. The translations are all my own, and doubtless there are a number of *gaffes,* for which I shall eventually be suitably chided.

This book is not heavily footnoted. In general, I have tried to indicate useful works available in English which deal with the period or particular authors, but I have avoided citing Russian references. The specialists know who they are, and the rest will ignore them in any case. Further, I have refrained from discussing most of the polemics which characterized the Romantic movement and its critical aftermath, because this information does not help much in understanding the works in question.

A work of this magnitude cannot hope to please everyone, and probably every reader will find too much of one thing or too little of another. I hope, however, the work will stimulate further study of Russian Romanticism, for there is much still to be done, and my own approach to this topic is but one of the many ways which may prove helpful and interesting.

John Mersereau, Jr.   *University of Michigan*

Nikolay Karamzin

Pyotr Vyazemsky

A dinner at the bookseller Smirdin's, Pushkin fourth from left

Stepan Shevyryov

Mikhail Pogodin

Nikolay Polevoy

Alexander Voyeykov

Fyodor Dostoevsky

Vissarion Belinsky

Kondraty Ryleev

Faddey Bulgarin

I. Fiction at the Turn of the Nineteenth Century. Karamzin's Language Reform. Sentmentalism—Karamzin, Klushin, Zhukovsky, Batyushkov. The Picaresque Novel—Narezhny.

This is the story of the coming of age of Russian fiction, which from its humble background in the first decades of the nineteenth century developed so rapidly and positively that it became the major European prose literature of the second half of the century. The period under consideration is roughly 1815 to 1840, and the term Romanticism (with a capital *R*) is applied to distinguish the prevailing literary mode from Neoclassicism and Sentimentalism as predecessors and Realism as its successor. The focus is upon the literary product of the period, and I deliberately avoid any effort to explain the "romantic" motivations of the authors or to theorize about the romantic spirit of the age.[1] Without delving into technicalities at this point, I will simply state that in the movement termed Romanticism certain genres and norms of composition were dominant, and the authors who employed these genres and implemented these norms are Romantics (again with a capital *R*).[2] One must, however, bear in mind that literature is in a constant state of evolution, rapid or otherwise, and there is, consequently, some difficulty in distinguishing between late Sentimentalism and early Romanticism or late Romanticism and early Realism. The evolutionary process in the latter case had been happily defined by the formula, "Realism is just Romanticism on all fours."

What about the proposition that there really was no Romantic movement as such in Russia? Those espousing this idea would reject our periodization of 1815-1840, claiming that these years represent a "transitional" period when no movement worthy of the name can be distinguished or defined. Let us leave aside Pushkin, Lermontov, and Gogol, temporarily acquiescing to the theory that they were not Romantics.[3] But what about the dozens of poets and prose writers whose works filled the many journals and almanacs of the twenties, the thirties, and even later, who had little to do with Sentimentalism and who cannot by any interpretive leap be called Realists? And what about the critics, often authors themselves, who very *self*-consciously considered themselves Romantics and saw their art as representing a movement distinct from trends prevailing at the turn of the century? That these self-styled Romantics were sometimes confused, that their definitions of Romanticism were vague, personal and even mutually exclusive, does not mean that there was no Romantic movement.[4]

Russian Romanticism developed, it is true, after German Romanticism, and it reached its zenith before French Romanticism did. It lacked the philosophical baggage of the German movement, but then it did not become mired in philosophy. It was a self-conscious movement, much more so than its counterpart in England. Its poets were not inferior to the English, and they were

15

better than the French or Germans. Russian Romantic prose lacked the richness of the English and French, but its fiction was as good or better than the romantic fiction produced in Germany. Moreover, the Russian Romantic fictionists prepared the ground for the Russian Realism which dominated European literature in the second half of the century.

In seeking the origins of Russian Romanticism, one can easily get lost in the minutia of cause and effect. Those who favor a typological definition of romanticism independent of period or movement can easily find romantic elements in the twelfth century epic *The Lay of the Host of Igor,* but this chameleon can also be used just as effectively by those seeking a typology for realism. Although the Romantic Movement spans roughly the years 1815-1840, it is useful to start our history in the latter part of the eighteenth century, for certain significant developments in the Russian literary language at that time were subsequently vital to the character of Romantic fiction. So that is where we shall begin.

Of critical importance at the end of the eighteenth century was the introduction of a new style of literary Russian destroying the authority of the Slavono-Russian which had been the vehicle for Neoclassical poetry. This reform, initiated by Nikolay Karamzin, challenged Mikhailo Lomonosov's[5] formulation, the so-called theory of three styles, which had sought to prescribe the proportions of Slavonic and Russian according to the nobility of the literary genre employed. So, for example, epics and odes should employ a "high style" based on Slavonic and Russian, elegies and middle genres should get along with standard Russian, and farces and other low fare might even use words and expressions found in the vernacular. Nikolay Karamzin, an enlightened disciple of European Sentimentalism, employed in his poetry and prose a middle style, eschewing Slavonic, which he considered barbaric, and also avoiding vernacular Russian, which was in his opinion much too coarse for polite communication. His "salon style," with simplified syntax patterned on French and English, vast numbers of words and phrases imported for the sake of expressiveness, and a new sensibility, was immediately popular. Moreover, it became the vehicle for translation of western European Sentimentalists, pre-Romantics, and Romantics. Vasily Zhukovsky, a poet blessed with a great original talent *and* ability as a translator, further developed Karamzin's language in his rendering of Gray's "Elegy" (1802) and later in translations from Schiller, Millevoye, and others.[6] Zhukovsky's Russification of Buerger's ballad *Lenore*, which he called *Liudmila* (1808), had enormous success, introducing not only a craze for ballads but increasing public appetite for smooth, sonorous, light, and emotion-charged verse.

Karamzin's salon style and the sentimentality and subjectivity which infused it were not favorites of everyone, and especially the die-hard Neoclassicists resisted these innovations, claiming that the glory of Russian eighteenth-century poetry was attributable to the retention of the Slavonic element in the poetic language and the distinction of high, middle, and low styles. In

1802 Admiral Shishkov, who later was to become Minister of Education, united a group of these literary (and political) conservatives in The Colloquy of Lovers of the Russian Word and joined battle with the Karamzinists. In particular they objected to barbarisms, or foreignisms, represented by unnecessary usage of foreign words, such as the substitution of the Russified French word *voyazh* for the perfectly adequate *puteshestvie*.[7] The Colloquy also objected to the pretensions to elegance of the Karamzinists, who ornamented their diction with periphrasis, inflating a simple statement such as "the moon shines" to "pale Hecate mirrors the wan reflections."[8] Moreover, the conservatives rejected what they considered petty genres cultivated by Karamzin's disciples.

Some of Shishkov's ideas were shared by a small but effective group of younger poets and dramatists, among them Pavel Katenin, Alexander Griboedov, Alexander Shakhovskoy, and Wilhelm Kuechelbecker.[9] These writer-critics shared with the Colloquy a kind of literary nationalism: for Shishkovites this meant the retention of eighteenth-century poetic norms and preservation of the Slavonic elements in the literary language; the concern of the younger archaists was that Russian literature and the literary language maintain their Russianness and not become the lackeys of western European masters. By the time this latter band took the field in the mid-teens, Karamzin was occupied with his monumental *History of the Russian State* and out of the contest. Therefore, they directed their darts at Zhukovsky, whose poetry and prose exemplified the foreign conceits of subjective Sentimentalism and the salon diction introduced by Karamzin. Zhukovsky found worthy support from his fellow members of Arzamas, a convivial literary group whose level of seriousness is evidenced by its name having been taken from a town famous for roast goose. Among those who gathered to read their satires on the odes and other pompous fare of the Shishkovites were Zhukovsky himself, Constantine Batyushkov, Prince Peter Vyazemsky, Denis Davydov, Vasily Pushkin, and his young nephew, Alexander.

Arzamas disbanded in 1818 after three years of fun, less from a surfeit of roast goose than an absence of worthy foes. The Colloquy of Lamers of the Russian Word, as Shishkov's group was facetiously known,[10] was no longer in real competition, and thus the *raison d'être* of Arzamas was gone. At the same time, the humor of Arzamas' lampoons had become a bit stale, since there was a limit to the laughs that one could get from parodying such Shishkovite gems as "Ode on the Return of My Beloved Brother From a Sea Voyage of Eighteen Months."

The appearance in 1820 on Alexander Pushkin's mock epic-fairy tale, *Ruslan and Liudmila*, to some degree rocked everyone's boat, literary liberal and conservative alike. Basically, the language derived from Karamzin, but many Slavonicisms were included for burlesque effects and, following the lead of the younger archaist Pavel Katenin, a spicing of vernacular Russian. A few years before, in 1816, Katenin had attempted to demonstrate to the

Karamzinists, and particularly to Zhukovsky, that the proper diction for ballads included vernacular, and Katenin's own adaptation of Buerger's *Lenore*, which he called *Olga*, was far more sinewy and folkish than Zhukovsky's smooth and decorous *Liudmila*.

Reaction to Pushkin's *Ruslan and Liudmila* was as varied as the work itself. Zhukovsky acknowledged the supremacy of his sometime pupil's verse with a portrait inscribed "To the Victorious Student from the Vanquished Teacher," but an anonymous critic of *The European Herald* said that the effect of Pushkin's work was just as if an uncouth peasant had intruded himself into an elite social gathering.[11] The Neoclassicists objected to the mixture of the heroic and the vulgar, voicing their disappointment that Pushkin had not provided Russian literature with a proper epic—an accomplishment which had proved beyond their own powers. The delightful humor and effervescence of Pushkin's verses were lost upon others, who became confused by the poet's playful vagueness and intentional mystification.

Irrespective of the enthusiasm, naivete, or indignation with which *Ruslan and Liudmila* was received, it clearly marked a new era in Russian poetry, later to be recognized as the Golden Age, which lasted two decades and was dominated by Pushkin and his Pleiad of art for art's sake poets, Yevgeny Baratynsky, Baron Anton Delvig, Prince Vyazyemsky, Denis Davydov, Nikolay Yazykov, Ivan Kozlov, and others.[12] Their contemporaries, the so-called "Civic poets," such as Kondraty Ryleev and Alexander Bestuzhev, also displayed fine poetic craftsmanship, but their voices were silenced after the Decembrist revolt of 1825. The majority of the poets of the Golden Age continued to write verse after 1830, but prose rapidly replaced poetry in the favor of the public, so the decade of the thirties was less brilliant than the previous one, at least from the public's point of view. The only new, first-rate poet to appear in the thirties was Mikhail Lermontov, and thanks to his talent the Golden Age lasted four and a half years after Pushkin's death in 1837.

Russian poetry had roots, a history, and its poets of the eighteenth century were not at all contemptible. The rapid developments which took place from 1790 onward, irrespective of whether they were based on Karamzin's reform or not, made use of the strong foundation laid during the earlier part of the century. The Golden Age did not float unanchored, it was not accidental, except perhaps for the genius of Pushkin, and even without him there would have been at least a Gold Plated Age. But the story with prose was quite otherwise.

For the Neoclassicists, poetry was the language of the gods, and they cultivated that language. Fiction was for clerks and literate house serfs, for only they could be interested in such salacious rubbish as Mikhail Chulkov's *The Comely Cook, or the Adventures of a Debauched Woman* (1770). The same went for Fyodor Emin's sentimental imitation of *La Nouvelle Heloise, The Letters of Ernest and Doravra* (1776), which might have titilated vulgar mentalities, sentimental girls, and the literarily naive, but had little value for the convinced Neoclassicist. In his opinion, if one had to write novels, then they should serve the cause of virtue, show the triumph of reason and duty. To create characters who were largely motivated by erotic considerations, that is, characters whose hearts ruled their heads, was a shady occupation and probably contributed to immorality. The dictates of the self-styled guardians of Parnassus were generally accepted, or at least given lip service, while many young girls and even society matrons shed a tear with Emin and kept his book hidden under a pillow.

Karamzin shattered these Neoclassicist prejudices, at least for many, and in effect he legitimized fiction. The date to remember is 1792, when his *Poor Liza* (*Bednaya Liza*) convinced his generation that "even a peasant girl can love." With that work and his *Letters of a Russian Traveler* (*Pis'ma russkogo puteshestvennika*), published the same year, he introduced into Russian prose the subjectivism, emotionalism, and sensibility of Sentimentalism. And, of course, both of these works were presented in the decorous language of the salon, a literary Russian made easier to understand because it seemed more French than Slavic.

Letters of a Russian Traveler, which derived from Charles Dupaty's *Lettres sur l'Italie* (1746-1788), had an enormous influence on domestic literary tastes and the development of the prose literary language. Here, suddenly, was a charming introduction to European habits, cuisine, towns, nature's spectaculars, and famous men, all presented in the pleasing style of a sensitive traveler. Most of his readers were really quite ignorant about Europe, and they were eager to learn, so much the more that in so doing they might share the author's tender sentiments, that they might shed a tear with him, as in the following passage, where he recounts the activities of the famous Swiss theologian and physiognomist, Johann Lavater (1741-1801):

Lavater surprises me more and more, my dear friends. Imagine, he never has a free hour, and the door of his study is almost never closed. If a beggar leaves, then some unfortunate person demanding consolation arrives, or a traveler, demanding nothing, but distracting him from his work. Moreover, he visits the sick, not only those living in his own parish but in other ones. Today at seven o'clock, having dispatched several letters to the post office, he seized his hat, ran from the room, and told me that I could go with him. "We shall see where," I thought, and followed him from street to street, and finally right out of town to a peasant's yard in a small hamlet. "Is she still alive?" he asked the elderly woman who met us in the entrance. "The soul scarcely remains," she answered with tears and opened for us a door into a room where I saw an old, wasted, and pale woman lying on a bed. Two boys and two girls stood next to the bed and were crying, but catching sight of Lavater they ran to him, took both his hands and began to kiss them. He approached the sick woman and asked her kindly how she was. "I am dying, I am dying," the old woman answered and could say no more, fixing her eyes on her breast, which was rising upwards in a frightening manner. Lavater sat down next to her and began to prepare her for death.

Karamzin's geographical sketches were also informative and emotional:

Early this morning I left Mainz in a large post carriage with five companions, and we arrived at Mannheim at seven in the evening, having followed the western bank of the Rhine through Oppenheim and Wurms.

This upper part of Germany may be called an earthly paradise. The roads are as smooth as a table, everywhere rich vineyards, everywhere trees laden with fruit. Pears, apples, walnuts grow along the road (a sight bringing ecstacy for a denizen of the north accustomed to see sad pines and orchards wet with steam, and Arguses standing guard with clubs!). And along these generous valleys meanders the honorable, wine producing Rhine, carrying on its wavy crest the blessed fruits of its shores, fruits which cheer the hearts of people in distant lands which have a less beneficent nature.

Speaking of Leipzig, Karamzin emotes:

Here, my dear friends, I had wanted to spend my youth. Here for several years previously my thoughts had yearned. Here I had wanted to gather what was needed to seek that truth about which my heart had anguished since my earliest years! But fate did not want to fulfill my desire. Imagining how I might have spent those years, in which, so to say, our soul is formed, and how I did spend them, I feel grief in my heart and tears in my eyes. That which is lost will never return.

It is amusing to compare Karamzin's reactions and style with those of Denis Fonvizin (1745-1792), the playwright whose satires on gentry ignorance, brutality, and egregious Gallomania put him at the top of Russian eighteenth-century dramatists. Fonvizin made a trip abroad about the same time as Karamzin, but whereas Karamzin saw only the good and the beautiful, Fonvizin saw mostly the bad and ugly. What impressed him about Leipzig were the baths with running water, the number of hunchbacks, and the abundance of beggars. Or:

In a word, gentry travelers lie unconscionably when describing France as an earthly paradise. No argument that there's much good in it, but I don't know that there isn't more that's bad.

At times his language becomes downright coarse:

The gentry (in Germany) doesn't know its snout from its ear. . . . The streets are narrow, the houses tall and packed with Germans, who have mugs a yard wide. . . . I asked for coffee. . . and such vile slops I've not seen since I was born—it would make a person vomit. . . . Paris itself is just a little bit cleaner than a pigsty. . . . Bedbugs and fleas tormented us barbarically.

For the twentieth century reader, Fonvizin's acerbity presents a pleasant contrast to the sometimes cloying effusions of Karamzin, but it was Karamzin's style which became fashionable.

Karamzin's *Poor Liza* merits discussion, not because it is part of Romantic fiction, but because it gave respectability to imaginative prose and, what is more, became a permanent allusion for subsequent Romantic and Realist authors. The immediate effect of its publication was that poor Liza became den mother to a whole fictional troop of poor Mashas, poor Mariyas, and even a deceived Henrietta, most of whom were shortly forgotten.[14] But Liza herself continued to be remembered, and when subsequent female characters were given that name, such as Pushkin's Lizaveta in *The Queen of Spades* or Dostoevsky's Lizaveta in *Crime and Punishment* (Raskolnikov's "unintentional" murder victim), there was always some implication of relationship to their earlier namesake.

Liza is a comely peasant girl, a paragon of filial piety who is determined to support her widowed mother:

"God gave me hands to work with," said Liza, "You fed me from your breast and watched after me when I was a child. Now it is my turn to watch after you. Only stop grieving, stop crying. Our tears will not bring Daddy back to life."
But often kind Liza could not restrain her own tears. Ach! She recalled that she had had a father, and that he was no more. But for her mother's peace of mind, she tried to hide her sadness and appear calm and joyful.

One day while selling lilies-of-the-valley on the streets of Moscow, Liza meets "a well dressed young man of pleasing appearance" who buys her flowers and impresses her with his gentility and generosity. The next day he appears at her cabin and introduces himself to her mother as Erast.

Now the reader must know that this young man, this Erast, was a rather rich nobleman with an unusual mind and good heart, good by nature, but weak and flighty. He led a confused life and thought only of his own pleasure, which he had sought in the diversions of society but seldom found. So he had become bored and complained about his fate. At the first meeting, Liza's beauty had made an impression on his heart. . . . It seemed to him that he had found in Liza that for which his heart had so long been searching. "Nature calls me to its embrace, to its pure joys," he thought, and he decided, at least for a while, to abandon high society.

Predictably, their meetings lead to declarations of love, and then one evening at their solitary rendezvous,

She threw herself into his embrace—and her chastity was shortly to perish! Erast felt an unusual agitation in his blood—never had Liza seemed to him so charming—never had her caresses touched him so strongly—never had her kisses been so flaming—she knew nothing, suspected nothing, feared nothing—the dark of evening nourished desires—not a single starlet gleamed in the sky—no light could illuminate the error—Erast feels an agitation within himself—Liza also, not knowing what is happening, not knowing what is being done to her. . . Ach! Liza, Liza! Where is your guardian angel? Where is your innocence?

Erast finds that his dream of idyllic bliss with his simple shepherdess is destroyed by dalliance, and he parts with Liza, lying to her that his regiment has been called into action. There is a tearful farewell, nights of anguished solitude, and then one day in Moscow she sees him riding in a carriage. She follows him to a mansion, where he tells her that he intends to marry another. In a daze she accepts the hundred rubles he puts in her pocket, is ushered

21

to the street, and there she faints. When she comes to, she wanders out of town and finds herself on the bank of a deep pond near the Simonov monastery. A young girl friend comes up, Liza gives here the hundred rubles (prudently assuring her the money was not stolen), and then she throws herself into the water.

Thus ended the life of one beautiful in soul and in body. When we are *there*, in a new life, we shall see each other, and I shall recognize you, tender Liza.

Poor Liza was almost immediately the inspiration for a tragedy from a higher sphere of society, Alexander Klushin's *The Unfortunate M—v* [*Neschastnyj M—v*] (1793). The title figure, a young man of erudition and taste, but without wealth or fame, becomes tutor to the daughter of a rich nabob, and they fall in love. The father discovers his daughter's breach of standards and the lovers are parted. M—v retreats to a garret, immerses himself in self-pity and *Werther*, and suffers "unimaginable tortures." A series of missives to the girl are the final expression of M—v, who at last shoots himself. The father is stricken with remorse.

Karamzin prefaced his tale with the declaration that "I love those things which touch my heart and cause me to pour forth tears of tender grief!" and Klushin's epilogue concludes, "All those who knew M—v suffered for him, all poured forth their tears, and I pour forth mine—and these minutes are the very sweetest in my life." The pleasures of melancholy and grief which Karamzin's and Klushin's narrators affirm is, of course, more convention than real sensibility. But the norms of the period required this, just as they required the presence within the story of the narrator (generally identified with the author) as commentator and guide, who had not only the right but the duty to warn or admonish his characters, as well as the task of interpreting their actions and pointing up the moral for the reader.

The potential for sentimental effusions is in itself rather limited, and writers who attempted the tale in the language of Karamzin soon began to repeat themselves. One substantial contribution of the Romantics was in broadening the prose literary language, of deepening its channels with respect to the depiction of emotion, a necessity which is very evident when one sees the stylistic poverty of the Sentimentalists in this respect. In Klushin's story we are virtually incinerated by the following series: "fiery tears," "the flame of love," "his heart burst into flame," "Sofia loved him, loved him tenderly, flamingly," "the fire of love," and several more similar locutions. The author is also very fond of *tremble*: "a trembling voice," "he feels a strong trembling," "he approached her with a tremble," and at least a dozen more variations are easily found. Palpitations combine with flame to produce: "With a tremble he leaned towards her, kissed her, and she kissed him on the cheek—and fire poured across his face."

The periphrastic elegance of Karamzin and his disciples, which was so irritating to the Shishkovites, is nicely demonstrated here with the following description: "A rosy dawn pours across the horizon; the magnificent luminary raises its proud forehead," the latter clause meaning "the sun rises." Elegance notwithstanding, the wording is further indication of Sentimentalism's lexical and locutionary poverty: Karamzin had also called the sun "the luminary of the day."

There is no reason to overkill with examples. Sentimentalism was extremely popular, and it was, at least at first, a unique experience for Russians to read stories in their own language depicting their countrymen in a prose which neither violated good taste nor offended madam with harsh Slavonicisms and crude vernacular. Karamzin's language, nonetheless, was circumscribed, limited, and soon even conservative. If the prose literary language were to prosper, it had to break the prohibitions implicit in the salon style, expand the lexical content by admitting words and phrases used beyond the drawing rooms of the *beau monde*. Then, too, the formulaic nature of Sentimentalism also impeded development, and prose needed new subjects, new types, as well as a new style. Romanticism provided these.

In *Poor Liza* the narrator's fatherly solicitude for his heroine, his "Achs" and his professions to love sweet melancholy, have often been understood as those of the author himself. This identification of the author with his narrator was typical of the readership at the time of Sentimentalism and continued through the Romantic period, when poets especially were credited with one hundred percent equivalence between what they as persons had felt and what they as poets had written. However, today we recognize that Karamzin's effusions were largely a conceit, a style adopted by him from western European models and translated into his reformed literary language. In this sense he was following in the footsteps of the greatest Sentimentalist fakir of them all, Laurence Sterne, whose crocodile tears had set all Europe weeping. Still, readers took Karamzin quite seriously, and they made pilgrimages to the Simonov monastery to view the site of Liza's last moments, pouring their own tears into the fatal pond to mingle with those of Karamzin, his narrator, Liza, Erast, and others.

It is not a criticism of Karamzin to assert that his Sentimentalism was a literary manner rather than an expression of his heart. On the contrary, it shows his perspicacity and modernity with respect to matters literary. This is further substantiated by his intimate knowledge of Neoclassical cliches, many of which also found a place in Sentimentalism. Take another work of that same year, 1792, *Natalia, the Boyar's Daughter* [*Natal'ia, boiarskaia doch'*]. Karamzin opens with almost Sternian playfulness:

I intend to communicate to my kind readers a historical legend or story, which I heard in the region of the shades, in the realm of the imagination, from the grandmother of my grandfather, who in her time was considered quite eloquent and almost every evening related fairy tales to the tsar's wife. . . . Ach! At this very minute I see an unusual light in my dark corridor, I see flaming circles which rotate with glitter and crackling, and, finally—oh, wonder! they form your image, an image of indescribable magnificence! Your orbs sparkle like suns; your lips are as scarlet as the dawn, as the peaks of snowy mountains at the rising of the luminary of the day. You smile, as a young creation in the first day of its life smiled, and in ecstacy I hear your *sweetly thundering* words: "Continue, my dear great great-grandson!" So, I will continue, I will. And, arming myself with a pen, I shall manfully sketch the story of *Natalia, the Boyar's Daughter.* But first I must rest. The ecstacy to which I was carried by the appearance of my great great-grandmother has sapped my spiritual strength. I shall put down my pen for several minutes—and these lines which have already been written will be an introduction or foreword!

Comparing Natalia to a rose, the fairest of flowers, he continues:

. . . But no beautiful girl could compare with Natalia, Natalia was the most charming of all. Let the reader imagine the whiteness of Italian marble and Caucasian snow, he still will not imagine the whiteness of her face, and imagining the color of Zephyr's beloved, he still will not have a complete idea of Natalia's scarlet cheeks. I fear to continue the comparison, not wanting to bore the reader with a repetition of that which he already knows, for in our magnificent age the store of poetic comparisons for beauty has been exhausted, and more than one writer chews on his pen with vexation, seeking but not finding new ones.

The story is a parody of the chivalric-adventure story, a genre of fiction popular (but not with strict Neoclassicists) in the latter part of the eighteenth century. The plot is simple, so simple, in fact, that Karamzin openly toys with the idea of making it more involved. Natalia, raised in innocence in medieval Moscow by her widowed boyar father, reaches the age when a husband is indicated. At church she sees a handsome young stranger, falls instantly in love, and although no words are exchanged, knows that he responds. The young stranger bribes Natalia's nurse and gains access to her tower, where, after some tender, passionate, and flaming kisses, the stranger reveals that his name is Alexey. He convinces her that she must elope with him that night or he will perish, and so they take the old nurse and flee in the wee hours, leaving behind a message for her father which explains that they will return only when Alexey has earned the right to call himself the boyar's son-in-law. After a secret marriage, they drive to a remote habitation in a forest, where they are greeted by armed men carrying torches. The old nurse is sure they have fallen into the hands of cut-throats:

Right towards them came five or six men with bundles of flaming splinters and armed with long knives which hung at their belts. The old nurse, seeing this wild, solitary habitation in the middle of an impenetrable forest, seeing these armed men and noticing on their faces something severe and violent, became terrified, wrung her hands and cried out, "Oh, ah! We've perished. We are in the hands of—robbers!"

At this point Karamzin tells us how he might have developed his story, had he not been so stuck on the truth:

Now I might have presented a fearful picture to the eyes of my readers, deceived innocence, betrayed love, an unfortunate beauty in the power of barbarians, of killers, the wife of the leader of the robbers, a witness to terrible crimes, and finally, after a life of torment, dying on the scaffold under the axe of justice in view of her unhappy parent. I might have presented all this in a believable and natural manner, and a sensitive person would have poured forth tears of grief and woe—but in that case I would have departed from the historical verisimilitude on which my narrative is based. No, dear reader, no! This time save your tears—calm yourself—the old nurse made a mistake. Natalia is not in the hands of robbers!

Rather obviously we are dealing here with an author—or he is dealing with us—who is quite aware of typical reader reactions and enjoys playing with them, deliberately withholding information for the sake of suspense. He can generate tears or not, as he wishes, and he cares not at all whether his implied reader likes it or not.

The story continues with prosaic verisimilitude. The newlyweds live blissfully in the woods until spring. Word then arrives that vicious Lithuanians have invaded Muscovy, and Alexey vows to regain his family's honor on the field of battle. Natalia accompanies him dressed as a boy. The scene shifts to Moscow, where the Tsar and Natalia's father anxiously await news of the conflict. A messenger arrives with word of victory. The army leader reports that just as defeat seemed inevitable, an unknown Russian, crying "We shall die or be victorious," inspired a counter-attack and himself captured the leader of the invaders. The report also mentioned the hero's younger brother, "a handsome lad," who had protected him with a shield. The army returns to Moscow, Alexey throws himself at the Tsar's feet and identifies himself as the son of the accused traitor, Liuboslavsky. The Tsar tells him that the Liubovsky name has long been cleared; Natalia is rejoined to her father; all live happily ever after.

The fairy tale nature of this plot is sufficiently evident, and the narrator's amused attitude toward his story is maintained throughout. The complete facetiousness of the narrator is underscored by the non-description of the wedding night: "My modest muse covers her face with a kerchief—not a word!" and the triviality of their existence at Alexey's hideaway: Natalia does handwork and Alexey sketches landscapes (heroes of the chivalric-adventure story were always artistic, but usually as musicians). He is free to idle away his time in this manner because it is no longer necessary to combat wild beasts which previously prowled the environs:

But Alexey no longer fought with wild beasts, for they (as if from respect for the beauful Natalia, the new inhabitant of their dense forest) did their roaring only in the distance.

A quite different variety of historical tale is Karamzin's *Martha the Mayor* [*Marfa posadnica*], written in 1802, which concerns Novgorod's defeat by Ivan III. Virtually from the time it had become Christianized,

Novgorod had enjoyed self-government. Its princes were elected by the *veche* (town assembly), which also dismissed those who proved unpopular or ineffectual, and after 1270 the town often did without a prince at all, relying on the elected mayor. History provides the plot and the central character, Martha Boretskaya, who rallied the Novgorodians against Muscovy's expansionist aims and who paid for her zeal with her life. The love interest is absolutely minimal: we are simply informed that Martha gives her daughter in marriage to the warrior Miroslav, who is chosen leader of Novgorod's troops and who perishes in battle. There is almost no dialogue, but there are several lengthy exhortations by Martha and others addressed to the populace. What Karamzin attempted here was to invest the bones of historical fact with a bit of flesh, a technique he later used to advantage in his *History of the Russian State*. Surprisingly, the sentimental potentials of this tale are not exploited, for the author does not see Martha as a victim of the oppressor Ivan III but rather sees them both as embodiments of opposing *raisons d'état*.

The language of the story, especially in the context of Sentimentalism, seems almost matter-of-fact:

> Delinsky died in battle, and the remnants of the army were hardly able to save themselves. The citizens and officials [of Novgorod] wanted to see Martha, and her broad courtyard filled with crowds of people. She opened the window and said, "Do what you want to!" and closed it. Feodosy, at the demand of the people, sent emissaries to Ivan: Novgorod would give him all its wealth, would withdraw from all territories, desiring only to preserve its own internal government. The Muscovite prince answered, "The Sovereign is merciful, but he will not accept conditions." Feodosy, in the deep night by the light of the torches, announced to the citizens the decisive answer of the Great Prince. Their gaze involuntarily sought Martha, involuntarily was fixed on her high tower. There a night lamp is extinguished. No one wanted to be the first to express agreement with the demands of Ivan. Finally his friends became emboldened and said, "God subject us to the Muscovite Prince. He will be a father to Novgorod."

Karamzin abandoned fiction in 1804 to undertake his monumental *History of the Russian State* [*Istorija gosudarstva rossijskogo*], which utilized an expository style more or less similar to that of *Martha the Mayor*. But at the time when Karamzin was abandoning the conceits of Sentimentalism, others were finding them still viable, as is clearly evident from the fiction of the poets Zhukovsky and Batyushkov, both of whom had a try at the historical tale.

Zhukovsky's tale, *Mariya's Grove* [*Mar'ina roshcha*] (1809) takes place in some misty period when shepherds lived idyllic lives along the Moscow River and were menaced only by crude warriors who inhabited gloomy towers.

> Good Mariya blossomed like a violet of the fields, upon the porch of her parental cabin, protected by her mother's love. For a certain time her soul had been filled with a secret flame, which enlivened in her all other feelings—love for the handsome Uslad. But this

feeling did not hinder her from being as happy as before, watering her flowers as she had done before, nurturing her raspberry bush, singing her happy songs as she sat with her mother knitting on the threshold of the cabin, laughing right from the heart when her friends told her their funny tales. The handsome songster felt a tender languor when he looked into the eyes of the kindhearted Mariya. Ach! He loved her passionately. Her dear image hovered before him when he was falling asleep, it appeared in his dreams, he saw it as the first glimmer of the dawning day. Uslad was melancholy when he saw her before him, alive, playful, happy. Mariya sighed, and her face showed deep and sincere feelings when her eyes met the eyes of Uslad. She rejoiced when Uslad convinced her of his tender love. Then she would kiss his rosy cheeks and say to him, "Good Uslad, you are my happiness."

Good Uslad has to go away for three moons, and while he is gone good Mariya catches the eye of a brutal knight, Rogday. Tempted by his wealth and his promise to take her to Kiev-town, Mariya gives her hand to Rogday, an act which merits the narrator's gentle admonition:

Ach! Who would have thought this, good Mariya? But why should one accuse her good heart? It had never betrayed Uslad. You were deceived, Mariya, when you convinced yourself that you no longer loved your friend. Your blindness will soon disappear; soon the previous feelings of love, to which you had become accustomed, with which you were so happy, will again arise in your soul. . . and what will happen then, innocent, deceived, unhappy Mariya?

When Uslad returns, he learns from Olga, Mariya's friend, that even before the wedding Mariya had second thoughts, and especially so after it. Yearning for Uslad, Mariya aroused Rogday's wrathful suspicions. He discovered the worst one day when his wife inadvertently called him "Uslad," declaring she loved him more than life itself. In Olga's words:

How can one describe the effect which her words produced in the soul of the terrible Rogday? His face purpled, his eyes gleamed like coals, he ground his teeth, fearsomely. "Uslad? What have you said, unhappy woman?" But Mariya was like an insane person. She didn't sense that Rogday even stood before her. With a spasmodic movement she pressed his hand to her heart and said,"Why should I love? I loved him more than life. All is finished!" Rogday trembled. In a fury he grabbed her around the body with one arm and flew, like a grey wolf with its prey, to the top of the mountain, to his fearsome tower. I wanted to follow. "Be off!" he roared in a hoarse voice, shining his beast-like eyes on me. My legs failed me.

In the abandoned tower Uslad finds mementos of Mariya's life, and a white apparition then leads him to a hermit's hut in a nearby grove. The hermit relates how Rogday had cast the dying Mariya from his horse and ridden away, later to drown while crossing a river. Uslad lives on with the hermit, buries him when he dies, and later dies himself, his head resting on Mariya's tombstone. In time the grove became known by the name of the innocent girl who perished there, Mariya's Grove.

The historical tale was to become one of Romanticism's major genres, but in order to do so it had to evolve from the saccharine fairy tale type of story to a narrative with a more specific historical background and characters who were more than abstractions. A link between Zhukovsky's type of tale and the full-blooded Romantic historical narrative is provided by Constantine Batyushkov's *Predslava and Dobrynya*, written in 1810 (although not published until 1832 in Delvig's almanac *Northern Flowers*). This is a tale of Kiev in the days of its glory under Prince Vladimir, Christianizer of Rus (old Russia, with Kiev at the hub), scourge of his enemies. The story opens with the return of Vladimir and his army from a victorious foray against the invading Pechenegs. The heroic warrior, Dobrynya, who is in love with Vladimir's daughter, Predslava, is denied her hand because his station is unsuitable. Against the girl's wishes, she is promised to the odious Bulgarian prince, Radmir. At a tournament Dobrynya bests Radmir in several contests, and he also soon beats him to the conjugal bed. The jealous Radmir surprises the lovers, and Dobrynya, caught with his *Panzer* down, is no match for Radmir, who slays him. Predslava falls upon his icy corpse, "like a lily plucked by the breath of inclemency, like a sacrificial victim consecrated to love and ineluctable fate."

What distinguishes this story from Zhukovsky's is the effort to recreate, albeit in a stylized manner, the image and atmosphere of life in old Kiev. The customs of the times, the clothes, the foods and amusements are all described, and in effect the plot and characters are simply a means of parading all this lavish detail before the reader. In this respect, *Predslava and Dobrynya* is an early variant of that group of Romantic historical tales which focused almost exclusively upon sociological and anthropological details in an effort to reproduce the way of life at a particular place and time in the past.

The lengthy discussion of Karamzin and the background of the historical tale have been pursued here in order to provide some general idea of the stage of development reached by the prose literary language and fiction in general around 1820. The examples reveal a definite poverty of style, a reliance upon cliches of expression, plot, and character. But the Karamzinian line was shortly to undergo revitalization, enabling fiction to move forward to a new stage, Romanticism.

The Karamzin—Zhukovsky—Batyushkov continuum (it will be extended later) was just one main current in the stream of early nineteenth-century fiction. A lesser, but still important, line of development was represented by the fiction of Vasily Narezhny (1780-1825), whose works derived from the didactic-adventure tale of the eighteenth century, in both its imported and domestic variations. The title of Narezhny's work of 1814, *A Russian Gil Blas* [*Rossiiskii Zhil Blaz*] provides more than a clue as to its model. Lesage's *Gil Blas* had been translated into Russian in the 1750's, along with a flood of miscellaneous western European and English authors including Talman, Prévost, and Richardson. From that point on, popular European works appeared in Russian translation without lengthy delay, and Narezhny had access not only to a translation of Lesage's picaresque novel but also translations of *Candide, Tom Jones,* and most of Rousseau. All of these find some echo in *A Russian Gil Blas, or the Travels of Prince Gavrila Simonovich Chestyakov.* It is the story of a well-meaning but incredibly naive provincial nobleman, a virtual pauper who, incongruously, is a prince, and his trials and tribulations as he travels in search of his unfaithful wife and their son. In a series of episodes presented in the typical picaresque string-of-beads fashion, he encounters a variety of persons, most of them incarnations of gentry foibles. All of his misadventures emphasize to him the Candidian moral, "One should trample one's own garden."

Only the first three parts of *A Russian Gil Blas* were published while Narezhny was alive. The final three parts were prohibited by the censor owing to their critical examination of gentry vices and implications hostile to the system of serfdom. They were printed for the first time in 1939!

Narezhny's novel has some domestic sources as well in the strong satirical tradition of Russian tales going back to the seventeenth century and the drama of the eighteenth century. An almost contemporary model was Alexander Izmailov's *Eugene, or the Pernicious Results of Bad Education and Companionship* [*Evgenij, ili pagubnye sledstvija durnogo vospitanija i tovarishchestva*] (1799-1801), a revelation of the seamier side of life accomplished with evident gusto by the author. Izmailov styled himself "Terniers No. 1," and when Narezhny appeared on the literary scene, he accorded him the right to be known as "Terniers No. 2."

"Terniers No. 2" had a manner quite distinct from that of Karamzin. About the only qualities they share were overt didacticism and occasional (for Narezhny) tears of joy, gratitude, and pity. Despite some Sentimentalist attitudes, Narezhny for the most part did not write in the dulcet tones of the Karamzin school, and he gave little indication of caring about the decorum of the salon. His characters speak vernacular Russian, and his uneducated gentry figures have their own colorful idiom. One of his most important contributions to the development of Russian fiction was exactly this broadening of the literary language to include speech from the lower classes, *declasse* gentry, or others from outside polite society, an effort that called forth criticism from literary purists. Anticipating the objections of the guardians of the Russian tongue, Narezhny lampoons the Academy in a delicious scene where Philolog, a caricature of Admiral Shishkov, proposes to eliminate foreign borrowings from Russian by replacing them with words derived from Slavonic roots. Thus "tragedy" (*tragediia*) finds its proper substitute in "grief-howling" (*pechal'novoishche: pechal'*–grief; *voi*–howl).

A Russian Gil Blas is a humorous social satire in the eighteenth-century manner. The characters have tag names (Kuroumov: *kura*–chicken; *um*–brain), and there is comic exaggeration of their dominant traits. The crudity of certain scenes denied Narezhny the approval not only of the effete Sentimentalists but also of the Neoclassicists, who generally discounted fiction (at

29

least publicly) and particularly so if it was earthy. His recognition as an important contributor to the development of fiction came only later when Vissarion Belinsky, the doyen of Romantic critics, declared that Narezhny's *Bursak* (1824) and *The Two Ivans* (1825) were "the *first* Russian novels.[15]

II. Liberalism and Romanticism—Glinka, Pushkin, Somov.

Some briefing in history is necessary at this point in order better to clarify certain qualities and developmental lines in Russian fiction in the early decades of the nineteenth century. Of immense significance was the fiasco of Napoleon's Moscow adventure in 1812 and his subsequent total downfall, for which the Russians rightly took a great deal of credit and which strengthened their self-assurance as a nation and as individuals. Moreover, Russian officers who found themselves in western Europe as a consequence of Napoleon's defeat were exposed to liberalism, republicanism, and human rights, which in general had been suppressed in Russia since the reaction which followed Catherine the Great's disenchantment with ideals of social reform. When these Russians compared their own position with that of their social counterparts in Europe, they were unavoidably aware of their subjugation and political impotence. It did not behoove the conquerors of the invincible Napoleon to play the thrall to anyone, and this idea gained currency as the aura of glory which had surrounded Alexander I was replaced by the fog of his own obscurantism and the despotism of his reactionary henchmen. Overt criticism was naturally impossible, but the gentry malcontents indulged their opposition at secret meetings, the more restrained advocating freedom for serfs and a constitutional monarchy while the most radical called for regicide and a republic. There were no media for propagandizing their ideas openly, but they became adept at insinuating their ideas, cautiously of course, into poetry, prose, and drama.

A preliminary goal of these reformers was to arouse in the gentry a sense of pride, of responsibility, of mission and then to mobilize this consciousness, if not for revolutionary purposes, at least to the support of attitudes favorable to reform from within the existing socio-political structure. The task of motivating a social elite whose goals were largely sybaritic, whose tastes were western European, and who, since Peter III, had had no obligation to serve the state, was enormous. The liberals attempted to instill a patriotic nationalism, appealing to Russia's heroic history of defense against Pechenegs and Tatars, its defense of Christianity, its manifest destiny. Topics and heroes were not hard to come by, since from the days of Rus the country had been reluctant host to a stream of uninvited guests. The Russo-Polish conflict of the seventeenth century provided a rich lode of events and personalities for "civic" literary treatment, involving as it did the Polish occupation of Moscow, the defeat of pretenders claiming to be the long lost son of Ivan the Terrible, the expulsion of the Poles, massive battles against the Polish-Lithuanian Union for control of the Ukraine. The Cossack hetman, Zinovy Chmielnitski, who later achieved the appellation of "Bogdan" or "God-given," was a perfect model for patriotic emulation, since he was not only a fierce defender of Orthodoxy (at least in legend), an indomitable warrior, but also a fighter for liberation, for freedom. Moreover, the Chmielnitski mystique was also connected in Russian minds with the traditions of Sech-Beyond-the-Falls, a Cossack military community whose leaders were elected, where majority views prevailed, where one was free to come and go.

One of the first to celebrate Chmielnitski in prose was Fyodor Glinka (1786-1880!), a retired officer who had acquired a distinguished reputation in the campaigns against Napoleon. He had published his experiences first in 1808 in *Letters of a Russian Officer*, [*Pis'ma russkogo oficera*], and he expanded this work in 1815-16 under the same title with details of the Fatherland War of 1812. In 1816 Glinka played a major role in founding the Petersburg Free Society of Lovers of Russian Literature, and he became its permanent president in 1819. Meanwhile, he had written a historical tale centering on Chmielnitski, and this had been published in 1817 in *The Emulator* [*Sorevnovatel'*], the monthly issued by the Free Society.

Zinovy Bogdan Chmielnitski, or the Liberated Ukraine [*Zinovii Bogdan Xmel'nickij, ili osvobozhdennaya Ukraina*] epitomizes the methods used by the liberal and radical writers to recreate history in the form of object lessons. In keeping with the high seriousness of its purpose, this variety of historical tale shuns the facetiousness of *Natalia, the Boyar's Daughter,* and there is no Sternean play with the reader. In his introduction the author excoriates the Poles for oppressing the Ukrainians and deplores the absence of a history of the Ukrainian Moses, Chmielnitski:

Captivated by the great deeds and fame of the Little Russian hero, I wrote a narrative based on historical legends: "Zinovy Bogdan Chmielnitski, or Little Russia Liberated." Florian's *William Tell,* Bitaube's *The Batavians, or the Liberation of Holland,* and similar compositions of this sort have always, unless I am mistaken, been very pleasing to readers.

Glinka never finished his story, and therefore we learn only of the hero's early life, his filial piety, his deeds of valor in Tatar ranks against the Turks, and his return to the Ukraine, where he finds that a haughty neighbor, the Polish Pan Czaplicki, has flooded out his family home, desecrated their church, and brought about his father's death. Chmielnitski goes to avenge these wrongs, and he finds the malefactor in his gardens:

"I am unknown to you," said Chmielnitski, "but hear me out. Zinovy Bogdan, son of Filomar Chmielnitski, asks the Lithuanian magnate: Who put my father in his grave? Who destroyed the temple built by him? Who covered with water the place of my birth and washed from the earth the as yet unmouldered bones of my ancestors? Answer! And judge what I should demand from the person who committed these deeds!" The eyes of the hero burned with that terrible fire of indignation which in the past had made whole detachments tremble. His blood boiled, and his sword, glittering with diamonds, shook at his hip. Czaplicki looked about him: there were no thralls around! The hero's appearance made him tremble. He hid his ire and answered with feigned humility:
"Restrain your anger, son of Filomar! Old age alone was the cause of your parent's

death, a spring flood of the river inundated your valley, and. . ."

"No," exclaimed Chmielnitski, "you, villain, you are the only one responsible! You sacrificed to your insatiable luxury the ancient possessions of peaceful families! You, daring blasphemer, destroyed God's shrine, you buried my parents alive! Oh, you snakes who suck the breast of my Fatherland! How long will you feed on our tears and blood? How long? But first you must receive retribution from the hand of the avenger of Little Russia. Draw your sword and defend yourself!"

Czaplicki let out a cry of despair and was numb with terror. Chmielnitski brandished his sword. . . when suddenly a piteous cry stopped him. A maiden, charming as an angel, rushes out from behind a tree, exclaiming through her tears: "Spare, spare my parent!"

Chmielnitski is so struck by girl's beauty that he drops his weapon, which his cunning enemy seizes. Defenseless, the future savior of the Ukraine is soon captured.

Apostrophe to readers, to characters, to nature, and to the Divinity were common to earlier Sentimentalist fiction, and Glinka expands the technique with apostrophes to abstract qualities such as friendship and patriotism. Otherwise, however, his effort at a Slavic *William Tell* shows little development beyond the stage of Batyushkov's *Predslava and Dobrynya.*

Fyodor Glinka, who was thirty-one when he published his *Zinovy Bogdan Chmielnitski,* incorporated just about all of the salient features of the typical historical tale, frosting his cake with patriotic pathos. We shall return to him from time to time, for he persisted as a writer throughout the period of Romanticism, compensated for his good intentions and literary limitations by a long life. His death in 1880 at the unusual age of ninety-four belies the idea that Russian Romantics died young—but then Glinka wasn't really a Romantic but rather a late blooming Sentimentalist.

Each additional year of Alexander's reign caused the reformers and radicals increasing exasperation and provided more compelling reasons for their opposition to the autocrat. Many young intellectuals, even while remaining outside revolutionary ranks, voiced their discontent at the absence of personal freedom, the repressive domestic atmosphere, the censorship, the secret police, the intrigues and denunciations that typified the hotbed of suspicion and fear that was Russia. Young Alexander Pushkin was typical of the disaffected youth, and in a series of poems and epigrams, which circulated only in handwritten copies, he proclaimed the advent of freedom and mocked the Tsar and his agents.[1] Ultimately these were seen by the authorities, and Pushkin, who in 1820 had just reached majority, was ordered to southern Russia. The conditions of his exile gradually became more stringent, and finally he was ordered to stay put at the family estate of Mikhailovskoe, and there he remained until 1826. Other writers were more circumspect in airing their ideology, and they suffered no reprisals. Meetings of the Free Society of Lovers of Russian Literature were one avenue for judicious expression of liberalism, and in general the Free Society was made up largely of literary and political liberals. It was this group that was in the forefront of those who welcomed Romanticism from abroad and fostered the domestic movement.

According to Belinsky, "dark rumors about some sort of *romanticism*, along with knowledge of an important English poet *Beeron*," began to appear in Russian journals around 1813.[2] Excerpts from *The Corsair* were translated in *The Russian Museum* in 1815, but long before that, of course, Zhukovsky had translated a wide selection of Schiller, Goethe, Uhland, and lesser German poets. Most of the young gentry naturally knew French and the ideas underlying the Romantic manifestation in France, especially those of Rousseau and Chateaubriand, were quite current in intellectual circles. As in France, Parny, Lamartine and Millevoye were favorites, Russian admirers particularly appreciating their subjective content, which made their poetry, irrespective of its antique form, seem novel. Along with Zhukovsky, Batyushkov was introducing foreign poets to Russia by means of translation, and with his own original verse, which he called "light poetry," he sought to make his native language as mellifluous as Italian. Both poets were mentors of Pushkin, and evidence of the influence of both can be found in *Ruslan and Liudmila*, whose appearance in 1820 has already been marked as a red letter event. The unusual and unexpected qualities of Pushkin's mock epic-fairy tale suggested its identification with other innovative works, and thus Alexander Voyeykov, a sometime Arzamasian, defined the poem as "romantic." In his assessment, the distinguishing elements of *Ruslan and Liudmila* were its qualities of the folklore heroic, the folklore fairy tale, and the comic. "Nowadays," he declared, "this type of poetry is called romantic."[3] A rival commentator advised Voyeykov to read Byron and see if his unique definition could be confirmed.[4]

Voyeykov's confusion was symptomatic of virtually all those who grappled with the problem of defining Romanticism. And grapple they did, with just about as many definitions as definers. One wonders why it was so important for Russian writers to pin down the term, when the English, for example, were content to do without it entirely. Prince Vyazemsky, who supposedly was the first to use the term in Russian criticism, summed up the prevailing confusion in a letter to Zhukovsky. Alluding to the Russian house spirit, a shy Poltergeist-like imp which bears the name *domovoy*, he declared:

Romanticism is like *domovoy:* many believe in it, there is a conviction regarding its existence, but what are its characteristics, how is one to define it, how is one to put his finger on it?

One of those who tried, and rather successfully, to "put his finger on it" was Orest Somov (1797-1833), a Ukrainian immigrant to the literary world of Petersburg and a member of the Free Society of Lovers of Russian Literature. In 1823 *The Emulator* carried in three installments his long essay *On Romantic Poetry* [*O romanticheskoi poezii*], which was the first[5] effort by Russian critics to provide a systematic treatment of the subject. Much of this essay derived directly from the ideas of Mme de Staël about national literatures, and Somov acknowledged his source as he paraphrased portions of her *De l'Allemagne*. Romantic poetry, in Somov's (derivative) conception, must freely express those qualities of its creators which distinguish them from other peoples. Essential to achieving this are qualities of national identity, or *narodnost'*, and locality, or *mestnost'*.[6] Somov sees ancient Greek drama as embodying *narodnost'* and *mestnost'*, whereas French Neoclassical drama, because it imitates the Greeks, does not. If poets are true to their individual national spirits and locales, each country will develop a unique romanticism, and this has been evidenced by Shakespeare and Byron in England and Zhukovsky and Pushkin in Russia.

The third part of *On Romantic Poetry* is the most original, a rather vehement exhortation to Russian poets and authors to forego imitation and avail themselves of the enormous potentials for an independent romanticism found in their own national identity and locality:

I have often heard the assertion that there cannot be a national poetry in Russia, that we began too late. . . that nature in our fatherland is flat and monotonous, that it does not have those glittering charms or those magnificent terrors which distinguish nature in several other countries. . . that the age of chivalry did not exist for us. . . that we have very few legends, and those are rather unpoetic, etc. etc. This unjust opinion falls of its own accord when we look around ourselves or contemplate *Russian antiquity*.

Somov sees the Russian chronicles as a rich source of information about the past, and he advises authors to read the annals of ancient towns such as Novgorod, Kiev, Chernigov, Vladimir, and Moscow. He asks that writers find material for their art through knowledge of the many and diverse peoples who inhabit the Russian land:

How many different countenances, temperaments and habits present themselves to the inquiring gaze within the compass of the totality of Russia. Not to mention the Russians themselves, here appear Ukrainians, with their sweet songs and glorious memories, there the militant sons of the quiet Don and the valorous immigrants of Sech-Beyond-the-Falls: they all. . . bear traits of difference in temperament and appearance. And what if we cast our gaze at the borders of Russia, inhabited by the ardent Poles and Lithuanians, by peoples of Finnish and Scandinavian extraction, by the inhabitants of ancient Colchis, the descendants of immigrants who witnessed Ovid's exile, by the remnants of the Tatars who once threatened Russia, by the many and varied tribes of Siberia and the islands, by the nomadic generations of Mongols, by the violent inhabitants of the Caucasus, by the northern Lapps and Samoyeds.

The conclusion of the essay rises to a fine rhetorical pitch as Somov exhorts the Russian poets to "do their duty":

The Russian people. . . must have a national poetry which is original and independent of foreign legends. Russian heroes established the fame of the fatherland on the field of battle, men of firm spirit have honored her chronicles with patriotic deeds. Let Russian bards occupy the position of the great bards of antiquity and recent times through their new and original poetic charms! Let there be reflected in their exalted songs, as in a pure stream, the spirit of the people and the qualities of a rich and magnificent language, by its very sounds capable of conveying victorious thunder, elemental combat, the ardent transports of unbridled passions, the quiet languor of hopeless love, cries of happiness, and the gloomy echoes of grief.

If Somov's essay sounded a rallying cry in the name of romanticism, it did not provide a distinctly designed flag which authors might follow. Romanticism's essential ingredients, *narodnost'* and *mestnost'*, were themselves sufficiently vague to promote further confusion. And confusion continued to reign, with all sorts of individualistic interpretations emerging. What Pushkin had to say on the matter is of particular importance, not only because he styled himself—rather vaguely, one must admit—a romantic, but because he was probably the most perceptive critic of his times.[7]

Until 1825 Pushkin did not publicly concern himself with the definition of romanticism, and before that date most of his remarks are found in correspondence with Prince Vyazemsky. While Pushkin had appeared to accept Vyazemsky's ideas on romanticism expressed in his preface to Pushkin's *The Fountain of Bakhchisaray*, now in 1825 Pushkin began to take issue with everyone, Vyazemsky included. Writing to him in May, he made an interesting prediction about French literature (later realized by Victor Hugo) and chided his friend about his understanding of romanticism:

You seem to love Casimir (Delavigne), I don't. Of course, he is a poet, but all the same not a Voltaire, not a Goethe. It's a far cry from a snipe to an eagle! The first genius there (France) will be a romantic and will carry the French away to goodness knows where. By the way, I have noted that with us everyone (and you, too) has the haziest notion of romanticism.

Included among that "everyone" were other friends, particularly Alexander Bestuzhev and Wilhelm Kuechelbecker. Writing in November to Bestuzhev, whose ideas on the evolution of literatures he had previously completely discounted,[8] he exclaimed:

Something important! I have written a tragedy [*Boris Godunov*] and am very satisfied with it. But I am terrified of publishing it—our timid taste will not stomach true romanticism. With us, when speaking of romanticism everyone means Lamartine. Whatever I read about romanticism is just wrong. Even Kuechelbecker talks nonsense.

The allusion here is to Kuechelbecker's article of 1824 in *Mnemosyne*, "On the Direction of Our Poetry," in which the critic had discussed the origins of romanticism and attacked that which was commonly identified as romantic in contemporary Russian literature. Not without foundation did Kuechelbecker criticize Zhukovsky, Pushkin, and Baratynsky, all of whom were his friends, for being parties to the imitativeness and repetitiousness of contemporary poetry:

36

An imitator knows no inspiration: he speaks not from the depths of his own soul, but forces himself to repeat another's concepts and feelings. Power? Where will he find it in the majority of our turbid, effeminate, colorless works, which define nothing? Everything is *a dream* or *a vision, everything appears to be* or *seems to be* or *gives an impression,* everything is only *as if, as it were, something or other.* Richness and variety? Having read one elegy by Zhukovsky, Pushkin, or Baratynsky, you know them all. . . . And the imagery is always the same: *a moon,* which, it goes without saying, is *melancholy* and *pale:* there are cliffs and groves where they never existed, a forest behind which a setting sun appears for the hundredth time, evening glow. Now and then there are long shadows, visions, something unseen, something unknown, banal allegory, pale, tasteless personification of *Labor, Bliss, Peace, Joy, Sadness,* the author's *Laziness* and the reader's *Boredom.* And in particular there is *fog:* fog over the pine woods, fog over the fields, and fog in the writer's head.

Later, in the draft of a rebuttal to Kuechelbecker, Pushkin was to say that this article had "served as the basis of all that had been said against romantic literature in the past two years."

Pushkin attempted a more formal approach to the matter of romanticism in an unpublished essay, "On Classical and Romantic Poetry." Here he attributed the confusion about romanticism to French journalists, "who usually related to romanticism everything that seems to them to be marked by the stamp of dreaminess and German ideology or which is based on the superstitions or legends of the common people. . . ," features which may be found in manifestly classical works. Pushkin rejected using the spirit of a work as a criterion for labeling it classical or romantic, and he proposed that form be the determining feature. Works which have forms used by Greek and Latin poets would be considered classical, those which do not would be considered romantic.

Pushkin's solution was not very helpful, especially as he did not discuss prose at all. However, his remarks about *Boris Godunov* do express rather clearly what he had in mind when speaking of romantic tragedy. In 1827 *The Moscow Herald* printed a scene from *Boris Godunov,* and the following year the periodical's critic, Stepan Shevyryov, provided a positive review. Other critics were not so kind, which rather surprised Pushkin, who had earlier decided that the idolators of Neoclassicism were dead. As a friendly response to Shevyryov's review, Pushkin drafted a letter expressing his aims and means in composing his drama:

Strongly convinced that the outmoded forms of our theatre demanded reforms, I constructed my tragedy according to the system of Our Father—Shakespeare, and as a sacrifice to his altar I brought two of the classical unities, scarcely sparing the third. In addition to this notorious trinity, there is a unity about which French criticism makes no mention (probably not supposing that its necessity may be disputed)—the unity of style. This is the fourth necessary condition of French tragedy from which the Spanish, the English, and the German theatre have been delivered. . . honorable Alexandrine verse was changed by me to iambic pentameter, in several scenes I even stooped to hateful prose, I did not divide my tragedy into acts, and I even thought the public would say *many thanks* to me.

Voluntarily refusing the advantages offered to me by a system of art vindicated by experience, established by habit, I tried to substitute for that a faithful rendering of persons and time, a development of historical characters and events—in a word, I wrote a truly romantic tragedy.

Particularly significant in this draft is the extension of Pushkin's earlier concept of romanticism being essentially a matter of form. Now he adds the criteria of verisimilitude (of characters and actions), absence of affectation, freedom of innovation.

Finally to sum up Pushkin's concept of romanticism, one must note that it was not static, not reduced to a question of form alone but more essentially to a question of *freedom.* For him the progenitors of romanticism were Calderon, Shakespeare, Lope de Vega, those who created a new set of literary forms while displaying creative freedom. The term romanticism was misapplied to works marked by melancholy, or German ideology, or legendary material, and it was misapplied to contemporary French poets, whose product, in Pushkin's evaluation, had suffered because they had valued affectation more than freedom and sincerity. For Pushkin, Goethe was a true romantic in the full sense of his definition, his *Faust* was for modern (read Romantic) poetry what *The Iliad* was for antiquity.[9]

The whole sticky question of romanticism was bound, as is perhaps already evident, to the equally troublesome concept of *narodnost'*, national identity, national quality, national essence, or what have you, and Russian critics were hardly less vehement, less confused, or less ideological in discussing it than in polemicizing over romanticism. However, the quidities of romanticism have sufficiently burdened our discussion at this point, so let us return to the conclusion of Somov's *On Romantic Poetry*, with its cry to arms for the sake of an independent Russian romanticism.

While the poets certainly had the language and background to fill Somov's prescription, and were well into maturity by 1823, the prose writers were still in adolescence. If there is one subject that perceptive critics keep harping upon in the early twenties, it is the poverty of the prose literary language. Pushkin was particularly aware of the problem, and as early as 1822, in an unpublished fragment, he had noted his dissatisfaction with the primitiveness of Russian prose:

Exactness and brevity, those are the primary merits of prose. It demands thought and more thought, without which brilliant expressions are of no avail. Poetry is another matter (however, it wouldn't be harmed if our poets had a fund of ideas far more significant than one usually finds. Our literature isn't going to get very far with reminiscences of lost youth).

Question: Whose prose is the best in our literature? Answer: *Karamzin's.* That's not much to brag about.[10]

This concern comes, one must remember, over a quarter of a century following Karamzin's original efforts at reform of the literary language. Poetry, with its strong roots in the eighteenth century, flourished with the new language, which it successfully implemented with an ever broadening lexicon. But with prose the story was otherwise. The salon style was sufficient for the sentimental tales of Karamzin and his immediate followers, but as the years passed no particular devlopment occurred. Fyodor Glinka's historical tale of 1817 for all intents and purposes might have been written at the turn of the century—its language was ossified. And so the would-be fictionist of the twenties finds himself more concerned with the actual problem of language than with problems of genre, plot, and character. Now the prose language did change, as we shall soon see, but the extent of its change depended largely upon the talents of the individual authors, specifically the ones who were dynamic enough to break out of the Karamzinian rut.

Vasily Zhukovsky

Fyodor Glinka

Constantine Batyushkov

III. The Literary Almanac *Polar Star* (1823-1825). The Travelogue—Glinka, Somov, Bestuzhev-Marlinsky, Grech, Zhukovsky, N. Bestuzhev.

The year 1823 is the next red-letter one (remember 1820 and *Ruslan and Liudmila*?) in this history of Russian Romanticism, because January of that year saw the appearance of *Polar Star for 1823 [Poliarnaia zvezda na 1823 god]*, a literary almanac which was to set the pattern for a host of imitations, thereby serving as a catalyst for the Romantic reaction. Literary almanacs, annual anthologies of fiction, *belles-lettres*, and poetry, had a tradition in Russia going back to 1787, when the students at the preparatory boarding school attached to the University of Moscow first issued their *Blossoming Flower*. At the end of the century, Karamzin published several commercial almanacs, such as *Aglaia*, including in them his own sentimental works, poetry by Kheraskov, Derzhavin, Kapnist, and translations from Homer, Ossian, Gessner, La Fontaine and Voltaire. Even Benjamin Franklin was represented in Karamzin's almanac for 1798, *A Pantheon of Foreign Literature*. Through the first two decades of the nineteenth century, each year saw at least one new almanac, most of them surviving only the initial issue.

Polar Star for 1823 was the brilliant brainchild of Alexander Bestuzhev and Kondraty Ryleev, both members of the Free Society of Lovers of Russian Literature and committed to liberalism. Bestuzhev (1797-1837) had been educated in the Mining Corps and later received a commission in the Life Guards. In the early part of his military career he had been stationed near Peterhof at Marli, which suggested the pseudonym *Marlinsky,* the name with which he signed his first important prose work, *A Journey to Revel* (1821). Bestuzhev was destined to become the most popular writer of the early thirties, and the name *Marlinsky* has come to epitomize Russian Romanticism.

Kondraty Ryleev (1795-1826) was retired from the army by 1823 and was a high official of the Russian-American Company in Petersburg. He and his family had an apartment in the company building on Galley Port, and there also *Polar Star* was edited, probably with the help of Orest Somov, himself a head clerk in Russian-American Company. Whether or not Ryleev and Bestuzhev specifically conceived their almanac as an organ to propagandize revolutionary ideas is open to question, since only after the appearance of the first issue did they become members of the secret Northern Society, Ryleev joining in 1823 and quickly assuming its leadership, Bestuzhev joining in 1824 and being elevated to the Supreme Council in the spring of 1825. Their deepening involvement in revolutionary activities distracted them from work on subsequent issues of their almanac, and it is clear that Somov's role as editorial assistant became more important as time went on.

The first number of *Polar Star* offered criticism, prose, and poetry by the very best talents that Russian literature could provide. Its poets included Pushkin, Zhukovsky, Vyazemsky, Glinka, Ryleev, Delvig, Baratynsky, and its prose was provided by Bestuzhev, Faddey Bulgarin, Nikolay Grech, Osip Senkovsky, Glinka, and Somov.[1] So successful was this venture that the next issue, *Polar Star for 1824,* was sold out in three weeks. Since royalties were not paid contributors, the profit potential was attractive, and literary entrepreneurs did not let *Polar Star* exist without competition for long. Therefore, in 1825 several similar almanacs appeared, among them *The Neva Almanac [Nevskii Almanakh]* and *Northern Flowers [Severnye Tsvety],* both destined to be rather long lived.[2] These almanacs provide us with a good, if not entirely comprehensive, view of the state of Russian prose in the first half of the 1820's. Be forewarned, however, that the view is rather like a desert, with but an occasional bit of green to hint at the lush terrain of the second half of the century.

Polar Star for 1823 includes Bestuzhev's historical tale *Roman and Olga,* his anecdotes connected with the Napoleonic wars in *An Evening on Bivouac,* Faddey Bulgarin's *A Military Joke. A Non-Fictional Anecdote,* which is pure fiction, his Eastern tale, *The Distribution of the Inheritance,* and Osip Senkovsky's *The Beduin: A Translation from Arabian.* Fyodor Glinka, an inveterate composer of allegories, presented his *The Unknown Woman* and *The Unknown Acquaintance,* both mercifully short. The rest of the prose in the almanac is non-fiction: Bestuzhev's literary criticism, Bulgarin's *The Liberation of Trembovla,* Kornilovich's *On the First Balls in Russia,* Somov's sketch *French Eccentrics,* and Nikolay Grech's *Letters from Switzerland.*

A digression in connection with this last contribution, which belongs to the genre of travel notes, is in order. Strictly speaking, travel notes are not fiction and thus lie outside the focus of this study. Still, their role in the development of a viable and flexible prose style is too important to neglect. Also, who knows how really non-fictional anyone's travel notes are, especially when it is common knowledge that travelers often permit themselves departures from the pure truth for the sake of enlivening their narratives?

From the time of Karamzin's *Letters of a Russian Traveler* right up through the twenties this genre retained its popularity, and Russian readers were treated not only to notes about trips to Europe but also to exotic spots such as the Crimea, the Caucasus, Siberia, or even the Ukraine, which at that time was not really familiar to most Russians. The range of material which could be included was almost limitless, and if picturesque landscapes, Baedeker-type information, sketches of eccentric traveling companions, descriptions of the populace and their customs did not suffice, then the traveler might include an anecdote related to him by a fellow traveler or chance acquaintance. At this point, the border between fiction and non-fiction becomes undefined.

We need not bother with those travel notes which simply duplicate the Sentimental formulae of Dupaty-Karamzin tendency: a surprising number of teary-eyed gentlemen felt impelled to record their travel impressions for the edification of contemporaries and posterity. On the other hand, there were more than a few travelers of a less emotional bent who provided amusing and informative accounts of their journeys, which retain their interest even today. These writers all contributed in some way to the development of the prose literary language.

One of these, Fyodor Glinka, recorded impressions of military campaigns against the French in 1805-1806, at which time he was adjutant to General Miloradovich (killed by the Decembrists in 1825 while serving as Governor-General of Petersburg). Glinka's *Letters of a Russian Officer*, published in 1808, and their continuation, concerning the campaign of 1812, are of considerable intrinsic interest as history and because of their obvious influence on *War and Peace*. A comparison of earlier entries with those from 1812 reveals also a definite diminution of Sentimentalist tone and content. The battlefield of Krems in 1805 was described in this fashion:

Yesterday I was surrounded by a thousand different deaths, I saw blood flowing incessantly, I heard the whistle of bullets—and I remained alive. Early this morning I walked about the battlefield: the noise had died down, a deathly silence reigned in the valley, the sun delayed its rising, as if it feared to gaze at the place where the war had raged. And how could one not become terrified? The whole shore of the Danube was covered with corpses! In one place they lay in heaps, in others separated. One had seized his crushed head, another had clutched at his breast from which his life had flowed along with his blood. All feelings were agitated at viewing the slain. Oh, how base the race of man seems at such a minute!. . . Struck by this sad spectacle, which I had no chance to notice yesterday in the heat of the battle, I hastened across the smashed weapons to the top of the hill. As I went further away from the place of terror, it seemed that a new life was pouring into my breast along with the fresh air. A melancholy wind whistled in the gorges of the cliff, and mingling with it were the pitiful moans of the wounded, which rose up from the closer of those huts which stood in the depths of the bloody valley.

The entry for November 14, 1812, reads this way:

We stopped in Borisov, which had been destroyed and was still smoking from the conflagration. The unfortunate Napoleonites crawl about the smouldering ruins and don't feel that their bodies are being burned! Those who are more healthy press into the huts and live under benches, under stoves, and crawl into the chimneys. They howl terribly when we begin to chase them out. Recently I entered a hut and asked the old owner to light the stove. "It's impossible to light it," she answered, "Frenchmen are sitting in there!" We called out to them in French that they should come out quickly to eat bread. This worked. Immediately three of them, black as Arabs, jumped out of the stove and appeared before us. Each offered his services. One asked to be a cook, another to be a doctor, and the third to be a *teacher*! We gave them each a piece of bread and they crawled under the stove. Indeed, if you have some urgent need of Frenchmen, then instead of ordering them for good money, send as big a cart as possible and take them for nothing. They are easier to catch than crayfish. Show them a piece of bread, and you will attract a whole column.

Lest the unornamented quality of this passage suggest that Glinka had abjured his Sentimentalist proclivities, recall that his *Bogdan Chmielnitski*, published in 1817, displays many Sentimentalist traits. While Glinka's style for travel notes developed away from Sentimentalism, his "high style" for fictionalized history preserved many features of Karamzin's affective manner.

One of the best of those authors of travel notes who began publishing in the late teens was Orest Somov, who recorded impressions of his European grand tour in 1819-1820 in a series of letters addressed to friends in Petersburg. These were published in *The Emulator [Sorevnovatel']* and in *The Well-Intended [Blagonamerennyi]*, the latter a publication of the Free Society of Lovers of Russian Literature, Science, and the Arts, a rather conservative literary club to which Somov, and also many other members of the Free Society of Lovers of Russian Literature, belonged. For the most part his exposition is unembellished, straightforward, with a buoyant or humorous tone, a style which contradicts his own later critical pronouncements about the wretched state of the prose language. In *A Walk Along the Boulevards [Progulka po bul'varam]*, he imaginatively adopts the role of a *cicerone* conducting the reader through Paris and calling attention to points of interest. Passing rue de la Paix, boulevard des Capucines, we arrive at a section called chaussée d'Antin, which throngs with people, vendors, beggars, and there is even a sword swallower. We visit the Chinese baths, where one may soak and eat ices, we walk through a shop of expensive bronzes. Finally we arrive at the St. Denis Gates, where something unusual is happening:

Let's see why all these people have crowded into the middle of the road. Has there been an accident? Men and women, young and old, push one another to fight their way through the crowd and see. . . what do you think? A donkey, having become obstinate, didn't want to go on and fell down in the middle of the street. The donkey's owner, meanwhile, has been beating the stubborn beast with a club as hard as possible and, as loud as possible, scolding the curious gapers. The donkey rolls about and has no intention of getting up, and the gapers answer the abuse with loud laughter and suggestions, each one funnier than the next and more absurd. The owner, seeing that he can't do anything with the donkey alone, calls a comrade, with his help heaves the donkey onto a cart and hauls it away, accompanied by the loud laughter and caustic jokes of the crowd of funsters.

Somov's letter about the Tivoli Gardens [*Prazdnik v sadu Tivoli*] in chaussée d'Antin is equally colorful, full of the joy and activity of that bustling amusement park. Acrobats, singers, cyclists, fortune tellers, magicians, theatres, restaurants, dance pavilions, boat rides are all detailed, and the account ends with a description of the fireworks display which marks the closing of the park:

. . . several wheels of fireworks have been set up at the top of a high column, and a rope has been stretched from the ground up to them. A daring tightrope dancer, without a pole, ascends the rope and sits down between the wheels. At that moment they are ignited, and, with his head and shoulder showered with ashes from the fireworks, he descends as if nothing special were happening.

Another important event in the history of travel notes occurred in 1821, when Alexander Bestuzhev, over the pseudonym Marlinsky, published his *A Journey to Revel [Poezdka v Revel']* in *The Emulator.* The work has as its theme the heroic past of Livonia, which courageously sought to preserve its independence from hosts of foreign invaders. The work also shows Bestuzhev's deep interest in history, an interest which we shall see developed in a whole cycle of historical tales about Livonia.[3]

A Journey to Revel is a remarkable potpourri of travel notes, interpolated anecdotes, poetry, and history, presented for the most part in an informal, even chatty, manner. The travel details are, from the perspective of the jet age, somewhat unusual, such as being thrown from an overturned sleigh and knocked unconscious, almost perishing in a snowstorm, and enduring other perils unknown to the modern traveler. Woven in are descriptions of the local natives, with whom Marlinsky is sympathetic but not uncritical:

Estonia begins beyond Narva. No longer are any opulent post stations visible, the horses and the people are small, the forest becomes sparser the closer one gets to Revel, and the road gradually becomes narrower. The rock slab huts of the inhabitants, scattered among the bushes, seldom form villages. Every two or three versts [a verst is equal to two-thirds of a mile] are seen smoky taverns, without floors and with a huge hearth in the corner. In these the smoky Estonians, with matted hair which hangs to their belts, take refuge along with goats and calves. The steam goes down and the smoke goes along the ceiling. Entering such a place I always imagined myself in the subterranean kingdom of Pluto, and when exiting into the pure air, I always said, letting my gaze linger on the black faces of the Estonians and their dirty walls, "Nature is good—when it is washed."

However, having formed, like Jouy, the habit of observation—the rule is: listen to the rich and make the poor talk—I learned that the condition of the local peasants has quite improved in moral and physical respects. The landowners, cooperating with the aims of a wise government, are receiving benefits from this: the tilling of land is blossoming in this region, distilling encourages this, and the Estonians little by little are losing their habits of drunkenness, laziness, and all those vices accompanying ignorance... But, my friends, I am not writing a book or from a book, so I advise the curious reader to read the work: *Essai critique sur l'histoire de la Livonie*, in which the present condition of all Livonia is described in detail.

Whether Marlinsky's friends followed his advise and read Comte François-Gabriel de Bray's book is unknown, but clearly the censor neglected to do so: the work speaks unequivocally of the Livonians' dissatisfaction with their servitude and their frequent efforts to achieve independence.[4] The plight of the Estonians is, in fact, an underlying theme throughout *A Journey to Revel*, and it finds strong expression in the lengthy passages devoted to the history of the land, a chronicle of avarice, brutality, and incessant conflict. The story begins around 1200, when the Danish king, Waldemar II, joined the Lithuanians and Teutonic knights with the aim of Christianizing or killing the aboriginal Estonians, but in either case taking their land. In 1219 the heights of Revel were fortified, and in 1223 the Teutonic knights usurped the castle from the Danes (the Pope made them give it back within a few years). In the rape of Estonia the German knights were assisted by the Sword Bearers or Livonian knights, another unholy order that soon merged with them. Russians, Danes and later Swedes fought for control of Livonia, with such commitment that, for example, the castle at Wesenberg, near Revel, was captured and burned not less than twenty different times. Some of the history of Revel and its environs finds a place in Bestuzhev's historical tales, and one of them *The Tournament at Revel [Reveles'skii turnir]*, derives directly from a synopsis presented in *A Journey to Revel*.

The contemporary scene in Revel also receives the author's close attention, and we are informed about matters of dress, the importance attached to education by gentry families, the absence of social pretensions, the poor quality of the theatre. *Baedeker* information is also included, such as the facts that Revel contains 1,700 houses, has 12,000 inhabitants, became a member of the Hanseatic League shortly after it was founded, received its name from either *Regenfall* (rainfall), an unlikely possiblity, or *Rehfall* (from *Reh*, or goat)[Marlinsky's error: *Reh* is deer], one of which fell from the promentory when wounded by some royal hunter, or most probably from *Riff* or reef, by virtue of the large number of submerged rocks in the harbor.

Marlinsky provides the physical details of the town with playful reluctance:

You complain, friends, in your letter that I do not write about the town—what strange people you are! If you read a poem of Pushkin's, do you ask about the cover? When smelling a rose, who worries about the flower bed in which it bloomed? But you want this, and I, submissive to the commands of friendship, will leave my dark street (*Dunkel-Strasse*) [*sic*] and woe to your curiosity. If my patience is equal to it, I will not spare a single corner, a single alley, a single cornice.

All the streets of Revel are crooked and so narrow that the cabbies are obliged to drive with bells ringing in order to avoid collisions. A curious and garrulous gossip can easily look across the street and see everything in the chamber of her neighbor, count her plates, and even note to which of her guests she is the most solicitous. The streets turn, interweave, develop out of one another, but none follows any other or even follows itself. There are two squares, and those are not large or regular. The houses are rather tall, with pointed roofs (covered with colored, glazed tiles), their windows and doors in little squares like chessboards. The windows onto the street, obviously, have been cut through recently, for in a military town, already cramped to lessen the extent of the battlements, it would be dangerous in case of attack to expose oneself to the fury of the besiegers by giving them an opening through the houses. Mercantile prudence finished what had begun as a military precaution: the living rooms are facing courtyards, and the storerooms are in front of the buildings for convenience in storing goods.

A Journey to Revel also includes an anecdote about an episode in which the author and his horse were almost victims of quicksand:

Returning home on horseback from Krasnoe Selo at 10:00 at night, and wanting to take the closest road to the village where our squadron was camped, I lost the winding path and proceeded as best I could. You know that Petersburg is surrounded with subterranean bogs on which floating moss and plants form a deceptive cover. Not noticing that my horse had begun to force his way through, I drove him on further and further, and finally he made another lunge, struggled, and sat down. Deceived by the grass, I thought to reach the bank in three steps, and with my spurs I forced him to lunge forward, to sink again. Too late I noticed my carelessness. My voice would be lost in the empty surroundings—that I knew! A cold sweat broke out on my face, my hair stood straight up, and in my imagination were depicted all the stories of similar accidents. My horse struggled and fought. A fountain of water splashed from the hole and bubbled under the crust, the area around shook, the abyss sucked. To die in this manner and at such an age—how terrible!

Finally I sprang from my horse and, not wanting to let the comrade of my misfortune perish, I encouraged him with voice and bridle. Continually freeing myself, with a joyous beating of my heart I finally stepped onto firm ground. Imagine what a celebration for me, what a treat for my horse!

Whether Marlinsky's face was actually covered with cold sweat or whether his hair did stand straight up will never be known, but the literary formula for describing fear used here was repeated in many of his later tales, whose heroes gushed gallons of cold sweat and whose hair snapped taut on numerous occasions.

The new tone in travel notes typified by the rejection of emotive subjectivism and the development of informal, objective exposition is found also in Nikolay Grech's (1800-1858) *Letters About Switzerland [Pis'ma o Shveitsarii]*, which appeared in *Polar Star for 1823*. Grech, editor-publisher of *Son of the Fatherland*, a journal of belles-lettres devoted to the Russian victory of 1812, was in good standing with the liberal camp, and many of the foremost poets appeared in his periodical in the twenties. His letters are dated September, 1817, and if one trusts this dating—and there seems no reason not to—we can see this as an even earlier example than those of Somov or Bestuzhev-Marlinsky of the avoidance of the Karamzin-Dupaty conceits. Grech's dominant style is matter-of-fact *reportage:* a tour of Rousseau's birthplace, the histories of various cantons, descriptions of the Alps, the Danube, the Rhine, Lake Geneva, and anecdotes about local figures. The passage on Ferney is representative:

After dinner we went to Ferney. One has to have a most ardent and creative imagination to visualize in this small, delapidated house the past *capital of the European Philosopher,* from which he corresponded with sovereigns, moved, amused, fooled and deceived Europe. This house, or castle (chateau), is constructed around a court and situated with its main facade not facing the best part of the local surroundings. It has two floors, each of not more than six rooms. A housekeeper, accustomed to receiving guests, led us inside and showed us the living room, bedroom, and study of Voltaire. The furniture was covered with a faded blue silk material. In the bedroom stands a bed of simple wood. Over it hang shreds of curtains, which in the course of forty years have been torn off by writers. Poorly drawn portraits of Frederick II, Lelain, Voltaire himself and others hang on the walls. In the corner stands a clay model for Voltaire's monument, with the inscription: *His mind is everywhere, but his heart is here.* The theatre is destroyed. The church is in ruins. It is worth mentioning that at the beginning of the revolution the French

Jacobins destroyed the well-known inscription at the church's entrance, *Voltaire to God*. It seemed too Christian to them! Having inspected all corners of the once famous Ferney and having repeated the remark about the brevity of fame in this world, we got into a *char-à-banc* (a bad imitation of a drozhky) and returned to Geneva.

Travel notes continued to be one of the main genres for succeeding issues of *Polar Star*, and the 1824 number included *Pleasures at Sea [Udovolstvija na more]* by Nikolay Bestuzhev, the seafaring older brother of Alexander Bestuzhev-Marlinsky, a short piece detailing the appealing aspects of shipboard life, and Vasily Zhukovsky's *A Journey Through Saxony's Switzerland [Puteshestvie po Saksonskoj Shvejcarii]*, dated 1821. Knowing Zhukovsky's early attachment to Sentimentalism, one might expect him to reproduce the style of the Karamzin-Dupaty *voyage,* but he does not. Although he is enthusiastic in his descriptions of the fabulous natural beauties encountered on his hike through the Bohemian forests and mountains, and although his descriptions are somewhat more poetic than those of the restrained Grech, he seldom effuses and never sentimentally. His most subjective moment is when he tries to depict the full power of the view from the Bastey, a precipitous promontory, and he concludes that the real charm of nature is in its inexpressibility. Typical is his passage on *Kuhstall,* a natural cave of considerable attraction to tourists:

Kuhstall. We didn't give in to the desire to indulge ourselves and therefore arose early and, having breakfasted, set off on our way. For a certain time—while it was possible and in order not to waste our energy for nothing—we rode in a carriage along the bank of the source of the Kirnich. Finally our road turned into a path, we proceeded on foot and began to clamber up the slope towards *Kuhstall.* Having reached the top with difficulty, we went along a path lined with pruned trees to the cave's entrance, or, to put it better, to the huge gates made by nature itself among the cliffs. These gates are called *Kuhstall,* because in the Thirty Years' War the inhabitants of the surrounding places hid their cattle under them from the plundering of the Swedes. And they are so large that one could hide a quite large herd under them. In our times this refuge for misfortune has become an object of carefree curiousity, and the memory of past terrors only animates the pleasure which is produced by the marvelous view of the cave and the abysses surrounding it. Its vault and walls seem like a mosaic, so variegated are they with names of travelers who everywhere want to leave an eternal trace of their momentary presence. And we, too, wanted to taste eternity, and while I occupied myself with the temporal, that is, allayed my hunger with a roast potato, O.....v scrambled up a ladder and for the benefit of the future sketched his own and my name on a spot beyond which no one's daring hand will ever reach. In the cave there is everything needed for this: brushes and ink. In one place in the walls a kitchen has been hollowed out, in another a cellar, and all through the summer people live here who regale travelers with dinner and coffee. There are even harpists.

Zhukovsky and Nikolay Bestuzhev were back again in *Polar Star for 1825* with more travel notes, Zhukovsky's concerning Swiss Switzerland this time. He covered some of the same ground as Grech, and it is interesting to compare their descriptions of Ferney:

I was in the chateau of Ferney, which now belongs to citizen Bedet. Only the living room and bedroom of Voltaire are preserved in their original state. In the bedroom stands a bed with half-rotted curtains, and on the walls are paintings of Frederick II, Mme du Chatelet, a portrait of Catherine, and several engravings. On the stove stands a wooden, rather badly made urn, in which at one time Voltaire's heart was preserved. Now there remains only the inscription: *Son esprit est partout et son coeur est ici*, only even that is half destroyed. The *son* has fallen off the beginning and the *ici* from the end, and the result is nonsense. In the living room, where a bust of Voltaire stands on an ancient stove, there are several quite bad pictures, among them one depicting Voltaire's apotheosis which is particularly noticeable for its monstrousness: Minerva, it seems, meets Voltaire, and the avenging geniuses are scourging his enemies, Freron and others, with snakes. The alley along which the hermit of Ferney used to walk and the lime grove planted by him are preserved entirely. The inscription which he made over the entrance to the church he built (*Voltaire to God*) was destroyed by the philosophers of the Revolution.

Readers of *Polar Star for 1825* may have found Zhukovsky's contribution rather bland in comparison with that of Nikolay Bestuzhev, whose *Gibralter* is a quite intriguing combination of guide book details, lyricism, *reportage*, and political allusion. It must be said that this author is much more successful as a writer of travel notes than as a fictionist, as will become evident later. But in the former category he ranks with the best, both as an observer and as a stylist.

One senses he is approaching the Spanish and Portugese shores: twenty miles from land the morning breeze bears the fragrance of orange and apple trees. It is an ineffable feeling, aroused by the inspiration of these aromas, by the spectacle of the cloudless sky and the sensation of life-giving warmth after the fogs of England, the smell of coal, and the constant bad weather which reigns in the English Channel. . . . From the English Channel itself we moved with a favorable wind and approached Gibraltar in twelve days. This was good sailing. Descending towards the straits, we came upon a view of Cadiz: The shore of average height is intersected by mountains in the distance. On the right a rather high mountain terminates the famous Cape of Trafalgar, and even further to the right the high African coast was visible. Before we came even with the straits, darkness fell, and, having decided not to pass at night through the narrows, where the currents are so changeable, we turned from the shore towards the sea, intending to enter the straits not sooner than sunrise. The clear and hot day was replaced by a dark, foggy, and cold night, which we passed in the vicinity of the African coast, turning towards it and moving away as soon as calculations showed it was close.

They passed Tangier, Tarifa, and entered the harbor. The captain of the port, Mr. Sweetland, received them hospitably and assured them that their seventeen gun salute would be answered, contrary to usual British policy. Bestuzhev then goes into considerable detail about Gibraltar, its name (deriving from *Gibel-al-Tarif*, or the cliff of Tarifa), its history, commerce and atmosphere.

The view of the town from the anchorage is beautiful: clean little houses with flat roofs rise one above the other in an amphitheatre almost to a third of the height of the mountain. In the anchorage were up to 400 vessels of various sizes, and among them a number of tartans, shebeks, cayuks, and other small Mediterranean vessels. It was almost impossible to move near to the quay, and one could scarcely walk along the quay itself, because from the one side sloops and cargo vessels crowded it and from the other a throng of people and carts, loaded or taking on goods, gave no passage.

The sun sets very quickly and leaves no sunset behind, so the transition from light to dark is almost without a twilight. While we were getting out of the carriage and taking the steps to the cliff in order to look at the sea and to set foot here on the southernmost point of Europe, the day was replaced by night, as in a theatrical effect. We drove back. Indeed, the entire picture had changed. The town sparkled with innumerable bright lights. The whole length of the Spanish shore was illuminated with various figures in several directions from the burning of the land to improve the soil. The fires on the ships and all the lights around the bay were reflected in the quiet surface of the sea, and, diffused in the light undulation of the rising tide, presented a sort of magical illumination. To complete the charm, deluded by the rocking of the carriage and seeing nothing below at the edge of the abyss, I imagined that I was flying under heaven itself in which the stars, lighted with a bright gleam not seen in our regions, seemed therefore twice as big and twice as close to one's head. This was a completely different heaven, different constellations! Our Great Bear was moving slowly along the horizon—but your Polar Star, my friends, was somewhat higher.

Then Bestuzhev, like a skillful magician, screens his allusions with an abrupt, prosaic, one sentence paragraph: "From beneath the heavens, we drove home to drink tea." But liberal readers could hardly have missed the reference to the fires improving the soil in Spain (the constitutionalists' revolution), the heavenly atmosphere of British Gibraltar, the slow moving Great Bear (Russia) over which shone the liberals' Polar Star (Ryleev's and Bestuzhev's almanac).

In his third letter, Bestuzhev directly deals with the uprising of the Spanish rebels, who were resisting foreign intervention and domestic tyranny.

The whole Spanish coast from Cadiz was in ferment for the entire time we were in Gibraltar. When passing the straits we had seen a French frigate lying off Tarifa, and we had heard shots from it and from the fortress, but we were not able to guess the reason. Finally, on arrival in Gibraltar, this was explained as follows: Remnants of Spanish constitutionalists numbering 700 men, persecuted everywhere, formed under the leadership of Lt. Colonel Valdez, attacked Tarifa, which had an insignificant garrison, took possession of the town, and closed themselves up in it with the firm intention of not giving up without a fight.

Deprived of all hope, the insurgents might have been able to defend themselves in the strong and almost impregnable fort had it not been that the lack of water, for which they hadn't been able to prepare during their brief control of the town, forced them to waver. Opinions differed. The exhortations of Valdez had no effect, the fear of a cruel death instilled despondency in the hearts of the scanty garrison. Grumbling spread, and they began to talk about opening the gates. Finally, obedience to the leader disappeared. Seeing such a state of mind, Valdez took advantage of the darkness of night and with six others fled to the African shore, and the remainder, who opened the fortress the next morning, were taken by the French and hanged. This was what was related in Gibraltar.

The extermination of this unit, the last hope of the insurgents, reestablished tranquility among the people. The seige, the taking of Tarifa, the capture of the fort occurred in the course of the five days of our stay in Gibraltar. From the height of the mountain, it was possible to see the smoke of the battle with a telescope. Valdez arrived in the night on the eve of our departure.

Writing these lines, Nikolay Bestuzhev was unaware that within a couple of years he would find himself in Petersburg's Senate Square as an insurgent constitutionalist, there to experience the frustration and pain of Valdez. However, Bestuzhev's fate was more bitter than the Spaniard's, who preserved life and freedom by seeking asylum in Gibraltar—Bestuzhev was condemned to penal servitude in Siberia.

Wilhelm Kuechelbecker

IV. The Historical Tale—Bestuzhev-Marlinsky, N. Bestuzhev, Kuechelbecker. The Military Anecdote—Bestuzhev-Marlinsky, Bulgarin.

If the genre of travel notes was a school for prose style in the twenties, not less so was the historical tale, which enjoyed a renaissance at that time. It was Alexander Bestuzhev-Marlinsky, who made this geriatric genre come alive by infusing it with innovative elements and stylistic elegance. His *Roman and Olga [Roman i Ol'ga]*, which appeared in *Polar Star for 1823,*[1] concerns the fourteenth-century conflict between Novgorod and Prince Vasily Dmitrievich, who styled himself "Grand Prince of Moscow, Suzdal, and Novgorod." Where Karamzin in *Martha the Mayor* had been open-minded regarding Novgorod's subjugation by Ivan III, Marlinsky eagerly supports Novgorod, which for him, and for liberals and radicals in general, epitomized freedom achieved by heroic self-sacrifice. It will be recalled that the citizens of that city-state traditionally elected their prince, if, indeeed, they chose to have a prince at all.

Paradoxically, Marlinsky was able to take the clichés of character and event which marked Karamzin's *Natalia, the Boyar's Daughter,* itself a parody of worn out situations and types from eighteenth-century adventure fiction, and to infuse them with new life. His hero, Roman Yasensky, has the pleasing appearance and courage found earlier in Karamzin's Alexey, and like Alexey's, his marriage to the heroine is impossible because of social prejudice. In this situation, Roman also insists that his beloved Olga elope with him. Olga is torn between love and filial duty, but love wins out and she agrees to flee with Roman. However, before they can accomplish this, Roman accepts a secret mission to Moscow on behalf of Novgorod and leaves without a farewell. The anguished Olga does not know whether or not she has been abandoned, but her lonely tears are requited when Roman, again like Alexey, achieves such fame through his military prowess that all obstacles to his marriage are removed.

Marlinsky successfully integrates the two themes of his story, personal love and love of country. The latter initially separates the hero and heroine, but in the end Roman's steadfast patriotism and sense of duty reunites him with Olga. Against this plot we have a colorful pageant of holiday games in Novgorod, a parade of various cavalry and knights in armor, fist fights in the old tradition, the assembly of the *veche*(as in *Martha the Mayor*), descriptions of clothes, occupations, the mores of the times. This sort of historical bric-à-brac was typical for the genre, and some authors in the late twenties even focused upon this sort of detail to the neglect of characterization and plot itself.

Marlinsky adheres to the conventional pattern of the historical tapestry, but he embroiders his design with finer stitches and more colorful threads than had his predecessors. His achievement is the creation of a dramatic story animated principally by broad use of dialogue. This was innovative, because although dialogue was certainly not new for the historical tale, before Marlinsky its use was limited mostly to reinforcement of the emotional content. Marlinsky uses dialogue as a means of characterization, both by having others speak of the hero's attributes but also by correlating (rather rudimentarily, it must be said) Roman's speech to his individualized personality. He uses dialogue to provide background explanation, and also to assist in advancing the plot, as when Roman persuades Olga to flee. Through this means, Marlinsky makes his readers *see* the action, to follow it as it develops in the same way they might experience the action of a play. He clearly is departing from the norms of his predecessors, whose narrators for the most part *told* the readers what had happened rather than *showing* them what was happening.[2]

Marlinsky was later to become famous as a prose stylist, and even in this early work we see evidence of his verbal facility. Before he appeared on the literary scene, no one had developed a prose quite so eloquent, so rich in striking metaphor, so capable of infecting the reader with the emotional tensions of the characters. The scene in the apple orchard when Roman proposes elopement is typical of his florid style:

"Olga," Roman then said, "I have brought unhappy news. I asked for your hand and was refused! I cannot live without you, and if your love is not simply empty words, let us flee to good Prince Vladimir. With him we shall find sanctuary, and in our hearts, happiness. Decide!"

Shocked and amazed by the news and by Roman's proposal, Olga sat silently. All was over! All those dreams, beloved friends of the heart, had perished. Happiness had forever disappeared, like a falling star, and so hopelessly, so unexpectedly! For a long time the mirror of wisdom was clouded by the breath of despair. Finally the terrifying thought of flight aroused Olga's attention.

"Flee, me flee!" she exclaimed sobbing. "And you, Roman, could propose a means which would be shameful for my family and clan and ruinous for myself! No, you did not love Olga when you forgot about her good name, the purity of her conscience. Flee! To commit an unheard of act, to abandon one's native land, to disgrace forever one's parents, to anger God and Saint Sophia! No, Roman, I reject love if it demands crimes, and even you, you yourself."

Tears interrupted her speech.

With threatening brow and wandering, flashing glances, the passionate Roman listened to the maiden's reproaches. "Women, women!" he cried with a wild smile, "and you pride yourselves on love, on constancy, on sensitivity! You, who are compassionate only in song, you, who capture the gullible out of vanity. Your song is merely a caprice, it is chattering and flighty as a swallow, but when it is necessary to prove love, not by words but by deeds, how full of excuses, how generous with advice, old wives' tales, and reproaches you are. . . ."

He continues his screed until he notices her tears, and then his "anger disappeared like melting snow on red-hot iron." Olga reevaluates her priorities and agrees to run away with him.

Marlinsky's style, or styles, merits attention for several reasons, not the least of which is its metaphorical elegance and periphrastic ornamentation. The preceding translation also conveys some of the original's cadence, its anaphoras, its parallelisms. In many respects this language is a continuation of the prose created by the Sentimentalists, but with more verve and sinew. And Marlinsky's success with this style established a tradition which had to be *overcome* before prose fiction could move out of its Romantic period. Later we shall see how Lermontov struggled to free himself from his tendency toward Marlinsky's style and to turn his prose towards that of Pushkin.

Here is how Marlinsky characterizes Olga's sense of abandonment during Roman's prolonged absence:

Quickly flow the words of a story; deeds are not done quickly. Winter passed, summer disappeared like morning shadows. Again winter storm arrived, and still, still Roman is not with Olga. The spring sun melted the blue ice on the Ilmen River; already playful swallows, rushing through the air, kiss the surface of the Volkhov river with their wings. Everything has come to life, everything is joyous, only Olga has no happiness! And for whom are the short nights not long when they are measured with grief? The beauty of the dear girl fades like a rainbow without rain, and pallor betrays her heartfelt anguish. In vain her father gives her Yakutsk sables, attires her in pearl embroidery, diamond earrings and bracelets, in vain her young friends amuse Olga with games and songs. She avoids the games of youth, and the hinges on her tower door rust little by little.

The poetic prose with which Marlinsky describes emotional states is somewhat modified in the direction of simple statement when he deals with historical exposition or summarizes events in order to advance the action between scenes:

Meanwhile, Roman rode further and further. Soon Torzhok and Tver, still glowing from recent fires, were left behind. The roads became empty, and wagons were but infrequently hauled along them. The proud Novgorodian's soul boiled with anger seeing how humbly the wagons turned aside for each Tatar, who, pivoting haughtily in his saddle, galloped on a stolen horse. Among the half-destroyed villages, each of two or three households, among the weed-choked fields, monasteries and churches stood out unharmed. The calculating Mongols did not dare to touch the shrines, the last refuge of the people they had enslaved, to whom they left one possession—life, one weapon—patience, one hope—prayer. The corruption of morals, that rust of gold, had not yet passed from the boyars to the poor. In smoky huts roofed with straw, Roman found hospitable lodging for the night, and a happy *Welcome* awaited him at the threshhold. His hosts regaled him with whatever God had sent them, and in the morning they accompanied him like a relative, from their hearts wishing him a good journey and happiness. "For me there is no happiness!" thought the gloomy Roman. "It deceived me with hope, like the song of the bird of paradise, and it has hidden itself like the glitter of a sword in the dark of night."

Marlinsky introduces a secondary character into *Roman and Olga*, the brigand Berkut, a penitent villain for whom life has become a burden. Like the hero and heroine, Berkut also speaks in metaphors:

". . . since then in vain have I sought to smother my conscience with the burden of great crimes. Everywhere I seem to see shadows, and laments, and the smell of corruption. By day the sun is bloody, and the stars at night are like the eyes of a dead man, and, it seems, the leaves in the forest whisper indistinct reproaches. Troubled sleep does not refresh my eyes, but burns them! Oh, how heavy are the torments of a murderer. He cannot forget the past or the eternal future!"

Berkut has a role in the plot, to free Roman from a Muscovite death cell, and, of course, he serves as an object lesson to point up the consequences of crime. He also serves as a contrast to Roman, who at his darkest hour can find consolation in dying for his love and his fatherland. When compared with Berkut, whose life is poisoned by his transgressions, Roman's image acquires a radiance in keeping with his surname, Yasensky, which suggests *bright*.[3]

Marlinsky had begun his apprenticeship as a writer of historical tales in 1821, at which time he was in Livonia, with the brief *Wenden Castle—An Excerpt from the Diary of a Guard's Officer [Zamok Venden—Otryvok iz dnevnika gvardejskogo oficera]*. Set in 1208, the story concerns the assassination of Winno von Rohrbach, the first master of the Knights of the Sword. It is a mishmash of Gothic atmosphere, theatrical dialogue, authorial sententiousness, and characters with no physical image at all, mere abstractions of coarse oppression and defiant rebelliousness. The Livonian cycle of historical tales was continued with *Neuhausen Castle—A Chivalric Tale [Zamok Neigauzen—Rytsarskaia povest']*, published in *Polar Star for 1824*. Again we have the Gothic mode, with dank castles, nocturnal scenes, gory details, stereotyped characters, inflated passions and inflated dialogue, in fact, everything which would make the story interesting to a pre-adolescent boy. The action, which takes place in the 14th century, involves a jealous knight, Ewald von Nordek, who is tricked by his evil "friend," Romwald von Mei, into believing that his wife, Emma, is in love with a Russian prisoner, Vseslav. Ewald insists upon a duel with Vseslav, but before it can take place, Ewald disappears—on the false accusations of Romwald, he has been seized and condemned to death by a secret clan (*Freigerichte*). Romwald also kidnaps Emma, who has aroused his libidinous instincts. The Russian, Vseslav, fortuitously escapes and joins a group of Novgorodians, led by his brother, and together they free Emma, who turns out to be their long lost sister. The finale is gruesome and grotesque—quite worthy of Matthew Gregory (Monk) Lewis, who probably inspired it. (The fiendish Romwald von Mei, who has Ewald in his power, speaks:)

"Now, know also that I slandered your Emma and blackened Vseslav, to make you hurt them. That's not enough, Ewald. Unsatisfied with insulting your name, and planting the tortures of conscience in your heart [for mistrusting his wife], I abducted your Emma. Now she is in my hands, and when I leave here, having murdered you, I will dry her tears with kisses. Emma is a woman, I guarantee that in two days she will already be playing with this dagger, which is about to drink its fill of her husband's blood."

"Outcast of nature!" exclaimed Ewald, clasping his hands, "Are you human?"

"Oh, of course I'm no angel," answered Mei malevolently, "but what creatures would not envy me. I delight in the torture of my enemy. . . Well, you've lived long enough Ewald, now I want to live in your place."

Romwald brandished his dagger, but suddenly the broken grating flew clanking to his feet. The murderer was rooted to the spot—and Vseslav, like the angel of vengeance, dashed into the dungeon and with one blow of his sword disarmed Romwald.

"Enough of your evil deeds, Mei!" he roared. "Your hour has struck. Throw this tiger out of the window," he said to his men, "so that he won't poison the air with his breath!"

It was not necessary to repeat the order to the Novgorod soldiers. They seized Romwald, swung him, and flung him from the tower window.

"The scoundrel won't drown," said Gedeon mockingly, listening to Mei's fall, "he has a real empty head: hear how it rings as it hits against the stones?"

"There won't be smithereens left of him," replied Ilya. "All the walls are festooned with palings."

"The brigand deserves his tortures," muttered Gedeon, "he was a great villain."

At the same moment, Vseslav broke Ewald's chains with the hilt of his sword, and Nordek knelt before him. "I bow my head before the innocent one whom I accused," he exclaimed, "and I embrace my stout-hearted savior!"

They gazed at one another with a feeling of ineffable rapture, and hot tears of surprise and penitence flowed together. "Hasten to Emma," said Vseslav, "She is innocent and good, as before. She is here below. . ."

With a cry of mad joy Ewald sprang to the wall, from it into the boat, and the happy, forgiven husband fell into the embrace of his enchanted spouse. For such scenes there are feelings and no tears.

The storm subsided, and our sailors had moved out from under the vault, when someone's moan attracted their attention. Vseslav sprang onto the stones in order to see who it was, and the most fearsome spectacle assailed his eyes: Romwald, prostrate, penetrated clear through by a sharpened paling, hung head down and flowed with blood. His hands were stiffened with a convulsive movement, and his lips pronounced unintelligible curses.

"Monster," said Ewald, shaking from horror, "you thirsted for others' blood, and now you are suffocating in your own." Covering his ears, averting his eyes, he fled. But for a long time thereafter, when falling asleep, he heard Mei's death rattle, and the picture of his execution appeared to him as in life.

Marlinsky was back again in the 1825 issue of his almanac with two more historical tales, *The Tournament at Revel [Revel'skii turnir]* and *The Traitor [Izmennik]*. The latter work can be passed over lightly. [4] Its protagonist is a Byronic avenger who, with the help of the devil, sells out Pereyaslavl to the Poles, and in so doing betrays his brother and the woman he loves. He dies, fittingly, reviled by everyone.

The Tournament at Revel has an underlying humorous quality which distinguishes it from Marlinsky's previous historical tales. The narrator in this story, obtrusive as usual, does not serve as a cheer leader to whip up the reader's reactions but rather provides facetious commentary and capricious digressions. His story is a cheerful one of the triumph of love over social prejudice. Edwin, a rich young merchant, seeks to marry Minna, the daughter of the haughty knight, von Burtnek, but he is refused, because Burtnek insists his daughter rates a wedding knight and not a merchant. Burtnek decides that whoever wins the annual jousting tournament shall have Minna's hand, thus inspiring hope in the coarse Donnerbatz, a drunkard who shares Burtnek's reactionary social values. Edwin, of course, is not a contender, since only knights may take part in the contest. On the day of the tournament, Donnerbatz profits too greatly from free drinks and passes out, thus permitting the knight Ungern, the mortal enemy of Minna's father, to best all challengers and claim his prize. But before Minna can be deeded to him, an unknown knight appears and taunts Ungern to a fight to the death. Ungern is defeated, and spared, but there is a scandal when the victor removes his helmet and turns out to be. . . Edwin.

None of this is taken very seriously, for the author is more concerned with his digressions than with his plot. There is even an incidental character, Doctor Loncius, a late blooming variant of the classical *raissoneur*, who figures in a number of humorous scenes.

[Doctor Loncius] had come to the north to try his luck in Russia and had remained in Revel, partly frightened by stories of the cruelties of the Muscovites and partly restrained by the town council, which did not like releasing either physicians or educators to hostile Rus. One must add that with his even temper and amusing wit he made himself an indispensible person in Burtnek's house. No one could carve a turkey at dinner better than he, and from Loncius alone did the Baron listen to the truth without becoming enraged. He amused the children by making shadow figures with his fingers and making a rabbit from a kerchief. He felt the pulse of the old aunt and lauded the past, and he made the cousin blush from pleasure by teasing her about some sweetheart.

Loncius is important to the author as a means of displaying his talent for amusing dialogue, his skill with repartée, his ability for word play. It is precisely in this area that Marlinsky did assist the development of the prose literary language. A good example occurs at the end of the tale, when Doctor Loncius strives to convince the obdurate Burtnek to keep his promise that Minna should marry the man who won the tournament:

Loncius. . . continued to persuade the blustering Burtnek, who swore to the entire world that he would not give his daughter to Edwin, even though he had been the victor.
"But your word, Baron, your knight's word!"
"But my ancestors, sir doctor, my ancestors! It is better to go back on one's word when necessary to uphold one's name. Putting it bluntly, Edwin assumed too much. Never, ever, will I give Minna to a man without a famous name."
"But with a good reputation?"
"To a man whose genealogy is an account book, who has no coat-of-arms?"
"He has thousands of them, Baron, and all on a field of gold."
"Let him be made of ducats, I will not agree to split my shield with a signboard."
"Remember, Baron, that with his blood Edwin returned to you that which Ungern had taken away. Certainly you wouldn't repay generosity with ingratitude?"
"Virtue is not a title."
"We shall promote him to commander of the Schwarzen-Haupter [the Black

Heads or merchant militia] ," the elders of that class proudly answered. "He has earned that distinction by his bravery."

"Do you hear?" said the doctor, "that's almost a knightly distinction!"

———

"He is rich, handsome, a commander, and brave. That will cut off evil tongues. Certainly you don't want to destroy your daughter and deprive a friend of happiness by changing your word? Moreover, your daughter's love is known to all the town."

"Let me think about it for a day, for an hour. . ."

"You will never think up anything better than what your heart tells you. . . . So, Edwin is your son-in-law?"

"Son-in-law and son. Edwin and Minna, my dear children, awaken to a new life!"

Chapter VI of this story is devoted entirely to a digression on the socio-political situation prevailing in Revel at the time the action of the tale takes place. Here we have a good example of the penetration of travel note material into fiction: this chapter might just as well have been composed for the non-fictional *A Journey to Revel*. And as in that earlier piece of travel literature, Marlinsky here expresses ideas which have relevance both to the historical material which is his apparent subject and to the contemporary Russian social and political condition. The Decembrist propagandist is clearly evident in the paragraphs describing the arrogant but worm-eaten class which ruled Livonia in the sixteenth century:

The events which I am presenting here took place in 1538, that is, fifteen years after the introduction of the Lutheran faith.

The order of Livonian Knights of the Cross had recently lost control of the Prussian Order, which had become attached to Sigismund, and already it had become feeble in its terrible isolation. The long peace with Russia had rusted the sword with which Plettenberg had once threatened her. Having become used to luxury, the knights knew only how to hunt and feast, and their military spirit was maintained only by infrequent skirmishes with Novgorodian horsemen or Swedish Varangians. If they did not inherit the manliness of their ancestors, still their pride grew greater and greater with every year. The spirit of that age divided even metals into noble and base categories, so is it any wonder that while convincing others the knights themselves became convinced, quite ingenuously, that they had been fashioned at the very least from noble porcelain? One must remember that the gentry, which was made up at that time of landowners, supported this idea. It sought to fuse with the knighthood, and consequently excited in the latter a desire to keep exclusively for itself those benefits which, God knows why, we call rights, and to degrade spiritually any new rivals. Meanwhile, the merchants, in general the most active, honorable, and useful of all the inhabitants of Livonia, with flattering ease became members of the gentry by purchasing real estate, or desirous of intimidating the gentry with splendor, abandoned themselves to luxury. The gentry, in order not to be outdone and to be on a par with the knights, had recently exhausted the estates they had acquired. The knights, in conflict with both groups, closed their castles, disarmed their vassals for good. . . and the fatal results of such unnatural class arrogance were imminent and unavoidable. Discord reigned everywhere. The weak undermined the strong, and the rich envied them. The military-trade society of Black Heads (Schwarzen-Haupter), as the city militia of Revel, enjoyed almost knightly privilege and consequently was hated by the knights. The hour of destruction approached: Livonia resembled a desert, but its towns and castles glittered with the bright colors of abundance, like an autumn leaf before falling. Banquets resounded everywhere, tournaments called the young men and all the beautiful girls together , and the Order noisily lived out its fame, wealth and its very existence.

Marlinsky ends abruptly with a rhetorical question which underscores the digressive character of this chapter: "Now just where had we stopped?" This is followed immediately by the epigraph to Chapter VII: "What will be, will be, and what will be is what God wills."[5] Significantly, the quotation belongs to Bogdan Chmielnitski, the liberator of the Ukraine, and it represents the entire text of his response to the Sultan's threat to destroy the Ukraine and all its inhabitants if Chmielnitski refused allegiance. Taken in context with the preceding chapter, it suggests the inevitability of an apocalyptic conclusion to the class conflict prevailing in nineteenth-century Russia.

The final story of Marlinsky's Livonian cycle has a curious history. *Blood for Blood [Krov' za krov']* was written during the first half of 1825 and was supposed to appear in *Little Star for 1826 [Zvezdochka na 1826 god]*, a somewhat smaller version of *Polar Star* with which Ryleev and Bestuzhev intended to conclude their publishing endeavors. Both editors had become increasingly occupied with revolutionary activities, and, moreover, they had been losing contributors to *Northern Flowers*. Therefore, they had decided to reduce the size of their almanac for the 1826 issue, and to withdraw from the field. Parts of *Little Star*, including Marlinsky's story, had already been printed before the Uprising of December 14, 1825. Immediately after the Decembrists had been crushed, the government seized all the printed portions of the almanac and baled them up. Orest Somov, as editorial assistant to Ryleev and Bestuzhev, had received proofs of the printed portions, which included his own story, *The Rebel [Gaidamak]*. Somov kept these proofs, and in 1826 sent to Aladin, editor of *The Neva Almanac*, the printed pages of his own story, inadvertently including *Blood for Blood*, unsigned and with a new title, *Eisen Castle [Zamok Eizen]*. Since convicted revolutionaries were not supposed to publish or be published, both Somov and Aladin had some questions to answer. Somov insisted he had sent Marlinsky's work to Aladin through an oversight. Aladin's excuse is not known.

Eisen Castle is a facetious historical tale whose original and pithy manner of translation is its most evident and important feature. According to a brief forward provided by Marlinsky, the tale was narrated to him by one of his fellow officers, "a well-known amateur of historical tales and ancient legends." And it is in the individualized language of this narrator that the entire story is presented.

The plot is properly preposterous and the dénouement ruthlessly violates the formulaic ending of reunited lovers. On reaching the age of forty, the heinous robber-baron Bruno decides to marry, and to expedite matters he usurps the fiancée of his nephew, Reginald. Luisa, the reluctant bride, finds life in Eisen Castle intolerable and her brutal husband more so. Falsely accused of infidelity, she then secretly justifies her husband's suspicions by having an affair with Reginald. The uncle and nephew quarrel over a trifling matter (Reginald refuses to shoot a serf to demonstrate his skill with the crossbow, and then becomes angry when Bruno hits the mark), and Reginald is cast into a dungeon to famish. Bruno leaves on a plundering expedition, and Luisa frees Reginald. When the Baron returns, he finds the lovers embracing, and they respond to his remonstrations by killing him. Later the guilty couple decide to legitimize their relationship by marrying, but as they are saying their vows the ghost of Bruno gallops up to the altar, tramples Reginald to death, and carries off the fainting Luisa. Shortly she finds herself buried alive at the spot where Bruno had been slain. Of course, it was not really a ghost but Bruno's brother who had come to extract blood for blood.

The fate of the protagonists is unimportant, since all are culpable, and, moreover, we learn so little about them that empathy is out of the question. Characterization is sufficient and no more. Bruno is coal black spiritually and physically, along with his armor and his horse, while Reginald and Luisa are so pale as to be barely discernible. Rather, it is the narrator's idiom which is intriguing. The same lightly humorous conversational tone is maintained throughout, regardless of the subject matter. This homogeneity of tone also obviates emotional reactions on the reader's part, since dire deeds are related with the same insouciance as mundane matters.

Yet a long time ago a castle stood here called Eisen, that is, *iron*. And by rights it was so strong that no tale could tell it and no pen describe it. Everyone said it got its name by its fur. The walls were so high that when you looked up at them your hat would fall off, and even the best archers couldn't shoot an arrow to the sphere on top of the tower. This gully on one side served in place of a moat, and on the other side thousands of poor Estonians spent entire seasons after harvest digging, and they dug down to active springs, and that's how they made the castle so there was no approach from any side. I won't even talk about the gates: oak planks set with nails like the studded sole of a Russian hiker. Thirty bolts with locks fastened it, and so many bushy-moustached men guarded it that there's nothing more to say. On each merlon was an iron stake, and even in the gutters there were gratings, so that not even a mouse would think to crawl here or there without asking. So why make such fortresses if you were living in peace with your neighbors? To tell the truth, peace in those days was worse than war is today. They'd shake hands with one hand and slap you in the face with the other, and then the fun started. And he who won out was right. And the knights were no fools. Just as they built their castles with other people's hands, so they spoke: this is for defense against foreigners , and when they had built their castles and settled in them, like in an eagle's nest, then it turned out that they were for pillaging their own land.

When the garrulous captain-narrator describes the appearance and habits of Bruno von Eisen, the results are more amusing than ominous:

He would get mad at a neighbor—then to horse with his servants and houndsmen, and he would trample the other's fields and burn his forests. God forbid meeting him at such a black hour! He would catch sight of an Estonian and gallop up to him with upraised sword.

"Recite 'I believe in the only one,' you good-for-nothing." And that peasant would faint to his knees, not knowing a word of German.

"Ey moista." (I don't understand.)

"Recite, I say!"

"Ah ha! So you're stubborn in your paganism, you animal! Then I'll christen you!" Bam, and the head of the poor fellow would fly to the earth like a bowling ball, and with a laugh the Baron would gallop on, saying "Absolvo te!" which is "Thou art absolved," because as spiritual knights they could at the same time kill the body and save the soul. That's how it was with outsiders, so how was it for his own people? Say he liked a peasant's horse:

"*Pergala!* (You devil!) Trade your horse for my lame bitch."

"Dear father and master! My occupation is hunting, and where will I get without a horse?"

"As far as the gallows, you good-for-nothing! You should be satisfied that I'm going to permit you to raise pups from her, and that your wife will breastfeed two of them for me."

This story must be recognized as one of the earliest examples in Romantic fiction of *skaz* narration, that is, the utilization of a narrator whose individual manner of expression is itself a dominant feature. In later, more highly intricate *skaz* tales, the narrator's voice served not only to relate events but also to provide something like a self-portrait. That is, the narrator emerged as a personality in his own right. In *Eisen Castle* the captain who tells the story remains undeveloped, and our interest in him relates solely to his manner of speech. Still Marlinsky's example, however rudimentary, does represent an innovation and one which was widely imitated.[6]

In addition to historical fiction, represented by *Roman and Olga* and his Livonian cycle, Marlinsky attempted another type of fiction in *Polar Star*. For want of a better pigeonhole, we shall call this work, entitled *A Novel in Seven Letters [Roman v semi pis'makh]*, an early variant of the society tale, keeping in mind that this "novel," which is so brief that it hardly qualifies as a short story, lacks the character development, the involved intrigue, and the circumstantial social setting of the canonical society tale.

The letters are all from the pen of a certain "S." to his friend George, and in them he chronicles the course of his tragic love for Adele, a capricious young lady of (in his opinion) considerable attraction. In letter five we find that "S." has a rival in Erast (shades of *Poor Liza*), in letter six we are told of a forthcoming duel, which, quite typically for duels in Russian literature, depicts the fatal shot as a sort of accident, with reconciliation, or an attempt at it, as part of the scenario:

We approached from twenty paces. I was walking steadily and already three bullets had whistled past my head. I was walking steadily, but without thinking, without any intention. Feelings hidden in the depths of my soul completely blacked out my mind. At six paces, I don't know why or how, I pressed the fatal trigger, and a shot resounded in my heart!. . . . I saw Erast shudder. . . . When the smoke had cleared, he was already lying on the ground, and the blood rushing from his wound, frothing, was coagulating on him. Be gone, be gone from my eyes this picture, remove from my heart the memory of it! I rushed to him. . . he moved away. . . looked at me without anger, gave me his hand, pressed to his lips a ribbon which was bound around his hand— it was Adele's belt. "Adele!" he pronounced quietly, and the light left his eyes. We listen. . . there is no pulse, we raise a sabre blade to his lips, there is no trace of breath: *he is dead!*

In anticipating the society tale, one of the most popular genres of the thirties, Marlinsky incorporated several elements which were to become *de rigueur* for the genre: a plot centering on a love affair, a triangle, gentry protagonists (at least one from the military), a challenge and a duel. In *The Test [Ispytanie]*, a work of 1830, Marlinsky develops the genre further and with considerably more success than with *A Novel in Seven Letters*.

Nikolay Bestuzhev, who traveled with his brother Alexander (Marlinsky) to Revel in 1820, was also bitten by the Livonian bug, with less effect. His rather short historical tale, *Hugo von Bracht. An episode from the Fourteenth Century [Gugo Fon-Brakht. Proizshestvie XIV stoletiia]* came out in *The Emulator* in 1823. The story material is similar to that used by Marlinsky: Von Bracht, a Livonian knight, returns from Palestine to find his castle destroyed, his wife dead, and his son missing. He himself has been condemned as a heretic, all this the result of his wife's refusal to submit to the advances of Hugo's supposed friend, Keller. The knight becomes a bandit and pirate, preying on shipping in the Gulf of Riga from his castle at Sonderburg, steeping himself in blood to overcome his grief. For fifteen years he carries on in this way. Then while attacking a Danish ship, he receives severe wounds from the sword of a young warrior, who desperately fights to defend his wife. However, the ship is taken and the slaughtered crew and passengers, among them the young Dane, are thrown into a boat and set adrift. Not unexpectedly, the young warrior turns out only to have been knocked unconscious, and he is able to steer the boat to shore and save himself. Seeking to free his wife, who has been given to Hugo as his share of the booty, he enters the pirate's service. When the young couple try to escape, they are apprehended, the Dane is garrotted in his wife's presence, and both are flung over the ramparts into the sea. The next morning Hugo himself is found dead, having ripped the bandages from his wounds in a paroxysm of grief and self-hatred: near his body are found rings and gold images identifying the young Dane as Hugo's missing son.

Notwithstanding the theatrical elements in the plot, which include Keller's attempted seduction, the immuring of Hugo's wife, the battle at sea, the murders, to mention just a few of the motifs, the story is almost totally undramatic. There is no exploitation of the potential for tension or terror, and the scenes which are developed are not always the critical ones. There is no dialogue, just three or four speeches in which characters summarize past actions. The story does have one feature not commonly found in the short historical tale, that is, an effort to convey some sense of the protagonist's psychological state, to show, in addition to his motivation (the destruction of the family), how he felt about what he was doing:

Despair gave voice to the oath [for vengeance], the desire for revenge led to crimes. Many castles were destroyed, and the bodies of Brach's enemies were thrown out as offerings to wolves and vultures. The knight's castle was transformed into a den of cut-throats. The knight was the ataman, and before the violence of his feelings had dissipated, he had already become a villain. At times, during those brief moments when his heart was at ease, Hugo desired to return to the path of virtue, but in the reveries of his conscience the shades of those who had been killed barred this road—and hatred for people again boiled in his heart. In every person he saw an instrument of his misfortune, and even those who surrounded him disturbed his soul. Had he wanted to flee, where could he have gone? The doors to this world were already closed to him. This new motive burned in his afflicted soul, and with new floods of blood he put out the flame which was consuming him. Thus a person desperately ill who is treated with terrible opium cannot leave it even after his recovery and to cause another's death serves to alleviate his suffering. Sometimes he seemed calm, but this calm was a pool in the quiet sea at which time the trusting sailor carelessly looks at the deceiving surface and does not see the indications of the approaching storm.

But all of this doesn't really help us to grasp the essence of this northern Corsair, because what we learn is vague and abstract. Nikolay Bestuzhev was trying to delineate his character's psychology, but the limitations of the language available to him crippled his effort. The vocabulary and the locutions are standardized and formulated, and the metaphors are cliches, even for 1823. The central figure of the story therefore remains an enigma to the reader, as arbitrary a character as Marlinsky's Bruno von Eisen.[7] Oddly, even Decembrist motifs, so typical of the Livonian theme, are absent from this work.

Yet another future Decembrist, Wilhelm Kuechelbecker (1797-1846), used Livonian history as a background for his fiction. Poet, critic, and literary conservative, he was one of the editors of *Mnemosyne,* the almanac of the Moscow intellectuals known as the Lovers of Wisdom [Liubomudrye].[8] Of German parents, he had been raised in Estonia, leaving there in 1811 when he was accepted by the newly established Lyceum at Tsarskoe Selo (along with Pushkin and Delvig, who became his closest friends). His *Ado,* published in *Mnemosyne* in 1824, differs markedly from Marlinsky's Livonian tales in its lack of dramatic action and, what is strange for an author who lived in Estonia until adolescence, in the absence of any real local color other than a few place names. The "ethnographic" content is almost exclusively connected with Estonian paganism, but the details are largely fabricated. As V.T. Adams has shown, the pagan Estonians were animists, they did not have priests, nor sacrifices, nor individual gods, all of which appear in the story.[9] Like Marlinsky, Kuechelbecker occasionally treats his dates and events with an ahistorical insouciance and even transposes actual events which happened elsewhere to the geographical area of his tale. The folksongs in *Ado,* we are told by Adams, in no way resemble the real thing.

What we have here, in fact, is a typical product of the future Decembrists' effort to exploit fiction as a means of promulgating their ideas of citizenship, freedom, and sacrifice, and all of these themes are included. Set in the 13th century, the action rambles from Estonia to Novgorod, now focusing upon the theme of Livonian independence, now upon the plight of the separated lovers, and, especially towards the end, upon the superiority of Christianity over paganism. The characters are pale, flat, and tedious. The exposition and dialogue are saturated with Slavonicisms and archaic forms.[10]

Ado, an Estonian pagan priest, is the leading spirit behind an effort to drive the Knights of the Sword, led by the cruel Ubald, from the region of Lake Peipus. Following an unsuccessful uprising, Ado's family are slaughtered. Only his daughter, Maya, escapes to break the dreadful news to her father—in the stilted manner of the opening scene of an inept tragedy:

Maya: The one who gave birth to me has moved to Yumala's dwelling [Yumala was the Zeus figure of the Peipus pagans]. The young ones, my brothers, followed her. Their blood purpled the threshhold of our hut. I was delivered from among the dead by Nor, son of Sur, my betrothed.

Nor, son of Sur, Maya's betrothed, goes to Novgorod to seek aid from Prince Yaroslav, but months pass without result. However, while there he becomes a Christian and is baptised "Yury." Meanwhile, Ado is captured and imprisoned to await the arrival of a high church official, a monk, who will properly condemn him to death at the stake. Maya, with the assistance of an Estonian in Ubald's guard, frees Ado. At the same time, Nor-Yury arrives with some renegades, led by the booty-hungry Purgas, and Ubald's castle is captured. Ubald and the monk are spared by Nor-Yury.

The father, the daughter, and his betrothed son returned to Loguz, which was noisy with the rowdy joy of the intoxicated victors. Suddenly Ado stopped and said solemnly to Yury, "I understand, Nor, why you withheld my avenging hand over the monk. You were not satisfied with his death and that of the evil Ubald. Their punishment must be tormenting! But extinguish in me my last doubt. You have control of Purgas's soul, so swear that you will convince him to hand over my enemies to me, swear by the awesome name of Yumala. Yury: I swear by the sacred name of Christ the Savior that his servant, although unworthy of his priestly rank, will remain unharmed and whole, and that not one hair on the head of Ubald will perish while I live!" Ado: Mother Earth, swallow me! Nor has betrayed his gods and his fatherland! Yury: No, no, Ado! I have not betrayed and never will betray my unhappy fatherland. To it belongs the last drop of my blood! But I have recognized the true God, and his testament speaks: Love thy enemies! I will boldly meet the armed oppressor of my brothers in battle, but disarmed he will find me his intercessor. Forgive me, Ado! He will find me his intercessor even against Maya's father.

And you old man—I have faith in the Lord—even you will know his sacred law someday: your great soul, without fail, must finally achieve his sanctity.

Ado wanted to be angry at Yury, but the youth's inspired face caused him involuntary, inexplicable reverence.

Yury was the intermediary between Purgas and his prisoners. They ransomed themselves and, leaving the castle, gave their sworn promise to be merciful to their subjects. Let us believe that the majority fulfilled this promise, since in general people are better than is usually thought.

The story continues with Maya's conversion, her marriage to Yury, and finally Prince Yaroslav's campaign against the Germans. Yury dies storming the walls of Yuriev, and his death so affects Ado that he becomes a Christian. Maya dies giving birth to a son, or, as the story puts it, "she passed from this vain and corrupt life into eternal life, whither her friend had preceded her."

The Christian emphasis here, and the special admonition to love one's enemies, suggest that the author of this work adhered to the Christian tenets of humility and turning the other cheek. Those who naively reconstruct an author's ethics on the basis of his works are in for a shock. On December 14, 1825, Kuechelbecker appeared on Senate Square and attempted to shoot both the Grand Duke Mikhail and General Voinov, but on each occasion his pistol misfired! Had he possessed a more reliable weapon, he doubtless would have hanged along with Peter Kakhovsky, who killed both General Miloradovich, the Governor-General of Petersburg, and Colonel Stuerler, the commander of the Life Guards Grenadier Regiment. As it happened, Kuechelbecker escaped to Warsaw, but he was captured there almost within a month after the rebellion. After ten years of solitary confinement in various fortresses, he was exiled to Siberia, where he was able to continue his literary work. The product of this second period, for better or worse, lies outside the scope of this study.

In striking contrast to the turgid nonsense of *Ado* is Kuechelbecker's *The Land of the Headless [Zemlia bezglavtsev]*, a Swiftian satire on contemporary Russia, which was published in the second number of *Mnemosyne* in 1824.[11] In a language which is as informal as its tone is familiar, the first person narrator describes his ascent in a balloon at a Paris fête, his loss of consciousness, and his subsequent awakening near Akardion (Heartless), the capital city of Akefalia (Headless). The satire is pointed and reasonably clever:

The greater part of the inhabitants of this country are without heads, more than half are without hearts. Well-to-do parents assign hirelings to the newly born children, and until they reach twenty the hirelings saw at their necks as well as try to rid them of their hearts. In Akefalia they are called educators. It is a rare neck which can resist their efforts; it is a rare heart that is armed against them with a sufficiently strong breast.

I remembered my own motherland and stood on tiptoes from pride, thinking about the superiority of our Russian education as compared with that of Akefalia. We entrust our children to honorable, intelligent foreigners, who, although they don't have the slightest notion of our language, or of our sacred faith, or of the time-honored customs of our land, do try in every way to inspire our youth with a devotion to everything Russian.

Kuechelbecker can't resist another shot at his literary friends, paraphrasing points made in "On the Direction of Our Poetry":

"Accordingly," you will say, "their literature is undeniably in a blossoming state!" And you are not wrong. Although I was only a short while in Akardion, I was able to note that they have quite a few political and scientific newspapers, heralds, fashion journals. The Akardion tribe of Grays and Tibulluses is particularly large; they constitute an entire legion. Still, it is somewhat difficult to distinguish an elegy by one from that by another: they keep on repeating the same thing, they are all sad and grieve that *two times two is five*. This idea, of course, is quite new and striking, yet it has become somewhat worn out under their pens. At least that's what one of the connoisseurs of their poetry assured me.

As a true son of my fatherland, I was overjoyed that our Russian poets have chosen a subject which is incomparably richer: from the age of seventeen in our country they begin to talk about their faded youth. Our poems are not burdened with thought, feeling, or imagery. Still, they incorporate some ineffable charm which cannot be comprehended either by readers or writers. Well, not everyone is a Slavophile, and anyone with any taste must be enraptured by these poems.

You will recall that Kuechelbecker was a literary fellow-traveler of Admiral Shishkov and his Colloquy, and that he favored the retention of Slavonic elements in the literary language. Moreover, in his poetic credo he supported revival of the ode, which in his opinion was the only suitable medium in which to sing the glories of heroes and the fame of the fatherland. *Ado* was his effort at an ode in prose, doomed to abort from the moment of conception. On the other hand, Kuechelbecker's critical and satirical prose displays an unexpected modernity, expository lucidity, and apparent ease of expression, and in this respect he must be ranked with those writers whose prose style contributed to the further sophistication of the literary language.

The inventory of genres of fiction which were established before 1825 must also include the military anecdote, usually a short-short story, often introduced as a digression into other prose forms, such as travel notes or memoirs. Marlinsky favored this form, and in *A Journey to Revel* (1821) we find an early example. The anecdote is incorporated here as a tale told to the author-traveler by another officer whom he encountered at a post station. In interpolating this story, the author sought to reproduce the colloquial style of the narrator. The story itself is inconsequential and implausible. Two young students, a Russian and a Prussian, become fast friends at Heidelberg. Later they separate and both become officers. After four years they meet again in Leipzig—but without recognizing one another!—there the Russian "insults" the Prussian's sister. There is a challenge, a duel, sudden recognition and reconciliation, followed by the marriage of the Russian to his friend's sister.

This rigamarole is similar to other unlikely adventures recounted in Marlin-sky's *An Evening on Bivouac [Vecher na bivuake]*, a duo of military anec-dotes appearing in *Polar Star for 1823*.

One of the more persistent anecdotists, whose works often became fully developed short stories, was Faddey Bulgarin. *Polar Star for 1823* contained his *A Military Joke—A Non-Fictional Anecdote [Voennaia shutka, nevymy-slennyi anekdot]*, which is obviously fabricated, with a plot that hinges en-tirely upon coincidence. The narrator, a Polish uhlan, is assigned quarters in the house of a German apothecary. To ensure that his host is generous with food and wine, he confides to him that his comrade in arms, Lieto, who is also lodged with the apothecary, is a violent person, and that once he had thrown an entire family out a window when he had been served inferior wine. The household is in fear, especially a pretty young relative who is staying with them. The officers do dine well indeed, and the narrator persuades the girl to sing. When Lieto hears her voice, he rushes into the room and throws himself at her feet: she is his long lost fiancée, who had been separated from him by the misfortunes of war. We learn that later they were married.

At best, anecdotes of this sort must be seen as a primitive form of fiction, something in the nature of an expanded incident with the stress upon the paradoxical or coincidental nature of the event itself. As Russian fictionists proceeded to a better knowledge of their trade, the anecdote, fleshed out with greater attention to setting and characterization, became the short story.

V. The "First Russian Novels"—Narezhny. The Supernatural Tale—Perovsky-Pogorelsky.

Vasily Narezhny, whose *A Russian Gil Blas* (1814) was mentioned earlier, reappeared on the literary scene in the early twenties with several more picaresque novels. The proscription in 1814 of the final three parts of that first work had its effect on the quality of the satire in these later ones, where the attacks against the abuses of the gentry and institutionalized oppression are definitely toned down. The author, who suffered poverty and deprivation as a petty clerk throughout his adult life, had obviously learned to restrain his rancor.

Aristion, or Reeducation [Aristion, ili Perevospitanie], which marked Narezhny's return to fiction in 1822, is the story of the reformation of a young gentry wastrel by exposure to Rousseauistic values and procedures, with added doses of religion and philosophy. Contrasted to the ultimately transformed Aristion and his multi-virtued mentor are a collection of ignorant provincial landowners, each embodying vices or passions which have brought themselves and their peasants to ruin. Among these, the miser Tarakh and the obsessive hunter Sylvester find a conspicuous place in the genealogies of Plyushkin and Nozdryov in Gogol's *Dead Souls*.

Gogol, the most "original" of Russian Romantic fictionists, seems to have read with equal attention Narezhny's last two novels, *Bursak* (1824) and *The Two Ivans, or A Passion for Litigation* (1825). You will recall that Belinsky called these "the *first* Russian novels," but they are essentially no different from *A Russian Gil Blas*, mastodons tramping forth from the glaciers of the previous century.

Bursak is a historico-didactic-picaresque novel set in the Ukraine at the time of her union with Russia. But the historical canvas is faded, and although the characters to some extent are involved in the events of their times, there is no effort, as in the novels of Walter Scott and his imitators, to paint a colorful mural of a particular place teeming with real and fictional characters. Major historical figures, such as the Grand Hetman of the Ukraine or the Voevoda of Kiev, do appear, but no dates are mentioned, no battles are named, and there is no discussion of the historical background to the cessation of Poland's control over the Ukraine. Everything is fiction, as in Gogol's *Taras Bulba*.

The story's main narrator, Neon, at the age of twelve is placed in a seminary to be trained as a village deacon, but, after he graduates a series of unlikely adventures culminates in his marriage and later promotion to a high rank in the army of the Grand Hetman. His tale is constantly interrupted by other narrators, whose flashbacks are like missing pieces in the larger puzzle. When all the tales have been told, we discover that Neon is actually the long lost child of the Hetman's daughter, who had fled with her lover to avoid marrying against her will. But there is simply no way to summarize the

69

plot, which is terribly contrived, with abductions, escapes, and many improbable encounters interwoven with cases of mistaken identity, failure to recognize close acquaintances, or even to tell the sex of men in women's clothing or vice versa. Characters alter their attitudes and personalities if the plot requires it. The narrative voice is always the same, whether Neon is speaking or renarrating the first-person account of one of the other characters. Nonetheless, *Bursak* is a pleasant adventure story with lots of humor and even burlesque.

Neon is something of a Ukrainian Tom Jones, and like his progenitor is prone to err, not from any innate wickedness but simply because he is thoughtless and very human. Most of his troubles stem from his seduction of the eighteen-year-old widow, Neonila, but a better side is revealed when he instantly marries her on learning that she is pregnant. Neon's good instincts ultimately lead him to fame and fortune, and even the skeptical reader is happy when the deserving hero is reunited with his real parents and finds happiness with Neonila and their child.

Although he is the central figure of the novel, Neon is less vivid than some of the minor characters, several of whom are quite charming in their villainy. Foremost among these is Neonila's father, Pan Istucharius, who for personal gain forced her marriage at age sixteen to the hideous, one-eyed Pan Pamfamir and later plots to marry her to Pan Varipsava, a seventy-year-old dwarf. The vengeful father pursues Neon and Neonila relentlessly, remaining obdurate in his antagonism even after he learns of their marriage and child. However, when he is told that Neon is the grandson of the Grand Hetman, Istucharius changes sincerely and becomes the soul of conciliation—and of no further interest.

There is a good taste of Ukrainian life in this novel, with its descriptive emphasis on traditional dress, regional customs, dwellings, taverns, food, and drink. The most specific details relate to Neon's life at the seminary, where he and a number of equally poor students live a communal life organized on republican principles. The boys are admitted free to the seminary and are provided shelter in the form of a large hut [*bursa*] lined with benches and heated with one or more large stoves. The students have to provide their own food, which they earn by singing in the streets or acquire simply by stealing. Neon's apprenticeship as a *bursak* fills the opening chapters, but in Chapter V we are simply told:

In this way, amid constant poverty and temporary satisfaction, amid studies and pranks, eight years flowed by. I was already finishing the course of philosophy and, therefore, enjoying unfailingly the rights of a philosopher [the top rank among students]. I was even drinking wine, smoking tobacco, and growing a moustache.

It is typical, however, of the author's lack of concern with any characterization in depth that our hero, Neon, has exactly the same mentality at twenty as he does at twelve, the age at which his story begins. In this case, maturation means growing larger, a necessary development preceding his subsequent involvement in seduction, marriage, fatherhood, and his military career. If *Bursak* can be faulted for weakness of historical color and shallowness of characterization, it can be commended for its pleasing comedy and bouyant mood. Narezhny has a good sense of the humor in life, and his satire is amusing. The scene in which Pan Istucharius discovers Neon and Neonila in compromising circumstances is very burlesque, culminating in the disclosure of marital irregularities on the part of Istucharius and libidinous activity on the part of his sniveling son, Epafras:

The summer was half over. One bright and beautiful night Neonila and I were relaxing luxuriantly on the sofa in the arbor. Suddenly close by a man's voice was heard, and shortly the door opened quietly and two people entered, although we were not able to see just who these vexatious visitors were. We held our breath.

"Dear Christodula!" said the man, and we immediately recognized Epafras, and as his lover an old maid who served Trifena, "Sit on the sofa, and I'll get something to eat and drink from the cupboard. Is it not true that I am clever in such circumstances? From time to time during the day I hid here plenty of pastry and a bottle of good drink."

He unlocked the cupboard and withdrew his supplies, just as the arbor door again opened and two more, a man and a woman, made themselves at home.

"Beautiful Kiriena!" said a voice, and instantly we recognized Istucharius and a young girl, a close friend of Neonila's, "Sit over here, on the sofa, and I'll get some light." With these words he uncovered a hidden lantern.

Let who is able imagine the tumult at that point. Neonila fainted for real, or at least it seemed so, for her eyes were closed and her breathing stopped. First of all Istucharius illuminated Epafras, who was holding a bottle in one hand and the dish with the pastry in the other.

"You good-for-nothing!" the father cried in great anger and boxed him on the ear so adroitly that the dish and the bottle fell out of his hands, and he stretched out with them. "With whom are you here, you scamp?" the old man continued with fury. "Is this possible? At your age? I don't know why Neon isn't looking after you. Somehow he's on the prowl away from home a lot."

Saying this, he illuminated the sofa and turned to stone. Christodula and Kiriena were sitting next to each other on the sofa and were covering themselves with their aprons. My dear, tender Neonila had nothing to do this with.

My guardian angel opportunely returned my senses. Taking advantage of Istucharius having become petrified, I jumped off the sofa, gave his hand a slap, from which the lantern flew to the floor and went out, and with the speed of a whirlwind flew from the arbor, locked the door with the key in the lock, and ran home.

The above scene is, admittedly, slightly salacious, but Narezhny's interest in the humor of the situation rather than in any prurient features. In general, like his hero, Narezhny seems to have a quite healthy, unneurotic attitude towards life, a gusto which is also evident in the story's inventories about food and drink. Even in the most trying circumstances, the characters hardly ever miss a meal, and they never lack for some intoxicating beverage to wash it down.

The Two Ivans, or A Passion for Litigation [Dva Ivana, ili Strast k tiazhbam] was Narezhny's final work, published in 1825, the year of his death. If *Bursak* has ties with Gogol's *Taras Bulba,* about which more will be said later, *The Two Ivans* is an important source for Gogol's *How Ivan Ivanovich Quarreled with Ivan Nikiforovich.* Although its form is not strictly picaresque, this novel seems cut from virtually the same cloth as Narezhny's earlier works. We have the same earthy situations, the same burlesque humor, the same concern with Ukrainian *byt,* or manner of living, the same didacticism. Again we have an involved and improbable series of events, but in this case, unlike *Bursak,* one can attempt a summary.

Having finished their studies at a seminary in Poltava, where they lived in the *bursa* for ten years, the two sons of two provincial landowners return home, where they are accorded a welcome befitting their rank of philosopher. While the boys, Nikanor and Koronat, have been away, their fathers, the two Ivans, have carried on an interminable feud with their neighbor, Khariton, each new act of vengeance being followed by retaliation, each new lawsuit followed by a counter suit. The origin of the antagonism is explained to the boys:

> "The husband of your aunt, Nikanor, at the time I mentioned gave a pair of rabbits to your younger brother, who was then five years old. He was allowed to put them in a hut at the end of the garden which served as a place to keep orchard and garden tools. The beasts began to multiply, and in the course of a little more than a year there was a small herd. After several weeks of spring had passed, when both our families were sitting after dinner under the flowering cherry and plum trees, listening to the tales of Ivan the Elder about his military exploits and calculating at leisure the quantity of our future crop, the sudden sound of a weapon's shot caused us to tremble. However, we quickly recovered, jumped up, and ran to the wattle fence which divides both gardens. Here again a shot followed, and we immediately saw that a bunch of rabbits was running right at us, one without a leg, another without an ear, a third without its teeth, all covered with blood. Your brother raised a howl: 'My rabbits!' and right then appeared Ivan's neighbor, the landowner Khariton Zanoza, with a weapon in his hands, and after him came his fifteen-year-old son, carrying half a dozen dead rabbits. Who can describe the extent of our displeasure and anger! 'What sort of bravery is this, Pan Khariton?' cried my friend Ivan, 'and how can you have dared to act so improperly?' Our neighbor, without taking off his cap—and you must know that we both were bare headed—approached the fence and said: 'We have enough game for tonight's supper. And I say to you, Pan Ivan, that if you don't move these damned animals, which have made holes from your hutch into my garden and have carried out a multitude of depredations against my trees and plants there, then first of all I'll finish them off, and, moreover, will summon you to court.'
>
> 'Ah, you boor, you lout, you dare to say this to a military man without taking off your cap!' my friend Ivan called out, and with the speed of the wind drew a stake from the fence, wound up, and the cap flew into the air. But as this was done hastily, the stake also hit the neighbor on the ear, then jumped to the temple, and the neighbor flew to the grass, his son raised a yowl, and triumphantly we each returned to his own house."

Since that modest beginning, there have been ten years of guerrilla raids on stock, field, dams, and mills, and with the return of Nikanor and Koronat whole apiaries and pigeon roosts become victims of the internecine struggle. Stratagem succeeds stratagem, and the principals sink deeper into fruitless litigation. Meanwhile, the youths discover that Khariton has two comely daughters, and they arrange to meet them. Clandestine meetings lead to seduction and eventually secret marriages, but when these liaisons are discovered by the two Ivans, their sons beat a tactical retreat to Sech-Beyond-the-Falls and enroll as cossacks. In Khariton's absence, the mother forgives the two girls, especially when she learns that their sins have already been absolved by ceremony. A climax is reached when Khariton and the two Ivans are dispossessed by the courts and turned out into the street. Happily, a pillar of virtue named Artamon, who had been vainly counselling the two Ivans to cease their nonsense, now appears and provides shelter and sermons to the victims. In time Artamon arranges the return of the seized properties, and, having learned their lesson, the litigants are reconciled.

This amusing tale is rather like a mock epic in prose, a chronicle of banal heroics, with everything on a reduced scale. The Homeric conflict between nations becomes the petty antagonism of provincial landowners, the very embodiments of self-satisfied mediocrity, with exalted feelings of their own rights and values. The battles of champions become name-calling contests and sneak attacks on pigeon coops, and the gods are reduced to the figure of Artamon, a *raissoneur* in the style of the eighteenth-century didactic novel. The paired characters are largely interchangeable, the two boys and two girls so similar as to be almost indistinguishable except for their names. Ivan-the-Elder and Ivan-the-Youner together are only just a match for Khariton. But all of this doesn't really matter, because the story that Narezhny tells doesn't demand individualized personalities but generalized embodiments of various moral and spiritual shortcomings which can be exposed by satire.

Narezhny's satirical tool is not a scalpel but a machete, so his characters are not only stereotyped but exaggerated, with each new scene reinforcing the individual's dominant features. The qualities of bull-headedness and blind commitment to futile causes associated with Khariton is demonstrated once again in the letter he writes to his family following the loss of his appeal to the Poltava regimental court:

Wife Anfisa and children: Vlad and Raisa and Lidia! I wish you all health.
You should know that the Poltava regimental commander is no wiser than the Mirgorod divisional commander, but the members of the regimental chancery are more brazen, more vicious, and more given to chicanery than the members of the divisional chancery. Is such a thing possible? They ordered that for the dishonor which I did to the clerk Anury in the presence of many witnesses—as if it were really a great dishonor for a chancery clerk to get a few blows on the back with a club from someone who is gentry born—I should pay two hundred *zloty*! Well, if I had beaten that scoundrel Anury to death, they couldn't have demanded more than twenty or thirty *zloty* for that kind of mutilation. Having heard such a stupid decision, I firmly refused to accept it, and these

merciless people decided to award him perpetual and hereditary possession of my farm with its peasants and all its premises. To tell the truth, since I began to litigate with Ivan Zubar and Ivan Khmara, this piece of property has lost its attraction because of its proximity to theirs. However, in order not to put my face in the mud, and not to shame such an honorable name, which I received from my enemies themselves, that is, the name of intransigence, I am setting off for Baturin today, where I intend to litigate to my last breath in the army chancery against the divisional and regimental ones. I would sooner agree to see you in rags, barefoot, raising your hands in supplication for a piece of bread, and even dying from hunger, than to give in to my enemies. When Foma reads you these lines, then know that I am already in Baturin.

Khariton Zanoza

This letter not only serves to reemphasize the stubborn conceit of Khariton, but it also shows the court to be a den of thieves. Satire against the judicial system has a long history in Russian letters, and the consensus seems to have been that being at the mercy of the court was about as desperate a situation as being in the hands of a physician. The following order of the court, which the triumphant clerk Anury reads to Khariton's family, satirizes not only the brazen venality of the court's servants but also pokes fun at the style of the document itself:

"The army chancery, having reviewed the decisions of the Mirgorod divisional chancery and the Poltava regimental chancery on the matter of the violent and illegal actions of Pan Khariton Zanoza, finds: as the clerk Anury is sufficiently satisfied for the beating on the neck and the blows with a club on his back by the awarding to him perpetual and hereditary possession of the farm of the said Zanoza, then justice demands satisfaction also for the divisional commander and the members of the divisional chancery, who were greatly dishonored by the most outrageous words pronounced by Zanoza on the evening when he accompanied Anury from his yard with a club; therefore it is necessary: having taken from Pan Khariton his Gorbilov house and the serfs, orchards, gardens and fields attached to it, give them to the possession of the divisional commander Gorday. And he is obliged in retribution to give from his treasury to all members of the divisional chancery, from the oldest to the youngest, one eighth of the salary of each. Pan Khariton Zanoza, as a danger to others and for the correction of his violent nature, is to be placed in the Baturin prison for six weeks on bread and water. As for the children of Khariton Zanoza, they then, on the arrival at their house of the divisional commander Gorday, have complete right to leave in those clothes which they are wearing. However, if because of ignorance or impudence they begin to protest, they are to be thrown into the street on their necks, and let them wander where they will."

At the time of his death in 1825, Narezhny was working on yet another didactic-picaresque novel, this one concerned with the life of Garkusha, the legendary Ukrainian bandit. With the usual salty features (seductions, brawls, beatings, intoxication, coarse language), the author traces the evolution of a simple shepherd into a robber ataman, his first small departure from rectitude leading to greater errors and finally to open rebellion against the law. Garkusha is portrayed with sympathy and his deeds are described with gusto, but still the author indulges in considerable tongue clucking. The story was un-finished, and an effort to publish it in 1835 resulted in a negative evaluation by the censor. Its fate was similar to that of the final three parts of *A Russian Gil Blas*—it was first published in 1950! Obviously, this novel had no overt in-fluence upon the development of Russian fiction, but it was probably known in some circles. In any case, it initiated a recurring theme for Romantic fic-tion, and we find Orest Somov, Alexey Perovsky, and others incorporating this figure of the Ukrainian bandit into their works.

In the twenties, French and Russian translations of E.T.A. Hoffmann and Washington Irving became available, and Russian authors, who were still working primarily with short forms, quickly began to imitate these imported works. From the mid-twenties on, the supernatural tale becomes one of the most popular types of fiction. Oddly, despite their obvious attraction to the supernatural, Russian authors almost always treated it satirically, ironically, or comically, exposing the supernatural as a hoax, a dream, an hallucination, or a mistake. Those few stories which presented the supernatural as "real," usually show satanic forces at work in the lives of simple people.

One of the first, and also one of the best, tales of the supernatural was Alexey Perovsky's (1787-1836) *The Lafertov District Poppyseed-Cake Ven-dor [Lafertovskaia makovnitsa]*, which came out in *The Literary News [No-vosti literatury]* in 1825 over the pseudonym "Antoni Pogorelsky." Here we have the somewhat unusual combination of the "real" supernatural de-picted in comic terms. The emphasis is upon the plot and stage effects, and the characters predictably fulfil their assigned roles. Thus we have the God-fearing Onufrich, a retired postman, his wife Ivanovna, a grasping shrew, their daughter Marya, an innocent and charming girl of seventeen. The demonic menace is provided by Onufrich's aunt, a hag who sells poppyseed cakes by day but by night tells fortunes and engages in witchcraft.

Onufrich, disturbed at rumors that his aunt is in contact with the Evil One, determines to persuade her to alter her ways and so goes to visit her:

> The old woman received him kindly. "Eh, eh, dear nephew!" she said to him, "What misfortune drove you out of the house so early and so far yet? Well, welcome, I beg you to sit down."
> Onufrich sat down next to her on the bench, coughed, and didn't know how to begin. At that moment the decrepit old woman seemed more frightening to him than a Turkish battery had thirty years before. Finally, he all at once gathered up his courage. "Aunty," he said in a firm voice, "I came to talk to you about an important matter."
> "Speak, my dear," the old woman answered, "and I shall listen."
> "Aunty, you don't have much more time on earth—and the time has come to reject Satan and his temptation."
> The old woman didn't let him finish. Her lips turned blue, her eyes became blood-shot, and her nose began to knock noisily against her chin. "Get out of my house!" she cried in a voice trembling with anger. "Get out, you cursed one! And if you set foot again on my threshold, may your damn legs forever fail you! " She raised a dry hand. . . .

Onufrich was frightened half to death. An earlier, long lost suppleness returned to his legs, and in one movement he jumped off the stairs and ran all the way home, not once looking behind him.

Although commanded by her husband not ever to mention the aunt again, Ivanovna is lured by thoughts of the old witch's rumored wealth, and she secretly takes Marya to visit her. The hag receives them, but tells Marya to come alone the following night at midnight. When the terrified girl appears, the old witch involves her in some mysterious ritual:

The old woman began to walk around the table, pronouncing the incomprehensible words of a drawn out tune. In front of them the black cat with the glittering eyes and upright tail moved along smoothly. Masha closed her eyes tightly and with shivering steps followed the old granny. Thrice three the old woman went around the table, continuing her mysterious tune, which was accompanied by the mewing of the cat. Suddenly she stopped and fell silent. . . . Masha involuntarily opened her eyes. Bloody threads still stretched through the air. But accidentally glancing at the black cat, she saw that it was wearing a green uniform frock-coat, and in place of its precious round feline head she saw a human face, which was fixing its wide open eyes directly on her. She cried out loudly and fell senseless to the ground.

When Marya recovers, her aunt promises her a fortune if she will marry the person selected for her. The bewildered girl returns home and tells her mother everything, and the greedy Ivanovna immediately begins to dream of a future life of luxury and position. Soon the aunt dies and is buried without incident, other than the corpse trying to bite Ivanovna's nose as she bends over it to impart the farewell kiss. Onufrich and his family move into the aunt's house, and there they are disturbed by knocking noises and spectral figures. One day a suitor arrives, and Marya is despondent, since she has recently fallen in love with a young man named Julian. Still, she obeys her parents and appears before the visitor.

Masha hastened downstairs in the same dress in which she had gone to the garret. She opened the door and became numb! On the bench next to Onufrich sat a man of short stature in a green uniform frock-coat, and that same face was staring at her which she had once seen on the black cat. She stopped in the doorway and could go no further.

"Come closer," said Onufrich, "What's the matter with you?"

"Daddy! That's granny's black cat," Masha answered and pointed to the guest, who was rolling his head in a strange way and looking fondly at her with almost completely squinted eyes.

"You've gone crazy!" Onufrich cried out in vexation. "What cat? This is Mr. Titular Counsellor Aristarchus Faleleyich Purrful [Murlykin], who does you the honor of requesting your hand."

At these words Aristarchus Faleleyich stood up, smoothly approached her and wanted to kiss her hand. Masha cried out loudly and moved backwards. Onufrich jumped up angrily from the bench. "What does this mean?" he cried out. "Such rudeness, just like a country wench!"

However, Masha didn't hear him. "Daddy!" she said to him angrily, "Have it your own way! But this is granny's black cat! Tell him to pull off his gloves and you will see that he has claws." With these words she left the room and ran to the garret.

Aristarchus Faleleyich quietly muttered something under his breath. Onufrich and Ivanovna were in extreme confusion, but Purrful went up to them all smiles. "It's nothing, sir," he said, lisping badly,"it's nothing, madam, please don't be angry! I will come tomorrow again, and tomorrow our dear bride-to-be will receive me in a better fashion." Following that he bowed several times to them, bending his roundish back charmingly, and then went away. Masha was looking out the window and she saw Aristarchus Faleyeich going down the stairs and walking off, moving his feet silently. But having reached the end of the house, he suddenly turned the corner and started to run like an arrow. With a loud bark, the neighbor's large dog tore after him at full speed. However, it was unable to catch him.

Shortly thereafter Onufrich turns up another suitor, the son of a rich friend, and Marya is given an ultimatum to settle for her father's choice or accept Purrful. She categorically rejects the frock-coated feline, and so imagine her delight when her alternative bridegroom turns out to be Julian.

This comic tale generated an amusing postscript when it was included in a cycle of stories Perovsky published in 1828, entitled *The Double, or My Evenings in Little Russia [Dvoinik, ili moi vechera v Malorossii]*, but that will be discussed later.

Vasily Narezhny

VI. The Uprising of 14 December 1825—N. Bestuzhev.

The attempt at revolution in 1825 which became known as the Decembrist Uprising was preceded by a sequence of strange and irresponsible decisions at the highest level of the ruling circles. When news of the death of Alexander I at Taganrog on 19 November, 1825, reached Petersburg, Nicholas I and his advisors, fearing a mutiny among the guards if there were an interregnum, took the oath of allegiance to Constantine, the oldest brother to the late tsar, who was at that time in Warsaw. However, Nicholas and his confidants knew that almost four years previously Constantine had renounced his right to succeed Alexander, in return for permission to divorce his wife and marry a commoner. The mock reign of Constantine lasted three weeks, while in Petersburg they awaited an official declaration from Constantine regarding the legitimacy of Nicholas' succession. However, Constantine had been angered by his younger brother's charade and refused to take any official action to clarify the situation. Word then reached Nicholas that a conspiracy had been uncovered in the southern army, and he determined to resolve his status by ordering that the oath of allegiance to himself be administered on the fourteenth. Meanwhile the radicals had been capitalizing upon the confusion by spreading rumors stressing the desirability of Constantine, who would, they said, shorten the term of military enlistment, free the serfs, grant a constitution, and institute other reforms. Such talk fell upon eager ears, because Nicholas was heartily disliked in the barracks for his disciplinary cruelty. The would-be revolutionaries believed that if they could occupy the Senate Square and prevent the senators from taking the oath of allegiance to Nicholas, they could force Nicholas to acquiesce to a constitutional monarchy. Therefore, they determined to move on the morning of the fourteenth.

Their efforts were too little and too late. Before eight o'clock on the morning of the fourteenth, the senators had already taken the oath, as had most troops in Petersburg. Some, however, refused the oath, and marched to Senate Square, chanting (allegedly) "Constantine and Constitution," apparently believing that "Constitution," which is a noun of feminine gender [konstitutsiia], was the Emperor's wife. On Senate Square, dominated by the equestrian statue of Peter the Great trampling a snake, the insurgents, in all about three thousand soldiers and thirty officers, formed a *carré*— and there they stood, all day. Other than to refuse repeated demands to surrender, the leaders seemed unable to act. Occasionally shots were exchanged as Nicholas moved loyal troops to surround the rebels. A cavalry attack was repulsed. Count Miloradovich, the Governor-General of Petersburg, and Colonel Stuerler of the Grenadiers were mortally wounded by Peter Kakhovsky, one of the few Decembrists not numbed by their own audacity and the freezing cold. The others waited and shivered, and meanwhile the Tsar had four cannons brought into position. As darkness was falling, the order was given to open fire with grapeshot.

A graphic description of the debacle is found in a fragment written by Nikolay Bestuzhev, who led a detachment of sailors to the square.[1]

I had long ago sheathed my sabre. I stood in the space between the Moscow *carre* and a column of Guards. Having pulled down my hat and crossed my arms, I repeated Ryleev's words that we were breathing freedom. With grief I saw that this breath was being stifled! Our freedom and the cries of the soldiers was more like moaning or a death rattle! Indeed, we were surrounded from all sides. Our inaction was intensified by a paralysis of the mind. We lost our spirit, for whoever once stops on this course is already half defeated. Moreover, the penetrating wind turned the blood to ice in the veins of the soldiers and officers who had been standing so long in the open. The attacks on us and our own firing ceased. The "hurrahs" of the soldiers became less frequent and weaker. The day grew darker. Suddenly we saw that the regiments facing us had moved to the side and a battery of artillery, with opened muzzles, stood between us, dully illuminated by the grey light of dusk. . . . The first cannon thundered, grapeshot scattered. Some balls hit the pavement and raised pillars of snow and dust with ricochets, others tore several ranks from the front lines, yet others whined overhead and found their victims in the people pressed together between the columns of the Senate building and on the roofs of neighboring houses. Broken windows tinkled falling to the ground, but the people who plummeted after them stretched out quiet and motionless. At the first shot seven men near me fell. I did not hear a single gasp, I did not notice a single convulsion, so terribly did the grapeshot cut them down at that distance. Complete silence reigned over the living and the dead. The second and third rounds cut down a pile of soldiers and the rabble which had gathered in crowds around our position. I stood exactly in the same stance, looked sadly into the eyes of death, and awaited the fatal blow. At that moment my existence was so bitter that to perish seemed a stroke of luck. However, fate had it otherwise.

With the fifth and sixth round the column trembled, and, when I looked around, already between me and those who were fleeing was the whole square with its hundreds of sacrifices to freedom, reaped by grapeshot. I had to follow the general movement, and, with a sort of dead feeling in my soul, I picked my way among those who had been killed. Here there was not a motion, not a cry, not a groan, only in the intervals between shots one could hear the hot blood streaming along the pavement, melting the snow, then crimsoning, becoming frozen itself.

A squadron of Horse Guards moved after us, and, when the fleeing people crowded together at the entrance to the narrow Galley Street, I reached the Guard Grenadiers, who had come up from behind, and ran into my brother, Alexander. At this point we stopped several dozen people so that we could resist and cover the retreat in case of a cavalry attack, but the Emperor preferred to continue firing down the long and narrow street.

Grapeshot pursued better than horses, and the platoon which we had put together was scattered. The corpses of soldiers and people piled up more and more with every step. The soldiers ran into houses, they knocked at gates, they tried to hide between the protrusions of the socles, but the grapeshot jumped from wall to wall and didn't spare a single cranny. In this way the crowd reached the first intersection and was met there with new fire from the Pavlovsk Grenadier Regiment. Not having seen where my brother went, I turned into a half opened gate on the right and encountered the owner of the house himself. Two nicely dressed people also rushed through the gate, and, at the moment the owner invited us to enter, grapeshot struck one of them and he fell, blocking our path. Before I could bend down to raise him, he closed his eyes forever. Blood sprayed from both his breast and back, since the shot had gone right through him.

Nikolay Bestuzhev was given sanctuary until later in the evening, when he returned to the naval base at Kronstadt. There he was arrested.

The Tsar was swift and deft in dealing with the "outcasts" who had planned his overthrow. By the time his investigation had been completed, it had reached even to the officers serving in the Caucasus, and over five hundred people had been questioned. Oddly, a number of the most vociferous conspirators suffered extreme cases of *mea culpa* and turned state's evidence, sometimes implicating the innocent in their zeal to heap ashes upon themselves. Trials were held for one hundred and twenty-one accused, and over one hundred were found guilty. Five of the ringleaders, including Kondraty Ryleev, were hanged, and the rest sentenced to various terms of penal servitude. Convict convoys of the condemned plodded towards Siberia under close guard, followed by a few intrepid wives and children, who voluntarily chose to share exile and privation with the prisoners.

The catastrophe of the Decembrist Uprising is like a watershed dividing the Romantic period into two parts, the first from somewhere around 1815 to December, 14, 1825, and the second from that fatal day until whenever Realism officially appears, somewhere around 1840. In the pre-Decembrist era, the anticipation of revolution conditioned the poetry, drama, and prose of all liberals, and after 1825 the memory of the debacle colored much of what was written. Before the Uprising there had developed under the censor's myopic eye a clandestine and sophisticated means of communicating liberal or radical values through literature. After 1825 the author who expressed even merely progressive ideology was threatened not only with proscription of his work but with actual exile. The post-Decembrist man of letters could contemplate the fate of his less fortunate writer-compatriots languishing in Russian fortresses or at hard labor in Siberia. No one was exempt from suspicion, and caution was the order of the day, since even the most innocuous idea might be misinterpreted.

If one can still find a measure of the old esprit in the works of those few authors who refused to acquiesce to tyranny, at the same time one sees on the part of the gentry society as a whole an attitude of conciliation, of pretending that nothing had happened, of public veneration for the Tsar and an acceptance of his "merciful justice." There was hardly a gentry family that was not somehow touched by the Decembrist affair, be it only through the involvement of a cousin or a nephew. But these families continued to cluster around the court, fearing lest their absence might lead to the Tsar's disfavor. The convicted relatives became non-people, they were not spoken of in public, and past association with them became a shameful stigma which had to be covered with the cosmetic of servility. A *beau monde* which before

1825 had all the ills common to high society now added voluntary and obsequious abasement to its seven deadly sins. This society, however, was soon to feel the stings of satire inflicted by a number of outraged and disgusted authors.

VII. Fiction of the Later Twenties. The Literary Almanac *Northern Flowers*. The Framed Tale—N. Bestuzhev, Pogodin, Polevoy, Bulgarin. The Supernatural Tale—Somov.

A dearth of fiction marked the immediate post-Decembrist period. *Northern Flowers*, the almanac which had inherited *Polar Star's* prestige and many of its collaborators, carried a number of travel accounts in its first three issues, but only two pieces which might qualify as fiction. Here we shall cease to accord honorary fictional status to travel accounts, which continued to proliferate and became even more interesting. Their role in the development of the prose literary language has been sufficiently stressed.[1]

The first piece of fiction to appear in *Northern Flowers for 1826* was entitled *The Inn Stairs [Traktirnaia lestnica]* and signed "Alexey Korostylov." Happily for Delvig, the author of *The Inn Stairs* used a pseudonym, for he was none other than Nikolay Bestuzhev, the naval officer whose grim memoir of events on Senate Square has already been quoted. Had his name figured in the almanac, the entire issue might well have been suppressed, appearing as it did just a few weeks after the Decembrist Uprising.

The story is of little artistic value but of interest as an example of Romantic hybridization of genres, combining the genre of travel notes with the personal confession. The latter was a rather embryonic version of what later was to become the so-called psychological novel or tale, not to be confused with the novel of psychological Realism. The travel element in *The Inn Stairs* centers on a trip by the narrator, a naval officer, to Copenhagen in 1815, which frames the confession of an old invalid whom he meets at his inn. The invalid's story concerns the sordid details of his extra-marital affair with a married woman and its distressing consequences, but Bestuzhev's effort to create a credible personality fails, since the motivation of the invalid remains obscure and his reactions seem quite capricious. The details of Danish life as seen by the visiting officer apparently are introduced to lend verisimilitude to the story of the interior narrator (the invalid), but in fact they distract the reader, causing his attention to focus upon the frame rather than on the picture.

This sort of story, in which a frame narrator reproduces the autobiography of some chance acquaintance in the teller's own language, became very popular among Romantic authors, and Mikhail Pogodin, Nikolay Polevoy, Orest Somov and others used this structure in introducing into Russian literature protagonists from the lowest social strata. In thus broadening the range of types suitable for polite fiction, they contributed to what Soviet critics call "the democratization of literature."

One of the first of these "democratizers" was Mikhail Pogodin (1800-

1875), historian and editor of the bi-monthly *Moscow Herald [Moskovskii Vestnik]*, which appeared from 1827 to 1830. Among his earliest works is *The Beggar [Nishchii]* (1826), a melodramatic life-history of a serf who had become a beggar after having been invalided from the army following twenty-five years of service. The autobiography is framed by the comments of a narrator who extracted the story from the beggar, the narrator's curiosity having been aroused by signs of nobility in the demeanor of the poor old man. In return for his story, the narrator provides him dinner. The beggar, who expresses himself in literate but simple language, marked by an occasional proverb, tells of his youth as a member of a well-to-do serf family and his engagement to Aleksasha, with detailed description of the matchmaking and pre-nuptial formalities. All is well until the unexpected appearance of their young master necessitates an overnight postponement of the ceremony. The next morning the would-be groom learns that the master has exercised his *droit de seigneur:*

> "The Fiend! He. . . Ach Aleksasha!" The beggar again fell silent. This moment was still alive in his imagination, and he shook all over, his eyes glittered. I was able to calm him with difficulty.

The infuriated serf attempts to knife his master, but he fails and is sent to the army. He serves heroically under Suvorov, receiving twenty wounds in one battle, and when his enlistment is over, twenty-five years later, he leaves the service. Gradually he sinks into poverty and becomes a beggar. His interlocutor's offer of assistance is politely refused.

If this story has any significance, it is in its attempt to utilize the life history of a serf protagonist as story material. Similar tales of drastic abuse had appeared much earlier, as in Radishchev's *Journey from Petersburg to Moscow [Puteshestvie iz Petersburga v Moskvu]*, but their literary qualities were dominated by the element of social protest. In addition, Pogodin's work shows authorial concern for the psychology of his pathetic narrator, as well as ethnographic interest in peasant *byt*, or life style.

Stories of a Russian Soldier [Rasskazy russkogo soldata], one tale by Nikolay Polevoy (1796-1846), is similar in structure and content. This is one of the works which brought the editor of *The Moscow Telegraph* recognition as a writer of fiction.

A simple freeholder from Kursk, a veteran of Suvorov's and the Napoleonic wars, uncomplainingly details the tragedies and suffering of his often lonely and painful life. His account is framed by the rambling discourse of a traveling merchant, who encountered the old veteran in a Ukrainian village, to which the soldier had retired after losing a leg. The veteran becomes garrulous and needs little prodding to pour forth his story, a litany of tribulations including his father-in-law's curse, his child's fatal bout with smallpox, the illness and presumed death of his wife, his volunteering for the army in place of his brother, his wife's sudden reappearance and a second, more painful parting, his loneliness as a soldier, battle, the death of his close friend, the loss of his leg, and finally his return home to find all friends and family gone.

Polevoy makes a very obvious effort to synthesize a lower-class narrative style for his protagonist, and so we have features in the old soldier's tale which are supposed to authenticate his humble origins. There is constant use of diminutive forms, proverbs and homey expressions, archaisms, locutions from folk laments, repetitions, but strangely no post-positive particles, which later were the hallmark of peasant speech. Notwithstanding all of these folksy elements, the reader will surely be disturbed by the appearance in the soldier's narrative of many of the same stylistic features which mark the "literary" exposition of the merchant, whose characteristic quality is the agglomeration of nouns and adjectives, parallel phrases, and constant alliteration.

Good old fellow!. . . Even now I can clearly imagine your grey hair, your so dearly deserved decoration [tvoi krov'iu kuplennyi krest] ; I still hear, it seems, the knock of your wooden leg, your voice; I see your expressive movements, the fire flashing in your eyes when you told me of defeats, and the tears which appeared in your eyes at the memory of parents once dear to your heart, the sad smile with which you looked on your situation [s kakoiu smotrel ty na svoe sostoianie] , and the smile of joy with which you spoke of the solace awaiting your bones in the bowels of mother earth.
I should like to convey to others some of your tales, but will they touch others as they touched me? With what shall I replace your expression, your look, your movements, your simple eloquent heart. In adding something *artificial*, I will only spoil your good-natured narration. But can I *retell* as you told it, can I replace your proverbs, your augmentations, your little tales, and that laughter through tears and those tears through laughter that so surprised me, who did not yet know that one may cry and laugh at the same time.

These passages waft of Sentimentalism, and it is therefore not unexpected that the old veteran should also be given to pathetic expressions and emotional outpourings. He recounts how he volunteered to be drafted in his brother's place:

I became sad when with one word I had forever decided my fate, and my countrymen and I bowed to each other, we embraced for the last time, they carried my respects to my brother, a bow to my mother and the graves of my son and wife, when I remained lone-oh-lonely, without parents, without friends, without a human greeting, so that were I to have died the next day, then there would have been no one to remember me, other than God's church: it is mother to everyone!

The veteran's account of his military training, his participation in battle, his meeting Generals Bagration and Suvorov, his brief encounter with Napoleon, are really anecdotal rather than informative. There is, however, despite the veteran's devotion and loyalty, a subtext revealing the terrible fate of those conscripted for military duty, who, even if they survived battles and privations, could scarcely hope to find their families alive after the usual twenty-five years of service. More openly discussed, and therefore more clearly conveyed, is the dire poverty which dominated the lives of peasants unfortunate enough to be born in areas where the earth was unfertile, the water poor, and the climate rigorous. The life of the peasant in these circumstances was little better than that of his animals, if he indeed could afford them, and he was constantly menaced by starvation and disease.

As if now I see my blessed homeland, although I left it long ago. On the bare steppe along a slope were several miserable huts, stripped, like after a fire. There weren't even small woods or young trees around, but only fields with poor grain. Next to the river were several hollows in the ground, where we used to wash in muddy water. There was a clayey walkway made of willow. The mud in the street was up to the knees, but in the winter everything was covered with snow, which was somewhat cleaned away from the entrance to each hut and piled in heaps against the walls. Without this we would have frozen to death from the cold, and it used to happen that during snowless and cold winters the only way to stay alive was to lie on the stove. On one side a windmill stuck up, as if mocking us for having nothing for it to grind, and on the other side several dozen cows, goats, sheep, and pigs wandered about near the village, thin as mice in the government office, where there was nothing for the clerks to eat except paper.

In the sentimentalized atmosphere of this story, a passage such as this commands attention with its straightforward description of poverty. The details suggest comparison with those found later in works of the Natural School or Realism.

Northern Flowers for 1827 included *The Almodavar Ruins [Razvaliny Almodavarskie]*, the work of Faddey Bulgarin (1789-1859), editor-publisher of the newspaper *Northern Bee* and virtual monopolist of Petersburg periodical publications. Again we have a frame tale, the exterior narrator recounting his experiences as a cavalry officer during Napoleon's invasion of Spain. In particular he tells of his near fatal encounter with a mad woman while exploring the ruins of Almodavar castle.

A sudden noise broke my reverie: sand and rubble sifted down from the top of a half-ruined vault. I looked around and saw a woman in a black dress with unkempt hair. She stood above my head and held a huge rock in her hands, ready to strike me! Our eyes met, and her wild look produced in me the same feelings as the glitter of a dagger over the head of a man suddenly awakened from sleep. An involuntary tremor ran through my veins, my blood congealed and my heart contracted. "Did you kill him," she cried in a threatening voice, and she raised the stone over her head. The moment was decisive, but a sudden inspiration saved me.

"No, not I!" I answered in a loud and firm voice, completely without understanding the question.

"Not you?" said the unknown woman, having lowered her voice, and slowly lowering the stone, she sat down on a piece of debris and fastened her black, glittering eyes upon me.

This melodramatic episode frames the insane woman's tragic history, which the officer hears from his Spanish guide. He recounts how her father had given shelter to a wounded French soldier, to whom she had become betrothed, and how French deserters had broken into their house and killed her fiancé. From that time she had become obsessed with a desire to avenge his death. All of this is narrated in a very touching manner. The story then reverts to the frame details and concludes with a crocodile tear:

> In silence I returned to the detachment, and for the whole journey I grieved, thinking about the unhappy girl. The ruins of Almodavar remained in my memory. "O people," thought I, "why do you torment one another, when by doing good you might be happy!"

Bulgarin demonstrated his versatility, if nothing else, as a writer of fiction with the historical tale, *The Fall of Wenden [Padenie Vendena]*, which came out in the 1828 edition of *Northern Flowers*. Again we are back in old Livonia, this time in the year 1577, when Ivan the Terrible, engaged in the pacification of rebellious towns, besieged Wenden, in whose castle the King of Livonia, Magnus, had taken refuge. The historical background for this tale clearly is drawn from Karamzin's *History of the Russian State*, but Bulgarin takes considerable liberty with the facts in order to achieve certain effects. Thus, although the event took place in summer, the fictionalized action is transposed to fall so that "autumn clouds" can be used to intensify the atmosphere. Bulgarin's portrait of Ivan the Terrible is a real *tour de force* of idealization in the face of incontrovertible evidence of the Tsar's maniacally vicious suppression of the Livonians.

Shortly after King Magnus fled to the castle at Wenden, he recanted his declaration of independence and threw himself upon Ivan's mercy. The German-Livonian defenders of the castle realized that capitulation would mean death, since Ivan had already sold entire Livonian towns into slavery and eradicated their leaders. To avoid capture and torture, the Livonians determined to blow themselves up, and their leader, Henryk Boysman, fired their powder magazine. Deprived of his prey, the outraged Ivan ordered the empalement of Boysman's corpse and the slaughter of the townspeople, though they had remained neutral during the siege of the castle.

In *The Fall of Wenden* these depressing facts are ignored, and, indeed, we are shown a magnanimous Ivan acting kindly towards his prisoners and even addressing the dying Boysman without rancour. The pardon of King Magnus is emphasized, and nothing is said of what happened to the populace of Wenden. Bulgarin was not affected by Karamzin's summary remarks:

> In one word, this *scourging of Wenden* belongs to the most terrible exploits of Ivan's tyranny: it doubled the hatred of the Livonians for the Russians. [2]

Into this adaption of history, Bulgarin interweaves a purely fictional plot involving a beautiful Livonian girl, Eleonora, who is in love with Vladimir, a Russian soldier held hostage by the defenders of the castle. Somehow they escape the explosion that ends the resistance, apparently not being worth the powder to blow them up. A more interesting character is that of Marko, a mysterious wizard who may be an older brother to Adam Mickiewicz's *wajdelota* in *Konrad Wallenrod,* published in 1829.[3] Marko is revealed to be the last descendent of a family of Livonian pagan priests whose mission was to avenge the German usurpation of Livonia, and in this he finds Ivan a convenient ally.

Bulgarin returned to *Northern Flowers* in 1829 with another eulogistic historical tale, *Peter the Great in the Naval Expedition from Petersburg to Viburg [Petr Velikii v morskom poxode iz Petersburga k Vyborgu]*, putatively non-fictional. Its motivation seems to have been similar to that of *The Fall of Wenden*: to demonstrate the super-patriotic attitudes of its author towards Russia's westward expansion. More will be said later regarding Bulgarin's apparently gratuitous patriotism for Russia, which rings off-key in a Pole whose parental estates and fortune had been confiscated by the Russians during the final partition of Poland.

In 1827 Orest Somov (1793-1833) made his debut as a writer of fiction, and two of his three stories concern the supernatural. *A Command from the Other World [Prikaz s togo sveta]*, appearing in the almanac *Literary Museum*, employs the same structure as *The Inn Stairs*, a frame of travel notes with an interpolated anecdote, but in a much more interesting and artistic fashion. The frame, as one might imagine, is very similar in its tone and humor to those letters which Somov sent from abroad to the Petersburg literary societies in 1819 and 1820. In fact, the details of the journey from Kaiserslautern to Helnhausen in this story were doubtless based on Somov's own observations of Bavaria on his return from France to Russia.

The play with the German language in the passage below heightens his humorous observation about Teutonic coachmen:

> German postillions wear clean clothes, and they play on coach horns. On the other hand, their irksome phlegm and their intolerable *langsam* torment the traveler. Even the most long-suffering person, it seems, will lose patience with them. Thus, angry and abusive, my companion and I traveled with them from Hamburg to Kaiserslautern. But neither abuse   nor endearments nor exhortations nor the smooth *chaussée*, along which one might have glided as on butter, nor the addition of a *Trinkgeld*—nothing stirred the ossified hearts of our tormentors.

The postillion's *langsam* precipitates his own punishment when he gets soaked in a downpour before they reach their destination:

> At that time we were entering the village of Helnhausen, which lies on a hillside in a quite picturesque setting. Our postillion, seeing the end of his suffering, placed the wet horn to his wet lips, and like the swan on the waters of the Meandre river, began

to play his final song at full blast. The horses, joyful at their forthcoming freedom from harness and rest in a cozy stable with fodder, echoed him by neighing. In such a fashion, with music and accompaniment, we drove up to the inn, the Golden Sun.

At the Golden Sun they meet the town worthies, most particularly the innkeeper, Herr Johann-Gottlieb-Cornelius Stauf, a man inordinately proud of his aristocratic heritage, Ernst German, the village teacher, and the crafty brewer, Nesselsamme, who persuades the innkeeper to relate to the travelers the tale of his summons from the other world. The vain Stauf enthusiastically details his connection to the illustrious Hohenstaufen clan, of which he is the last male descendent. In fact, this heritage was the reason he had at first forbidden his daughter, Minna, to marry the teacher, Ernst German, who though honorable and solid could hardly have aspired to be the husband of even a distant descendant of the Hohenstaufens. Meanwhile, in accordance with a family legend concerning periodic visitations by a ghost of his ancestor, the innkeeper was preparing for a meeting with the spectre of the exalted Georg von Hohenstaufen. One night a page clothed in black armor appeared in his bedroom and gave him a scroll appointing a rendezvous three nights hence at the ruins of the Hohenstaufen castle. With trepidation but resolve the innkeeper fulfilled the summons, and at the castle the same page conducted him to a chamber where he was greeted by his awesome ancestor. The ghost commanded him to guarantee the continuation of his family line by permitting Minna to marry Ernst, who, he insisted, was of even more distinguished lineage than the Hohenstaufens themselves, since his was the family from which Germany had taken its name.

The humor of the story derives not only from the self-importance and pompousness of the innkeeper, whose remarks reveal his hopelessly bourgeois nature, but also from his unawareness that he was the victim of an elaborate hoax: his illustrious ancestor was none other than his friend the brewer, who had organized a conspiracy to obtain the innkeeper's permission for the marriage of Minna and Ernst.

In this story Somov reveals a talent for creating a graphic external image of his characters by the use of circumstantial detail:

The host, a man over fifty, with a most pleasing old-German face, walked sedately around the table carrying his pipe, with each step seeming to raise himself closer to the ceiling, for nature begrudged him a stature which suited his pompous deportment. He was wearing clothes of a special cut, which might be called a compromise between a dressing gown and a camisole: extra wide sleeves, but skirts which hung somewhat below the knees. This new kind of tunic was made from a chintz cloth with large arabesques of bright color, the kind that in Russia is used to upholster furniture, and it was fastened from top to bottom with huge buttons. Our innkeeper's greyish hair was covered with a black silk nightcap. Seeing us, the host approached and bowed most grandly. . . .

The brewer, Nesselsamme, "a short, heavy man with a round and red face, a nose that inflated like a blacksmith's bellows with each breath, roguish eyes under an awning of heavy, reddish brows, and with a most cunning smile," provides an introduction for the inn keeper:

"The honorable host of this house," continued the cunning brewer," is Herr Johann-Gottlieb-Cornelius Stauf, a humble branch of the ancient Hohenstaufen line." At these words, our host seemed to grow whole inches. First he rubbed his hands, then he tried to hide a smile of satisfaction behind some strange grimace which crossed his face—in a word, he was beside himself. Finally his tongue became untangled. With all the noble modesty of an ambitious provincial, he said to us:
"Exactly so, dear gentlemen! Under this humble roof, in what are, one might say, almost tatters, you see the descendant of a once famous clan." His voice shook, and try as he might, he was unable to conclude this eloquent introduction.

The external portrait is reinforced by what we learn of the innkeeper's psychology from his own tale, a mixture of pompousness and completely naive forthrightness, both of which combine to produce a perfect type for projecting the ironical essence of the anecdote.

VIII. Fiction of the Later Twenties (continued). The Physiological Sketch and Society Tale—Somov. The Story Cycle—Perovsky-Pogorelsky. The Supernatural Tale—Titov.

Somov's other story of 1827, *The Holy Fool [Iurodivyi]*, appeared in *Northern Flowers for 1827*. Admittedly, in some respects *The Holy Fool* fails to realize its potential as a study of human psychology, and there are some regressions to Sentimentalist formulae with respect to style. Nevertheless, the innovative qualities of this work imply a progressive author who is unafraid to assay new techniques and experiment with form. The story's structure incorporates two types of fiction which in 1827 were still new for Russian prose, or at least under-developed—the physiological sketch and the society tale. A few words about each are appropriate here.

The physiological sketch originated in France with Etiènne de Jouy's sociological encyclopedia of Paris in five volumes, *L'ermite de la chaussée d'Antin*. Constantine Batyushkov tried his hand at a similar type of writing in 1816 with his *A Stroll to the Academy of Arts*. Several of the letters sent by Somov to *The Emulator* and *The Well-Intended* in 1819-1820 follow Jouy in their concern with the sights and peoples of European cities. In Russia the sketch became very popular, focusing primarily upon individuals associated with a particular trade or occupation, and *The Holy Fool* incorporates an early version of this genre.[1] The title in Russian is *Iurodivyi*, the word identifying a type of religious mendicant in Orthodox countries notable for eccentric or even insane behavior, feats of piety, and ability to prophesize. Somov created a physiological sketch of the *iurodivyi* and integrated his character, Basil-the Half-Wit, into the general plot line of a society tale.

The society tale shared first place with the historical novel in the hearts of Russian readers during the thirties. Basically, it derived from Balzac's intimate views of French Parisian and provincial societies, its typical representatives, its dress, activities, mores, and amusements. The earliest Russian varieties of this genre, of which *The Holy Fool* was one, were generally didactic. This quality is evident in Somov's work and Alexander Marlinsky's *The Test* (1830) often considered (incorrectly) the first of the genre. The society tale later developed its typical formulae, usually involving a comely countess or princess who was unhappily married to a rich but otherwise unattractive husband. (Advanced age, obesity, and stupidity were common defects.) Seeking to rise above the banality of her daily existence, the heroine would form a sometimes guilty liaison with a young man of unusual but unrecognized (often artistic) talents. Their relationship usually had an unhappy dénouement. Typically the society tale involved a general picture of the activities of the *haut monde*, with scenes of balls, clandestine rendezvous, challenges, duels, banquets, gossip, and gambling. The society tale was of great importance in the development of Russian fiction, for it was the basic form to which other genres were joined to create the novel of psychological Realism.

The society tale component of *The Holy Fool* concerns a young officer, Melsky, whose rather innocent jests with a young lady at a ball lead to a challenge by a jealous artillery officer. Before Melsky departed for the ball, Basil-the-Half-Wit, a *iurodivyi* whom Melsky had sheltered at his quarters, had enigmatically warned him "Our tongue is our enemy." Basil had also revealed an uncanny knowledge of Melsky's past and had predicted that he, Basil, would lead Melsky to the grave of the officer's aunt. At the duel, the *iurodivyi* appears and, just as the antagonists fire, he throws himself between them, receiving their bullets. The duelists, shaken by the consequences of their pride and intransigence, are reconciled, and they take the wounded man to a peasant's hut for treatment. There he lingers for several days, but, when Melsky comes to visit him on the fourth day, he finds the *iurodivyi* has disappeared. A search finally discloses his lifeless body in the cemetery on the grave of Melsky's aunt.

Leaving aside the plot itself, one finds in this story an unusual emphasis on the individual psychology of the protagonist, Melsky, who is projected as a congenial but heedless young man, one who embodies that code of values peculiar to his military calling. Early in the story there is a long description of Melsky's inchoate thoughts as he vainly tries to free his mind of the *iurodivyi*'s haunting image, and this disclosure of the mental anxiety of the officer is far more complex than one generally finds in fiction of the twenties. There is also in this story a strong suggestion of the inner emotional states of the various characters, conveyed by their dialogue. Again, Somov's achievement must be judged in the context of such popular authors as Marlinsky, who in the early twenties was capable of creating witty repartée but seemingly unable to have his characters express their emotions in any sort of natural language. Somov's challenge scene is illustrative. At the ball Melsky and his *vis à vis*, Sophia, idly amuse themselves by poking fun at the other guests, but their conspiratorial snickering does not pass unnoticed:

Several paces from them stood an artillery officer, holding his fingers to his mouth as if he were biting his nails, and looking with a severe expression now at Melsky and now at Sophia. Everything comes to an end, and the cotillion, which sometimes lasts until dawn, and especially so in the provinces, on this occasion ended rather quickly. Sophia disappeared from Melsky's view, and he, wishing to breathe some fresh air, went towards the glass doors leading into the garden. There the artillery officer, obviously waiting for him, blocked his path.

"Excuse me," Melsky said quite politely.

"First permit me to learn from you, kind sir, what your lady was saying to you and what she was laughing about?"

"That's a fine thing!" answered Melsky, not yet losing his patience. "Has the lady been entrusted to your care? And if so, then I expect that you know enough about the laws of chivalry. . . ."

"My dear sir!" the artillerist interrupted heatedly, "I demand from you the facts and not empty chatter."

"And I demand from you, sir," Melsky interjected with the same tone, "to tell me where you get the right to interrogate me?"

"I'll show you my right at the proper time."

"And I'll show you that I know how to get rid of annoying people who ask too many questions."

"You're impertinent!" and word followed word, the noise became louder and louder. A circle of curious people pressed around the two officers, everyone asking what the quarrel was about. But neither Melsky nor the artillerist was able or willing to disclose the cause at the root of their quarrel.

The scene in which Melsky is joined by his insouciant seconds, led by the dueling enthusiast Svidov, has a strong illusion of reality deriving from the natural quality of the dialogue and the straightforward, impersonal exposition:

A light tap on the shoulder aroused him [Melsky] from his obliviousness. Starting, he looked around. Before him stood Svidov, his second; further away were both witnesses to the duel on his behalf, officers of their regiment.

"Enough meditating on the vanity of this world," said Svidov to him cheerily. "It's now half past five. We have an hour and a half to go. Order some vodka for us and a bite to eat. We can't give you anything, brother. Don't get peeved, just wait a while. Such games as these you play with an empty stomach."

In decisive situations the calmness and cheerful disposition of a comrade's spirits act strongly on others, and so it was now. The three officers cheerfully occupied themselves with the proffered breakfast. Melsky sat with them, although he ate nothing. Svidov enlivened the conversation. He joked, made his companions laugh at Melsky, saying that he had purposely tried to cut out a lachrymose mask for himself, because he was planning to read his adversary's funeral service, and so forth. Melsky himself became quite cheerful, especially towards the end of the breakfast when Svidov, followed by the other two officers, poured full glasses of wine, raised them, and loudly cried, "To your health, Melsky."

"I shall thank you, gentlemen, in two hours, and not before," Melsky replied unconstrainedly.

Svidov looked at his watch. "Oho, friends, we've been feasting for some time. It's half past six. Melsky, order your pistols and charges. I, as the organizer of your life or death—don't get pale, dear friend—want to find out if the ammunition is in proper condition."

The pistols were inspected, the horses brought up, and in ten minutes, the four comrades were already outside of town.

The sketch of the *iurodivyi* is quite complete and includes all of those features distinctive of the fool-in-Christ: monkish garb, unkempt hair and beard, turbid and roving eyes, (appearance of) feeblemindedness, prophetic pronouncements, total disregard for rank or social station manifested by tactless candor in addressing others, lack of concern for personal comfort, and the physical constitution to withstand the elements and privation. Somov cleverly integrates this figure in his story by showing him from Melsky's point of view, and the *iurodivyi*'s inexplicable knowledge of private affairs, his

93

enigmatic remarks, his predictions are all presented as the young officer perceives them. The omniscient narrator is not obliged to explain anything more than Melsky's subjective reactions, which are confused and indecisive. This creates in the reader's mind a strong tension between belief and disbelief in the apparent occult powers of the *iurodivyi*, making the tale more suspenseful and engaging.[2]

The year 1828 marked Perovsky's second appearance in print with *The Double, or My Evenings in Little Russia [Dvoinik, ili moi vechera v Malorossii]*, a work structurally and thematically inspired by E.T.A. Hoffmann's *The Serapion Brothers*. Perovsky had spent almost two years in Dresden shortly after Napoleon's first defeat, and it has been surmised that probably he met the popular German author at that time.[3]

Like many authors, particularly in the early Romantic period, Perovsky was concerned with "motivating" the genesis of the tales forming his work, so he created a frame in which the narrator, Antoni P., a provincial landowner thirsting for intellectual companionship, exchanges stories with his double, a gentleman resembling himself who fortuitously appears for several hours each evening. At the time Perovsky was writing, the *Doppelgänger* had yet to be introduced into Russian literature, so he was obliged to create his own term, *dvoinik*. The stories are loosely unified by variations on the theme of the supernatural, and Antoni and Double function not only as raconteurs but also as a "chorus," commenting upon the stories themselves.

The First Night sets the stage, the narrator explaining the circumstances of his isolation in the country and introducing us to the accommodating Double, who assures Antoni that the appearance of one's double is not necessarily a sign of imminent death. The tone is light and slightly humorous, especially when Double provides "rational" explanations for supernatural events. The Second Night opens with Antoni reading his *Isadore and Anyuta [Izador i Aniuta]*, a sentimentalized and melodramatic anecdote set in Moscow during the French invasion. The poet Ivan Kozlov recorded in his diary that Perovsky had read this story at his house in 1825,[4] so its composition preceded publication by a significant period. In fact the tale does have many of the stigmata of Sentimentalism, especially in connection with the hero's agonizing over his dilemma, whether to hide his officer's uniform and stay with his fiancée, Anyuta, and dying mother or to observe his oath and retreat with the army. A sense of duty, supported by the threat of a maternal curse, determines his choice of the second alternative, and he departs. Six weeks later he returns with the victorious Russians to find his house gone and no sign of his loved ones. Guided by the remains of an elm tree which had graced his garden, he locates the spot which had been his home, and there he communes with something known only to himself.

This unpromising story is relieved only by the comment of Double, who objects to the ending, which hints that Isadore is visited by Anyuta's ghost. Following this, however, the First Night continues with at least five more brief stories, a sort of can-you-top-this of supernatural anecdotes. Things pick up considerably on the Third Night, when Double presents "*The Pernicious Consequences of an Uncontrolled Imagination*' [*Pagubnye posledstviia neobuzdannogo voobrazheniia*], whose characters are closely modeled on those found in Hoffmann's *Der Sandmann*. But despite uncontestable similarities, Perovsky's story is essentially different, because its philosophical point of view is quite unlike that in Hoffmann's tale. Hoffmann's protagonist, Nathaniel, is a victim of fate and a weak constitution, whereas Perovsky's Alcest is the victim of a murder plot capitalizing upon his imagination, over which his common sense has no control.

A rich and handsome young Russian, Alcest, is sent to Leipzig to complete his education under the direction of Colonel F. There he "accidentally" encounters a paragon of beauty, who, he is enraptured to learn, lives just across the narrow street. When Colonel F. insists on knowing why Alcest has become withdrawn and disinterested in his favorite pursuits, the young confesses his secret love:

"Ach!" he exclaimed, "this is not a girl, this is an angel. I know neither her name nor her calling, but I am convinced that both one and the other correspond to such heavenly beauty! You will see her, dear F. . . , and my passion will no longer surprise you."

He led me to the window, drew aside the curtain, and, indicating the house opposite ours, continued with ecstacy.

"Look and admit that you have never seen such an angel!" My eyes quickly followed the direction of his finger. I saw a girl sitting at the window, and indeed I was astounded! I had never seen such a beauty even in my imagination. Grimm Street was not wide, and I could study all the features of her charming face. In careless curls her black hair fell to her shoulders, white as Carara marble. An angelic innocence shone in her glance. No! Neither the genius of Raphael nor the flaming brush of Corregio, the artist of the graces, nor the most inspired chisel of the unknown sculptor of Venus di Milo had ever produced such a face, such a waist, such a collection of inexpressible charms! She looked at us and smiled. What a look, what a smile!

Inquiries reveal that the girl, Adelina, is the daughter of a Neapolitan savant, Professor Androni, a specialist in mathematics, astronomy, and mechanics. On the pretext of enrolling in his forthcoming lecture course, Alcest and Colonel F. became acquainted with Androni, whom they find exudes an aura of evil and mystery. Ultimately they meet Adelina, who is extremely reticent, shy, and emotionless, although she plays the harp beautifully and even dances a fandango at a ball given by her father. But she is never allowed to be alone with Alcest. While Colonel F. is away in Dresden on urgent business, he is informed that Alcest and Adelina are to be wed. Rushing back to Leipzig, he arrives after the couple have retired to their bridal chamber, and Androni will not hear of their being disturbed. Later that night the troubled F. is astonished when Alcest bursts into his room to report that Adelina had broken open in his nuptial embrace and appeared to be full of cotton. They rush back to Androni's apartment and find him sewing up her breast, while his accomplice, the vile Venturino, is winding her up with a large key:

> The villain was so occupied with his work that he did not notice our entrance into the room.
> I hadn't yet collected myself when, with a wild cry, Alcest threw himself at Androni. His face dispayed fury. . . . He swung at him with his cane and might have killed him on the spot had not Venturino stayed his hand. Androni went into a frenzy of anger. He seized a heavy hammer lying next to him and struck Adelina right on the head!. . . In one instant her face was completely transformed! Her charming nose was crushed, her pearly white teeth were scattered from her shattered jaws!. . .
> "There is your wife!" announced Androni, continuing to hit Adelina with the hammer. . . With one blow her beautiful blue eyes leaped from their sockets and flew off to one side. . . . Poor Alcest was seized by madness. . . . He grasped one of his Adelina's eyes from the floor and fled the room, laughing loudly and gnashing his teeth!. . . I followed him. Having left the house, Alcest paused a moment, then let out a pitiful wail, and suddenly, like an arrow, ran headlong down Grimm Street.

Later we learn that the evil Androni had deliberately ensnared Alcest with his "living doll" in revenge for some offense committed by the youth's father. Androni's plot is completely successful, for the sensitive Alcest disappears forever, apparently a suicide, and his father, who had learned too late of Androni's scheme, joins him in death.

Although Perovsky has paralleled Hoffmann with Alcest's suicide, he has added a new feature in the unusual method which is used to render Alcest suicidal: *effigiecide*. The scene of Adelina's "murder," incidentally, is worthy of a disciple of *l'Ecole frénétique,* a movement which was to exert noticeable influence upon Russian Romantic fiction in the early thirties.

In discussing this tale with Double, Antoni asks how it is possible for anyone to fall in love with a doll, especially an intelligent person such as Alcest. Double replies:

> . . . can a person fall in love with a doll? It seems to me there's nothing to wonder about here. Look at society. How many dolls of both sexes will you meet, who are totally unable and who cannot do other than to walk along the street, dance at balls, curtsy and smile. Nonetheless, at times people fall in love with them and even prefer them to people incomparably more worthy![5]

Part Two opens with the Fourth Night, which is more essay than fiction. As promised, Double attempts to answer how apparently intelligent people can make stupid mistakes. With the aid of pie-shaped diagrams and degrees of intensity on a scale of 1 to 15, he demonstrates that the attributes of intelligence, such as common sense, sagacity, foresight, clarity, memory, and so forth can be entirely negated by various sins and weaknesses, such as hatred, anger, baseness, greed or vanity. Without being specific, alas, Double asserts that thus it is possible for intelligent people, such as Voltaire, to be led into errors which would be obvious to persons of the most ordinary intellect.

The allusion to Voltaire is apropos, since the whole disquisition seems very much in the eighteenth century rationalistic mode.

Still, the Fourth Night does provide a comment upon Alcest's extravagance and inability to perceive the obvious (Colonel F. saw more, such as Adelina's absence of emotion, but apparently he was not so intelligent as his ward), and any dullness visited upon the reader is more than compensated for by the Fifth Night, which is the charming story *The Lafertov District Poppy Seed Cake Vendor*, which had been published in 1825. In this collection, the story is credited to Antoni, who mentions to his *vis à vis* that the tale had appeared in *The Literary News* published by *The Russian Invalid [Russkii Invalid]*.

Since the story has been discussed previously, nothing more need be said about its content here. However, there is an amusing circumstance connected with its publication in 1825, and this is alluded to in the frame as soon as Antoni has finished his tale:

"This story," said Double, "pleases me more than *Isadore and Anyuta*. It's too bad, however, that you didn't add a denouement. Some people might think that Masha's grandmother was a witch."

"You don't provide denouements for superstitious people," I answered. "Besides, whoever absolutely has to know the denouement of my story, let him read *Literary News* of 1825. There he will find a denouement composed by the honorable publisher of *The Invalid*, which I didn't relate to you because I don't want to appropriate someone else's property."

What in fact had happened was that the publisher, assuming that Perovsky's tale was some sort of object lesson on the excesses of superstition, appended explanations for all the fantastic content—that Masha was drugged and imagined things, and that Mr. Purrful's appearance and actions just seemed like those of the cat. This naive reaction obviously amused Perovsky, and thus his allusion to it here.

Antoni and Double then engage in an extended discussion about superstition, divination, astrology, witches, and wizards, and the difference between ancient and modern attitudes toward witchcraft. Double even provides a translation of a supernatural episode from Apuleius.

The Sixth Night opens as follows:

"Today," began Double when we met the following evening, "I will relate to you a true adventure which happened to a certain Muscovite friend of mine. I wrote it all down in his very own words. Here it is: A JOURNEY BY DILIGENCE."

Double's Muscovite friend is, in fact, primarily a link to yet another interior narrator, Colonel Fritz vander K., whom he meets while traveling from Moscow to Petersburg by diligence. The Chinese-box structure, with Antoni as the exterior surface, Double inside the frame, then the Muscovite, and finally vander K., provides sufficient distance between Perovsky and the events of the innermost box to relieve him of responsibility for them: vander K.'s tale, although hardly supernatural, is highly unusual to say the least.

Vander K.'s narrative is presented in a very forthright manner, without rhetorical intensification except when he describes his emotional reactions. Briefly, he tells of being raised in Borneo, where at the age of four he was abducted by apes, with whom he lived for the next four years, adopting their habits and acquiring a real love for his simian foster-mother, Tutu. One day while foraging he stumbles upon his parents' home and is repatriated. Three years later Tutu begins to visit him clandestinely at night, an act fraught with danger owing to his parents' excessive hostility towards apes. One night his father surprises the animal in the boy's room and hacks off a paw before it can flee. Vander K. does not see Tutu again until after the death of his parents, when he and the ape reestablish their relationship. Vander K., now twenty, unexpectedly falls in love and becomes engaged. His fiancée, Amalia, suspicious of his daily sojourns in the jungle, accuses him of infidelity, and he is obliged to reveal the true nature of the object of his attentions. Sharing the simiaphobia typical of settlers on Borneo, she demands he choose between Tutu and herself. The distraught youth goes to the jungle:

> There Tutu met me. Poor Tutu tried to show with joyous capers and grimaces that she was happy to see me! But I stood before her like stone, with hanging head. Tutu was not used to seeing me in such a state, and she began to caress me even more and with her paw accidentally touched the cord on my neck on which Amalia's portrait hung. It fell to the ground. . . . My friend, I looked at her charming features, then involuntarily looked at Tutu, and at that moment Amalia won out over the ape. I picked up the portrait, and for the first time in my life I shoved Tutu away. Then I turned from her, wanting to leave the forest. I intended to go to Amalia. Having taken several steps, I looked about. . . Tutu was quietly following me. I yelled at her angrily, took several more steps, looked around and saw that she was still following me. . . . I was seized with rage. . . I imagined that she was in a mood to seek me out even at Amalia's. My thoughts became confused. . . . I did not know what I was doing. My gun was loaded; one instant—a shot rang out. . . . Poor Tutu fell at my feet, and at the same time I fell to the earth, deprived of my senses.

From that time forward, vander K. becomes a homeless wanderer, tortured constantly with the memory of his vile deed, and so intense is his remorse he even imagines that his victim, the selfless ape, visits him at midnight.

In the introduction to the volume, *Antoni Pogorelsky*, N. L. Stepanov states, "The fourth and last story in *My Evenings in Little Russia*, 'A Journey by Diligence,' is a sentimental narration of the tender attachment of a human for an ape." He goes on to say that this tale is typical of early romanticism[6] in demonstrating how civilized society destroys the best instincts in man. While it is true that in some instances we can point to sentimentalist qualities in Perovsky's tales, it is certainly open to question whether *A Journey by Diligence* is a *serious* sentimental narration. The conclusion of the Sixth Night suggests otherwise:

"I will not criticize the story you have told," I said to Double, "both because of my natural politeness and also because it actually seemed to me quite remarkable. All the same, I cannot but mention that all your stories smack of a certain originality not pleasing to everyone. A few days ago you spoke about a count who went mad from love for a doll. And now you've gone one better. . . . A colonel, a military man, used to the horrors of war, loses his mind because he once shot an ape! Well, if that's the way you want it, honorable Double, but such occurrences are somehow not natural."

Double insists the contrary, and the frame ends this way:

"Goodbye, honorable Double! If you were not so tired, then I should like to learn from you if indeed the apes on the island of Borneo are as vander K. describes them?"
"I will gladly satisfy your curiosity. But let us leave th. . is. . . con. . . versa. . tion. . . until. . . tomor. . row. Goodbye!. ."
Double disappeared, and his last words were so unclear that I still don't know if he actually said them or that it only seemed so to me.

This facetious closing of the curtains suggests that Perovsky, far from being an author of sentimental proclivities, was actually parodying the theme of the noble savage, which was already extremely passé at the turn of the century. At the same time this story seems to play with the love triangle, the "other woman" not even a rival, but a one-pawed ape. Moreover, the final details of Tutu's death seem a parody of the stock scenes of forgiveness and remorse:

I do not know how long my fainting spell lasted. When I again came to myself, Tutu was lying next to me, swimming in blood. Her dying gaze met my gaze. . . . I threw myself toward her to bind her wound. Alas, it was already too late! One more time she licked my hand, the hand of her slayer, and she died in my embrace. Now the furies of despair seized me. I had killed my benefactress, my second mother!. . . I expected that the earth would open under me, I was unworthy to live on earth.

What strikes us when we read Perovsky and try to synthesize an image of an author is that we are dealing with a man who does not take himself or life too seriously and who most of all values common sense, the virtue which his Double puts above all other intellectual qualities. Such being the case, we are fairly safe in assuming that the tragic tale of Tutu, jungle mother, is presented tongue-in-cheek. Rather interestingly, there is a similar example of parodic Sentimentalism in Jules Janin's *L'Ane mort et la femme guillotinée*, which, although written to mock the excesses of *l'Ecole frénétique*, was taken seriously by the public, which thenceforth associated Janin's name with the movement he had burlesqued. The death scene of the ass, Charlot, reminds one of Tutu's demise. As Janin's narrator walks past the dying beast, he tells us:

99

I received from its broken leg a feeble kick, an inoffensive kick which resembled a sweet and tender reproach, the ultimate and sad farewell of a friend whom you have offended and who forgives you. Sobbing, I left the fatal spot. "Charlot, Charlot!" I cried, "is it really you! You, dead, you, formerly so lively and nimble!"

There is no question of influence here, although both probably remembered their Sterne. Perovsky's Tutu anticipated Janin's Charlot, for *L'Ane mort* first appeared (anonymously) in 1829.

The 1829 issue of *Northern Flowers* carried a lengthy story of demonic coercion entitled *The Isolated Little House on Vasilievsky Island [Uedinnenyi domik na vasil'evskom]*. The piece was signed "Tit Kosmokratov," the pseudonym of Vladimir Titov. Here we have one of the few examples of a "serious" tale of the supernatural, where the demon is actual and his influence fatal.

An ailing widow and her daughter, Vera, live quietly in remote Petersburg suburb, where they are occasionally visited by Paul, a distant relative. Unaware that Vera is in love with him, Paul introduces his strange acquaintance Bartholomew to the family, and soon this rich but mysterious man becomes a favorite visitor. Meanwhile, Bartholomew has involved the irresponsible Paul with a mysterious princess, the better to have Vera to himself. The cunning Bartholomew completely captivates the mother, and his solicitude for her poor health endears him to Vera also. However, his demonic nature is suddenly and cruelly manifested when he denies the dying woman her last rites and immediately after her death proposes a shameful alliance to Vera. When she indignantly refuses, the house bursts into flames, and she barely escapes. Shortly thereafter Vera herself dies, leaving a remorseful and sometimes insane Paul to ponder the consequences of his relationship to Bartholomew.

The characters are conventional, and this applies even to Bartholomew, who is a rather banal demon. Somehow, no one's fate is of any great importance. It is darkly hinted that the mother had disposed of her husband. Vera is vapid, and the reader is hardly concerned as events demonstrate that "the sins of the mothers. . . ." The best feature of this story is the straightforward narrative style, unencumbered, for the most part, with metaphorical ornamentation or authorial hand wringing. When one does encounter a stylistic retrogression, such as the periphrastic description of Vera's death, the effect is parodistic:

Spring had not yet succeeded in adorning the meadow with new green when this flower, which had promised a luxuriant development, concealed itself irrevocably in the bosom of all-embracing nature.

The most interesting thing about this story, as reported in the memoirs of A.I. Delvig, is that Titov wrote it down after having heard Pushkin improvise one evening at the Karamzins'. Some commentators have seen substantiation for this in a brief outline, *The Enamored Devil*, found among Push-kin's papers dating from the early twenties. There is some vague similarity between this and Titov's narrative:

Moscow in the year 1811.
An old woman, two daughters, one innocent, the other romantic—two friends visit them. One is dissolute; the other is the Enamored Devil. The Enamored Devil loves the younger and wants to destroy the young man. He provides him with money, takes him everywhere. *Nastasia—a widow* witch. Night. The coachman. The young man. He quarrels with him—the older daughter goes insane from love for the Enamored Devil.[7]

In any case, *The Isolated Little House* as reproduced by Titov seems miles away from Pushkin, both in content and treatment. Pushkin's prose, as we shall see, is condensed, pared of all non-essentials, whereas Titov rambles along for almost 8,000 words. In both of Pushkin's tales with supernatural themes, *The Undertaker* and *The Queen of Spades*, the treatment is highly satirical, and Pushkin does not resort to Sentimentalist pathos, except to be humorous.

IX. Fiction at the End of the Twenties. The Picaresque Novel—Bulgarin. The Tale of Merchant Life—Polevoy. The Society Tale—Sumarokov. The Historical Novel—Zagoskin.

The end of the twenties was appropriately marked by the appearance of a literary dinosaur, *Ivan Vyzhigin. A Moral-Satirical Novel [Ivan Vyzhigin. Nravstvenno-satiricheskii roman]*, the work of Faddey Bulgarin (1789-1859). Parts of this novel had appeared in *The Northern Archive [Severnyi arkhiv]* as early as 1825, when they were entitled *Ivan Vyzhigin, or a Russian Gil Blas*. Appetites whetted by these *hors d'oeuvres,* the public devoured the four volumes of the complete work as they came from the presses, and, for better or worse, *Vyzhigin* became Russia's first best seller.

We have met Bulgarin before, as author of military anecdotes, historical tales, and Eastern tales, but now he deserves a little biography, if only to put into perspective this enormously controversial figure, who, with Grech and Senkovsky, virtually monopolized Russian periodical publication during the heyday of Romanticism. A man of massive personal animosities, a bald-faced liar, a conniver and calumniator, he was also a literary critic, feuilletonist, and dramatist. Much of his fiction is second-rate at best, but, quality not-withstanding, Bulgarin was, with the possible exception of Marlinsky, the most popular author of the 1830's.

Of Polish extraction, Bulgarin was educated in the Corps of Pages in Petersburg and commisioned. Subsequently, and inexplicably, he turned up as a cavalry officer in Spain fighting on the side of France. Captured after the fall of Napoleon, he somehow made his peace with the Russians and by 1820 had settled permanently in Petersburg. He seems to have had a natural-born facility as editor and publisher: in the twenties he founded a number of journals, *The Northern Archive* (1822-1828), *Literary Leaflets* (1823-1824), *Son of the Fatherland* (1825-1840), and was editor and publisher of the only newspaper permitted to publish political news, *The Northern Bee,* which appeared regularly from 1825 until the year of his death. Although he was not a Decembrist, he had many acquaintances among the conspirators and visited Kondraty Ryleev on the eve of the insurrection. Bulgarin was a contributor to every issue of *Polar Star*, and, as we have seen, his prose appeared in Baron Delvig's *Northern Flowers* in the later twenties. It wasn't until the turn of the decade that he achieved notoriety as a calumniator and informer.

One of the more amusing aspects of Bulgarin's *Ivan Vyzhigin* is the way in which the author, by means of his foreword, seeks to defang his critics *avant la lettre*. With considerable prescience, he identifies features of his story which will arouse reaction. At the same time, he casts himself in the role of a moderate social reformer, humane philosopher, and literary innovator. To justify his satirical approach, he traces the genealogy of Russian satire from Peter the Great and Prince Antioch Kantemir to the present, noting that enlightened monarchs themselves favored the corrective effects of salubrious satire:

> Well-intentioned satire fosters the perfection of morality, representing vice and eccentricity in their true form, and revealing in its magic mirror that which must be avoided and that which one must follow. That is the aim with which the novel *Ivan Vyzhigin* has been created.

Probably sensing that his satire might be misconstrued by some Russians as an attack against their institutions and national qualities, especially in view of his Polish origin, Bulgarin opens his novel with a portrait of the Polonophile Gologordovsky (Barepride), a Byelorussian, who is depicted as arrogant, cruel, gullible, ambitious, and profligate, a detractor of all things Russian.

In the foreword the author also excuses himself for not having idealized his hero, sensing that some of his readers would blame him for Ivan's human failings, as indeed some of them did. His hero, the author declares, is innately good, but sometimes weak, as are all mortals, and that is the way he has described him. Bulgarin concludes with a request and a declaration which are rich in overtones:

> Let the defects be excused because of the good intentions, and because *this is the first original Russian novel of its kind*. I dare to assert that *I imitated no one*, copied no one, and wrote that which was conceived in my mind alone.[1]

Be Mr. Bulgarin's intentions what they may, his assertions of originality must be challenged. As he himself noted, the tradition of satire in Russian literature was well-rooted, and the "true to life novel" *[bytovoi roman]* and the "moral-didactic" picaresque novel were not new to the Russian scene. Chulkov's *The Comely Cook, or The Adventures of a Debauched Woman,* itself a cousin to Defoe's *Moll Flanders,* preceded Bulgarin's novel by sixty years. Vasily Narezhny's *A Russian Gil Blas* (1814) or *The Two Ivans* (1825) were contemporary examples of the genre. So Bulgarin's claim that he neither imitated nor copied anyone is a good example of the gentleman protesting too much, especially since the parts of *Ivan Vyzhigin* published before 1829 mention *Gil Blas* in the title. And Lesage was not the only source, for, as Pokrovsky has demonstrated, *Vyzhigin* was also a bourgeois adaptation of Bishop Krasicki's *Pan Podstoli* (1778), on which it relied heavily in conception and details.[2]

There is no way adequately to summarize or condense the content of *Ivan Vyzhigin,* whose four volumes chronicle the events in the life of a serf gooseherd who ultimately turns out to be the illegitimate son of a rich nobleman. As we follow our "hero," who is no better than he should be, from Byelorussia to Moscow and Petersburg, from Venice to Istanbul and the Kirghiz steppes, we watch him endure privation, corruption, captivity, slavery, and other trials and tribulations. The plot is involved, with characters popping up unexpectedly from time to time, and the story is filled with coincidences, not the least of which is Ivan's ultimate discovery of the true identity of his father, a circumstance which repeats the plot of Narezhny's *Bursak* (1824). There are numerous interpolated autobiographies related by those whom Vyzhigin encounters in the course of his wanderings. Vyzhigin himself and these lesser narrators all recount their adventures in the same undramatic manner we have seen in the novels of Narezhny, with sparing use of dialogue. This sort of boxes-within-boxes structure does function as a means of retardation, for a tense moment in Vyzhigin's tale will be left unresolved while we are treated to the past history of some relative or chance acquaintance who has just bobbed up in the hero's life.

Today the popularity of this novel is difficult to explain, but in some ways it was a spot of green in the arid literary scene of 1829. Further, it catered to philistine tastes and contemporary prejudices (anti-Semitism), and its revelations about the life of society in the capitals doubtless appealed to the meaner instincts of the herd.

Ivan Vyzhigin spawned a number of derivative works, and so the public was soon treated to *Pyotr Ivanovich Vyzhigin*, *The New Vyzhigin*, by Guryanov, *Vyzhigin's Children*, and Orlov's *The Death of Vyzhigin*. Pushkin prepared chapter titles for *The Real Vyzhigin*, which alluded to some undisclosed details in Bulgarin's checkered career, and he threatened to complete the work if Bulgarin's vicious and base personal attacks against him did not cease. Bulgarin, who played the role of super-patriot following the Decembrist Insurrection, could not afford any reexamination of his service to Napoleon and, accordingly, ceased at least public attacks against Pushkin.

The year 1829 also marked the appearance of one of Mikhail Pogodin's better known (but far from his best) stories, *The Black Affliction [Chernaia nemoch']*. The story concerns life in the merchant class of Moscow, a milieu well known to Pogodin, for his father, a freed serf who had prospered in business, had assumed the traditions of this intransigently conservative estate. The title derives from a popular term for epilepsy, but in this case it is used by a merchant's wife to describe a consumptive melancholy which is destroying her son Gavrilo. Seeking help, the mother calls upon the family's priest, and his questioning of the youth opens up the floodgates of an impassioned personal confession. At this point the story acquires the form of the so-called psychological novel of the period, a first-person confession or *profession de foi* focusing upon significant experiences in one's formative years.

Gavrilo tells of his unusual curiosity as a child, his boring education founded upon religious readings, his apprenticeship at his father's shop, and his gradual loss of interest in the routine of mercantile life. What he really wants to do is study, but he doesn't even dare to ask his fearsome father to send him to an institute, because the tyrant has more than once damned all educational institutions as agencies of corruption. The priest is sympathetic and promises to intercede, but Gavrilo returns home that very day to find his parents closeted with a matchmaker. The priest's efforts are in vain, and Gavrilo is forced into the pre-nuptial routines typical of his class, including the "inspection" [smotr] during which the bride and groom and the parents of each give one another close scrutiny. All of this is too much for Gavrilo, and, after a final unsuccessful plea to change his parents' plans, he drowns himself. Overall the story is rather dull, as is typical of the nondramatized confession. Its real value lies in the revelation of the mores of the merchant class, and in this respect it has sociological value. Best of all is the opening scene in which the mother tries to tell the priest what is wrong with her son, while the priest's wife, bitter at having been pointedly excluded from the conference, eavesdrops from the next room. Also charming is the description of the smotr, where the two betrothed are dumb with painful shyness while the parents "lay it on" to impress each other.

In the spring of 1829 *The Moscow Telegraph* published an epistolary novella entitled *Coquetry and Love [Koketstvo i liubov']*, the work of Pyotr Sumarokov (dates uncertain, 1800-1860), an author totally forgotten over the decades. This work is of considerable interest, because it is a society tale of provincial gentry life, yet it precedes Bestuzhev-Marlinsky's *The Test* (1830), usually credited with being the first fully developed example of this genre. This story was republished in 1833 in three volumes entitled *Tales and Stories of Pyotr Sumarokov [Povesti i Rasskazy Petra Sumarokova]*, which also included other provincial society tales such as *Prejudice [Predubezh-denie]*, *The Well [Kolodets]*, and *The Ring and the Note [Kol'tso i zapiska]*.

Coquetry and Love consists of the letters of four persons—the handsome hussar cornet, Count Alexander Slavsky, Liudmila Lidina, an orphan raised by the Count's cousin, and Captain Schmidt, a bumbling giant from Estonia. Aglaida, the villainess of the piece, writes the final letter, a grudging confession of her evil machinations. She concludes:

What will happen to me if this story becomes known in society? What then will our honorable little neighbors do to me?. . . They will probably gossip half a year about this subject, which will provide such inexhaustible work for their tongues! Here they will find love, and virtue, and rivalry, and—even a duel. Is it not true that this is a whole novel? And rather absurd, wouldn't you say? Well, my dear, we have read many like it which are even more stupid than this one.

The action opens with the return of Alexander to the family estate after an absence of three years. There he finds his former love, Liudmila, apparently about to accept Captain Schmidt's proposal. The humiliated young officer turns to Aglaida for consolation, and the pretty young schemer uses every trick to make him fall seriously in love with her. Finally, she provokes a duel between the Count and the Captain in which the Count is wounded. As he convalesces under Liudmila's watchful eye, the misunderstanding between the two lovers is resolved. Liudmila believed that the Count's mother, her benefactress, wanted to marry her off to Schmidt to keep her from marrying Alexander, which would have precipitated his proposal and presumably have caused trouble between mother and son. Liudmila purposely acted coldly towards him. When it becomes clear to Liudmila that the Count's mother is not opposed to their marriage, she confesses her love and all ends happily.

The letters contain a considerable amount of dialogue, an element not usually found in actual correspondence but conventionally introduced into epistolary fiction to provide dramatic content. Sumarokov has also made some effort to distinguish the styles of correspondents, particularly in the case of the stork-like Schmidt, who expresses his preference in women in a letter to his brother:

It is true, I was never a ladies' man, but that was only because I never found a girl to my style. Polish women seemed to me too flighty, and their behavior always made me blush. There is not much use for young Russian ladies. They are almost all too extravagant, they love fancy dress, and don't like housekeeping. I should like my wife not to be embarrassed to frequent the kitchen and know how to prepare beer soup and goose with cabbage. For this reason I had not even thought about women, I had been occupied only with the service and my company, and I had not intended to marry other than some good and modest countrywoman upon my return to Revel.

In the same self-confident tone he goes on to declare his attraction to Liudmila, whom he prefers to Aglaida.

Aglaida is not at all bad looking: a blonde, with big blue eyes, a sharp little nose, turned up at the end, with blonde curls as smooth as silk, and with the most charming scarlet mouth, in short, a beauty. And this very beauty, would you believe it, has deigned to fall in love with me. However, I have withstood the temptation and prefer Liudmila to her. You probably will think it strange why I chose a girl of insignificant origin in exchange for the countess? It is because Her Grace seemed to me too witty and cunning, and I am certain that soon after her marriage her husband will wear horns. And in my opinion, that is not the trifle that many think it is.

The two lovers, Alexander and Liudmila, are not particularly interesting. The Count mopes about and misconstrues everything, and Liudmila, too, is really the victim of her own misconceptions. Perhaps the most attractive character is Alexander's mischievous and witty sister Julia, who writes no letters but plays an important role in reconciling the lovers. Her comments about Schmidt are sharp and amusing, and she quickly sees through Aglaida's machinations.

Though there may be a bit of social protest implicit in Liudmila's presumed obligation to smother her love for her benefactor's son because of her poverty, a role realized by Tolstoy's Sonia in *War and Peace*, the social satire so apparent in later society tales is not evident here. This is essentially a love story, and as such is successful on a modest scale.

The cult of Walter Scott in Russia never reached the proportions that it did, for example, in France, where from April to August of 1822 one hundred and fifty historical novels were published.[3] Still, a large number of Russian writers and quilldrivers paid their respects to the Scott tradition by attempting at least one long piece of fiction in the style, they hoped, of the master. Few really succeeded, at least from today's perspective, but at the same time several enjoyed at least a transitory popularity, which must have seemed vindication of their efforts.

The historical novel's moment of glory in Russian literature was indeed just a moment. As a genre distinct from the historical tale, which had its own development from the time of Karamzin, the historical novel first appeared in 1829 with Mikhail Zagoskin's *Yuri Miloslavsky, or the Russians in 1612* but, notwithstanding its immense popularity, it was almost a dead genre by the time Pushkin published *The Captain's Daughter* in 1836. Meanwhile, just about everyone had tried his hand, including Ivan Lazhechnikov, Faddey Bulgarin, Nikolay Polevoy, Alexander Veltman, Constantine Masalsky, Rafail Zotov, Mikhail Lermontov, Nikolay Gogol, Ivan Kalashnikov, Nikolay Grech, and others. Sad to say, all of this effort was largely in vain, and, while these and other authors may have amused their generation, with few exceptions as historical novelists they did practically nothing to advance the art of fiction, to develop the prose literary language in the areas of psychologization or naturalness of emotional expression.

Mikhail Zagoskin (1790-1852) began his career as a civil servant in Petersburg, fought with the Petersburg militia in 1812, and in the teens, while holding a modest government job, wrote several comedies which enjoyed success and gave him entry to conservative literary circles. Moving to Moscow in 1820, he continued writing plays, but real acclaim was achieved only in 1829 when his historical novel, *Yuri Miloslavsky, or The Russians in 1612 [Iurii Miloslavskii, ili Russkie v 1612 godu]* captured the attention of all literate Russia. Pushkin wrote to him,

> I congratulate you on a complete and fully justified success, and I congratulate the public on having one of the best novels of the present period. Everyone is reading it. The ladies are in ecstacies. Zhukovsky spent an entire night with it.

One secret of Zagoskin's success was that he provided his compatriots with a lively and colorful tale from their own historical past, a tale of patriotism, sacrifice, devotion, and morality, qualities about which Russians needed reassurance after the Decembrist debacle of the recent past. The following year when Zagoskin published his second novel, *Roslavlev, or the Russians in 1812 [Roslavlev, ili Russkie v 1812 godu]*, he unabashedly asserted his purpose in writing both works:

> In publishing my second historical novel, I consider it my duty to express the deepest

feelings of gratitude to my compatriots for the flattering reception which they accorded *Yuri Miloslavsky*. In undertaking to compose these two novels, I had in mind to describe Russians in two noteworthy historical epochs, similar but separated by two centuries. I wish to prove that although the external forms and features of the Russian nation have completely changed, what have not changed are our unshakable loyalty to the throne, our adherence to the faith of our ancestors, and love for our native country.

Yuri Miloslavsky is set against the background of the final years of the "time of troubles," a period stretching from the death in 1598 of Fyodor, the feeble-minded son of Ivan the Terrible, to the election of Mikhail Romanov as tsar in 1613. In that interval Russia suffered violent social upheavals, pretenders, civil war, a plague, and occupation by the Poles. In the vain hope that order would be restored, the population of Moscow took an oath of allegiance to Wladyslaw, the adolescent son of Poland's King Sigismund. It turned out, however, that Sigismund intended to rule Russia himself, and, when this was discovered, the Polish troops in Moscow were beseiged in the Kremlin. Meanwhile, at Nizhny-Novgorod the butcher-patriot Kuzma Minin successfully incited opposition to Polish rule, the militia formed under Prince Pozharsky successfully combatted bands of renegade Cossacks, and ultimately Moscow was liberated.

The novel opens at the time opposition to Polish rule was rising in Nizhny-Novgorod. Our hero, the title character, has reluctantly taken the oath to support Wladyslaw, hoping that peace will come to ravaged Russia. Yuri is ordered by the Polish military dictator of Moscow, Gosiewski, to go to Nizhny-Novgorod and dissuade Minin and his followers from opposing Wladyslaw. The plot thickens when Yuri discovers that the beautiful Anastasia, with whom he is in love, is the daughter of the vicious boyar Shalonsky, and that the traitorous father has betrothed his daughter to Gosiewski. Even without knowing that Yuri and his daughter are in love, Shalonsky takes an immediate dislike to the youth, and his antipathy inspires efforts to assassinate Yuri, his encarceration, and an attempt to starve him to death. Yuri is rescued, and, convinced that Anastasia can never be his, he takes the vows of a monk, an act which frees him from his oath and enables him to fight for Russia against the Poles. In a cliff-hanging conclusion, Yuri finds Anastasia about to be gibbeted by partisans who connect her with Gosiewski and the enemy, but she is saved by a quick wedding ceremony which makes her Yuri's wife. The hero then helps Pozharsky free Moscow from the Poles, and he and Anastasia are reunited as man and wife when he learns that his monastic vows were incomplete and hence not binding.

The historical novelist had to provide his readers with morally and physically attractive heroes and heroines, faithful but somewhat foolish servants, thoroughly reprehensible villains, and a cast of supporting players with interesting and exaggerated features of behavior. Accordingly, the handsome Yuri is a paragon of virtue, his beloved Anastasia is beautiful and demure, and the villainous boyar Shalonsky is a man of violent temper, a debaucher murderer, and supporter of King Sigismund, the enemy of Russia. Yuri's servant, Alexey, is a lesser Sancho Panzo, devoted, stingy with his master's money, stubborn, and opinionated. In this respect he anticipates the similar figure of Savelyich, in Pushkin's *The Captain's Daughter.* One of the more intriguing characters in Zagoskin's novel is the Cossack Kirsha, a fearless and cunning daredevil who becomes an invaluable ally to Yuri in his quest for Anastasia and defense in Russia. The initial description of the Cossack is indicative of his conventionalized behavior throughout the story:

Kirsha was a daring horseman, he loved to brawl, to get drunk, to raise havoc, but in the very heat of battle he would spare a disarmed enemy, and he would not amuse himself, as did his comrades, with captives, that is he didn't cut off their ears or their noses but only set them free to go where they pleased, having stripped them from head to foot and left them only their shirts. It is true that this happened sometimes in winter, in crackling frosts, but on the other hand in the summer he behaved with them with the same mercy and patiently bore the mockery of his companions, who called him "Father Kirsha" and said that he was not a Cossack-from-beyond-the-falls but an old woman. To avenge eternally any insult and never to forget a good deed, that was the rule which Kirsha never changed for his whole life.

Zagoskin's novel has many incidental characters of comic substance, among them a village wizard whose domination of his superstitious brethren is broken by Kirsha, a greedy peasant woman who overcharges Yuri for her milk and then becomes despondent when Kirsha tells her they were ready to pay ten times what she had asked, a braggart Pole who seizes a goose roasted for Yuri and then is forced to eat the entire bird as punishment for his ill-considered greed. These colorful types are joined by others in a series of dramatic scenes set in wayside inns, peasant villages, a bandit's lair deep in the Murom forest, the Trinity Monastery, the houses of Nizhny-Novgorod boyars, and along the highways and byways of old Russia.

Walter Scotts's evocation of the past, which his readers took on faith as a reconstitution of the true details and atmosphere of the times, was emulated by his successful disciples, and Zagoskin was no exception. Pushkin, with perhaps more enthusiasm than was justified, stressed the reality of the novel:

Mr. Zagoskin has transported us precisely to the year 1612. Our fine people, boyars, cossacks, monks, turbulent rabble, all of this has been divined, all of this happens, seems as it had to happen and seem in the troubled times of Minin and Avraamy Palytsyn.

One supposes that Zagoskin researched his real-life characters, and that the appearance and behavior of his historical figures correspond to fact. But in his portraits of Minin, Pozharsky, and other Russian patriots, there is a definite conventionalization which emphasizes their particular virtues. Nowhere is this more obvious than in the depiction of Avraamy Palitsyn, the chronicler of the Trinity Monastery:

The meek and yet magnificent aspect of the elder, his looks which flashed with intelligence and were filled with kindheartedness, his pleasant, sonorous voice, but most of all his piety and his flaming love for his fatherland, known to all Russia, aroused in Yuri's soul a feeling of the deepest respect for this immortal champion of the virtuous Dionysus. Remaining silent for a while, Miloslavsky said in a timid voice, "Father Avraamy, I do not dare to hope that you will fulfill my request."

"Speak boldly, my child," the old man answered, "is it for us, the sinful, to reject the requests of our brother, when we ourselves hourly, like small children, run with vain prayers to our mutual father?"

The holy man does as Yuri requests and accepts his vow:

"Yuri, from this hour you no longer belong to the world, and I, in the name of the Lord, release you from all worldly promises and oaths. Stand up, lay brother of Elder Avraamy. Henceforth you must blindly fulfill the will of your pastor and mentor. Go to the camp of Prince Pozharsky, arm yourself with worldly weapons against our mutual enemy, and if the Lord does not deign to adorn your brow with the crown of a martyr, then at the conclusion of hostilities return to our abode for acceptance of the angelic image and service to the Lord, not with weapon in hand but in the spirit of meekness, peace, and love.

"Thus," cried out Yuri, bathed in tears, "I can again fight for my homeland! Ach, I feel that nothing touches my conscience! My soul is calm. Father Avraamy, you have returned life to me!"

Clearly, we are dealing here with a stylization, a feature very typical of the historical novel.

The representation of the past, of course, involved more than simply parading historical personages across the stage of one's fictitious world. Again, it was Scott who set the pattern for the depiction of setting, especially well-known locales, which are described not only physically but with reference to their legendary heritage, the popular beliefs surrounding them, their pervading atmosphere. By the time he wrote *Bryn Forest [Brynskii les]* in 1845, Zagoskin was adept at this technique:

At the end of the seventeenth century among the impenetrable forests which once covered the larger part of Russia, one of the first places was occupied by the dense forest located in what is presently the province of Kaluga, through which flows the small river Bryn. And even today Bryn forest, which is often mentioned in popular fairy tales and proverbs, is represented in the imagination of simple people as some sort of unknown wilderness, the gloomy and deserted haunt of shaggy bears, hungry wolves, forest spirits, werewolves and cutthroats. In this respect it takes precedence over the famous Murom forest, and if the peasant of a steppe province wants to say about some runaway that he has disappeared completely from sight, he often expresses this as follows: "Who can find him, friend? He must have gone off to Bryn forest."

After *Roslavlev,* for which he received over one thousand rubles, Zagoskin's material situation improved considerably, he was appointed Gentleman of the Bedchamber, given the post of Director of Moscow Theatres, and elected to the Russian Academy. He continued an active literary career, producing another historical novel set in the times of Prince Vladimir entitled *Askold's Tomb [Askol'dova Mogila]* (1833), a comedy, a collection of fantastic sketches in 1836, and a philosophical novel, *The Seducer [Iskusitel']* (1838), but his popularity was never so great as it was with his initial success. Still he persevered, and in the forties, while he held the post of director of the Armory Museum, he composed sketches of Moscow life, *Moscow and Muscovites [Moskva i moskvichi]*, and two more historical novels, *Bryn Forest* (1845), a tale set in 1682, and *The Russians in the Beginning of the 18th Century [Russkie v nachale XVIII stoletiia]* (1848). By that time the historical tale had long since lost its popularity. Zagoskin's final efforts were among the last of this genre.

The Georgian Military Highway, 1837-38, painting by Lermontov

Alexander Bestuzhev-Marlinsky

Mikhail Zagoskin

X. Fiction of the Early Thirties. *The Literary Gazette*. The Supernatural Tale—Somov. The Later Fiction of Bestuzhev-Marlinsky.

Without being excessively arbitrary, one can mark 1830 as the year when prose decisively displaced poetry as the passion of the Russian reading public. To a certain extent, this reorientation of interest was brought about by the abundance of good poets and good poetry during the twenties and the overabundance of their less talented imitators, who saturated the market and sated the readers. Poetry had both won its victory and exhausted its resources, and so beat a dignified retreat to winter quarters, Pushkin and his Pleiad ably defending the rear. Meanwhile, the adolescent fiction of the twenties had begun to lose some of its gangling postures and appeared able to take a few firm strides without stumbling over his own feet.

The thirties are marked by the entrenchment of new genres, some of which, to be sure, had rudimentary beginnings earlier. The decade opens with an avalanche of historical novels, and later come society tales and the related *Kuenstlernovellen*, or artists' stories. The family chronicle takes to print, as does the (usually) brief psychological sketch. One must bear in mind that all of these are deeply concerned with class peculiarities, mores, social injustice, and the sociology of urban and country life at all levels. In this decade authors crossbreed genres more than ever, but now they do so not out of ineptitude but as a result of artistic self-confidence. Fictionists are prepared, both technically and mentally, to improvise.

Significant economic changes occurred in connection with the business of literature in the early thirties, namely creation of a real literary market place, complete with producers, retailers, and purchasers. Until this time *belles-lettres* had been largely a labor of love, and in general authors were not paid. The six thousand rubles which Pushkin received for *Count Nulin* in 1827 from *Northern Flowers* was an exception to the rule, and the example was not enthusiastically approved by publishers of almanacs and other literary material. However, the situation changed quickly thereafter, and with the introduction of payment for poems and stories the literary producers themselves changed. No longer was literature almost exclusively the occupation of men of leisure, or at least those with leisure time. Plebians could enter the ranks of the literati, and they did, as publishers, editors, and authors. At the same time, the reading public began to expand both outward and downward, which made the phenomenon of the first best seller, *Ivan Vyzhigin*, possible in 1830.

However, we should note that the numbers involved in these ventures were miniscule by present standards. The most widely read newspaper in the twenties, Bulgarin's *Northern Bee*, enjoyed ten thousand subscribers, while in 1831 the editors of the last issue of *Northern Flowers*, the most prestigious and popular almanac of its kind, determined that a tirage of 1200 copies would suffice. Even the sensational success of *Ivan Vyzhigin*, whose sale was exceeded only by Karamzin's *History*, concerned a mere six thousand copies.[1]

The year 1830 is also memorable for the appearance on 1 January of the first issue of a new newspaper devoted to literature, *The Literary Gazette*. For the next year and a half it was published every five days in eight pages. *The Gazette* was the creation of the Pushkin-Delvig faction in literature, and with it they hoped to challenge the hegemony of the Bulgarin-Grech periodicals and to provide an antidote to Polevoy's *The Moscow Telegraph* and Pogodin's *The Moscow Herald*, both of which had somehow failed to fulfill their expectations. *The Telegraph* had been initiated in 1825 as a bi-weekly and had enjoyed the patronage of Prince Vyazemsky, who encouraged its orientation to French Romantic literature, especially Victor Hugo. But in the opinion of the Petersburg literary mandarins, Polevoy had reacted improperly regarding Karamzin's *A History of the Russian State*, as evidenced by his polemical *A History of the Russian People [Istoriia russkogo naroda]* (1829-1833). Polevoy's criticism of Karamzin as artistically dated, lacking in philosophical ballast and *narodnost'*, was too great an act of *lèse majesté* on the part of the plebian Muscovite, and the Petersburg literati ceased to have anything to do with him. *The Moscow Herald* was launched in 1827 by several of the Lovers of Wisdom Society [Liubomudrye], and its Romantic inclination was towards Germany, with emphasis upon Goethe, Hoffmann, Jean-Paul, Tieck, and Schiller. Pushkin published heavily in *The Moscow Herald,* but within a couple of years the original collaborators had dispersed, leaving the journal to Pogodin, a professor of history whose scholarly interests increasingly circumscribed the periodical's content. *The Literary Gazette*, therefore, was in a sense the product of deceived expectations. Its editor, Baron Delvig, was assisted by such luminaries as Pushkin, Prince Vladimir Odoevsky and Prince Vyazemsky, among others, with Orest Somov acting as he did in *Northern Flowers* as a sort of managing editor. Prose was featured in this new paper, including original and translated fiction, criticism, bibliography, and miscellaneous tidbits connected with letters, and each issue also presented one short poem.

A goodly portion of the fiction in *The Gazette* was provided by Somov, who was also largely responsible for the critical and bibliographic sections. All of his original stories in the 1830 issue of *The Gazette* (he translated several pieces, as well) have the subtitle *From a Traveler's Tales.*[2] which suggests their inspiration was Washington Irving's *Tales of a Traveller*. The least interesting of these is *The Posting Station in Chateau Thierry [Pochtovyi dom v Shato-T'erri]*. Here a traveler-narrator learns from the station master of that French town the story behind his marriage to a deaf-mute. This account, conveyed as a first person narrative, is filled with pathetic situations and sentimental language as the station master tells of saving the poor girl from marauding soldiers, the death of her benefactress, and their ultimate marriage.

The most attractive part of this whole work is the frame, in which the traveler details his conversation with a garrulous French coachman.

The Fearful Guest. An Anecdote [Strashnyi gost'. Anekdot] is a conventional tale of the supernatural in which the ghost that steps from a painting (shades of Irving and Hoffmann!) to terrify the protagonist turns out to be a dream spectre, the product of a troubled conscience. The frame is more interesting, because the description of the anecdote's narrator seems to be a portrait-tribute to Adam Mickiewicz, the Polish Romantic poet whom Somov surely heard improvise tales in the style of Hoffmann at Petersburg literary gatherings.

> The guest was a man of around thirty. His pleasing, noble features bore the stamp of pensiveness or creative fancy. He was not a handsome man, but at first sight his languid eyes, in which shone a gentle flame of intelligence, drew one to him by a fascinating, almost magnetic attraction, and one's glance involuntarily rested on his lips which protruded slightly in a pleasing way. It seemed that these pressed lips contained the sweet sounds of Poetry, ready to burst from the soul, agitating the mouth with a slight, involuntary movement. From his accent it was evident that he was one of our southwestern compatriots, but his words, which indicated a delicate feeling of refinement and a soaring inspiration, animated his speech and lent it an unusual power of persuasion.

The ideas expressed by this narrator in the discussion which precedes his improvisation are quite in keeping with Mickiewicz's Romantic credo. Asked his opinion of the supernatural, he replies that a poet's convictions cannot be at variance with his imagination:

> "Poetry is the daughter of fancy. If Poetry doesn't trust what fancy shows her, then her creations will be either cold or too vague. In either case , she will lose her power over the heart, which alone has ears for her sounds."

The poet then begins his tale of the supernatural, "inspired by the genius of improvisation."[3]

The longest (11,55 words) of Somov's contributions to *The Literary Gazette* in 1830 was *The Suicide. A Tale [Samoubiitsa. Povest']*, which ran in five installments in the autumn issues of the paper. The exterior narrator is an estate manager who travels in the provinces. On one of his journeys, he is obliged to spend the night in the house of a village constable when his coachman refuses to drive past a supposedly haunted manor house. In search of entertainment, the traveler encourages his host to tell him the story behind the superstitious fear which surrounds the manor, and it is the constable's own words which form the rest of the tale.

The initial frame, in addition to explaining how the traveler comes to meet the person whose story he re-narrates, is extended to embrace the whole first installment. In this we learn not only of the problem caused by the reluctant coachman, we are also presented a full and circumstantial characterization of the constable. Anticipating a means used by Turgenev in the earliest of his *A Sportsman's Sketches*, "Khor and Kalinych," Somov first introduces us to the constable's agreeable young son, who greets the traveler with openness and cordiality. The tidiness and cleanliness of the hut reflect upon the character of the orderly host, and we learn even the titles of the small library of books, which, the son tells us, the constable had been allowed to choose for himself from the manor after the death of the master. With this background, which is reinforced by some further remarks by the son on his father's erudition, we are introduced to the constable himself:

> I entered the room and was met by a man of about forty in a long-tailed frock coat of grey cloth. This was the master of the house. I had expected that this philosopher-autodidact would also be an orator-autodidact and would meet me with a lengthy congratulatory speech, or at least some pretentious greeting, but instead I heard the usual village host's gratitude that I "had not scorned his house and hospitality." For a few moments this confused my plan of attack against the weak side of my literate host, but at the same time it gave me a much more favorable opinion of his intelligence than before. I threw off my cloak and sat down on the bench, and my host, having taken the cloak, carefully folded it and put it aside, stood off at a respectful distance by the stove and seemed to await my questions or orders. In so doing he gave me complete freedom to look him over. He was a man of middle height and strong physique with a healthy, fresh face. The expression of this face and of his sharp black eyes revealed innate intelligence, penetration, and even a certain cunning, but his stance and manner indicated studied civility and the behavior of one who was accustomed to deal with those of higher station.

After dinner the constable unburdens himself of his grievances against the estate executors, whose indifference and greed had worked sorely to the peasants' disadvantage. Here Somov again anticipates the technique of social criticism used by Turgenev in *A Sportsman's Sketches*, where, after establishing the humanity and good character of his peasant protagonists, the author shows how they had been victimized by the profligate and even cruel gentry. In *The Suicide* the constable's quiet dissatisfaction with those whose neglect had been ruinous for the peasants makes very powerful social criticism, just because the reader already has a strong empathy for this man and appreciates his innate dignity and self-discipline.

The language of the constable is stylized to reflect his personality, his peasant origins, and his unusual, but limited education. In sombre and matter-of-fact tones, he tells of the return of the Old Master from abroad, his deep melanchholy, his conflict with his wastrel nephew, and his refusal to permit the youth to marry an Italian actress, which intensified their quarrel. The Old Master firmly insisted he would disinherit his nephew and free his serfs if he were disobeyed. They parted angrily.

> "The next morning around seven o'clock, the time the Old Master usually awakened, the dwarf was standing at his door and waiting for him to ring. The dwarf stood there for a long time, surprised that the master had overslept but thinking that maybe

the cause was a long period of insomnia the previous night. But then it struck eight o'clock, and still no ring was heard. . . . Timosha the dwarf was by nature impatient. He began to knock on the door and call out, "Master, master!" There was no answer. Then he ran to us in the vestibule and told us his worry about the health of the Old Master, calling on us to go with him in order, if need be, to give our general assistance or to send for a doctor as fast as possible. We waited in the corridor while the dwarf unlocked the door and went into the bedroom. But he had scarcely entered when we heard his wild, piercing cry. We rushed in. Lord, my God! On the floor was heaped a bloody pillow, there was clotted blood on the sheets, and the master, our kind Old Master, lay on the bed with his throat cut!"

The tone of the constable's narration then changes as he satirizes the various district officials who arrive to conduct the inquest. From a purist's point of view, this violates the consistency of narrational voice, but the humor of the passages more than compensates for this. The Secretary and his two clerks are the worst of the lot:

"But the most wicked weed of all was the Secretary, Tit Panfilovich Koscheyev [the name suggests "Skinflint"]. About this nickname it was said, *a dog is called according to his fur.* Even at birth he was already bathed in ink and swaddled in papers. . . . In the office where he worked he was known as *Cunning conniver,* and the cunninig conniver couldn't have justified his reputation better. Wherever you needed someone devious, a hypocrite to twist the law, he was your man. He was so dried up, just as if he were pressed together from the dust of archives, it was hard to see how he stayed alive. He was not tall and by nature or habit stooped, so that when he stood and hung his head forward, his shoulder blades were almost on a level with his ears. His face was the dark color of a dried mushroom. Under his grey, beetling brows two tiny eyes sparkled and darted like a viper's. His voice was consumptive and broken by a choking cough. And the long, lean fingers of his hands were truly like quills which had been knocked out of the inkwell onto the floor, where they had shriveled and dried up.
The two petty clerks who arrived with him also belonged, as the saying goes, to the nettle family. Wherever they saw a chance for profit, their fingers automatically became clawlike, as if ready to catch bribes in flight."

If one were to write a book on the image of the physician in Russian literature, it would be proscribed by medical associations everywhere. With very few exceptions, until Chekhov somewhat rehabilitated the doctor at the end of the century, Russian authors created them as incompetent, indifferent, vain, and pompous. Somov's caricature is typical:

"The doctor was a young man who had gone abroad to be saturated with the wisdom fashionable at those times. For him, apparently, it was all the same whether to cure a man or send him to the next world, only that in either case there should be profit for himself. . . . The doctor began to examine the body and declared that the wound could not have been made by another's hand, that the cut indicated a free movement of the hand which made it, that if there had been violence, that is, if it had been done by a hand other than that of the deceased, it could not have been made from this side, nor could the interval between the vertebrae of the throat have been chosen so successfully that the entire *operation*, as he called it, might be completed in one attempt.
'From my observation of the wound, I see, gentlemen,' he continued, turning to the District Inspector, the Attorney, and the Secretary, 'that the person undertaking this *operation* had to have a basic knowledge of Anatomy. We know that the deceased

was an educated person and probably knew Anatomy. From this I conclude, and I request that you enter my opinion in the inquest report, that no one other than he himself could so deftly and successfully have completed this *operation* and that consequently he committed suicide.' "

The story is resumed in the constable's original style when he describes the funeral of the Old Master. As the bereaved peasants are carrying the coffin to a grave outside the churchyard, a greyish figure resembling the Old Master appears and silently accompanies the procession. As soon as the interment is completed, the frightened mourners hasten away. When the nephew hears the report of the peasants, he becomes distraught. As the weeks pass he becomes totally anguished, tortured by secret fears and, along with the rest of the household, frightened by the ominous bangings which rock the manor house. The constable remarks that the nephew's terror gradually led him to the awful suspicion that the Old Master had met with foul play, but he kept this to himself. After six months of agony, the nephew cuts his own throat and dies. At his burial, the greyish ghost appears and accompanies the coffin to the grave.

Although Somov almost invariably treats the supernatural ironically or satirically, in *The Suicide* the ghost cannot be explained away, especially since our informant is the sober-minded, reliable, and educated constable. One wonders why the author took this approach, since the ghost could easily have been justified as the product of the murderous nephew's conscience and the superstitious fear of the peasants. Be this as it may, this work remains one of the few *de facto* ghost stories by an established author.

The prolific Somov published yet another tale of the supernatural in 1830, the most interesting and innovative of his works in this vein, worthy to be ranked among the best of the genre. *Kikimora—The Story of a Russian Peasant on the Highroad [Kikimora. Rasskaz russkogo krest'ianina na bol'-shoi doroge]*, was included in *Northern Flowers for 1830*. *Kikimora*, which freely translated means *monster*, in popular superstition is a demonic female force. It shares the peasant pantheon with such creatures as *domovoi*, or house spirits, *leshie*, or wood sprites, *Baba-Yaga*, the hag who lives in a hut supported by chicken legs, and other diverting creations of the folk imagination. *Kikimora* is a fully developed *skaz* tale, with the emphasis upon the quality of narration as much as upon the events described. Somov's narrator is a peasant coachman, Faddey, whose language is alive with the expressiveness of his class. In his racy and colloquial idiom he tells the story of a family in his village strangely plagued by *kikimora*, which at night would wash and comb their little daughter, Varya. Although *kikimora's* attentions were not harmful, the family was nervous and asked the priest to exorcise the spirit, but he refused even to believe in its existence. They then turned to the bailiff, who took their money and lots of rum, but even his energetic antics failed to rid them of *kikimora*. Meanwhile, the monster's behavior was becoming malicious toward everyone except Varya. Then one day the girl fell into a trance, climbed to the rooftree of their hut, and jumped to her apparent death. As she was being prepared for burial, an old crone appeared and pronounced a spell over the body, and the child returned to life. The crone then exorcised *kikimora* by making it hide in a peasant's coat, which was then carried out of the village on a sledge.

The tale opens directly with an unmarked dialogue (that is, without "he said," etc.) between Faddey and his passenger:

"Well, you see, little father, sir, that was some time ago, I still ran around barefoot and played knucklebones. And truth to tell, I was a master player. It happened that whatever target you set, I'd take it away like with my hand."

"You're forever getting sidetracked from your story, my dear Faddey! Hold to one thing, don't bring in anything extraneous, or, so you'll understand better: right down the highway, don't turn aside, and don't cut new paths with your wheels on the plowed or unplowed ground."

"My mistake, little father, sir! Lively now, my dovies, downhill, up hill, the master'll stand a drink, he will. Well, what then were we talking about, little father, sir?"

"Well, it's already a good half hour since you promised me to relate something about *kikimora*, and we still haven't got to the matter."

"And that's the truth, little father, sir. I see myself that it's my fault. Be kind enough to listen, benefactor."

Only when one is half way through the story is there an indication it is being re-narrated by the coachman's passenger: "Faddey grumbled and silently began to shake the reins." At the end of the story the passenger, our exterior narrator, comes to the fore as he recounts his unsuccessful attempt to get Faddey to declare whether or not he personally believes in *kikimora*, a tactless question which causes the coachman to retreat into his shell:

Here Faddey crossed himself and then yelled at the horses, waved his whip, and rushed along at full speed. Try as I might, I couldn't get another word from him. And in that stubborn silence he conveyed me to the last station, where he also taciturnly thanked me with a bow when I gave him the stipulated additional fare.

From the structural point of view, this story must be considered a framed tale lacking its initial frame. Somov might have done without it entirely, leaving the work as the coachman's monologue, but the story would have lost something had he done so. The work presents a rather complicated system of perspectives, each one giving a different interpretation to the supernatural content. From Faddey's account we deduce that the villagers are far less sophisticated than he. He, after all, was not impressed at all with the foreign bailiff, who, as the others said, "had plenty in his nose." His own attitude toward the existence of *kikimora* remains undisclosed until the passenger tries to explain away the grooming of Varya as a trick played by jealous neighbors. He says he did not personally see *kikimora* as it was being hauled out of town on the sledge, but at the same time he comes to the defense of his fellow villagers when their belief is challenged by the passenger's scepticism. Thus, the presence of the frame permits three views of the story material: the complete credulity of the peasants, the non-committal but somewhat defensive position of Faddey, and the incredulity of the passenger. Further, what we learn of Faddey in the action and dialogue of the frame identifies him, gives him substance, and makes him a more interesting personality than he would have been if we had been able to hear only his voice.

Of course, that voice is quite special in its own right, and the principal delight of this story is the colorful language of Faddey. Alas, translation here is more unsatisfactory than ever, since the cadence and tone of this unique personal style are lost. Still, a sample may convey some of the flavor:

> We had a bailiff in our settlement at that time, I don't know what he was, a German or a Frenchman, from Mitava. By name and patronymic he was called *Vot-on-Ivanovich* [Vot-on means "there he is," and was probably a phrase used by the foreign bailiff to open his sentences, on the order of "Well, now."] but I don't know how to say his last name at all. Our constable, Elisey, what was then up at the counting house at the manor, also called him Mr. *Von-Baron*. This *Von-Baron* was a great wind-bag. When, like it happened, that we take a rest after working for the master, well then he gives out with stories about foreign folk no bigger than an ell with goat's feet, about bewitched castles, about corpses that wander about at night without heads. . . . What didn't he tell us? You couldn't have put it all in three baskets. He didn't speak Russian awful well either. Sometimes you could crack your skull and still not figure out what he was talking about. . . . The peasants were convinced that *Vot-on* Ivanovich had *plenty in his nose*. As for me, I never noticed nothing but snuff. . . . Truth to say, he did think up some sort of machines there in the master's yard for sowing and threshing grain. Only his thresher almost threshed his own head, and no matter how much a dozen men worked on it, they still couldn't thresh a single sheaf.

One point might well be reiterated: *Kikimora*, which is narrated for the most part in this kind of individualized vernacular, with emphasis on the language and the unique personality of the speaker as well as upon the content of his anecdote, qualifies fully as an example of *skaz* technique. What is more, it is evidently the first sustained *skaz* tale in nineteenth-century Russian literature, and thus may be considered the precursor of later works by Gogol, Dostoyevsky, Remizov, Zoshchenko, and others. Among Somov's many innovations in the form and style of Russian prose fiction, his experiments in *skaz* ought to have secured his lasting reputation.[4]

In the history of Romantic fiction, 1830 was a remarkable year, and one of the most important developments was Alexander Bestuzhev's return to print. As a convicted Decembrist, Bestuzhev could not publish under his own name, but he was allowed to use a pseudonym, and the true identity of "A. Marlinsky" was an open secret. His return to literature was a society tale, *The Test [Ispytanie]*, his first fully developed example of this type of story. He had anticipated this genre as early as 1824 with his *A Novel in Seven Let-*

ters [Roman v semi pis'makh], but now he presented a fully fleshed tale of intrigue in the fashionable circles of Petersburg society.

Generally speaking, the story is wildly improbable, the characters are puppets, and the didactic element is primitive in conception and incorporation. Pushkin, as we shall see later, answered *The Test* with *The Queen of Spades*, a work of justly acclaimed artistic value and generally overlooked polemical force.

The entire plot of *The Test* is downright silly. A certain Gremin persuades his fellow officer, Strelinsky, to attempt to win the affection of Alina, a wealthy young widow with whom Gremin had previously been in love. The tester succeeds too well, which seems rather *de trop* to Gremin, who issues a challenge. Meanwhile Gremin has fallen under the spell of Strelinsky's sister, Olga, fresh from the Smolny Institute. Through Olga's intercession, a pointless duel is avoided and everyone lives happily ever after.

The motivations of the characters are either unexplained (Gremin's justification for such a test) or simplistic (the cause of the duel). Once the characters have been wound up and set in motion, they work to articulate the plot. There is no psychological complexity, and even the dialogue, which might be a key to personality, remains unrevealing—except to disclose the wit of the author. Olga is particularly mechanical, programmed for sententious speeches and timely swoons. Here again we encounter those stylistic features typical for Marlinsky: lyrical flights in poetic language, a quest for striking metaphor, didactic commentary with heavy emphasis upon proper conduct and service to the people, and narrational digressiveness. The entire second chapter is a digression, a genre description of the Petersburg food market no way connected with the story. While faulting Marlinsky for the many weaknesses of this work, one must credit him with his repartée, which is lively, clever, and witty. The conversation between Alina and Strelinsky at the masked ball is quite well done, especially since even in 1830 few conventions had been worked out for the representation in Russian of conversations almost certainly carried on in French, a task of great difficulty since Russian equivalents for French conversational standbys did not exist. Four years later Prince Vladimir Odoevsky still lamented the difficulties facing an author who wished to include social conversations in a novel of manners.

Ammalat-Bek, A True Story from the Caucasus [Ammalat-bek. Kavkazskia byl'] is probably Marlinsky's best known work, a colorful tale set in an area ranging from the high Caucasus to Derbent on the Caspian Sea. For better or worse, it created or at least reinforced an image of the Caucasus and its peoples which captivated generations of Russians. In Tolstoy's *The Cossacks [Kazaki]*, the protagonist, Olenin, arrives in the Caucasus under the spell of Marlinsky's work, as Tolstoy himself perhaps did.

Marlinsky began work on the story in May 1830, while serving in Daghestan as a common soldier. He completed it only in September of the

121

following year, an unusually long period of composition for this author. Nikolay Polevoy serialized it in his *Moscow Telegraph* in 1832.

The basic story is factual: a Tatar youth, Ammalat-Bek, taken prisoner in a raid against the Russians, was spared at the behest of a Colonel Verkhovsky, who sought to instill in him Christian ideals. Meanwhile, Ammalat fell in love with Seltaneta, daughter of the unpacified Avarian leader, Sultan Achmed-Khan. The Sultan demanded Verkhovsky's head in return for his daughter's hand, and Ammalat indeed killed his benefactor. The night following Verkhovsky's funeral, a grave (not his) was opened and the head removed from the corpse. Meanwhile, the Sultan had died, and his wife refused to honor his agreement with Ammalat. Subsequently, Ammalat wandered from place to place and was finally killed by the Russians at the seige of Anapa in 1828.

These facts are embellished by Marlinsky to provide excitement and suspense, so, for example, we see Achmed craftily force Ammalat's first break with the Russians by murdering a Russian officer in the youth's house, and later we watch the development of the conniving Sultan's plot to turn Ammalat against Verkhovsky by spreading the rumor that Verkhovsky has agreed to exile Ammalat to Siberia for life. In Marlinsky's version, Achmed is still alive when Ammalat arrives to claim Seltaneta, which permits a more dramatic confrontation, and the final scene, in which Ammalat is slain by Verkhovsky (actually, the late colonel's brother), is pure invented melodrama.

One of the reasons for the success of *Ammalat-Bek* was its rich exoticism, for at that time the Caucasus was an intriguing and exciting land for most Russians. Regardless of rampant hyperbole and anthropomorphism, Marlinsky's descriptions of nature accorded with the accepted image of storm-shrouded, icy peaks and savage, untamed rivers. The depiction of the Terek is typical:

Wildly beautiful is the roaring Terek in the gorge of Daryal. There, like a genius drawing its strength from the heavens, it struggles against nature. At places it is clear and straight, like a sword cutting through the granite wall, it flashes between the cliffs. At places, black with anger, it roars and roots like a savage beast under the ageless mosses. On a stormy night when the belated horseman, hunched in his shaggy cloak, surveying the ground, rides up to the bank overhanging the Terek's whirlpool, all the terrors born of an active imagination are nothing in comparison with the true terrors which master him. With a dull noise torrents of rain twist underfoot, fall from the cliffs lowering above and threaten momentarily to crush one's head. Suddenly, like lava, lightning flashes, and with terror you see above only a black, torn thundercloud and below the yawning abyss, crags along the sides, and right before you from the precipice is the roaring, spurting Terek, sprinkled with fiery foam.

Ethnographic information is stuffed into the narrative not for padding or retardation but for its own sake, because Marlinsky, an avid student of foreign languages and cultures, found it interesting and wanted his reader to share this interest:

The Avarians are a free people. They do not recognize and do not tolerate any power over them. Each Avarian calls himself a lord, and if he has a *yessir* (captive) he considers himself an important master. They are poor, consequently, and brave to the extreme. Good shots with a rifle, they do very well on foot. They ride horses only when on raids, and then only a few of them do so. Their horses are small but unbelievably strong. Their language has fragmented into many dialects, but basically it is Lezghian, for the Avarians are of the Lezghian tribe. They recall the Christian faith, for it has not been one hundred and twenty years since they first bowed to Mohammed, and until now are poor Moslems: they drink vodka, *buza*, frequently grape wine, and most often brandy, which they call *dzbap*. The fidelity of the Avarian's word has become proverbial in the mountains. Their homes are quiet, hospitable, happy, they hide neither their wives nor daughters. They are ready to die for a guest and ready for vengeance to the end of generations. Vengeance for them is a shrine, robbery is fame.

In addition to longish digressions of this sort, there are numerous bits and pieces of information injected into the story or tacked on as footnotes:

Ur, *ura*—means "kill!" in Tatar. There is no doubt that this cry came to be used during the Mongol domination and not at the time of Peter, who supposedly borrowed "Hurrah" from the English.

In Belinsky's *Literary Reveries [Literaturnye mechtaniia]*, the critic's first major survey of Russian literature, he aptly noted the essential sameness of all of Marlinsky's heroes. Ammalat, notwithstanding his exotic trappings, his stylized speech, his Moslem values, really doesn't seem much different from Roman the Novgorodian or other Marlinsky protagonists:

This leader of the Turks was a tall, well-built youth, with an open face. Black *zilfliars* (curls) wound about his ears from under his hat, a faint moustache darkened his upper lip, his eyes sparkled with proud affability. He was sitting on a fabulous steed, which spun beneath him like a whirlwind.

Ammalat-Bek provides numerous examples of the endless rhetoric and emotional excesses typical of Marlinskian dialogue. As the wounded Ammalat flees to a mountain stronghold with Sultan Achmed-Khan, his horse founders, and the exhausted youth loses spirit. He begs Achmed to save himself and leave him to die:

"You must not speak such foolishness, dear Ammalat, and only your fever excuses you. We are created to live longer than our fathers. . . . To avenge ourselves against the Russian is a sacred duty: revive yourself for that alone. And what if we have been beaten in war, that is not a novelty. Today success falls to them, tomorrow it will fall to us. Allah gives happiness, but man creates fame for himself not with happiness but firmness. Take heart, friend Ammalat. . . . You are wounded and weak, I am accustomed to being strong and am not tired from our flight. You mount my steed, and together we shall more than once again fight the Russians!
Ammalat's face became fiery. . .

123

"Yes, I will live for revenge against them!" he cried out, "for revenge both secret and overt. Sultan Achmed-Khan, only for this reason do I accept your generosity! Henceforth I am yours. . . . I swear on my father's grave I am yours! Lead my steps, direct the blows of my hand, and if I, sinking into luxury, forget my oath, remind me of this minute, this peak: Ammalat-Bek will awaken, and his dagger will be lightning!"

The thematic and stylistic petrifaction of Marlinsky's art is apparent in a comparison of *Ammalat-Bek* with *Roman and Olga,* written almost a decade earlier. Like Roman and Olga, Ammalat and Seltaneta encounter an obstacle to their marriage in the person of the girl's father. Unless Ammalat abjures his allegiance to the Russians, Achmed-Khan will not permit his daughter to marry. Ammalat suggests that she flee with him:

"If you love me, let us flee from here!. . ."
"Flee, a khan's daughter flee like a captive, like a criminal! That is terrible!"

In old Novgorod the dialogue went like this:

". . . let us flee to good Prince Vladimir. With him we shall find sanctuary, and in our hearts, happiness. Decide!"
"Flee, me flee!" she exclaimed sobbing. "And you, Roman, could propose a means which is shameful for my family and clan and ruinous for myself!"

Of course, in the end both Seltaneta and Olga acquiesce.

The author does make some attempt to individualize Ammalat, who is seen from several points of view. Least important is the opinion of Seltaneta, for she simply idolizes the youth. Achmed-Khan's perspective is simply that of someone who wishes to exploit Ammalat's martial prowess and who cannot understand his acceptance of Russian domination. Verkhovsky, in a series of letters to his fiancée, provides some tentative insights into Ammalat's character, at the same time revealing a violent antipathy for what he considers typical Asiatic proclivities toward tyranny and vengeance. One may note that the contrast between Verkhovsky and Ammalat is basic to the didactic content of the story, which seeks to show the superiority of Christian forgiveness and mercy over Islam's eternal enmity and revenge.

In addition to Verkhovsky's letters, we are also provided translations from the Tatar of Ammalt's notes, which reveal a confused young man whose old value system has been almost destroyed but whose new values are not fully accepted. They also reveal the depth of his suffering when away from Seltaneta, but this is nothing new:

I recall every dear feature of your face, every position of your shapely waist. . . and that little foot—the seal of love, and that bosom—a grenade of bliss. The memory of your voice makes my soul vibrate like a string ready to break at a high note. . . . And your kiss! The kiss in which I quaffed of your soul! It sprinkles roses and coals on my solitary couch. . . . I am aflame. Hot lips suffer with thirst for a kiss. My hands want to embrace

124

your waist, to touch your knees! Oh, come, fly hither, that I might die of pleasure, as I now am dying of boredom!

Although it may be true that Marlinsky did not significantly develop as a fictionist through his career, he certainly maintained that journeyman talent for storytelling indicated in even his first pieces. Vivid scenes were one of his specialties. The final encounter between Ammalat, Sultan Achmed-Khan, and Seltaneta is representative. With his bloody trophy, the severed head of Verkhovsky, Ammalat arrives at Khunzakh, the Sultan's village, eager to claim his bride, but there he finds Achmed-Khan on his deathbed:

In the middle of the room the khan was lying on a mattress, disfigured by his sudden illness. . . . His breast would rise high and then fall back heavily; his breath wheezed in his throat. . . . The spring of life had already broken, but the wheels turned irregularly, one moving another. . . . His wife and daughter were on their knees sobbing beside his couch, his oldest son, Nutsal, in silent despair, was sitting cross-legged, his head resting on a clenched fist.

All this, however, did not strike or impress itself upon Ammalat, who was overflowing with one thought alone. With firm step he approached the khan and said to him loudly:

"Hail, Khan! I have brought you a gift which would bring a corpse to life. Prepare the wedding. Here is my ransom for Seltaneta! There is Verkhovsky's head!" With this word he threw it to Khan's feet.

The familiar voice momentarily aroused Sultan Achmed from his final sleep. With difficulty he raised himself to look at the gift, and an involuntary tremor ran over his body when he caught sight of the corpse's head.

"Let he who regales a dying man with such terrifying food eat his own heart!" he pronounced almost inaudibly. "I must make peace with my enemies, and not. . . . Ach, I am burning! Give me water, water. . . . Why did you give me to drink of hot oil? Ammalat! I curse you!. . ."

The effort wasted the khan's last drops of life: he fell back on the bolster a lifeless corpse. The khan's wife had looked with displeasure upon Ammalat's bloody, inopportune gift, but when she saw that it had hastened her husband's death, all her grief exploded in a fire of anger.

"Envoy of hell!" she cried, her eyes flashing. "Feast your eyes, there are your great deeds. . . . "

And then when Seltaneta announces, "Goodbye, Ammalat, I pity you but can never be yours," the would-be hero is totally defeated.

Marlinsky composed *The Frigate "Hope"* [*Frigat "Nadezhda"*] in 1832, and the work was published the following year in *Son of the Fatherland* and *Northern Archive*. This didacto-tragic tale tells of the love affair between the unhappily married Princess Vera and Captain Pravin, master of a Russian frigate. Their love develops against a background of Petersburg salons, where the unsophisticated but noble captain is, indeed, out of his element and finds himself involved in rumor, gossip, intrigue, and a duel. The sensitive Vera is attracted by his rectitude and inner strength, and ultimately their love leads to transgression. When Pravin's frigate is posted to the Mediterranean fleet, Vera persuades her husband to accompany the *Hope* to England. Once there, Pravin irresponsibly leaves his storm endangered ship to join Vera at an English coastal inn. Her husband discovers them and delivers an admonishment which cools their ardor. Duty prevails and Pravin returns to his foundering ship. The ship survives, but the captain is fatally injured when his skiff smashes against the *Hope's* side. Vera dies while still in England.

Glimpses into the special world of shipboard life add some additional interest to this otherwise conventional society tale, though the heavy use of marine jargon burdens the reader.

Marlinsky made considerable efforts to provide psychological motivation for Vera's and Pravin's mutual attraction. In the two letters which open the work, Vera castigates the frivolity of Petersburg society and relates how she met Pravin while on an excursion to the fleet, where his heroic rescue of a drowning sailor reinforced love at first sight. In a letter to his first mate, Nil Pavlovich, Pravin himself lavishes praises upon Vera, who completely captivates him when he later visits her. The indifference of her husband acts as a catalyst to their passion. Still, Marlinsky is unable to get into the minds of his characters in other than traditional ways, such as the inclusion of letters. As an omniscient narrator he employs his usual tumid grandiloquence to describe their mental states. Here is Pravin's mental agitation as he realizes his culpability for Vera's moral destruction:

> "You, you," his conscience cried, "have destroyed this precious vessel, you have thrown this myrrh into the fire in order to enjoy one minute of fragrance. You knew that within her was locked the talisman of happiness, the testament of inexorable fate, the fame and life of your beloved. You knew—and impudently you broke the seal, as a child breaks its toy in order to see its interior. Look now upon the soul of Vera, destroyed by you. . . !!"

The Romantics' conceptual and stylistic orientation toward metaphor is clearly evident in this story, which is in essence an allegorical recapitulation of the Decembrist debacle. The significance of the ship's name requires little comment, other than that the loss of *Hope* is connected with the irresponsibility of Pravin, who puts personal interests above duty. The Russian name Vera means *faith*, and one sees that the captain destroys faith through his selfish act. The surname Pravin contains several allusions: *pravilo* is a rudder or helm, *pravil'nost'* is rectitude, *pravda* is truth, and *pravo* is justice. All this may suggest that a man fit to lead in the name of truth and justice may deny the very possiblity of their triumph by indulging his passions at the moment he should be bolstering faith and restoring hope.

Less interesting are Marlinsky's other novelettes of the sea, the adventure stories *Lieutenant Belozor [Leitenant Belozor]* (1831) and *Nikitin the Sailor [Morekhod Nikitin]* (1834), both of which are loaded to the gunwales with expressions and terminology typical of naval or maritime occupations. They might still serve today as exciting reading for adolescent boys.

XI. Pushkin's *Belkin Tales.*

The best authors of the Romantic period began their careers as poets, and among them only Perovsky-Pogorelsky was exclusively a prose fictionist. Not surprisingly, Alexander Pushkin displayed an extraordinary gift for prose, although his talent in that area was hardly recognized during his lifetime—Marlinsky was more to the public taste. It was in the later twenties that Pushkin turned to prose with *The Negro of Peter the Great [Arap Petra Velikogo]*, a fictionalized biography of the author's African great grandfather, Abraham Hannibal. The piece, which breaks off in the middle of the seventh chapter, displays from its first lines that laconicism so typical of all his prose:

Among the young people sent to foreign countries by Peter the Great for the acquisition of the knowledge needed by the reformed State was his godson, the Negro Abraham. He was trained in a Parisian military academy, released as an artillery captain, distinguished himself in the Spanish war, and, severely wounded, returned to Paris. In the midst of his vast labors, the Emperor never ceased to keep himself informed of his favorite and always received flattering reports about his success and behavior. Peter was very satisfied with him and constantly called him back to Russia, but Abraham did not hurry.

Abraham's liaison with a French countess, the birth of their illegitimate child, his decision to return to Russia and subsequent journey are provided as reported background. The story really gets started after Abraham's arrival in Petersburg in Chapter II, when two dominant themes begin to develop, one stressing the role of Peter the Great as the creator of modern Russia and the other concerning Abraham's marriage to the daughter of the boyar Rzhevsky. The historical background includes descriptions of Peter's assemblies, where contemporary European social niceties were forced upon reluctant boyars and where those who broke the rules or incurred the Tsar's displeasure were obliged to down the contents of the huge Chalice of the Big Eagle.

In *The Negro of Peter the Great* Pushkin exercised his poetic license, changing circumstances to enhance the plot. Thus, Abraham's liaison with Countess D. was probably fictitious, and, though Peter himself serves as matchmaker for his Negro in the novel, history tells us that Abraham did not marry until a number of years following Peter's death, and, moreover, his wife was not a boyar's daughter. The novel ends at the point where Natalia, Rzhevsky's daughter, first glimpses her "official" fiancé, as she recovers from the shock of being told whom she must marry.

During Pushkin's life, only two parts of this work were published, but the entire piece, including the uncompleted seventh chapter, did appear in *The Contemporary* in 1837.[1] *The Negro of Peter the Great* had minimal effect on the course of Russian fiction, but it has been mentioned here primarily as the first extended example of Pushkin's imaginative prose.

A Novel in Letters [Roman v pismakh] was apparently intended to be a literary-political tract in the form of an epistolary society tale. The piece dates from 1829 and contains a number of Pushkin's ideas on literature and, especially, the author's personal views on the duties of the gentry with respect to their serfs, views which are reiterated in his personal correspondence, his criticism, and his notes on history written at about the same time. The literary opinions would hardly have excited the concern of the censors, but the remarks on the *parvenu* aristocracy and its indifference to the welfare of the serfs would have prevented publication of the work had Pushkin finished it. Probably this knowledge, and perhaps a realization that political tracts do not lend themselves to integration in a work of fiction, led the author to abandon his efforts.

The story's initial emphasis on the psychological state of the heroine, Liza, is of some interest, however. Raised and educated in Petersburg as the companion to a wealthy princess, she has recently joined her grandmother in the country, and it is there that she pens her first letter to her confidante, Sasha.

Of course, dear Sashenka, you are surprised at my unexpected withdrawal to the country. I hasten to explain everything frankly. The dependence of my position was always burdensome to me. Of course, Avdotya Andreevna raised me as her niece's equal. But in her house I was nonetheless a ward, and you cannot imagine how many petty miseries were unavoidable in that position.

She continues with some specific examples, and then adds: "Now, I live *at home,* I am the mistress—and you cannot believe what a real pleasure this is for me."

Pushkin's interest in the psychology of his character is visible also in a device which parallels one found in *Eugene Onegin*: Liza finds the books that her adorer, Vladimir, had read when he visited the country several years previously, and these books with his marginal notes reveal to her important facts about his personality. Sasha, Liza's correspondent, also provides comments upon the motivation of both Liza and Vladimir, which further deepens their characterization. This concern with inner motivation rather than external action is an important development in fiction and is a harbinger of Romanticism's evolution toward Realism.

The *Belkin Tales* [Povesti Belkina] are probably the best known of Pushkin's prose, with the exception of *The Queen of Spades*. He composed the five stories and their introduction in several weeks during the fall of 1830 when he was confined to his father's estate at Boldino by a cholera quarantine. The introduction, which explains very circumstantially that the stories were transcribed by a provincial gentleman, Ivan Belkin, after he had heard them narrated by various persons, was apparently written as an afterthought

128

to insulate Pushkin from any direct attacks by the critics. But the anonymity of the tales also led to their being ignored, and by the time Pushkin's name was connected with them the critics were distracted by more recent works.

The manuscript dates indicate that the *Belkin Tales* were composed in the following sequence: *The Undertaker, The Station Master, Mistress Into Maid, The Shot, The Snowstorm [Grobovshchik, Stantsionnyi smotritel', Baryshnia-krest'ianka, Vystrel, Metel']*; the introduction was written last. The stories were arranged by the author with *The Shot* and *The Snowstorm* first and the rest following in the order of their composition. Some efforts have been made to justify Pushkin's plan in ordering the stories, but most explanations are unconvincing.

Pushkin was not only concerned with externally intriguing plots and characters but engaging in covert play with literary types, themes, and clichés. Unfortunately for his reputation as a prose writer, the critics of his time based their interpretations on the obvious externals, misunderstanding the stories and dismissing them as pleasant but unimportant trifles.

Professor Waclaw Lednicki has demonstrated[2] that the central figure in *The Shot*, the enigmatic Byronic Sylvio, is a psychological imposter, whose revenge against a truly natural leader of men, a certain Count D. , becomes the entire purpose of his life. Thematically the story relates to Pushkin's *Mozart and Salieri*, one of the "little tragedies" written in Boldino that same fall, in which the composer Salieri, consumed by envy of Mozart's natural genius, poisons his rival. As for its structure, *The Shot* provides an interesting example of how a story can be organized to achieve the utmost in mystification, suspense, and characterization. Here we are given a multiple view of the central character, with the story presented by three narrators. Sylvio and the Count relate their tales of past events to a certain Lieutenant I.L.P. (remember, Belkin only wrote down stories told by others), who in turn incorporates their narratives into the framework of his story, which details his own meetings with both men. The character of the narrator himself is very important, for he must be naive enough to be attracted to Sylvio and yet sufficiently perceptive as a reporter to enable the reader to penetrate the real personality of the story's anti-hero.

The Shot, all of which is presented retrospectively, opens in a provincial garrison town, where the narrator, at that time a junior officer, has become attached to Sylvio, a civilian retired from the army, who has acquired a reputation among the officers for his hospitality and skill with the pistol. However, the narrator is surprised and disappointed one evening when a newcomer to Sylvio's circle insults his host and does not even receive a challenge. One day Sylvio receives a letter and immediately announces his departure, at the same time inviting the officers to a farewell dinner. They all attend, and as they are leaving, Sylvio asks his young friend to remain. He then explains to the narrator that although he would surely have exterminated the rude newcomer in a duel under normal circumstances, he could not expose himself to the slightest risk because of a more pressing question of honor. Five years previously, he explains, he was serving in a cavalry regiment and had acquired quite a reputation for his abilities as duellist, drinker, and rake:

"You know," continued Sylvio [to the narrator], "that I served in the *** Hussar regiment. My character is known to you: I am accustomed to be first in all respects, and this has been my passion since childhood. In our day brawling was fashionable, so I was the foremost brawler in the army. We prided ourselves on drunkenness, so I outdrank the famous Burtsov, whose praises were sung by Denis Davydov. In our regiment duels took place by the minute, and in all of them I was either a second or a participant. My comrades idolized me, and the regimental commanders, who were replaced by the minute, looked upon me as a necessary evil."

"I was quietly (or unquietly) enjoying my fame, when a young man from a wealthy and well-known family (I don't want to name him) was assigned to us. From the day of my birth I had never met such a brilliant child of fortune! Imagine youth, intellect, good looks, the wildest kind of gaiety, the most reckless courage, a resounding name, and money, whose extent he did not know and which was never exhausted, and imagine what kind of effect he was bound to produce upon us. My prominence tottered. Seduced by my fame, he tried to gain my friendship. But I received him coldly, and without the slightest regret he withdrew from me. I came to hate him. His success in the regiment and in feminine society brought me to complete despair. I began to seek quarrels with him. He answered my epigrams with epigrams which always seemed to me more unexpected and sharper than mine and which, of course, were incomparably more humorous. He was jesting while I was being spiteful."

Here in Sylvio's own words is the essence of his conflict with the Count, who, naturally and without trying, achieves what Sylvio has taken years of role-playing to accumulate. Finally, the exasperated Syivio challenges the Count, who appears at the duelling site casually eating cherries and, having won the right to the first shot, just as casually puts a bullet through Sylvio's forage cap. Sylvio then aims at his adversary, but the Count faces him fearlessly, continuing to eat cherries and spitting the pits across the barrier.[3] This is too much for the would-be Byronic avenger, and he postpones his shot until such a time as the prospect of death will mean more to the Count. Now, five years later, Sylvio informs the narrator that he has heard of the Count's recent marriage and that he is leaving to take his revenge. The narrator remarks that Sylvio's tale caused "strange, conflicting feelings" to agitate him.

Another four or five years pass, during which the narrator retires to his estate in the country. His closest neighbor is a Countess B., who had been absent from her estate since shortly after her marriage several years before. However, one day she and her husband return to resume residence there, and the narrator visits them. In the course of their conversation, it turns out that the husband is Sylvio's old enemy, the Count, and he now tells the narrator what happened when the duel resumed. Sylvio had suddenly reappeared at the estate, demanded his shot, but hesitated as he aimed at the accommodating Count. Finally he determined they should begin anew. Once

130

more they drew lots, the Count again winning first shot. Under some strange domination by Sylvio, the Count's shot pierced a picture on the wall. As Sylvio began to aim, the Countess rushed in and threw herself at his feet. The Count angrily told her to rise and demanded that Sylvio either shoot or stop his mockery. Sylvio responded that he would not shoot, since he was sufficiently satisfied with seeing the Count's agitation and apprehension. Hardly aiming, Sylvio put his bullet into the same hole made in the picture by the Count's shot and then departed. The narrator laconically reports that it was later said that Sylvio had died in battle during the Greek Insurrection.

The psychology of the envious, vindictive, obsessed Sylvio is naturally more intriguing than that of the Count, so it is on the former that Pushkin focused his story. And it is the manifold presentation of Sylvio, whose masks are peeled off to reveal his diseased soul, which makes this story so unusual, especially for the year 1830. Sylvio is seen from four different points of view: his own, which does not change and is lacking any self-awareness, the Count's and the narrator's which change as they learn more about Sylvio, and the reader's, which is abstracted from the others. Our view of Sylvio is continually evolving: at first we are intrigued by this mysterious figure who seems to be a natural leader, we are puzzled at his refusal to challenge the newcomer for his insult, and surprised at the extent of the malice revealed in his own story. Our feelings of dismay are further intensified when we learn that Sylvio spares the Count, but his act is not one of compassion. Rather, he does so because he expects that the Count will find his future life poisoned by the memory of Sylvio's domination. In declining his shot, Sylvio declares:

"I am satisfied. I have seen your confusion, your alarm. I forced you to fire at me. That is enough. You will remember me, I leave you to your conscience."

But the irony is that Sylvio's long awaited "revenge" is ineffective. Sylvio attributes to the Count the kind of reaction which he, himself, would have had under the same circumstances, that is, a galling sense of frustration and humiliation. But the Count lives on happily, the episode with Sylvio reduced to the level of a bad dream. Although shaken, the Count has again proved his natural superiority to the psychological impostor.

Although *The Shot* incorporates Romantic themes and situations, and although its central character, Sylvio, is close kin to such excessive Romantic figures as Byron's Lara, Tieck's Eckbert, or even Scott's Black Monk, the tale's ultimate effect is quite unlike that of typical Romantic fiction. The mysterious and intriguing aura surrounding the central figure is the product of the naivete of the narrator, who is impressed by Sylvio's mask. But if the reader understands the story, the fog gradually disappears and he gains a clear view of an obsessive personality, repulsive in its malignity and frightening in its violence.

The story concludes with Pushkin's private ironical twist:

It is said that Sylvio led a detachment of hetaerists during the revolt of Alexander Ypsilanti and was killed in the battle of Skulyani.[4]

Skulyani was a disaster and a fitting apotheosis for Sylvio, whose personal qualities were insufficient to sustain his impersonation of the natural leader. The direct reference to Alexander Ypsilanti reinforces the irony, since Pushkin had a low opinion of him as a commander. In *Kirdzhali*, a historical sketch published in 1834, Pushkin had this to say about the Greek revolutionary:

Alexander Ypsilanti was personally brave, but he did not have the qualities necessary for the role which he undertook so passionately and imprudently. He did not know how to get along with the people he had to lead. They had neither respect for nor confidence in him. After the unhappy battle in which the flower of Greek youth perished, Iordaki Olimbioti advised him to withdraw and himself took his place. Ypsilanti galloped to the borders of Austria and from there sent his curse to the people whom he called rebels, cowards, and scoundrels. These cowards and scoundrels for the most part perished within the walls of Seko monastery or on the banks of the Pruth, fighting desperately against an enemy ten times stronger.

Without suggesting any direct connection between Ypsilanti and Sylvio, it should be noted that neither name is Russian, and, like Sylvio himself, Ypsilanti served for a time as an officer in the Russian army.

The Shot is introduced with an epigraph from an anecdote included in Marlinsky's *An Evening on Bivouac* (1823): "I swore to shoot him in accordance with the duelling code (I still had a shot to follow his)." The earlier story is a sentimental tale involving an officer, Vladimir Lidin, who is gravely wounded in a duel with a captain who maligned the girl he loved. After a lengthy convalescence, Vladimir returns to his regiment to learn that his adversary and his girlfriend have been married. Since he still has one shot, he vows to continue the duel, but friends see to it that he is posted to some distant place. Later he learns that the wife was also the victim of the captain, who abandoned her to die penniless. Like *The Shot,* Marlinsky's tale has multiple narrators, but the potential for contrastive characterization is not exploited as it is in Pushkin's work. Further, Marlinsky seasons his work, as usual, with overt sentimentality and sententiousness, qualities antithetical to Pushkin's art. One may see *The Shot*, therefore, as Pushkin's restrained polemic with Marlinsky, the same plot nucleus built into a tightly crafted tale emphasizing the protagonist's obsessive personality and leaving it for the reader to decide the point.

The Snowstorm involves fate and mistaken identity, each theme emerging from the rather preposterous plot. Still, the atmosphere is more serious than frivolous, though not so serious as *The Shot*. Mariya, the daughter of a wealthy provincial family, falls in love with their poor neighbor, Vladimir, but her parents prohibit their marriage. The two lovers scheme to elope, and one stormy night Vladimir sends his sleigh and coachman to convey Mariya and her maid to a nearby church, where arrangements had been made for their wedding. Meanwhile, Vladimir sets out alone and becomes hopelessly lost in the storm. A hussar officer on his way to Wilno also loses his way because of the blizzard and ends up at the church, where the fainting bride, the anxious priest, and witness mistake him for the tardy bridegroom. The officer nonchalantly permits himself to be married to the girl, who, only after they are wed, recovers sufficiently to discover that her husband is a total stranger. The hussar then drives away, and Mariya returns home. Her parents are blissfully ignorant of her adventure, and when she falls ill and raves deliriously about her love for Vladimir, they have a change of heart and reconsider their opposition to her marriage. They write this good news to the young man, but he responds madly that he will never see them again and wishes he were dead. Shortly afterwards they learn he has rejoined the army. Four years pass. Vladimir has perished in the War of 1812, and Mariya has moved to another village. There she meets a Colonel Burmin, a wounded veteran of the victory over Napoleon, and the two are quite attracted to each other. One day Burmin declares his love, but he explains that marriage is impossible because of a heedless act in the past, when during a snowstorm at some unknown village he had married an unknown woman. All is happily resolved when Mariya declares that she is his anonymous bride.

The caprice of fate is one of Pushkin's favorite themes. In Burmin's account there is a special note of his apparently *fated* role in the whole episode:

"At the beginning of 1812," said Burmin, "I was hastening to Wilno, where our regiment was stationed. Having arrived at some post station once late in the evening, I was about to order that horses be harnessed as soon as possible when suddenly a terrible snowstorm arose, and the station master and the drivers advised me to wait. I followed their advice, but an inexplicable agitation took possession of me. *It seemed as if someone were pushing me.* [Italics mine]. Meanwhile, the storm did not abate. I became impatient, again ordered the horses to be harnessed, and set off into the tempest. The driver got the idea of traveling along the river, which would have shortened our way by three versts. The banks were drifted, and the driver passed the place where we should have turned onto the road, and in that way we ended up in some unknown region. The tempest did not abate. I saw a small light and ordered to be driven towards it. We drove into a village. There was a light in the wooden church. The church was open, behind the wall stood several sleighs, people were walking around the porch.

'This way, this way!' cried several voices. I ordered the coachman to drive up to them. 'For God's sake, where have you been?' someone said to me, 'the bride is in a faint, the priest doesn't know what to do. We were on the point of going back. Get out as fast as you can.' Without responding, I jumped from the sleigh and entered the church, which was weakly illuminated with two or three candles. The girl sat on a bench in a dark corner of the church. Another was rubbing her temples. 'Thank God,' she said, 'you've arrived at last. You almost tormented the young lady to death.' The old priest hurried. Three men and the maid supported the bride and were occupied exclusively

133

with her. We were married. 'Kiss each other,' we were told. My wife turned her pale face toward me. I was on the point of kissing her. . . . She screamed, 'Ai, it isn't he, it isn't he!' and fell senseless. The witnesses fastened their frightened eyes upon me. I turned, left the church without any hindrance, jumped into my kibitka, and cried out, 'Drive on!' "

Is it fate again which reunites the husband and wife and leads them to discover their paradoxical relationship, or is it merely coincidence? Or is perhaps Pushkin playing with the whole Romantic concept of fated lovers, mistaken identity, and implausible coincidence? Notice the careful attention to details in the hussar's account, which seeks to justify Burmin's being mistaken for Vladimir: the darkness of the night, the dim candle light in the church, the fainting bride, who distracted everyone's attention from Burmin. If this story is a crypto-satire on outworn Romantic cliches, as its somewhat facetious tone might suggest, then all this justification is simply a red herring, a part of Pushkin's private joke.

Regardless of the author's intent, the story is cleverly constructed to keep the reader guessing until the very end. Burmin does not appear until the dénouement, and until his story is told we do not know what happened at the church on that fatal night, only that it brought about Mariya's spell of delirium and Vladimir's incoherent response to her parents' letter, incoherent not because he no longer loved the girl but because he knew he could never marry her: the morning after her marriage to Burmin he had learned that the wedding had taken place and that the groom had disappeared.

If we wished to see some special purpose in Pushkin's arrangement of the Belkin stories, we could claim that the third in the series, *The Undertaker*, is a work linking the sombre psychological study of *The Shot* and the less serious case of mistaken identity of *The Snowstorm* with the mock serious psychological study of *The Station Master* and the totally frivolous case of mistaken identity of *Mistress Into Maid*. *The Undertaker* is a tale of the supernatural based on a variant of the cliché, "Speak of the devil and he shall appear."

Having moved to a new section of town, an undertaker, Adrian Prokhorov, is invited by a neighbor, the cobbler Schultz, to attend a party in honor of his silver wedding anniversary. At the celebration, which is thronged with German tradesmen of various callings, a great deal of beer is consumed, followed by toasts with sparkling wine. Finally a fat baker raises his glass "To the health of those for whom we work, *"unserer Kundleute!"* In jest, one of the guests calls out to the undertaker, "What's this? Drink up, little father, to the health of your corpses." Adrian is offended, and after the party is over he returns home angry and drunk. In a fit of pique, he declares that he won't invite his neighbors to his housewarming but rather "the people for whom I work, the Orthodox dead." Despite his servant's remonstrances, he persists and issues an invitation. The next evening the surprised undertaker finds his house crowded with his former customers. Although the spectres are somewhat macabre, there is no element of terror except for the host.

The room was filled with corpses. Through the window the moon illuminated their yellow and blue faces, sunken mouths, dull, half-closed eyes, and projecting noses. With terror Adrian recognized in them the people buried through his services. . . . All of them, ladies and gentlemen, surrounded the undertaker with bows and greetings, with the exception of one poor fellow who had recently had a free funeral. Somewhat conscience stricken and embarrassed by his rags, he did not approach but stood quietly in a corner. . . .

At this moment a small skeleton squeezed through the crowd and approached Adrian. Its skull smiled pleasantly at the undertaker. Bits of light green and red cloth and rotted linen hung here and there upon it as on a pole, and its bones rattled in its big jack boots like pestles in mortars. "You don't recognize me, Prokhorov," said the skeleton. "Do you remember the retired sergeant of the Guard, Peter Petrovich Kurilkin, the very one to whom in 1799 you sold your first coffin, moreover a pine one instead of oak?" With these words the corpse offered its bony embrace, but Adrian, collecting himself with difficulty, cried out and shoved it away. Peter Petrovich staggered, fell, and scattered about. A murmer of displeasure arose among the corpses. All of them stood up for the honor of their comrade, they surrounded Adrian with abuse and threats, and the poor host, deafened by their cries and almost crushed, lost his presence of mind, and he himself fell onto the bones of the retired sergeant of the Guard and lost consciousness.

Descriptions of all this spectral haunting are quite facetious, even to the skeleton named Peter Petrovich who falls apart. The revelation that this was Adrian's dream, brought on by overindulgence at the cobbler's feast and irritation at the fancied insult to his profession, disarms the supernatural element.

Some efforts have been made to relate *The Undertaker* to works of E.T.A. Hoffmann, but the ties, if any, are tenuous. Pushkin's tale is more closely connected with his own *The Stone Guest*, one of the "little tragedies" written at Boldino in 1830, in which the brazen Don Juan invites the statue of the commander to stand guard over his rendezvous with the commander's widow:

> *(to the statue.)* I, commander, bid you come
> To the widow's house, where I'll tomorrow be,
> And stand and guard the doors. Well? Will you?
> *(The statue nods its head)*
> Oh, God!

Another source is indicated by an allusion in the story to the watchman Yurko, who "for twenty-five years served his calling with trust and truth, like Pogorelsky's postman." In *The Lafertov District Poppyseed Cake Vendor* (1825), Perovsky-Pogorelsky presented a story of the supernatural set against the background of the Moscow lower bourgeoisie, and, although the supernatural in that tale is "real," the tone is facetious, as it is in Pushkin's work.

Pushkin's enthusiasm for Perovsky's work is indicated in a letter written to Leo Pushkin in March, 1825:

My soul, grandmother's cat is really charming! I read the whole tale twice in one breath, and now I'm obsessed with Trifony Faleleyich Purrful. I move forward smoothly, squinting my eyes, rotating my head, and arching my back. Pogorelsky is certainly Perovsky, right? [5]

Generations of readers have been deceived by *The Station Master*, which only goes to prove that most readers see in a work what they wish to see. On the surface this story seems to be about a poor station master of the lowest rank, Samson Vyrin, whose beautiful daughter, Dunya, the light of her old dad's eyes, is abducted by an officer and taken to a life of sin in Petersburg. This touching tale is related by a traveler who visits the posting station on three occasions. The first time he is smitten, as are most voyagers, by the beauty and spontaneity of Dunya, whose charm animates the entire household. A second visit three years later reveals a haggard station master, a broken man, who when plied with punch tells of the perfidious officer, Minsky, who pretended to be ill in order to win Dunya. Tearfully he recounts how he urged his daughter to ride in Minsky's carriage to the village church and how she never returned. He followed her to Petersburg, learned where she was being kept, even saw her, but Minsky would not let him speak to her. The station master tells also of his anger when Minsky tried to buy him off with a handful of bills. The traveler-narrator leaves the station consumed with gloomy thoughts of Dunya's ultimate fate and the sorrowful image of her desolate father. A final visit discloses that the station master died from drink. The narrator's inquiries reveal that once a woman in an expensive carriage with children and servants had come to the village and visited his grave. The narrator also goes to the bleak cemetery and ruefully surveys the last resting place of Samson Vyrin, the victim of his daughter's sins and a rich man's callousness.

The Station Master presents an early example of the unreliable narrator. He does not deliberately try to deceive his audience but rather he is too naive, too conventional, to see the true import of the facts he relates. Happily, he is a comprehensive reporter who provides the reader with all essential information, but, unhappily, too many readers accept his judgment uncritically and, along with him, shed their tears pointlessly.

The meaning or point of any story must be developed from the entire story, and interpretations which are based on only a portion of the story are simply incorrect. A story is an organic whole, and its meaning derives from that whole. The Soviet scholar, M.O. Gershenzon, who is responsible for the dictum that the art of good criticism is the art of slow reading, was puzzled by one aspect of *The Station Master* which did not seem typical of Pushkin's prose. Gershenzon noted that one seldom finds digressions, inessential details, or superfluous qualifiers in Pushkin's fiction. Therefore, the critic was struck by the lengthy passage in which the narrator describes in detail the four pictures ornamenting the walls of the station. These depict the Parable of the Prodigal Son.

At this point he [the station master] undertook to transcribe my travel orders, and I occupied myself by looking over the pictures which decorated his humble but tidy abode. They depicted the story of the prodigal son: in the first a venerable old man in a night-cap and robe is taking leave of a restless youth, who hastily accepts his blessing and a bag of money. In the second was depicted in clear features the dissolute behavior of the young person: he was sitting at a table surrounded by false friends and shameless women. Further, the wastrel youth in rags and a three-cornered hat was herding swine and sharing their banquet. On his face was depicted deep sadness and repentence. Finally there was represented his return to his father. The kind old man in the same night-cap and robe was running out towards him: the prodigal son was kneeling, and in the background the cook was killing the fatted calf and the older brother was asking a servant the cause of all the joy. Under each picture I read appropriate German verses. Until now I have retained all this in my memory, along with the pots with balsam, and the bed with the motley screen, and the other things which surrounded me at that time. I see, as if now, the host ʃhimself, a man around fifty, fresh and vigorous, and his long green frock coat with three medals on faded ribbons.

In telling of his subsequent visit, the narrator again mentions these pictures, more or less in passing. But everything else has changed, for the station itself is gloomy and the master crushed. In Samson's story of Minsky's deception and the search for Dunya, he continually refers to his daughter as "my strayed lamb," "my poor Dunya," and the narrator in turn calls the master "the poor father," "the poor station master," "the unfortunate one." The old man concludes his tale with these pitiful observations:

"It's already been three years," he concluded, "that I have been living without Dunya, and there's not been a word about her. Whether she's alive or not, God knows. Anything is possible. She's not the first or the last to be lured away by some traveling scoundrel, kept there a while, and abandoned. There are many of them in Petersburg, foolish young girls, today in thick silk and velvet, and tomorrow, take a look, they are sweeping the streets with tavern beggars. When I sometimes think that maybe this will happen to Dunya, then against my will I sin and wish her in the grave."

And so he takes to drink and dies. But why? Because he believed the pictures in his house, because he was certain that Dunya had to follow the descent of the prodigal and fall into poverty and misery. The irony is, however, that his dire prediction did not come true, quite the contrary. On the narrator's final visit, he asks to see Samson Vyrin's grave and is taken there by a small boy, who tells him:

"Well, nowadays there are few travelers. . . . But in the summer a lady passed through, and she did ask about the old station master and went to his grave."
"What lady?" I asked with curiosity.

137

"A beautiful lady," answered the little boy. "She was traveling in a carriage with six horses, with three little young gentlemen and a wet nurse, and with a black pug dog. When they told her that the old master had died, then she began to cry and said to the children, 'Sit quietly, and I'll visit the cemetery.' And I was about to lead her there. But the lady said, 'I know the way myself!' And she gave me a silver five kopek piece— such a kind lady!"

So Dunya is alive and well in Petersburg supported in style, with a coach and three children, a wet nurse, and a lapdog. And for that Samson Vyrin drank himself to death.

Nothing Pushkin ever wrote would suggest that his was a sentimental mentality. Rather, he always mocked that inclination, and often his characters were victims of their confidence in the verity of Sentimentalist cliches. He considered Richardson's Clarissa Harlowe an absolute fool (she willed herself to death after having been "dishonored" by Lovelace), and, regardless of the narrator's attitude toward Samson Vyrin, Pushkin must have seen the station master's self destruction as the epitome of folly.

All of the Belkin tales have their elements of irony, but in *The Station Master* irony becomes the essence of the piece. In addition to the irony of the pointless sacrifice, there are minor ironies, for example, the master's first name, Samson, which implies strength, and his surname, Vyrin, which possibly suggests *escavate* [vyryt']. In any case, Samson was done in by a woman and Vyrin does dig his own premature grave. Irony figures also in the origin of his tragedy, for it is he who insists that Dunya accompany Minsky to the church in his carriage: " 'What are you afraid of?' her father said, 'surely his honor is not a wolf and won't eat you up. Take a ride to church.' " And there is irony also in the scene of Samson's righteous indignation when Minsky tries to give him money to leave Dunya alone:

> For a long time he stood without moving. Finally he saw behind the fold of his cuff a roll of papers. He withdrew them and opened up several crumpled five and ten ruble bank notes. Again tears came to his eyes, tears of indignation! He wadded the notes into a ball, threw them to the ground, trampled them with his heels, and went on. . . . Having gone several steps, he stopped, thought a bit. . . and turned around. . . but the bank notes were not there. A well dressed young man, catching sight of him, ran up to a cabby, hurriedly took a seat, and cried out, "Drive on!"

Samson's second thoughts about the payoff money completely cancel out his earlier tears of indignation, and his heedless sacrifice of the banknotes, which is motivated by misplaced emotions, presages his later unnecessary death.

If one wishes further substantiation of Gershenzon's interpretation, note that *The Station Master* is a subtle parody of *Poor Liza*, with the victims raised one notch in social status. Instead of Liza's widowed mother, a peasant, we have Dunya's widowered father, a civil servant at the bottom of the scale.[6] Liza's mother and Vyrin are devoted to their offspring, who are not only uncommonly pretty but pretty free with their kisses. As malefactors we have Erast, a wishy-washy young gentleman who gambles to penury, and Minsky, who is obviously from the real *beau monde* and one who knows what he wants. Karamzin's refrain of "poor Liza" is matched by the station master's "poor Dunya," a phrase which Pushkin's narrator also reëchoes. The attempt to pay off the offended party is virtually the same in both stories. "[Erast] took her by the hand, led her to his study, locked the door. . . ," while "Minsky took him by the hand, led him to the study, and locked the door behind him." Readers raised on Karamzin would certainly have expected that Dunya would come to no good end, but the wily Pushkin led them by the nose and reversed the anticipated ending.

Mistress Into Maid, the last of the Belkin group, is yet another ironical treatment of *Poor Liza* and, at the same time, a variation on the themes of fate and mistaken identity found in *The Snowstorm*. Its pervasive facetious tone implies its parodistic essence. Ivan Berestov, a widowed landowner of patriarchal principles, is at loggerheads with his neighbor, the Anglophile Grigory Muromsky, the father of seventeen-year-old Liza. When Alexey Berestov returns home from the university, he instantly captivates the local gentry misses with his Byronic poses:

> It is easy to imagine what kind of an impression Alexey was bound to create in the circle of our young ladies. He was the first among them to appear gloomy and disenchanted, he was the first to talk to them about lost happiness and about his faded youth. Moreover, he wore a black ring with the image of a death's head. All this was quite new in that province. Girls lost their heads over him.

Liza Muromskaya seeks an opportunity to meet this fascinating and handsome young neighbor, and, learning that he has an eye for peasant girls, she puts together a suitable costume, creates a cover story about being Akulina, the blacksmith's daughter, and goes into the forest to be encountered "accidentally" by Alexey. Their initial meeting leads to others, and Alexey is progressively more fascinated by his peasant beauty, whose moral rectitude and skill in learning to read and write (so they can correspond) are simply amazing. Meanwhile, their fathers have become reconciled, and Liza is forced to meet Alexey at her father's house. Heavy applications of powder and eyebrow pencil, in addition to an outlandish costume and artificial hair pieces, prevent Alexey from recognizing her. In fact, the impression she creates is so negative that Alexey flatly rejects his father's demand that he marry the girl. He then writes to his peasant Akulina proposing marriage. Hoping to enlist Liza to oppose the match which their parents are forcing on them, Alexey goes to Muromsky estate to talk to the young lady. Imagine his surprise to find his peasant maiden, now transformed into a pretty provincial miss, reading his letter in her father's drawing room.

There are several allusions to Karamzin in this story which suggest its parodic quality. Alexey teaches Liza Muromskaya "to read" using *Natalia, the Boyar's Daughter*, whose hero is also an Alexey and who eloped with Natalia to the Murom forests. The Liza of *Mistress Into Maid* is not destined to become yet another "poor Liza," and part of Pushkin's irony is in the fact that Liza-Akulina is not seduced and cast off. However, hidden in this story there is an actual victim of Alexey's attraction to lower class girls. Here there is a remark in passing about a letter written by Alexey:

> The young ladies looked at him and some feasted their eyes. But Alexey was little occupied with them, and they ascribed his insensitivity to a love affair. Indeed, there was passed from hand to hand a copy of the address of one of his letters:
> To Akulina Petrovna Kurochkina, Moscow, opposite the Alexeyev monastery, the house of the coppersmith Savelyev, and I most humbly request that you deliver this letter to A. N. R.

Who was this A.N.R., a gentry girl or something less elevated? Recall that when he arrived in the country Alexey immediately disdained the provincial misses and started chasing peasant girls. As Liza's maid reports:

> "They say the gentleman is handsome, he's such a kind person, so cheerful. One thing is bad: he likes to chase girls too much. Well, as for me, there's nothing wrong with that. In time he'll settle down."

One may surmise that this letter to A. N. R. contained expressions of undying love, but that the next one would rationalize an end to their liaison. While Alexey and Liza are rejoicing in the provinces, somewhere in Moscow a young girl's dream has been shattered.

While writing the Belkin tales, Pushkin was also working on a satirical piece called *A History of the Village of Goriukhino [Istoriia sela Goriukhina]*. He did not finish the work, but it did appear in *The Contemporary* soon after his death in 1837, and thus has a place in Romantic fiction.

The Petersburg literary mandarins, you will recall, were unhappy with Polevoy for his denigration of Karamzin's *History of the Russian State*, expressed polemically in his own *History of the Russian People*. Pushkin's "history" is a parody of the pretensions of Polevoy's pedestrian work, and to some extent it is also a lampoon on that author-critic-publisher himself.

The village of Goriukhino was the ancestral holding of the Belkin family, and Ivan Belkin, transcriber of tales, retired there after an uneventful career in the army. The first part of *A History of the Village of Goriukhino* is an amusingly tedious account by Belkin of his efforts to serve literature, his original aspirations to be an epic poet yielding gradually to the realization that his talent, at best, was sufficient only to equip him as a village historian. He begins his history with a pseudo-scholarly explanation of his sources, which range from old calendars to village gossip:

> Here I put forth a list of sources which served me in compiling the History of Goriukhino Village: 1. A collection of antique calendars. *54 parts*. The first 20 parts are

filled with antique script and titled. This chronicle was composed by my great grandfather, Andrey Stepanovich Belkin. It is distinguished by clarity and succinctness of style: for example: May 4. Snow. Trishka beaten for rudeness. 6. The chestnut cow croaked. Senka beaten for drunkenness. 8. Weather clear. 9. Rain and snow. Trishka beaten because of the weather. 11. Weather clear. Newly fallen snow. Hunted 3 hares....

This register of incredible triviality continues in an exposition that is archaic, bookish, and naive, a marvelous exaggeration of Polevoy's style:

The land which is named Goriukhino after its capital occupies more than 240 dessiatins on the earthly sphere. The number of its inhabitants extends to 63 souls. To the north it is bounded by the villages of Deriukhovo and Perkukhovo, whose inhabitants are poor, emaciated, and stunted, but the proud proprietors are devoted to the military exercise of coursing hares. To the south the river Sivka divides it from the holdings of the free Karachevsky grain farmers—restless neighbors known for the turbulent cruelty of their customs. To the west it is surrounded by the flowering Zakharinsky fields which thrive under wise and enlightened landowners. To the east it comes in contact with wild, uninhabited places, an impassable swamp, where only bogberries grow and where legend proposes the habitation of a certain devil. N.B. This swamp is called *The Devil's Swamp*. It is related that a half-witted shepherdess used to stand watch over a herd of pigs not far from this remote spot. She became pregnant and was quite unable to explain satisfactorily this occurrence. Public opinion accused the swamp devil, but this fable is unworthy of a historian's attention, and after Niebuhr it would be unforgivable to believe it.

The benighted and earnest Belkin is also a perfect vehicle for Pushkin's gibes at serfdom. Later in his history, our chronicler tells how the villagers prospered when left largely to themselves but were impoverished virtually overnight when put under the control of a venal estate manager. Pushkin's social consciousness did not extend to the emancipation of the serfs, but he did demand elementary justice for them. In his unfinished *A Novel in Letters* (1829), he unequivocally expressed the conviction that the masters had a responsibility to ensure the welfare of those in their possession.

Ivan Lazhechnikov

XII. The Historical Novel—Kalashnikov and Lazhechnikov.

Among the better-than-average historical novelists was Ivan Kalash-nikov (1797-1863), whose youth in a Siberian merchant family provided a personal acquaintance with some exotic places and a class that, with some few exceptions, including that of Pogodin, had been little treated in Russian Romantic fiction. Judging by the introduction to *The Daughter of the Merchant Zholobov—A Novel Drawn From Irkutsk Legends [Doch' kuptsa Zholobova. Roman izvlechennyi iz irkutskikh predanii]*, published in 1831, the author's primary concern was to acquaint his readers with the real life of his native region, about which the public was, in his opinion abysmally ignorant, or worse still, misinformed:

> In publishing this novel, I had in mind to acquaint my readers with a region distinguished by its richness of products and its variety of nature and inhabitants, which until the present time is still a little known and almost fairy tale country. Recently one of our better newspapers wrote that in Irkutsk people ride on dogs. If that is the way people who are engaged in scholarship think, what can one expect from the rest?

While emphasizing his desire to set the record straight, as it were, Kalashnikov concludes this introduction by resorting to the authority of Scott himself for the license he took in telescoping historical events to include them within the temporal frame of his work:

> In conclusion, I admit to the sin of having united in one frame several events which occurred at different times, but I hope to be forgiven for two reasons: *first,* the happenings which I described are not as historically significant as, for example, the taking of Kazan or the battle of Poltava, which if united in one period of time would mean to engage in obvious absurdity; and *second,* the progenitor himself of the modern novel, the inimitable Walter Scott, did the same thing, which every educated reader of his works knows.

Indeed, Scott's shadow lies across the structure of this work, its episodes, characters and connective tissue. At the same time it is a social history, a novel of mores, a grab bag of ethnological, geographical, gastronomical, and meteorological information. Heavily seasoned with regional terms, many elucidated by footnotes, the story barely gets moving—as a novel—by the end of the first volume. Pared of its exotica, it might well pass for one of Pogodin's short stories of the life and loves of the merchant class.

Alyosha, an orphan, is raised by a kind lady who was also the nurse to Natalia Zholobova, only daughter of a rich merchant. When the story opens, Alyosha is about twenty, handsome, and making a good career for himself as a chancery clerk (the author is at pains to insist that he did not share the dissolute habits of his colleagues). He falls ill from love of Natalia, and she, in turn, confesses her love to her father. Unlike the typical merchant paterfamilias, he approves her choice, especially since he has had a dream foretelling catastrophe. Meanwhile, the scheming and besotted Zapekalkin, a clerk who hates Alyosha for his rectitude, frames him by stealing stamped government paper. Zapekalkin is also in cahoots with the dishonest merchant Gruzdyov, who wants Alyosha out of the picture so his wastrel son, Grigory, can marry Natalia. The *smotr* is held (here called *smotreniye* as in Siberian custom) and Alyosha and Natalia engaged, but an earthquake disturbs the festivities. Alyosha is further distressed by knowledge of the charges against him, which he has kept secret from Natalia. The scene now shifts to Lake Baikal, where three travelers are parting, Natalia and her father to return to Irkutsk and Alyosha to proceed to Nerchinsk, where he has been assigned to serve in perpetuity as punishment for stealing the paper. After leaving Baikal, the merchant and his daughter are seized by bandits, and volume I ends with the cutthroats deciding to take their captives to their leader, Buza, to determine their fate.

The Scottian pattern is established—separation of lovers by forces of evil, and we may expect that the next three volumes will detail Alyosha's efforts to free Natalia from Buza's control—and embrace. The expected peripheral characters are also here: the nurse, the conniving clerk, the dishonest merchant, the mad woman who makes enigmatic prophecies. Also in the manner of Scott, Kalashnikov digresses upon the character of the landscape, the history of the region (with emphasis upon "the way things used to be") and introduces all manner of bric-a-brac to lend historical verisimilitude. Yet, nothing comes to life as it does in Scott—the characters are simply abstractions of virtue or vice playing out their roles, and one has the feeling that the "play" could be staged with entirely different exotic scenery and remain essentially unchanged.

Still, it is the scenery and ethnographic content which prove—at least for this reader—the most engaging components of the novel. There is, for example, a lengthy description of the aboriginal Buryats' pagan holiday:

Many thousands of the Brotherly Ones (the name the Russians give the natives) gathered for the celebration of the *Autumn* festival [Sange-Gaara] at Goose Lake, where from time immemorial the main encampment of the *Selengin clan* has been. The locale favored this festival: a vast hilly plain surrounded the lake on all sides. After the acceptance of the Tibetan religion by the Brotherly Ones, large *kumirni*, or temples, were built next to the lake, but at the time we are describing the Selengin clan still adhered to the *shaman* faith. The shaman. . . stood with a tambourine at the place of sacrifice, e.g., on a platform made of boards under the open sky. Countless crowds of people stood around him in devout silence. The shaman, straining his motionless gaze to the East, seemed to be awaiting the first rays of the sun. Finally its golden edge appeared from behind the mountains, which showed blue in the distance. The shaman struck the tambourine, and all the people fell face downwards. For a long time the dull sound of the tambourine resounded in the pervading silence. Then the shaman, assuming that the gods must already be listening, began a prayer, and the entire assembly, having risen to its feet, chanted after each section of the prayer: *Go!* [listen] *Gegea!* [Help, have pity!] . Then the shaman intoned the following:

"O Burkhan and Okodil! You, Irgekiny, Ongony, Nagaty, gods and great spirits, good and evil, who inhabit the mountains and forests, the water, and the nether regions! Send us health! Preserve us from falling from mountains, from drowning in water! Provide us with children and cattle, game and fish, tea and clothing!"

You, O sun! Give us clear and bright weather, so that we can successfully engage in trade with animals!"

"You, sacred spirits of shamans! Don't refuse us your help and defend us from all dangers visible and invisible."

"As a token of our sincerity, we bring you, oh gods and spirits, a sacrifice of twenty horses, fifty cows, and a hundred each of sheep and goats!"

At the conclusion of this prayer they brought to the shaman the animals consecrated to sacrifice, and he began to stab them in the breast with a knife: blood poured in a river over the place of sacrifice.

As an Orthodox Christian, Alyosha, who witnesses this ceremony, thinks, "What a false and beastly idea of God!" The reader, however, will probably find the scene of anthropological interest.

As we proceed further into the story, and move with it deeper into the wilderness, we involuntarily think of James Fenimore Cooper and his romanticization of the nature, the natives, and the stalwart settlers of America. Kalashnikov also presents a heroic pageant of the intrepid Russians who conquered Siberia, wresting control from the elements, the natives, and beasts. One of his more vivid scenes describes a combat between man and bear:

The shot resounded, but the bullet only lightly wounded the beast, and, filling the forest with its roar, it fled from the fire. "Don't leave us," shouted Bragin, who together with Batur ran after their enemy.

Following the bear, the hunters approached a small hollow, where, standing on its hind paws, it threateningly prepared for battle, its infuriated eyes glinting in the darkness. "Your turn now," said Batur, "Well, with God begin."

Although Bragin felt an involuntary terror, remembering that this was his *fortieth bear* [in Part I, page 137, a footnote had informed the readers that "In Siberia there is a belief among huntsmen that the fortieth bear always eats the hunter."], on which his life depended, according to the legend instilled in him from childhood. Still, ashamed of appearing a coward in the eyes of his comrade, he manfully left the forest and, letting the bear come within a few paces, he fired the rifle. Unfortunately, his shaking hands betrayed him, and the bullet flew whistling into the thicket, breaking off tree branches. At that moment the bear flung itself upon him, seized the weapon, and broke it like a straw. The agile huntsman grasped the knife hanging at his belt, which had always been his trusty comrade when he had grappled with a bear at those times he had his usual strength. But now no weapon could help him, for he lacked the most important mainspring of all combat—confidence in victory. With one gesture, so to say, the bear knocked the knife from him, and setting its claws into the back of his head, was ready to pull the skin off to cover his eyes, for the eyes of a human, from some strange instinct, are greatly feared by bears.

"Batur! Help!" the huntsman cried in a desperate voice. Another shot filled the empty thicket, and the bullet, hitting the bear in the side, passed clear through it. The badly wounded animal tumbled backwards with a roar, releasing its victim.

"Did the devil strike you?" grumbled Bragin, wiping away the blood which poured from the back of his head. "You must have see that the bear had almost begun to scalp me, but you didn't shoot!"

"How could I shoot," answered Batur, "when you were screening it? So, then I'd aim at a crow and hit a cow!"

After their little set to, the huntsmen quickly removed the bear's skin, and getting onto the road, dragged it to the encampment.

The next three parts are devoted to the continuing tribulations of Alyosha and Natalia. In Part II we also have the introduction of another Scottian standby, the rough and ready companion of the hero who is ever ready to sacrifice life and limb for his friend or the heroine. This Neudalin, in fact, completely displaces Alyosha in Part III, where the hero does not appear at all.

After many adventures, Alyosha tracks the bandit Buza to his hideout and defeats his band, but Natalia is not there, and one bandit says that she drowned. The dejected Alyosha heads for Nerchinsk, but on the way encounters Zholobov—Natalia is alive and well. The girl and her father return to Irkutsk, but then the dishonest Gruzdyov conspires with an Inspector Krylov to accuse Zholobov of witchcraft by conjuring up a fiery snake, in the hope of seizing his fortune. The poor merchant is found guilty, and Natalia barely escapes the Inspector's libidinous clutches, thanks to Neudalin. Given a chance to escape, the merchant refuses on the grounds of honor, and for his righteousness suffers death by torture. Natalia is led to believe that Alyosha has married and agrees to marry Grigory Gruzdyov.

Here we have one of the more sensational scenes. At the *smotr*, the Inspector, who has been drinking heavily because of his guilty conscience, gets drunk and makes a toast to the bride. She refuses to look at him, but when forced to, denounces him as a villain and flees. He falls into a fit, smoke pours from his mouth, eyes, and ears, and he quite literally *burns up*. Here the author, who had been so upset that educated people really believed the inhabitants of Irkutsk rode about on dogs, insists in a footnote that the human body can be subject to internal combustion:

Spontaneous combustion of the human body is a most unusual event, but nonetheless does occur in nature. It results from the use of internal and even external alcoholic substances. The body burns without any external flame having touched it.

Dickens, I believe, describes a similar phenomenon, and in *Dead Souls* one of the serfs Chichikov purchases reportedly died in this way. However, such effects from overindulgence in fiery spirits had not been attested in this century.

The last part of the novel is largely devoted to the history of Nerchinsk, Russia's outpost on the Amur river. There Alyosha pines for Natalia and, learning that she plans to marry Grigory, becomes engaged to a local girl. Owing to some meddling by schemers, he is called away on official business in the middle of his wedding; his disappointed bride drowns herself. For his faithful service and timely rescue of the governor of Irkutsk Province, Al-

146

yosha is pardoned and returns to Irkutsk, but Natalia has already taken vows. Meanwhile, Zapekalkin and Gruzdyov, the architects of his misery, have been captured by bandits: the former is drowned in a sack and Gruzdyov has his feet cut off before help arrives. Taken home to die, he requests last rites and then falls speechless. His son Grigory is concerned only that his silent father impart to him the secret of his money's hiding place.

The disappointed son, despite the priest's protests, wrote on a slip of paper: "Show, if you can, where your money is hidden," and presented it to his father. The latter looked at him angrily, gathered his last strength, took the paper, put it into his mouth, chewed it, swallowed, and closed his eyes forever.

Natalia is allowed to break her vows, because she took them while deceived by the lie that Alyosha had married another, and so all ends happily. Somehow we knew it would.

The reader shall be spared any lengthy discussion of Kalashnikov's next novel, *The Kamchatka Girl [Kamchadalka]*, which appeared in 1833. The author's own words will suffice to give a general idea of the content:

The public's kind reception of my first novel, *The Daughter of Merchant Zholobov*, and especially the flattering reviews by men-of-letters—our own and foreign ones—gave me the courage to publish another novel written in the same form and spirit. Not in its development but by its locale this novel in a certain sense is a continuation of the first: in both the action takes place in Siberia, and thus both novels acquaint the reader with Siberian nature and the native inhabitants. In both I tried to preserve traces of the Siberian dialect, but as a large part of the Siberian words used in the present work have already been explained, I didn't consider it necessary to make a second explanation.

The setting, he goes on to say, is at the end of the eighteenth century, when the Kamchatkins still retained their customs and faith. Since then things had changed for better and for worse: an epidemic had decimated the population (he notes that fifteen out of a hundred survived, sometimes less), the populace had accepted Christianity and Russian habits, and the governmental administration of them had been modified to accord better with their situation.

Kalashnikov's story is again one of parted lovers, with a number of interesting details of Eskimo *byt*. Amateurs of the graphically ghastly are advised to seek out the scene in which a drug-and-drink-crazed Kamchatkin slits his own throat before the indifferent eyes of his family, who then drag his corpse from the igloo with a rope and fling his remains into a snowbank.

Few of the Russian historical fictionists had the imagination, information, and dedication to compose novels with the scope of Scott's, and so many works of the thirties in this genre, though running to four parts, were less than one hundred thousand words. One of the real "quickies," whose two parts together total less than fifteen thousand words, is *Vasily Delinsky, or Novgorodians in the XIV Century. A Historical Novel, the Composition of S. Sh. [Vasilii Delinskii, ili Novgorodtsy v XIV stoletii. Istoricheskii roman, sochinenie S. Sh.]*, which was published in Moscow in 1833.

The story, set in 1396, opens with two brothers discussing the merits of Vasily Delinsky, a patriotic, courageous, handsome, articulate young man. One brother is trying to persuade the other to give his daughter, Natalia, to this paragon of virtue, but the second brother, although an admirer of Delinsky, is determined that Natalia marry a rich man, which Delinsky is not. Failing to persuade the obdurate father, the first brother departs to break the bad news to Delinsky. The scene then shifts to a rendezvous between Delinsky and Natalia, and he tells her that they must elope. She at first insists she will never dishonor herself or her family in such a shameful way—and then agrees.

At this point the familiarity of the material cannot be ignored, and one begins to anticipate that the further development of the work will follow the lines of Bestuzhev-Marlinsky's *Roman and Olga* (1823). In fact, the entire work is, if not a word for word plagiarism, a paraphrase in which every aspect of Marlinsky's historical tale is paralleled, including plot, characters, individual scenes, and even such free motifs as the activities of the *veche*, the public banquet following the *veche's* decision to reject the demands of the Grand Prince of Moscow and his Lithuanian ally, Vitovt, the tournament, fist fights, etc.

Chicanery in literary affairs was, of course, fairly common in that period, but usually involved publication of an author's works without his knowledge or permission, like Alexander Voyeykov's pirated selections from Pushkin's *The Robber Brothers* or Aladin's unauthorized printing of Somov's *The Rebel* and *Giant Mountains*.[1] On occasion the work of one author would be credited to another. Selections from De Quincey's *Confessions of an English Opium Eater* were published as the work of the then better known Charles Maturin, the Irish doyen of *l'Ecole frénétique*. To capitalize upon the popularity of Veltman, his name was put to the novel *Lieutenant Chernoknizhnik, or Moscow in 1812*, a work which he, prolific as he was, did not write.[2] In the case of *Vasily Delinsky* an unscrupulous author, or publisher, or both, took advantage of the fact that *Roman and Olga* had been out of print for ten years (since its original appearance in *Polar Star for 1823*) and that Bestuzhev, serving as a common soldier in the Caucasus, was hardly in a position to make an effective complaint.

Ivan Ivanovich Lazhechnikov (1792-1869), one of the most popular historical novelists, modestly styled himself "the grandson of Walter Scott." Raised in patrician style by his well-to-do merchant father, who lived in the manner of the provincial gentry, Lazhechnikov took an active part in the War of 1812 and was among the Russians who subsequently occupied Paris. After leaving military service in 1819, he began an on-again-off-again career as a provincial public school official. He first became known for his *Campaign*

Notes of a Russian Officer [Pokhodnye zapiski russkogo ofitsera], which appeared in periodicals from 1817 and were published separately in 1820, but his reputation was founded on his historical novels written in the thirties: *The Last Novik [Poslednii Novik]* (1831-1833), set in Lithuania against the background of Peter the Great's conflict with Sweden; *The Ice Palace [Ledianoi dom]* (1835), a tale of palace intrigue during the reign of Empress Anna, and *The Infidel [Basurman]* (1837), devoted to the time of Muscovite Grand Prince Ivan III. A drama of the early forties, *The Bodyguard of Ivan the Terrible [Oprichnik]* was proscribed by the censorship (but later adapted as an opera by Tschaikovsky).

Although Lazhechnikov was early on the scene as a Russian historical novelist, he cannot be credited with any real advancement of the genre, which, at least in the context of European literature, was well into middle age before its vogue in Russia. But he was a competent writer who researched his plots and historical figures, and his stories had a tasty seasoning of that kind of horror popularized by *l'Ecole frénétique* and its disciples. The second novel, *The Ice Palace*, provides a representative example of this author's product.

The story takes place in Petersburg during the final winter of the reign of Anna Ivanovna, the widowed Duchess of Courland who found herself Empress of Russia from 1730 to 1740. The title refers to an elaborate mansion entirely of ice constructed at the Empress's order to serve as a place to marry one of her jesters to a hideous Kalmyk woman, an act of whimsicality typical of that sovereign. Lazhechnikov slightly alters this historical fact in his narrative, but he is true to the spirit of Anna's reign in his scenes of court life and intrigue. The villain of the piece is Ernst Buehren, known as Biron in Russia, who was Anna's policy maker and lover. Biron, whose repressive measures made him hated in Russia, is opposed in his quest for control by Artemy Volynskoy, a cabinet advisor respected by the Empress for his rectitude and patriotism. Into this political intrigue is interwoven a love story involving Volynskoy and Marioritsa, a favorite of the Empress, who is believed to be a Moldavian princess but is actually an illegitimate gypsy. Volynskoy's infatuation with Marioritsa is exploited by Biron to discredit him with Anna, since the cabinet advisor is already married. To make a long story short, Biron and Volynskoy see-saw for power, and when Marioritsa discovers that her continued presence in Volynskoy's life will bring about his defeat, she poisons herself. Her effort is in vain, for Volynskoy is arrested and executed.

The characters are simplistic, their motivations and even their appearances predictable. Here is a description of Marioritsa after a romp in the snow:

They sat the princess [Marioritsa] down in the huge presidential chair, whose antiquity and worn, reddish black velvet more sharply accentuated this charming, youthful creation, flushed by the frost, in a glittering dress, half unfastened as if in order to disclose her shapely feminine body. This was a rosy leaf which had fallen on a monk's cassock, a swan resting in dark reed-grass. Surrounded by her friends, who looked as if they wanted for themselves, one—her damp hair, which wound in black ribbons around her neck to her waist, another—her rosiness, a third—her waist, shoulders, and God knows what else. Noticing in their eyes the involuntary tribute to her preeminence and seeing this preeminence in the mirror. . . Marioritsa seemed like some eastern princess surrounded by her subjects.

Volynskoy, who is considerably older than the girl, is conventionally depicted as handsome, commanding, a devoted patriot, whose Achilles heel is his passion. The Empress is presented as a woman whose heart is in the right place but who is ill, indecisive, and able only momentarily to free herself from Biron's spell. Biron himself is persistently scheming, cruel, vengeful, and evil, a depiction for which Pushkin chided Lazhechnikov: "He had the misfortune to be a German. He has been charged with all the terror of Anna's reign. . . . However, he had a great mind and great talents."[3]

Unlike some historical novelists, Lazhechnikov does not stylize the language of his characters to convey the impression of early seventeenth-century speech. Rather, his characters express themselves in what was for Lazhechnikov contemporary Russian, often more bookish than vernacular.

In recreating the Petersburg of 1739-1740. Lazhechnikov provides many scenes of circumstantial description, rather as if he were transferring into words the details of an old engraving. These set pieces are, of course, standard for historical tales and novels, a part of the *realia* of the genre. At the same time he incorporates material which provides a feeling of the times, for example, the scene of the appearance of "The Tongue." An abridged selection cannot convey the rather effective mood of terror which infuses the description:

Suddenly from somewhere a sentry's cry resounded. It seemed like a warning cry that the world is coming to an end. After it everything becomes still, all movement dies out, the pulse stops. . . . Everyone listens intently.

Again the exclamation resounds, surges, rises as if by steps, closer and closer. Already one may distinguish the word "The Tongue!"

They are bringing "The Tongue," hundreds of voices repeat with terror.

The word "The Tongue" moans through both levels of the Central Bazaar, through the streets, it becomes weaker, it gains strength and is communicated like the plague. Almost every person echoes it. Goods and money are thrown down, shops are locked, they lock themselves up in them, they shove one another, they flee headlong. . . . And in several moments the Grand Prospect, the Central Bazaar, all that part of town is empty, as if dead.

Only on the square, opposite the Central Bazaar, are seen two people. . . . These two people are our gypsies [Marioritsa's mother, Maruila, and her male companion].

They turn around.

At them, directly at them, accompanied by a convoy on horseback, comes some sort of monstrous being. At least it seems so at a distance.

The gypsies think to flee, but where? It is already too late. . . . The monstrous being is closer and closer, now several paces away. One can tell that this is a person covered from head to foot with a sack of rough cloth in which there are openings only for the eyes and mouth. . . . With reason do flight and abandonment precede him. He is the same as the plague, an earthquake, a flood. When from the small opening in the cloth are heard the magical *word and deed* [a formula of arrest used by the secret police], it leads to questioning, torture, and execution, it kills before death. No less terrible is the cry of the crocodile which has opened its maw to swallow its victim. This was one of the legal evils from which Catherine the Great freed us. It was called "The Tongue."

What was "The Tongue"? A capital criminal, led through the town in the raiment described above, in order to point out those who had participated in his crime. It goes without saying that this terrible means was used for fulfilling one's own purposes, greed or thirst for power, revenge or the desire to confuse the court.

The Tongue approached the frightened *gypsy* woman and denounced her with the fateful *word and deed.*

Nothing comes of the interrogation of Maruila by Biron's henchmen, as the wily gypsy woman avoids implicating herself in any conspiracy on behalf of Volynskoy. Still, she realizes that the striking resemblance between herself and her daughter, Marioritsa, may lead to the discovery of their relationship, the exposure of Marioritsa's true identity as a common gypsy. The mother therefore determines to alter her own appearance, which she does in a manner worthy of the best of *l'Ecole frénétique*: she destroys half of her face with acid!

Such fictional scenes are hardly more gruesome than reality. The historical Volynskoy was originally condemned to having his tongue cut out and being impaled, but his sentence was mitigated to having his limbs cut off before decapitation. His tongue had already been pulled out during the torture which preceded his execution.[4]

Although Lazhechnikov was no innovator in the genre he chose, he must be credited with detailed research of his period and thus historical verisimilitude, at least in so far as setting is concerned. *The Ice Palace* is really a *proper* historical novel, in that most of the characters are actual people, a circumstance which naturally puts constraints upon the author. Irrespective of how much he admires Volynskoy, Lazhechnikov must show his life ending with defeat and execution. An author who primarily dramatizes fictional characters, and whose historical figures are in the background like portraits on a wall, is much freer to develop his intrigue and perhaps thus be more entertaining or engrossing. Lazhechnikov took the more difficult road, but one can fairly say that he overcame the natural obstacles.

Arbitrarily, but perhaps to the reader's relief, I have chosen to limit the number of historical novels considered in this study. A few of the best, by Gogol, Pushkin, and Veltman, will be treated subsequently. The others are fairly standard representations of the genre. Among these are Faddey Bulgarin's *Dmitry the Pretender[Dmitrii Samozvanets]* (1830) and *Mazeppa* (1833), Nikolay Polevoy's *The Oath on the Lord's Tomb [Kliatva pri grobe gospodnem]* (1832), Constantine Masalsky's *The Musketeers[Strel'tsy]* (1832) and *The Black Box [Chernyi iashchik]* (1833), and Rafail Zotov's

Leonid, or Some Features from Napoleon's Life [Leonid, ili Nekotorye cherty iz zhizni Napoleona] (1836), *The Mysterious Monk, or Some Features from the Life of Peter I [Tainstvennyi monakh, ili Nekotorye cherty iz zhizni Petra I* (1836), *Niklas Bear Paw, Smuggler Chieftain, or some Features from the Life of Frederick II [Niklas Medvezh'ia Lapa, ataman kontrabandistov, ili Nekotorye cherty iz zhizni Fridrikha II]*(1837), and others.

XIII. The Novel of Manners—Perovsky-Pogorelsky, Ushakov. The Parodic Travelogue—Veltman.

As the Russian proverb goes, "In a place where there's no fish, even a crayfish is a fish." Accordingly, owing to the dearth of novels in domestic manufacture, Bulgarin's *Ivan Vyzhigin* was lauded to the skies and became a best seller, its author modestly asserting that his work was the first original Russian novel of its kind. Some similar, if less extravagant, claims greeted the appearance in 1830 of part one of Alexey Perovsky's *The Smolny Institute Graduate [Monastyrka]*, which, despite Bulgarin's earlier presumptions, the March 17th number of *The Literary Gazette* hailed as "probably the first real novel of manners in Russia."

The title refers to the central figure, Anyuta Orlenko, a Ukrainian orphan of gentry parents who was educated at the institute attached to the Smolny monastery in Petersburg. But the novel really concerns life among the Ukrainian provincial gentry, a milieu to which Anyuta returns after graduating from the institute. This is a lively and colorful picture of gentry life, first presented through the letters of the sophisticated Anyuta, and then through the omniscient narratation of Antoni Pogorelsky, who in the epilogue to part two identifies himself as the husband of one of Anyuta's cousins and thus privy to information about the family.

Perovsky, from behind the mask of Pogorelsky, manifests that particular attachment to the Ukraine which is typical of Little Russian authors, such as Narezhny, Somov, and Gogol, and like them he depicts Ukrainians with a gentle smile of ironic condescension. An early scene of the narrator's vain argument with the functionary in charge of a posting station is representative:

Finally at the next to the last station they told me categorically that there were no horses other than a troika reserved for couriers, which I couldn't have. I impatiently jumped out of my calash and requested the clerk to give me the logbook, so I could find out whether or not I was being deceived. In Little Russia not all stations have a civil servant as station master. The fat, moustachioed Ukrainian, not answering a word, grimaced, scratched his shaven head, slowly walked into the next room, and in five minutes brought back a soiled piece of paper, which, among other things, probably had served him for penmanship lessons and on which, besides orders for post horses, so much was scratched that I would have needed special skills to extract from that calligraphic labyrinth what I wanted to know.

"What sort of nonsense is this?" I cried with chagrin, throwing the paper he had given me onto the floor. "Surely you have a proper logbook?" The clerk bent down indifferently, picked the paper off the floor, and gave it back to me, not saying a word. "Why don't you answer me? Don't you have another logbook?"

"Taint none."

"What do you mean, 'taint none'? Haven't you been ordered always to keep a clean book for logging orders for post horses and keeping track of horses out on trips?"

"Yes."

"Well, why don't you have one?"

"Eh, mister, not everything's done that's ordered."

"What's that?" I cried with increasing fury. "It looks to me as if you're laughing at me. So you take pride in the fact that you don't do as you're ordered?"

"No, mister, I'm not prideful of it."

"Then how do you dare not carry out your superior's orders?"

"Well, what's to be done when there ain't no paper, mister?"

My threats failed to change one bit of that stubborn Ukrainian's physiognomy, but he got rid of his deafness when, having decided to try other means, I quieted down and shoved a silver ruble into his hand. Then he bowed low and declared that although he really didn't have any horses, it was possible to hire a pair from the priest and another from the Jewish tavern keeper. . . .

Anyuta's letters to her friend reveal her culture shock, when, after the institute's finishing-school ambience and an introduction into Petersburg society, she returns to her Ukrainian village of Barvenova and becomes reacquainted with her barefooted aunt and red-faced cousins, all of whom speak a language which she scarcely remembers. Her initial attitude of superiority is evident in her description of the local ball:

It was very pleasant at the ball. It began at six o'clock and we danced until almost dawn. No one knows any French quadrilles here. Polish dances, ecossais, and simple quadrilles, seemingly that is all. And even those are not at all like what we learned from Mme. Didelot! We danced the mazurka, but badly! My cavalier was an arithmetic teacher at the local regional academy. He stamped his feet a lot, and his boots smelled terribly of tar. That odor is most displeasing, but my aunty and cousins say it is good for health. The teacher is considered the best of the local dancers, and apparently he himself is convinced of that. In the mazurka, you know, when the cavalier puts a hand around the lady and rotates her around himself, he swung me so that I flew away from him and almost fell. Aunty says I myself am to blame, because I have such a tiny waist that people here don't know how to put a hand around it.

The plot begins to take shape in Anyuta's last letter, in which she questions her correspondent about a certain Guards officer, Blistovsky, who has been sent to the Barvenovo area on a remount mission. The letters are then followed by Pogorelsky's account, which opens with a biography of Anyuta's father, a Cossack officer who had retired to the Ukraine after winning honors under Suvorov. Shortly after Anyuta's birth, she was orphaned and came under the guardianship of Klim Sidorovich Dyundik, a sanctimonious liar and scoundrel, who had conned his way into the gullible father's confidence. Dyundik totally ignores his ward, leaving her to be raised by her aunt, but later he sends her to the Smolny Institute to spite the aunt and to mollify his wife's intense hatred of the child, sight unseen!

In the course of time Anyuta and Blistovsky become engaged, but the aunt insists that Anyuta's guardian must give his blessing. Blistovsky sets off to Dyundik's estate to appeal for permission, but he goes with serious apprehensions, having met the Dyundiks the previous year at a fair in Romny, where he had inadvertently insulted them. We now have another flashback, a particularly amusing one as we follow Blistovsky from his acquaintance with Klim Sidorovich at the fair through his adventures with Dyundik's wife, Marfa Petrovna, and their two gauche daughters. Although Dyundik is a rogue and liar, he is totally under the thumb of his aggressive wife, whose opinion is law, whose temper is hair-triggered, and who secretly uses rouge. The mother is delighted to have a guest from Petersburg, particularly one who is able to appreciate her girls' command of French, an achievement in which the parents take almost pathological pride. However, when Blistovsky hears Sofia addressing her sister Vera as *Fois*, he begins to wonder about their teacher, and his fears are confirmed when *Qu'est-ce que c'est que cela* comes out *Kesse-kesse-kesse lya*. Since he can't understand them, the girls and their mother think he doesn't know French, and, when they later hear him speaking the language at a ball, they assume he had been mocking them previously. His popularity with the family is not increased when he apprehends the Dyundik's nephew, a dandy named Pryzhok, pouring acid on ladies' gowns and has him arrested.

Back to the present. Arriving at Dyundik's estate, Blistovsky is espied by the girls and their mother. The conversation which follows was certainly adapted by Gogol for *The Inspector General [Revizor]*.

> With curiosity they strained their eyes in that direction.
> "It must be the secretary of the regional court or the Commisar," said Marfa Petrovna.
> "No, Mommy," Sofia noted, "he's wearing a military cloak."
> "And as if you didn't know that they all like to dress in the military fashion?"
> "Mommy!" Vera Klimovna suddenly cried, "It looks like Blistovsky!"
> "Well now," replied Marfa Petrovna with acid mockery, "It's about time you forgot about him! Why the devil would he come here?"
> "Mommy! It is Blistovsky! My God, Blistovsky! I recognize his moustache and sideburns. Mommy maybe he has come for my ha. . ."
> "Shut up! What sort of nonsense has gotten into your head?"
> Marfa Petrovna wasn't able to continue her speech, for at this time the carriage entered the court and all of them, to their extreme surprise, saw that Vera had not erred in her supposition.

Vera's conjecture that Blistovsky has come as a suitor gains him a warm reception, and when the next morning he asks for permission to marry Anyuta, Dyundik is so shocked and chagrined that he storms out of the room, knocking down Marfa Petrovna, who had stationed herself at the keyhole. Marfa Petrovna, takes to her bed, Dyundik closets himself with her, and Blistovsky must depart without an answer. Thus ends part one.

Those who were curious as to the fate of Anyuta and her would-be fiancé had to wait until 1833, when the second part of the novel appeared. Part two created much less of a stir than the first part, and rightly so, for what had been a humorous novel of manners with a love intrigue was continued as a Ukrainian Gothic tale, replete with an abduction, a pursuit, a remote lodge in a dense forest, a secret room, apparent supernatural happenings, and mysterious gypsies.

Now the emphasis is upon Marfa Petrovna, who forces Anyuta to come to her house and sever relations with her aunty. Having isolated their ward, the Dyundiks fraudulently insist that her father's testament promised his curse if she married without her guardian's permission. The brainwashed Anyuta is prepared to accept this, but she balks at marrying their nephew, the idiotic Pryzhok. To avoid interference from Blistovsky or the aunty, they carry her off, and the rest of the story details the flight of the Dyundiks with their prisoner and the pursuit by Blistovsky and the aunty.

The real value of part two lies in the further development of the terrible Marfa Petrovna, the *bête rouge* of the Ukraine. She becomes worse and worse, and more comical, and finally receives her fitting reward in the narrator's epilogue.

Marfa Petrovna, on hearing of Vladimir's marriage [to Anyuta], choked from anger in the strict meaning of that expression. Having read Anna Andreevna's [the aunty's] letter, she turned red, then blue, blood rushed to her head, and she fell off her chair. They picked her up, put her in bed, and sent to the nearest town for a doctor. But before he could arrive, she died, vainly gathering all her strength to say something. Just before her very end she succeeded in pronouncing several disjointed words. Klim Sidorovich, who was fussing over her and inseparable at that time, heard her say to him, "Goodbye, my dear!" but other witnesses unanimously assert that she said, "Scram, you fool!"

It is unfair to expect of Perovsky more than he provided, an unusually lively adventure novel of manners. Still, considered as a whole *The Smolny Institute Graduate* is disappointing, because it never realizes its potential as a psychological study. At first, the story seems to point in that direction, since Anyuta's letters supply interesting clues as to her personality. But after that intriguing beginning, we learn little more about her other than that she adapted well to the resumption of life in the Ukraine and developed a genuine affection for her aunty and cousins. After the appearance of Blistovsky, she becomes simply a maiden in love.

This pattern recurs in part two, where the author initially seems to make an effort to get inside her head. Dyundik's efforts to blackmail her emotionally with her father's bogus testament are paralleled by her private thoughts, and there is a long dream sequence which comments upon her distressed state. Her wavering between submission and revolt is well motivated, but again, as the story progresses, the psychological aspects of her dilemma give way to physical problems connected with her incarceration and abduction, and from that point on Anyuta becomes primarily just another damsel in distress.

The portrait of Blistovsky reveals some effort on the author's part to make him a credible personality, but withal he remains a totally wooden *raisonneur*, whose glamor is largely in the eyes of the beholder, Anyuta. The other characters are, of course, stylizations, with certain features highlighted through repetition. Thus, Marfa Petrovna's basic tone is arrogant pettiness, and this is struck in scene after scene until she remains etched in the mind's eye of the reader as a vivid, if two-dimensional, figure. Klim Sidorovich is also memorable, and he is important as one of the first fully developed portraits of the classic *poshliak,* the epitome of self-satisfied mediocrity clothed in sham rectitude.

Klim Sidorovich considered himself the oldest of his clan, and from all his family, which was without wealth, he demanded special respect, although his spiritual qualities gave him less right to that than anyone. He was deceitful and cringing to those of higher station, haughty and arrogant to those of equal or lower station, moreover evil, vengeful, stupid and grasping. But he owned three thousand serfs and enjoyed a certain respect, once even having been elected regional Marshal of Nobility. He took more than a little pride in this, although he was not reelected for the next three year term, according to him because of his firmness of character and his refusal to give in to the Governor of the Province, but according to others because of his complete inability to handle the job, his stupidity, and arrogance. However, with all his weakness of intellect, he did not lack either cunning or a certain cleverness in achieving his intentions.

A skinflint and welcher, Klim Sidorovich has created the fiction that he maintains a five-hundred bed clinic for the poor, but he is vague as to its location. He also prevaricates at length about his services to Anyuta's father and his concern for "the poor orphan." Yet, despite his deceitfulness and unctiousness, he is not really sinister, and only his abject fear of the Medea-like Marfa Petrovna keeps him from abandoning his plan to have her marry Pryzhok. The author spares him in the epilogue, punishing him only by burdening him with spinster daughters.

If Klim Sidorovich has no grandchildren, he does have a literary descendent in Russian literature's epic *poshliak,* Pavel Chichikov of Gogol's *Dead Souls.* Those acquainted with both will be struck by the family resemblance, not that the scrawny Dyundik looks at all like the rotund and pink-cheeked Chichikov, but in their souls they are the same—morally vacuous and congenitally covetous. Their high opinions of their own cleverness in the face of their amazing fatuousness lead them to become their own victims.

Vasily Ushakov (1789-1838) was educated in the Corps of Pages and had an active military career, including participation in the Battle of Borodino. He retired as a junior captain in 1819. His novelette *The Kazakh [Kirgiz-kaisak]*, published in 1830, was something of a novelty at that time owing to its focus upon society and its theme of discrimination.

The story concerns the frustration of a love affair involving a well-to-do young officer, Victor Slavin, and the Princess Liubskaia, daughter of a wealthy nobleman. When it is revealed that Victor was, in fact, not gentry born but actually the son of a Cossack soldier and a Kirghiz nomad, the Princess's father prohibits the marriage. The rejected Slavin finds death in battle, and Princess lives on with a broken heart.

While generally enthusiastic about this work in his review in *The Literary Gazette*, Somov chided the author for violating verisimilitude, contending that racial discrimination of this sort was alien to Russians when the fiance was as wealthy as Slavin:

Another remark: Prince Liubsky, whom the author wanted to present as a hateful fool, generally acts like a wise person, and he expresses himself intelligently, even wittily. For example: "The disavowal of prejudice is fine in a melodrama, and were I composing a theatrical play, then of course I would stage such a magnanimous scene. But it is not actors, who at the end of the spectacle remove their famous titles along with their costumes, that are acting in this circumstance. No, *mon cher!* I will not disgrace my family. Besides, you'll find among us many Kalmyks, Kirghiz, Kara-Kalpaks and other steppe emigrants who are bought like apes and parrots for amusement alone. Would you ask them to marry the most famous young ladies of our fatherland, princesses, countesses. No, brother! I don't follow that fashionable philosophy."

Count Reshimov should have answered that (as we have said earlier) a lieutenant of the Guards, having two millions in Lombards, is not a miserable little Kirghiz purchased like an ape. But in the novel Prince Liubsky remains correct.

Notwithstanding that, *The Kirghiz* belongs to that small number of novels worthy of attention and the public's approval. The story is a very good one. There is generally much truth and art in the details. Many scenes are lively and remarkable. The meeting of Victor with his mother is unusually touching.

Ushakov's *Poor Seraphima [Bednaia Serafima]*, a society tale appearing in *The Library for Reading* in 1836, concerns a different kind of prejudice, that of society against those suffering from physical disabilities. The work is tiresome and implausible but does contain a relevant admonition for those reading it: "Despondency is a great sin" [Unynie—tiazhkii grekh].

This formula is the dying admonition of a widow to her three daughters. The oldest, Hope, marries and is soon widowed, while the second, Faith, marries a rich Muscovite named Pronsky. Love, the youngest, dies in childbirth, leaving behind a daughter, Seraphima, a paragon of beauty except for a repulsive crossed left eye, which exposes a red membrane. The child's father rejects the unsightly offspring which cost him the life of his beloved wife, and she is raised in the country by her Aunt Hope. Masking her deformity with a patch, she circulates freely in company, and so popular does she become with everyone that Aunt Faith insists she be brought to Moscow. A rich young officer, Prince Leodorov, sees Seraphima's portrait (with the head turned to hide the left eye) and falls in love with her at once. Later he meets her at Aunt Faith's house and finds her even more captivating than imagined.

Moscow society is also taken with this pathetic freak, which they call "the interesting cross-eyed girl."

This was a victory both for mothers and for their not so comely daughters. They could sincerely sympathise with the charming girl who was so terribly disfigured but who was consequently in no way dangerous. In a few days it became fashionable throughout Moscow to fawn upon 'poor Seraphima. This was considered a humanitarian and most Christian deed.

Prince Leodorov decides to test his ability to make Seraphima fall in love with him, an experiment which ends grotesquely when her eavesdropping French governess bursts in and rips the patch from the girl's eye. The Prince flees in confusion, and Seraphima remains convinced that she has no hopes of ever being loved.

We are now introduced to Potemkin (our first indication of the temporal setting), who had been a friend of Seraphima's father. When he learns of the girl's misfortune, he determines that she shall have a glass eye implanted, as he himself has had. He has her kidnapped [!] and taken to Petersburg, where her crossed eye is removed—we are spared the details—and replaced with a beautiful orb of French manufacture. Seraphima now enters society, encounters Prince Leodorov at a masked ball, dallies with him a bit, and ultimately they are married with Potemkin's blessing.

Potemkin patronizes the young couple, in particular seeing eye to eye with the bride:

> Not long before his departure, Prince Grigory Alexandrovich [Potemkin], while caressing Seraphima, asked her if she were satisfied with him. Seraphima fixed her single eye on the single eye of the Prince. He burst out laughing. [And so do we.]

The story ends with the anticipated moralizing:

> Finally, then, she was amazed at the grace of Providence which so often strikes us with misfortune in order to teach us to appreciate future felicity. The Princess [Seraphima] came to the conviction that her marital bliss would not have been half so valuable to her had she not previously been deprived of all hope of such happiness. And to all similar conversations there was one and the same conclusion, that her deceased grandmother had spoken a sacred truth: "Despondency is a great sin!"

Trudging through the often arid landscape of Romantic prose, one is delighted and refreshed by his encounter with the ebullient Alexander Veltman (1800-1870),[1] certainly one of the most imaginative writers of the thirties. His *The Wanderer [Strannik]*, published in three parts in 1831-1832, is a parodic revival of the travel notes genre, a combination of an imaginary journey taking place on a map in the narrator's study with details derived from a real journey over the same territory some years before. The reader is moved from past to present and back at the whim of the author, who delights us with his witty "closet" journey, his often erudite digressions and parodistic poetry, at the same time providing an engaging travelogue. The area of his journey is Bessarabia, Moldavia, and Wallachia with which Veltman was intimately acquainted, having served there from 1817 until 1831 as a military surveyor. Soon after the conclusion of the Russo-Turkish war of 1828-1829,

Veltman retired as a lieutenant colonel and left what he termed his "Bessarabian captivity" for Moscow.

The Wanderer is divided into days, each containing the thoughts which occur to the "traveler" as he sits contemplating his map, his memory carrying him to Jassi or Kishinyov or wherever. His bits of memory or flights of imagination are often arrested by external circumstances normally connected with eating or sleeping, such as his dinner being served or having to retire. The segmentation into days is not absolute, and on one occasion he points out, lest the reader miss the joke, that the "day" actually contained forty-eight hours. Consider the beginning of "Day IV":

XXIX.

What is better than a detailed, reliable map? During wartime for the strategic consideration of a colonel, for dispatch of troops to an officer of the General Staff, and for me, for a peaceful, scholarly journey! I love to encompass with one glance the area where I have been, am, and will be!

Having thus explained my involuntary joy in glancing at that entire part of the world subservient to man, I shall be seated in my canoe and float down the course of the Dniester. . . .

XXX.

What a frightening shore is visible over there at the bend! A cliff hangs over the river, and what are those caves which show darkly at its summit? I shall immediately satisfy your curiosity, although Horace has commanded us to flee from all curiosity as from an immodest man. Let us ascend the rocky path. Permit me to catch my breath! Well, onwards, there is a path through an orchard. The Dniester, like a little stream, winds below us. We are now at the top of that cliff which from below had frightened you so much. Be more careful in descending this stairway cut into the face of the cliff! Hold onto the railing, and don't look down, for your head might start spinning and, God forbid, you might be dispatched to the source of power, as the author of *Metamechanics* puts it.

XXXI.

Do you see?. . . Oh what carelessness!. . . What a terrible flood in Spain and France. . . . That's what comes from setting a glass of water on the map!. . . but who would ever have thought I would knock it off the Pyrenees with my elbow?

Of course, this kind of play with the levels of his narrative can't be sustained indefinitely, and after a while we get down to some circumstantial information about the places he visited, especially Jassy and Kishinyov. At this point the tone is similar to that of the usual informal travelogue:

XLIV.

Day had already been managing its affairs for six hours on our hemisphere when I awakened. I had scarcely dressed when a crowd of Jews rushed into my room. What

160

do you want, damn you! "Well, maybe you need something?" they all answered. "Here are kerchieves, pomade, perfume, you can buy something—towels, napkins, knives, please to inspect." "Be gone, you locusts! Take yourselves to the devil! " "And where does the devil live?" a wise Jewish question responded. "Hey, you lead them to the devil!" Not waiting for a guide, all the Jews flocked onto the street and all became silent.

XLVI.

The initial step on the street of an unfamiliar town is a difficult moment, in which a person looks all around and usually after a short or long hesitancy, goes willy-nilly in the direction that most of the people are moving.

The first thing that struck me were the taverns and small shops. In almost every house bottles of wine and vodka stood in the little windows, and on the large, lowered shutters were tobacco, sulphur, nails, shot, ropes, meshti, kushmy, pipes, kochkoval, butter. . . . "God Almighty!" I thought, "Everywhere here things are sold. Where do the people who buy things live? *Plachinda, plachinda!*" a wild voice suddenly sounded behind me. "You're a *plachinda* yourself, damn you!" And just so: a Moldavian, with a face burned like the crust of a roll, smeared with butter, like a pancake, was carrying a hot, greasy pot on a copper tray and crying out, "*Plachinda, plachinda!*" This is breakfast for passersby.

Notwithstanding some paragraphs of factual description or *reportage*, the reader is seldom allowed to forget that he is a pawn of the author's whimsy, which affects even the structure of the work. One chapter consists only of the Sternean declaration, "I should like my journey to make me famous. . . and etc." The "Foreword," which is Chapter VI, is cut off at the pockets in the following manner:

Every lover of reading knows well how insufferable any foreword is, especially when Mr. Author, as yet uncertain that anyone will take the trouble to read his book, asks that we be merciful and pardon it and then excuses its shortcomings as a result of all the circumstances of his life. That is why I don't want to continue this foreword.

In one of his more capricious moods the author erases part of his manuscript and deliberately declines to correct it:

In order profitably to complete a journey over the Arctic and Antarctic hemispheres of the globe which represents the earth, one must carry on a detailed description of everything that meets his eyes, for example:
N.B. There was an example here, but I erased half of it and scratched out the rest. Its prosaic quality didn't suit me. However, one can always find similar examples in old calendars, account books, reports, in memoirs and notebooks.

This author is a veritable mill of digressions, and there seems to be no subject, if it occurs to him, on which he fears to express an opinion, often an erudite one. Noah's ark, the identity of Alexander the Great's real father, Hebrew religious tradition, the Kishinyov Jewish dialect, Bessarabian history, dreams, all are treated in passing or at length, seriously or facetiously. Still, one must admit that no matter how refreshing it is to listen to the wanderer, after a while his kaleidoscopic manner proves a bit wearing, and one wishes for a *vis-à-vis* whose personality didn't transmit quite so strongly.

Between 1831 and 1840, Veltman produced a prodigious number of historical novels, fantastic tales, and short stories, many of which are marked by originality of concept, unabashed whimsicality, stylistic variegation, and, it must be said, a certain amount of superficiality. To name just a few of his titles published in the thirties, *The Year MMMCDXLVIII. A manuscript of Martin Zadeka [MMMCDXLVIII god, rukopis' Martyna Zadeki]* (1833), *Koshchey the Deathless [Koshchei bessmertnyii]* (1833), *The Sleepwalker [Lunatik]* (1834), *Sviatoslavich, The Devil's Nursling [Sviatoslavich, vrazhii pitomets]* (1834), *The Ancestors of Kalimeros, Alexander of Macedonia, Son of Philip [Predki Kalimerosa: Aleksandr Filippovich Makedonskii]* (1836), *Heart and Thought [Serdtse i dumka]* (1838). To keep the discussion within limits, only a few of his most representative stories can be treated.

Following *The Wanderer*, which was an immediate success, Veltman turned to the historical novel (in his case, the pseudo-historical novel), publishing in 1833 *Koshchey the Deathless*, which was universally popular.[2] The work, like much of Veltman's corpus, combines fantasy and reality, this mode extending even to the language of narration, an arbitrary combination of Old Russian and the contemporary language. The story is a variant of the *Don Quixote* and *A Russian Gil Blas* themes: the hero, Iva, a medieval gentryman who confuses reality and fancy, believes his fiancée has been abducted by Koshchey the Deathless, a malefactor from Russian fairy tales, and Iva's adventures in pursuit of her compose the story. The novel is filled with folkloristic and annalistic elements, often with ironical intent, a feature missed by many contemporaries. The critic Belinsky, while generally applauding Veltman's effort, noted that the image of ancient Rus was presented not as it actually was but as a visionary impression. More recently, B. Buchstab called it "a variegated mosaic of fragments from an ancient way of life."[3]

Veltman had no monopoly on originality or whimsy, and they are found in abundance in the work of another   onetime   disciple of Laurence Sterne, Nikolay Gogol.

XIV. Gogol's *Evenings on a Farm Near Dikanka.*

Nikolay Gogol is the prime example of the Romantic fictionist, although there is still a gaggle of die-hard commentators who insist that he be
included in the ranks of critical realists. The source of their misconception
can be traced to Vissarion Belinsky and his disciples, the radical critics,
who saw what they wanted to see in Gogol's works and ignored those things
which did not fit their preconceptions.

Chernyshevsky and Dobroliubov, Belinsky's immediate followers,
imposed upon literature the obligation of exposing social ills, especially serfdom, and they evaluated the works of their contemporaries in accordance
with the thrust for reforms which these works embodied—or seemed to em-
body. To give the devil his due, the radical critics were not without analytical
acuity, especially Chernyshevsky, but they stubbornly insisted that Gogol's
works represented a real image of Russian life and that the author's purpose
was to expose the negative features of a society based on serfdom. Shortly
before his death in 1848, Belinsky was dismayed to read Gogol's obscurantist
pronouncements in *Selected Passages from a Correspondence with Friends,*
because what Gogol stated directly in this "correspondence" contradicted
completely the message which the critic had earlier derived from the author's
fiction. Instead of being a reformer, Gogol now defined himself as an apologist for autocracy and Orthodoxy. Belinsky's response was his famous "Letter
to Gogol," in which he bitterly assailed the author for having recanted his
supposed liberalism. Gogol in turn was mortified that Belinsky should so un-
graciously respond to the truth in his *Selected Passages.*[1]

Because his stories are replete with sordid or "dirty details" and popu-
lated with "heroes" from the lower classes, Gogol was credited with founding
the so-called *Natural School*, a modest literary current that came to the fore
in the 1840's with an avalanche of physiological sketches, a genre lying between imaginative fiction and the essay and concerned for the most part
with plotless portraits of typical occupational types: the water carrier, the
postman, the organ grinder, the batman, the cook, and so forth. The underlying objectivity of these sketches caused them to be associated with canonical Realism, which was a mistake. The Natural School's concern for the
downtrodden, which developed as it explored the urban lower classes, its
focus upon the seamy side of life and its sentimentalized treatment of the
victims of the establishment, all implicated Gogol with its formation. However, as we shall see, the practitioners of the Natural School, while in fact
concerned with depicting much of life's least attractive aspects, misread their
Gogol as much as did the radical critics.

At the end of the century Dmitry Merezhkovsky and Vasily Rozanov
demonstrated clearly that Gogol was really quite outside the tradition of

Realism, but not everyone was convinced. Even today there is a stubborn insistence that Gogol was not a Romantic but a Critical Realist, and as such—naturally—qualified for a prominent place in the genealogy of Socialist Realism. Happily, this dogma has not prevented some Soviet scholars from providing significant interpretations and insights relevant to Gogol's fiction. Unlike most Romantic authors, Gogol has received competent treatment from non-Soviet literary historians. Of most interest to the English reader are Vladimir Nabokov's *Nikolai Gogol* and Victor Erlich's *Gogol.*[2] A number of ideas that follow derive from these books, and from studies utilized by Nabokov and Erlich.[3]

Following his secondary education in the sunny Ukraine, Gogol arrived in Petersburg in the winter of 1828-1829 brimful of hopes for a career as an actor or public servant. The frozen north quickly chilled his hopes, as no suitable job was forthcoming. His original optimism was further dampened by the total failure of his idyl *Hans Kuechelgarten*, which was so unenthusiastically received that the would-be poet felt obliged to buy up the edition and burn it.[4] Probably owing to the solicitude of his fellow countryman, Orest Somov, Gogol's "A Chapter from a Historical Novel" appeared in *Northern Flowers for 1831*. Signed this time with a cryptic *OOOO* (derived from Nikolai Gogol-Yanovsky), the piece is an excerpt from an unfinished historical novel, *The Hetman*, set in a foggy Ukrainian past. The effort clearly reveals Gogol's familiarity with the techniques of Walter Scott and his imitators. We have a hero on a dangerous mission, a meeting with an enigmatic stranger later revealed to be an important conspirator, and many details of local color and lore, with circumstantial description of clothes and habitations. The speech of the characters is stylized to suggest occupation and class origins. Gogol also seems to have remembered Charles Maturin's *Melmoth the Wanderer*, a rambling tale of demonic depravity which outdid the Gothic tradition and even inspired a group of French imitators called *l'Ecole frénétique*. In the tradition of Maturin, Gogol has suspenseful nocturnal scenes with *chiaroscuro* illumination, a peasant with fiery eyes, and even a pine tree which drips blood.

Contrary to enthusiasts' assertions of Gogol's originality, he was a compulsive lifter of motifs, types, and themes from other authors. If the reader roots about in the literature of the late eighteenth and early nineteenth centuries, he will encounter all sorts of prototypes for Gogol's characters and many of his devices as well. Gogol had no prejudice in this matter, and his sources are found not only in Russian and Ukrainian literature but also in German, French, and English. Before the Gogolophiles become too riled, I shall qualify that statement by saying that Gogol *was* most original and inventive in the combination and treatment of this appropriated material, and in that lies his artistry and uniqueness.

From the historical novel, a genre to which he was to return, Gogol moved to the short story, probably in emulation of Somov, whose Ukrainian tales were appearing in Petersburg almanacs and periodicals. Paradoxically, Gogol was soon to be accorded the prestige of ethnographer on the basis of his early narratives about life in Little Russia, but his letters to his mother and sister importuning them for detailed information about the lore and habits of his countrymen show that he was poorly informed about the traditions and customs of the Ukrainian lower classes.

Gogol's initial success as a writer came with the publication in 1831 of four tales comprising the first part of *Evenings on a Farm Near Dikanka* [*Vechera na khutore bliz Dikanki*]. The collection was purportedly the work of a Ukrainian bee keeper, a rustic counterpart to Pushkin's Belkin,[5] who provided an introduction in his homey and unliterary style. He himself can't explain why he is called Rudy (Red), since his hair is not red, but such are nicknames, once given they last forever. Rudy explains that the "evenings" take place when fall work is finished, when the bees have been put in the cellar for winter. Then people gather to dance and tell stories, and the best tales of all are spun at his house, especially by Foma Grigorievich, the church sexton. Thus Rudy rambles on, creating a comfortable atmosphere for his auditors, who are invited to attend one of the evenings and partake of the goodies his wife prepares. The thoughtful beekeeper even provides directions on how to find his house.

The stories display a variety of moods and styles, ranging from rowdy slapstick and pithy abuse to highly literary effusiveness and ornamental prose. Nabokov, for one, does not think much of these tales, and he attributes Pushkin's initial laudatory reception, "an astonishing book," to the general dearth of appetizing fictional fare. Erlich is more charitable and feels that Pushkin was attracted by the Breughel-like qualities of Gogol's tales.

The Fair at Sorochinsk [*Sorochinskaia iarmarka*] is a lusty rustic musical comedy with stock characters from the Ukrainian puppet theatre and exaggerated incidents. Gogol has divided his tale into thirteen scenes, many of them introduced by lyrical passages dedicated to the beauty of the Ukrainian landscape or to the excitement and animation of the country fair. The opening of the story has long been an anthology piece, a bit of Gogolian spellbinding which hypnotises the reader and permits the author to do with him as he will:

How captivating, how luxurious is the summer day in Little Russia! How oppressively hot are those hours when midday glints in the silence and sultriness, and the immeasurable blue ocean, bending over the earth like a sensuous cupola, seems to have fallen asleep, all immersed in delight, embracing and pressing the beautiful one in its airy embrace! Not a cloud in the sky, not a word in the field. Everything has as if died. Only above, in the heavenly depth, a lark trembles, and its silvery songs fly on airy steps to the enraptured earth, and in the distance the cry of a gull or the tinkling voice of the quail remains in the steppe. Lazily and thoughtlessly, as if wandering without aim, stand the towering oaks, and the blinding blows of the sun's rays burn whole picturesque masses of leaves, throwing a shadow as dark as night on others, which are sprinkled with gold when the winds blow strongly.

The love affair between the ocean of the sky (Gogol had to resort to a metaphor here, since *sky* is neuter in Russian while *ocean* is masculine) which sensuously embraces the feminine earth hardly qualifies this passage as a circumstantial description of the Ukraine. Nonetheless, apparently this prose poem has the power of suggesting the illusion of Ukrainian landscape to those properly conditioned by life in Little Russia, which includes heeding the Ukrainian high school teachers who insist this passage is realistic.

This lyrical overture carries us to the countryside where peasants are congregating for the fair at Sorochinsk, among them Solopy Cherevik, whose eighteen year old daughter, Paraska, is anticipating her first fair. A handsome young man in a white half-caftan immediately takes notice of the girl's beauty, and he and his friend audaciously antagonize her step-mother, whose tongue is as long as her temper is short. The crude language of her response to the gibes of bystanders represented a new element in fiction, which until then had presented only a decorous variety of peasant speech:

"See how she scolds!" said the youth, looking at her with wide-open eyes, as if puzzled by her unexpected greeting, "and how come the tongue of this century-old witch doesn't ache from saying such words."

"Century old!" the elderly beauty repeated, "You heathen! Go wash yourself first! You useless harebrain! I never saw your mother, but I know she was trash! And your father was trash! And your aunt was trash! Century old! Why the milk is still wet on his lips."

This sally is answered by a handful of mud which hits its target, and the old scold is still yelling as she is carried out of earshot on Salopy's cart. The farce continues as Gritsko, the youth in the white half-caftan, seeks permission to marry Paraska, a proposal agreeable to Salopy but opposed by the stepmother. Gritsko enlists the aid of gypsies, who capitalize on a rumor that a devil's red half-caftan is hidden somewhere around the fair and that the devil himself, disguised as a pig, is seeking it. Since pigs run rampant on the fair grounds, the place is in a constant hubbub, and there is even a rout when a pig's snout intrudes into Solopy's cabin, causing him to put a pot on his head instead of his hat and to rush blindly into the alley, literally hag-ridden by his terrified wife. The evil step-mother, who was also engaging in a bit of hanky-panky with the priest's son, is defeated, and Gritsko gets the girl. Gogol rings down his curtain with a musical finale:

A strange, inexpressible feeling would have possessed any witnesses at the sight of how with one sweep of the violin bow by the musician in the coarse half-caftan with the long curling mustaches everything willy-nilly was transformed into unity and became harmonious. People whose gloomy faces, it seems, hadn't been crossed by a smile in ages stamped their feet and shook their shoulders. Everything flew, everything danced. But even more strangely, even harder to understand would be the feeling aroused in the depths of one's soul at the sight of the old folks, on whose ancient faces wafted the indifference of the grave, who were pushed among the new, laughing, alive people. Carefree people, even without childlike joy, without a spark of sympathy, who are forced by intoxication alone, as a mechanic forces his lifeless robot to do something which seems human, they quietly nodded their drunken heads, dancing behind the festive people, not even turning an eye on the young people.

The noise, laughter, and songs became quieter and quieter. The violin bow was dying, becoming weaker and losing its indistinct sounds in the emptiness of the air. Somewhere the stamping of feet was still heard, something resembling the murmur of the distant sea, and soon all became empty and mute.

Where did these zombies, these ancient automatons activated by alcohol, come from? Why does Gogol have them tag along at the end of his pageant? And why does he present this whole passage as a hypothetical situation, whose witnesses *would have* responded with ineffable feelings had they seen this sight? Why, because it never existed, doesn't exist, and can never exist, except in the world of the author's manuscript, as he intoxicates himself with the brilliant color and sound and action of his fantasy.

But there is an end to lyricism and an end to intoxication. In a manner which will become typical for Gogol's art, the final paragraph completely erases the joyous mood and arbitrarily confronts the reader with a pathetic (or bathetic) reversal of moods:

Is it not so with happiness, that beautiful and inconstant guest, which flies away from us, and in vain the isolated sound seeks to express joy? It hears melancholy and emptiness in its own echo and frantically attends it. Is it not so with the playful friends of stormy and unfettered youth, who singly, one after another, lose themselves around the world and finally abandon their one elder brother? It is dull for the one left behind! And his heart becomes heavy and melancholic, but there is no help for it.

Gogol's devils are of two sorts, comic ones who can be duped by clever mortals and sombre ones who stick to their demonic calling of collecting human souls. *Saint John's Eve, A True Story Narrated by the Sexton of *** Church [Vecher nakanune Ivana Kupala. Byl', rasskazannaia d'iachkom ***skoi tserkvi]* tells of the orphan Petrus, who takes money from the devilish Basavryuk in order to gain permission to marry Pidorka, the daughter of his employer. Following the tradition of Orest Somov, whose *The Water Sprite [Rusalka]* (1829) and *Saint John's Eve [Kupalov vecher (Iz Malorossiiskikh bylei i nebylits)]* (1831) had utilized motifs from Ukrainian folklore, Gogol fills out his conventional love plot (the same plot as the previous story) with legendary material of various sorts, including witches, the hut on chicken legs, transformations from animal to human or vice-versa, wandering fires, not to mention such fairy tale cliches as the poor orphan who loves a girl of higher station, the timely intercession of the devil with a proposition, the task set by the devil, the success of the youth, and the final accounting with the Evil One.

Gogol presents this story as told to Rudy Panko by the sexton Foma
Grigorievich in the words of his grandfather. If Foma Grigorievich can be
trusted to "tell it as he heard it," his grandfather had a markedly pithy
manner of narration. This is how Foma retells his grandfather's account of
how the devilish Basavryuk sent Petrus to Bear's Gully to pick a blossoming
fern:

"Now is the time!" thought Petrus and extended his hand. He takes a look—
from behind him hundreds of shaggy hands also stretch towards the flower, and in
back of him something runs from place to place. Everything became quiet. Basavryuk
appeared sitting on a stump, all blue, like a corpse. If only a finger would move. His
eyes were fixed motionlessly on something only he alone could see, his mouth was
half open, and not a response. Nothing stirs around there. Whew, it's scary! But then a
whistle was heard which made something inside Petro go bang, and it seemed to him the
grass was making noise, the flowers began to converse with reedy little voices like tiny
silver bells, the trees began to roar with abuse. Suddenly Basavryuk's face came to life,
his eyes flashed. "You've returned at last, you hag!" he muttered through his teeth.
"Look, Petro, a beauty is now standing before you. Do everything ordered, or you're
lost forever!"
   At this point he parted a thorn bush with his knobby cane, and, as they say,
a hut on chicken legs appeared before them. Basavryuk struck it with his fist and the
wall fell down. A large black dog ran straight out, and whining, it turned into a cat and
leaped at their eyes.
   "Don't get so mad, don't get so mad, you old she-devil!" said Basavryuk, spicing
this with such a word that any good person would have covered his ears. Then, instead of
a cat there is an old woman with a face as wrinkled as a baked apple, all bent into a
bow, with her nose and chin like the pincers of a nutcracker.
   "What a beauty!" thought Petro, and ants ran down his spine.

Goaded by his need for Basavryuk's money, Petrus insanely accedes to
the demand of the unholy pair and slaughters a child. When he recovers his
senses at home, he finds bags of gold about him, and in less than no time he
and Pidorka are wedded. But soon the bridegroom succumbs to increasing
melancholy, he is tormented by a vague memory, and when the next Saint
John's Eve occurs he recalls the crime that made him rich. Confronted with
the spectre of his innocent victim, he burns to a cinder.
   Up to this point the satanic influence of Basavryuk is treated earnest-
ly, but now a Gogolian change of mood occurs. One day a group of village
worthies are drinking in the tavern while a ram is being roasted. Suddenly this
ram raises its head and "everyone immediately recognized Basavryuk's mug
on the ram's head. My grandfather's aunt even thought it was about to order
some vodka." Other uncanny things occur later, and finally:

Well now, on this very place where our village stands, it seems everything is calm.
Still not even so long ago my late father and I remember how an honest man couldn't
walk past the tumbledown tavern, which the evil tribe repaired at their own expense a
long time afterwards. From the soot-blackened chimney a column of smoke poured, and,
having risen so high that one's hat would fall off to look at it, sprinkled the entire steppe

168

with hot cinders. And the devil—he shouldn't be mentioned, the son of a bitch—was sobbing so piteously in his hovel that the frightened blackbirds rose in flocks from the nearby oak forest and swept through the sky with wild cries.

May Night, or The Drowned Girl [*Maiskaia noch', ili Utoplennitsa*] is a rambunctious farce in which a Cossack youth, Lenko, tricks his libidinous father, the one-eyed village headman, into letting him marry the local beauty, Ganna. This *mélange* involves wilies, or drowned girls, a step-mother witch, and crowds of "extras" who rush hither and yon propelled by rumor, fear, curiosity, and mischief-making. The story opens with a rhapsody extolling the beauties of evening in the village, when "the thoughtful evening dreamily embraces the blue sky, turning everything into indefiniteness and distance." The second chapter is initiated with another anthology piece, the famous "Do you know the Ukrainian night," which is followed by a long rhapsody honoring "the enchanting night," "the divine night," when:

The entire landscape sleeps. And above everything breathes, everything is marvelous, everything is triumphant. And there is something unembraceable and wondrous in one's soul, and crowds of silver visions harmoniously arise from its depths. A divine night! An enchanting night! And suddenly everything becomes alive, the woods, the ponds and the steppe. The magnificent thunder of the Ukrainian nightingale is scattered about, and it seems that even the moon in the heavens attends the sound.

This turgid description is matched by the characters and the action of the story, so everything is more or less on the same plane. The story is gaudy, but consistent. Even when Gogol gets to the description of such prosaic matters as the supper at the cabin of the headman, he inevitably rises to exaggeration:

Only one cabin was still lighted at the end of the street. This was the habitation of the headman. The headman had long ago finished his supper and, doubtless, would long ago have gone to sleep, but he had a guest at this time, a distiller, sent to build a distillery by the landowner who had a small parcel of ground in among the free Cossacks. Under the very icon stand, in the place of honor, sat the guest, a short fattish little person with small, always laughing little eyes, in which, it seemed, was written that pleasure with which he smoked his stubby pipe, continually spitting and pressing with his finger the tobacco which had turned to ashes and crawled out of it. A cloud of smoke quickly grew above him, wrapping him in greyish smoke. It seemed as if a wide chimney from some distillery, having become bored with sitting on its roof, had thought to take a stroll and had decorously taken a seat at the table in the headman's cabin. Under his nose projected a stubby thick moustache, but it showed so indistinctly through the tobacco atmosphere that it seemed like a mouse which the distiller had caught and was holding in his mouth, undercutting the monopoly of the barn cat.

Here we have some typical Gogol: a distiller is transformed into a perigrinating chimney which has usurped the prerogative of the barn cat and is holding a mouse in his mouth which isn't a mouse but really the moustache as half seen through the dense smoke.

The final story of Part I of *Evenings* is *The Lost Document*, subtitled *A True Story Narrated by the Sexton of ***Church [Propavshaia gramota. Byl', rasskazannaia d'iachkom ***skoi tserkvi]*. On this occasion Foma Grigorievich, rather than retelling a story heard from his grandfather, as in *Saint John's Eve*, relates how his grandfather, the headman's courier, had to play fools with witches to recover a message for the Empress, which he had lost while sleeping off the effects of a carousal. The work is motley, with genre scenes of a somnolent fair in early morning, a tavern yard packed with freight wagons, gypsies around a fire, a static description of a *real* Cossack from Sech-Beyond-the-Falls, and finally grandfather's impression of the imperial palace with its vast chambers. Best of all are the witches:

There was such an avalanche of witches like sometimes it happens with a snowfall at Christmas. Bedizened and smeared like misses at a fair. And all of the, however many there were, drunk and dancing some devilish trepak. God save us from the dust they raised! A Christian would take to trembling just to see how high that Satan's tribe was jumping. Despite the danger, grandfather took to laughing when he saw devils with dog snouts on German legs, curling their tails and twisting around the witches like young blades around pretty girls. And the musicians pounded themselves on their cheeks with their fists like on drums and whistled through their noses like on bugles. As soon as they saw grandfather, a horde of them rushed at him. Pig, dog, goat, crane, horse snouts, all lined up and then they crawl up for a kiss. Grandfather just spit, what abomination!

Colorful as they are, this unholy crew is hardly on a par with the monsters at the Sabbath celebration in Somov's *Kievan Witches*.

When Part II of *Evenings* appeared in 1832, it contained four more tales, *The Night Before Christmas [Noch' pered rozhdestvom]*. *The Terrible Vengeance [Strashnaia mest']* , *Ivan Fyodorovich Shponka and his Aunt [Ivan Fedorovich Shponka i ego tetushka]*, and *The Enchanted Place [Zakoldovannoe mesto]*. The garrulous beekeeper, Panko, again provided an introduction, this one ending on a note of loneliness:

Comes to mind that I promised you my own tale would be in this booklet. And just so, I was about to do that but I saw that my tale would require, at the very least, three such booklets. I was thinking to print it separately but changed my mind. I know you. You would start to laugh at an old man. No, I don't want to! Goodbye! We won't see each other for a long time, and maybe never. What of it? It's all the same to you even if I had never been on earth. A year will pass, another, and none of you will remember or pity the old beekeeper, Rudy Panko.

The Night Before Christmas and *The Enchanted Place* are just more of the stylized folklore found in the earlier tales such as *St. John's Eve* and *May Night*. But both *The Terrible Vengeance* and *Ivan Shponka* are distinctly new. The former is an eclectic work belonging to the tradition of literary Satanism, and it has, nowithstanding its Ukrainian setting, more than a little in common with the *Maerchen* of Ludwig Tieck or the disciples of *l'Ecole frenetique*. Some critics purport to find deep currents of symbolism,

170

Freudianism, and demonism in this work, which is well and good, but my own feeling is that it is a rather silly piece of *juvenalia* and so patently imitative as to preclude further comment.

On the other hand, the *Shponka* story is wonderful, a preview of Gogol the Great, the unmasker of the *poshlust* (for the time being, read "banality") which has permeated to the very core of life and subverted man from his high mission. Nabokov has provided a lengthy and delightful disquisition on the meaning of *poshlust,*[6] a term which encompasses such concepts as self-satisfied mediocrity, mock-emotional responses (false humility, enthusiasm, indignation, etc.) pretentiousness in many forms, to name just a few aspects. *Poshlust* can be found everywhere, in the righteous indignation of political speeches, in the artificial camaraderie of talk-shows, in advertisements which cater to elitist instincts, in efforts of those to the manor born to be just plain folks, and in sermons from pulpits too. Gogol believed in the Devil, but his Devil was not a sulfur and brimstone figure with black wings and flashing eyes but rather an insidious Devil which entrapped man by making him succumb to the *poshlust* of everyday living. A life devoid of spiritual quality, concerned only with food, sleep, comfort, was a life of *poshlust,* a life of passivity, absence of enthusiasm, was a life of *poshlust.* And Ivan Shponka was his first *poshlyak,* the embodiment of this affliction which is non-fatal but so very dangerous for the soul.

The story presents many of the features associated with Gogol's Petersburg cycle, his comedy *The Inspector General [Revizor]* (1836), and that picaresque descent to the seventh circle of provincial *poshlust, Dead Souls [Mertvye dushi]* (1842). One outstanding characteristic is the use of razorhoned verbal irony, here applied to our passionless hero, Shponka, his purposeless life, his vulgar military companions, his masculine aunt, his bullying neighbor, his vapid fiancée-to-be, or anyone else who crawled from day to day engaged in pounding sand or gratifying mundane appetites.

Shponka's problem is that he is a nothing, absolutely devoid of passion or enthusiasm, talent or aspirations, and his "success" in life has been based on keeping quiet:

When he was still called Vanyusha [Johnny], he studied in the Gadyach district school, and it must be said that he was a most well-behaved and most industrious boy. The teacher of Russian grammar, Nikifor Timofeevich Deeprichastiye [Mr. Gerund], used to say that if all his pupils were as industrious as Shponka, then he wouldn't have to carry to class the maple ruler with which, as he himself admitted, he was tired of beating the hands of lazy and mischievous boys. His exercise book was always very clean, properly lined, and not a spot anywhere. He would always sit quietly, having folded his hands and fixed his eyes on the teacher, and he never hung bits of paper on the back of anyone sitting in front of him, and he didn't whittle on the bench, and he never played *squashed granny* before the arrival of the teacher.[7]

Having more or less finished his schooling, Shponka entered the P*** infantry regiment, which was in no way inferior to other infantry regiments

171

in that its officers drank fortified spirits, could abuse Jews no worse than hussars, and some of them could even dance the mazurka. But poor Shponka could not even do these things:

Having dealings with such comrades, however, in no way diminished Ivan Fyodorovich's timidity. And since he didn't drink fortified spirits, preferring a glass of vodka before dinner and supper, and not dancing the mazurka and not gambling, then naturally he was always alone. Thus. . . sitting in his quarter, he practised occupations suitable for a modest and good soul: now he would polish his buttons, now read a book on fortune telling, now set mouse traps in the corners of his room, now, having taken off his uniform coat, he would lie on the bed. Moreover, no one in the regiment was more punctual than Ivan Fyodorovich, and he commanded his platoon in such a way that the company commander always put him up as an example. Therefore, in a short time, eleven years after having received his ensign's rank, he was promoted to sub-lieutenant.

Shponka's military career is terminated when he returns home to manage his estate, which previously had been run by his aunt, Vasilisa Kashparovna Tsupchevska, a domineering and mannish female of giant proportions, who is able to tackle anything from rowing the fishing boat or shooting game to shaking pears from her orchard. Her rustic counterpart, a neighbor, Grigory Grigorievich Storchenko, has usurped a piece of Shponka's patrimony, and the wily aunt hopes to regain the lost property and improve her nephew's fortunes by marrying him to Grigory Grigorievich's daughter. The ludicrous crudity which is a hallmark of Gogol's descriptive art appears here in connection with almost everything Grigory Grigorievich does. A bully and complainer, he is always shouting about something, always dissatisfied, and always tactless. At a dinner for Shponka and his aunt, the host quickly gets into an argument with another guest, the landowner Ivan Ivanovich, a deprecator in his own right.

"Hmmm, what sort of turkey is this!" Ivan Ivanovich said in an undertone with a look of disparagement, turning to his neighbor. "Is this the way turkeys are supposed to be? If only you could see my turkeys! I assure you that the fat on one of them is more than that on ten of these kind. Would you believe, my dear sir, that they are so fat it is even revolting to look at them when they walk about my courtyard!"

"Ivan Ivanovich, you're lying!" pronounced Grigory Grigorievich, having overheard his speech.

"I tell you," Ivan Ivanovich went on to his neighbor, giving the impression of not having heard Grigory Grigorievich's words, "that last year when I sent them to Gadyach, I received fifty kopecks for each. And didn't want to accept even that."

"Ivan Ivanovich, I tell you that you're lying!" Grigory Grigorievich pronounced, syllable by syllable for greater clarity and louder than before.

But Ivan Ivanovich, giving the impression that none of this had to do with him, continued as before, but only quite a bit softer. "Just so, my dear sir, I didn't want to accept it. In Gadyach not one landowner has. . . . "

"Ivan Ivanovich! You're stupid and that's that," Grigory Grigorievich said loudly. "Certainly Ivan Fyodorovich knows all this better than you do and most likely doesn't believe you."

At this Ivan Ivanovich was thoroughly offended, fell quiet, and set to picking at his turkey, notwithstanding that it wasn't so fat as those at which it was revolting to look.

The rich *poshlust* of petty gentry interests and occupations is illuminated fully in the course of the story, culminating in the bewildered Shponka's reactions to his aunt's manifesto that he must marry. The cunning aunt arranges it so that the prospective bride, Grigory Grigorievich's blonde daughter, must remain alone with the quaking suitor:

The blonde young miss remained behind and sat down on the couch. Ivan Fyodorovich was sitting on his chair as if on needles, he blushed and lowered his eyes. But it seemed that the young miss didn't notice that at all and sat on the couch, studiously looking at the windows and walls, or the cat, which had cowardly run under the chairs.

Ivan Fyodorovich got up his courage a bit and was about to start a conversation. But it seemed that all his words were lost along the way. Not one thought came to his mind.

The silence continued about a quarter of an hour. The young miss continued to sit as before.

Finally, Ivan Fyodorovich got up his courage. "There are very many flies in summer, mam," he pronounced in a half quavering voice.

"A great many!" answered the young miss. "My little brother purposely made a swatter from mamma's old shoe. Still, there are very many of them."

Here the conversation again ceased. And Ivan Fyodorovich in no way could find his voice again.

The story ends unfinished, because as Rudy Panko explains, his wife, who was illiterate, had inadvertently used half the manuscript on which to bake her *piroshki*. Again the source is Pushkin. In the introduction to the *Belkin Tales* we read:

Besides the stories which you have deigned to mention in your letter, Ivan Petrovich left a number of manuscripts, part of which I have and part of which were used by his housekeeper for various domestic needs. Thus last winter all the windows of her wing were pasted over with the first part of a novel which he never finished.

In any case, the promise of the last sentence, "Meanwhile in the aunt's head a completely new idea took shape, about which you will learn in the next chapter," is unfulfilled, and we never learn what became of our diffident hero.

Shponka and Grigory Grigorevich are reincarnated as even more extreme figures in the vapid Manilov and the bellicose Nozdryov of *Dead Souls*, while the aggressive aunt and empty blonde became prototypes for Gogol's females, who are either masculine tyrants or wholly idealized china dolls, pretty and hollow.

Vladimir Odoevsky

XV. Odoevsky's *Kuenstlernovellen* and Other Fiction.

The so-called *Kuenstlernovelle*, a story whose protagonist is an artist of one sort or another—painter, poet, musician—developed concurrently with the society tale and "psychological novel," genres with which it has a number of things in common. Like the society tale, the *Kuenstlernovelle* usually has its setting in the upper strata of society. Its artist-protagonist is usually an outsider of less patrician or even plebian origins whose talents are ignored or scorned by the *haut monde*, except for a married woman from that milieu who finds him an interesting diversion. The first person confession which is typical of the "psychological novel" is often found in the *Kuenstlernovelle*, either interpolated or forming the entire work itself.

Prince Vladimir Odoevsky (1804-1865), a member of the pre-Decembrist Lovers of Wisdom Society and co-editor with Wilhelm Kuechelbecker of *Mnemosyne*, may perhaps be credited as the source of the stream of *Kuenstlernovellen* in Romantic fiction, although his works in that direction are quite unlike the typical ones in many respects. First, his three major stories of this sort are based on real-life artists, Beethoven, Piranesi, and Bach. They are marked by deep philosophical content, and show Odoevsky's acquaintance with Kant and Schelling. Odoevsky's brand of *Kuenstlernovelle* was not imitated by others.

It is fair to call Odoevsky "the Russian Hoffmann," for he seems to reflect the German Romantic's art more consistently and clearly than any other of the so-called Russian Hoffmannists, most of whom are only tenuously linked to their master. Odoevsky's *Weltanschauung* derived from German idealistic philosophy, and like Hoffmann he sought for the realization of the ideal in music. His tale *Beethoven's Last Quartet [Poslednii kvartet Betkhovena]*, which appeared in *Northern Flowers for 1831,* has as its epigraph a quotation from Hoffmann's tale about the seemingly mad Krespel.

Odoevsky's treatment of Beethoven is unusual to say the least, for instead of an imposing portrait of the great composer, who was affluent and admired during his lifetime, we are shown a shabby and starving old man, misunderstood, scorned, and neglected, a being of frantic energy oblivious to the world around him. Odoevsky manages to infect the reader with the frenzied condition of his protagonist without resorting to the usual tumid Romantic diction for such depictions. A certain laconic quality makes the whole tale more poignant, and there is an unusually graphic quality to the scene of the insane and decrepit old man, clad in torn bathrobe, playing a new composition on a broken down and stringless harpsichord.

In 1832 Odoevsky continued his cycle of *Kuenstlernovellen* with *Opere del Cavaliere Giambatista Piranesi*, also published in *Northern Flowers.* The title figure is the eighteenth century Venetian engraver of Roman monuments, who also aspired to the creation of architectural masterpieces. This person, or his ghost, or someone claiming to be Piranesi, is encountered by the narrator, a bibliophile, in a Petersburg bookstore. The Venetian modestly asks for 100,000,000 (the currency is not specified) to build an arch between Mt. Etna and Vesuvius, and he then continues with a frantic monologue which comprises almost the entire rest of the story. His tale is fantastic, with such details as his early study with Michelangelo and the claim that his engravings of projected architectural extravaganzas have become the habitation of evil spirits, which have tortured him and prevented his death. That is why he is also The Eternal Jew. Mocked by the magnificent constructions of his rivals, he tries to shake down the dome of St. Peter's or pull over the leaning tower of Pisa. The eccentric finally departs with the bibliophile's small contribution, which will be added to the amount being collected for the removal of Mt. Blanc, whose presence interferes with his plans for a castle.

Hoffmann is reflected here in the general themes of genius and insanity, the gulf between the ideal and reality. Norman Ingham has also noted that the spirits of Piranesi's majestic plans, which haunt him because they feel constricted in their engraved version, are derived from Hoffmann's Johannes Kreisler.[1] The fate of the ludicrous but sympathetic Piranesi is that of all men of genius, who can conceive of perfection but who are frustrated by reality. The vast creative powers of Piranesi have even enabled him to triumph over death (the story takes place after 1778, the year he died), perhaps thus symbolizing the immortality of artistic creativity.

In 1833 Odoevsky joined the family of story cyclists with his *Motley Fairy Tales, With a Pretty Little Word, Collected by Iriney Modestovich Gomozeyko, Master of Philosophy and a Member of Various Scholarly Societies, Published by V. Voiceless [Pestrye skazki s krasnym slovtsom, sobrannye Irineem Modestovichem Gomozeikoiu, magistrom filosofii i chlenom raznykh uchenykh obshchesv, izdannye V. Bezglasnym]*. Gomozeyko, Odoevsky's *alter ego* and *porte parole*, is an impecunious philosopher who frequents society in order to lay on the truth.

The fairy tales are brief exposes of human frailties, little nuggets of satire illustrating the statements of their titles, which are imaginatively designed to provoke one's curiosity. *The Fairy Tale of Why It Was That Collegiate Counselor Ivan Bogdanovich Relationship Was Unable to Wish His Superiors Happy Easter [Skazka o tom, po kakomu sluchaiu kollezhskomu sovetniku Ivanu Bogdanovichu Otnoshen'iu ne udalosia v svetloe voskresen'e pozdravit' svoikh nachal'nikov s prazdnikom]* relates how an exemplary civil servant was so addicted to cards that he played even on Easter eve, with the result that he and his partners were bewitched and obliged to play all Easter day. Ivan Bogdanovich Relationship's failure to pay courtesy visits to his superiors on the holiday was noted with surprise in all the chanceries, and presumably tarnished his zealously polished image as a model civil servant.

The Fairy Tale About the Corpse Which Belonged to Who Knows Whom [Skazka o mertvom tele, neizvestno komu prinadlezhashchem] is a whimsical sketch about a venal clerk and his strange encounter with a disembodied spirit, the corpse's normal occupant, who had carelessly detached himself from his usual habitat and had lost his body. The satire is directed against the chicanery of provincial officialdom, with some amusing parody of the impoverished style of provincial officialese.

The Fairy Tale About Why It Is Dangerous for Young Ladies to Walk in a Crowd Along Nevsky Prospect [Skazka o tom, kak opasno devushkam khodit' tolpoiu po Nevskomu prospektu] pokes fun at those who sacrifice themselves at the altar of foreign fashions, becoming simply brainless and heartless dolls demanding constant amusement.

The blend of humor and the fantastic at the service of satire which characterizes the *Motley Fairy Tales* puts them prominently in the genealogy of Gogol's Petersburg cycle, which followed in 1835.

Sebastian Bach completes Odoevsky's trilogy of *Kuenstlernovellen,* and its real-life prototype joins it, along with this author's *Beethoven's Last Quartet* and *Opere del Cavaliere Giambatista Piranesi,* to the genre of fictionalized biography. The Bach tale was composed in Revel in 1834 and published in *The Moscow Observer* in 1835, where it was signed with the pseudonym "Voiceless" [Bezglasnyi] .

The story opens with the description of an eccentric who has spared neither time nor money in his search for collections of pictures, engravings, and music. We are told that he is convinced of the existence of a secret language known to artists, without knowledge of which one cannot understand their works. All artists have a common goal, all speak the same language, and all understand one another. The narrator then laments the fact that in transcribing the tale related by this eccentric lover of arts he is unable to:

preserve the heartfelt conviction of the truth of the words he spoke, his dramatic participation in the fate of artists, his particular art of rising gradually from a simple matter to powerful ideas and powerful feelings, his bitter mockery of the ordinary occupations of ordinary people.

Our inner narrator, the eccentric collector, opens with a categoric argument that the life of artists cannot be written in the usual manner of historians, for their lives exist in their works:

The materials for the life of any artist are one and the same: his works. Be he a musician, a poet, a painter, in them you will find his spirit, his character, his expression, in them you will find those events which evade the genealogical pens of historians.

Sebastian Bach reads like lives of saints, and in incident and structure the work resembles canonical examples of that hoary genre. Just as the spiritual qualities of the saintly hermit or monk are emphasized, Odoevsky is primarily concerned with Bach's mystical-musical development. This is presented in a series of revelatory incidents: the youth's clandestine study of modern composition in defiance of his conservative mentor's admonitions, his transcendental vision in the cathedral following his first contact with organ music, his intuitive understanding of the instrument maker Albrecht's pious efforts to create organs which would inspire exalted feelings, the discovery of his true vocation as composer. Odoevsky deliberately sacrifices the true details of Bach's married life, his two wives and twenty children, so that the mythic aspect may be emphasized. Contrary to fact, the love between Bach and his wife, Magdelena, is destroyed when the Venetian Francesco seduces her from the harmonious world of her husband's music with his modern Italian arias and *canzionetti.* Her Italian blood, inherited from her mother, is aroused, she falls in love with Francesco and his music, and after his departure the evil coal of her affection burns on, hidden under an ash of domesticity. Dutifully she succors her husband as he loses his sight, but ultimately she is consumed by the flame of her passion and dies.

Implicit in this dénouement is a criticism of the new music of Italy, a music at the service of passion rather than the spirit. Odoevsky seeks to establish a qualitative difference between the compositions of Bach, who was scarcely known in Russia at that time, and works of the Italian school, which enjoyed wide popularity. The eccentric inner narrator explains it this way:

I have already told you that inspiration did not act upon him violently; its quiet fire burned in his soul. At home at the clavicord, in the chorus of his pupils, in friendly conversation, at the organ in a chapel, he was everywhere true to the sanctuary of art, and never did mundane thoughts or mundane passion interfere in its sounds. For this reason, today, when music has ceased to be prayer, when it has become the expression of mutinous passions, leisure amusement, the allurement of vanity, the music of Bach seems cold, devoid of life. We do not understand it, as we do not understand the indifference of martyrs on the pyres of paganism, we seek something understandable, which is known, compatible with our indolence, the comforts of our lives. Deep feeling is frightening, as deep thought is frightening.

The ending of the story is pathetic, with Bach widowered, enfeebled, blind, isolated, and devoid of inspiration.

The language of this tale is markedly different from the author's tale about Beethoven. Whereas the earlier work was notable for its matter-of-factness, here we have a not very satisfying combination of straightforward, even laconic narration, with cliches of the following sort:

Albrecht's words fell upon Sebastian's soul. He was often lost in their mystery. He might even have been unable to repeat them, but he understood the feeling and was strengthened in its fiery inner activity.

178

Odoevsky attempts to excuse the motley aspect of the language of the inner narrator by pointing out that the eccentric's

> habit of fusing within himself all kinds of sensations, his habit of assuming the feelings of others, produced in his speech dregs of ideas and concepts often completely diverse. He became angered that he lacked the words to make his speech intelligible to us, and he used anything at hand for his explanation: chemistry, hieroglyphics, medicine and mathematics. From a prophetic tone he would descend to the emptiest polemics, from philosophical considerations to trade jargon; everywhere there was variety, variegation, strangeness.

If Odoevsky's explanation for the yawing style of this story is of questionable utility in resolving the reader's uneasiness, one cannot fault him for the innovative manner in which, here and in the Beethoven piece, he illuminated the inner world of the artist and revealed how different its spiritual content and focus were from those ordinary mortals. Certainly here we have a demonstration that for this purpose, at least, Romantic diction was perfectly suitable.

The Sylph [*Silfida*] is probably Odoevsky's closest approach to Hoffmann's ideology. The tale was published in Pushkin's *Contemporary* in 1837. The underlying theme is that an ideal world is found beyond the limits of sanity, and that this is preferable to the mundane pleasures of conventional living. The contrast between normal, prosaic occupations and the transcendental experience of the world of the imagination is embodied in the opposition of the protagonist's desire to maintain contact with the supernatural realm of sylphs and the well-intentioned efforts of his friends to make him conform to their own standards of behavior. Ultimately he is "saved" from insanity and unenthusiastically adopts the routine typical of a provincial landowner.

The Romantics' conviction that no sensitive person could exist in a mundane environment without some flights into the revitalizing atmosphere of the Good, the True, and the Beautiful, which they associated with poetry, idealistic philosophy, profound music, and masterpieces of art, is expressed directly by Odoevsky's Iriney Modestovich Gomozeyko in *The Vision [Prividenie]*, a late version of the supernatural tale, published in 1838 in *The Literary Supplement to The Russian Invalid*:

> . . . Our mind, worn out by the prose of life, involuntarily is attracted by these mysterious happenings which make up the current poetry of our society and serve as proof that no one in this life is able to isolate himself from poetry any more than from original sin.

The story, which Iriney tells to three traveling companions, presumably is responsive to man's desire for escape from the mundane, but that is not what interests us at this point. It is the structure of the tale which makes it unusual, for its plot and characters seem quite conventional.

The daughter of a capricious widow elopes with her lover and is cursed by her mother. After the birth of a son, the young woman's mother is reconciled to her, but she is admonished always to wear an amulet which abjures the curse. Years pass, her son grows up, enters the army. To celebrate his return home on leave, a ball is held at family castle. Tiring of the festivities, the son leaves the party and goes to the bedroom, which is presumably haunted. To punish him for leaving the party so early, his mother and some guests dress as ghosts and enter his room. Awakened suddenly, he seizes a pistol and fires, shooting his mother. Her final words report that she had failed to wear the amulet.

Such are the details, but the story is presented ingeniously through the use of four narrators, whose contributions form a set of Chinese boxes, with each smaller box having a temporal setting more distant than the one which surrounds it. A first person narrator establishes the external setting with his initial sentence: "Four of us were in the diligence, a retired captain, a department head, Irenei Modestovich Gomozeyko, and myself. Odoevsky's *port parole* then relates how an old acquaintance of his, a man of Voltairian rationalism and a disbeliever in the supernatural, narrated at a soirée an anecdote about the young officer who shot his mother. However, there is yet another retrospective level, for the Voltairian learned of the details of the elopement and the curse from his landlady, and he retells her story in her own words. The story shifts from one level to another, which it must be said, can be confusing, especially so since the voices of the narrators all sound the same. However, the anecdote which emerges from the Voltairian's words has a special function in Odoevsky's structure: when the Voltarian has finished his tale, Iriney Modestovich relates that a young man who had listened silently then informed the group that he knew the family in which the tragedy occurred and that the mother was alive and well. He also added that everyone who told the story was doomed to an early death. Iriney then reports that the Voltairian soon fell ill and ceased to appear at their gatherings. The passengers in the diligence then comment upon the story, quite ineptly, and the story closes with Ireney's answer to the exterior narrator's question as to whether the Voltairian did in fact die. "I didn't say that," replied Iriney.

Odoevsky might have told his story utilizing just the Voltairian and the woman who provided him the background facts, but then we would simply have had a typical tale of the supernatural. The young man's revelation changes our whole understanding of the event, for if the mother was not shot, then it indeed was a ghost which led the group to the son's bedroom. The prediction of the Voltairian's speedy death and his disappearance suggest the existence of demonic forces emanating from the castle, but that interpretation must be changed when at the very last we learn that the Voltairian did not die.

One may question whether the game is worth the candle, whether this involved structure is really justified by the prankish conclusion. Nonetheless, the tale serves well in suggesting the elusiveness of any categoric affirmation or denial of the supernatural—now you see it, now you don't. In its own way it also provides that "poetry of life" which Iriney Modestovich informs his fellow travelers is so important for our spirits, stifled by the mundanity of our lives.

A number of Odoevsky's stories published in the thirties, including all of those discussed in this group, were incorporated into an omnibus work published in 1844 with the title *Russian Nights [Russkie nochi]*, which represented Odoevsky's last major literary effort. In the context of this collection, the stories reinforce one another, and their thematic significance is more clearly displayed. Odoevsky provided an organizing frame of philosophical discussions carried on by some young intellectuals, Rostislav, Viacheslav, Victor, and Faust. The form seems to derive from Hoffmann's *Serapion Brothers*, as some of Odoevsky's contemporaries noted, but in the introduction to his work he insisted that he had conceived his structure long before Hoffmann was known to him. There is no reason not to believe this assertion, just as there is no reason not to presume that Odoevsky *was* familiar with Perovsky's *The Double,* whose structure did derive from Hoffmann.

The late date of *Russian Nights* puts it beyond the limits of this study of Romantic fiction, but one should be aware of its importance as a capstone for Odoevsky's visionary Romanticism and the summation of his major achievements.[2]

СРЕДА. ТОМ. I. № I. ЯНВАРЯ 1го.

ЛИТЕРАТУРНАЯ ГАЗЕТА.

1830 ГОДЪ.

Выходитъ
черезъ
каждые пять дней.

Цѣна годовому изданію,
состоящему изъ 78-ти №,
№ въ С. П. Б. 35 руб.,
съ пересылкой и разно-
скою 40 рублей.

Въ Январѣ Газета сія выходитъ въ слѣдующіе дни: 1-го числа (въ Среду), — 6-го (въ Понедѣльникъ), — 11-го (въ Субботу), — 16-го (въ Четвергъ), — 21-го (въ Вторникъ), — 26-го (въ Воскресенье) и 31-го (въ Пятницу).

МАГНЕТИЗЁРЪ.

(ОТРЫВОКЪ ИЗЪ НОВАГО РОМАНА, соч. Антонія Погорѣльскаго.)

ГЛАВА I.

[Текст сильно повреждён и частично неразборчив.]

Ч. I. № 1.

The 1st page of the 1st issue of the *Literary Gazette* of Baron Delvig, with Chapter I from a new Pogorelsky novel. Dated January 1, 1830.

XVI. Somov's Novellas of Manners.

In the last two years of his life, Orest Somov published three tales deriving from the manners of the Ukrainian provincial gentry. While not so developed as Perovsky-Porgorelsky's earlier *The Smolny Institute Graduate*, they present interesting types and amusing situations, marked by a similar gentle tolerance toward the foibles of this group. Although not canonical society tales, they have some features of that genre, especially *A Novel in Two Letters [Roman v dvukh pis'makh]* published in Baron Rosen's almanac *Alcyone for 1832*. A work of more than 7,000 words, it consists of two long letters written by a young nobleman to a friend in Petersburg. In these he recounts his meeting, courtship, and marriage to a provincial gentry girl. A partial frame is provided by an "editor's" afterword, which comments on the origin of the correspondence:

> Unexpectedly there came into my possession these two letters of Lev Konstantinovich. I don't know his surname, for both were signed simply *Leon*. I have not tried to correct the style, which is sometimes careless, nor to give Russian translations of the French insertions with which it is sprinkled. I could collect a whole hundred volumes of similar correspondence of our young men of the world, who often write as they speak, that is, half in French and half in Russian. I don't know, or guarantee, that the reading of this correspondence will be pleasing or useful. I am publishing these two letters because what they contain is a complete episode.

Leon is a rather supercilious young man who identifies himself with Eugene Onegin, the blasé youth of Pushkin's narrative poem, and, in fact, he alludes to this work on more than one occasion. Returning to the Ukraine after four years abroad and in Petersburg, he finds his provincial relatives and their friends totally unstimulating. When he learns from his aunt that she intends to marry him to a certain Nadezhda, the daughter of a neighbor, he flatly refuses. However, he accidentally encounters the girl just after he saves the life of a crude neighbor, Avdey Kochevalkin, who had fallen into a bog, and the girl's simplicity and freshness attract him. His interest flags at a ball, where she is trite and reticent, but later at a dinner he finds her charming. On Nadezhda's name-day, Leon secures his parents' blessings and then steals off with her to church, where secret arrangements have been made for their marriage. Once wed, they return to her house and announce their marital state, to everyone's astonishment and eventual joy.

The story is presented retrospectively in three narrative blocks, covering Leon's activities from the middle of May, when he first arrived in the Ukraine, to his wedding day in mid-September. The first two fall within the initial letter; owing to the correspondent's carelessness, his original epistle lay forgotten in his room for three weeks, and, when he rediscovered it, he appended an account of his subsequent activities during that period.

In the first part of his original epistle, the hero expresses a general antipathy for young ladies from the provinces and categorically vetoes his aunt's intention that he marry. The continuation of this letter tells of his rescue of Avdey and his first encounter with his "intended." The second letter details the vicissitudes of his relationship with her and his surprise marriage. The total reversal of Leon's attitude is an important element of the psychological content of the work, and the three stages of his change of opinion mark progress from "never" to "maybe" to "positively." One might also remark, however, that Somov could just as well have had his hero write three separate epistles and have changed his title accordingly.

Contrary to what is stated in the afterword, Leon does not write "half in French and half in Russian": in both letters there are scarcely more than a dozen intrusions of French. However, these are sufficient to give a Franco-Russian flavor to his style. In general, the protagonist employs a simple expository style with a lightly facetious tone:

> I arrived here at the best season, in the middle of May, when everything was in bloom: orchards, woods, the meadows, and the cheeks of the village beauties. You laugh and say that I have become a bucolic poet? Well, laugh, and I shall prove to you that my expression is completely accurate. The faces of the village girls were blooming then—with freckles and spring sunburn.

The humor is maintained by overstatement, as when he calls the river near his uncle's village a "Hellespont" and his daily swim "a Byronic exploit." There is burlesque hyperbole in the reference to a flock of ducks as a "web-footed encampment" entrusted to "the supreme command" of Akulina, the village poultry herd. His aunt's conference with her confidants is termed "a female congress" and the confused speech of the Avdey is effectively characterized as "muddy eloquence." Not a little of the humor derives from the several pithy monologues of Leon's aunt and the rather coarse speech of the rustic Avdey Gavrilovich, examples of which are quoted below.

Leon's initial predisposition to take a lightly ironic view of everything he encounters in the provinces makes him an ideal vehicle for the author's gentle satire directed at the provincialism of the Ukrainian gentry, their ordered but mundane daily schedule, their eating habits, amusements, dress, manner of speaking, and their pragmatism. The ball where Leon is introduced to Nadezhda provides an excellent opportunity for him to describe the gaucheries of the local worthies (and, unknowingly, to reveal his own confident self-centeredness). He prefaces his account of this fête by saying that it was exactly as the one depicted in Chapter V of *Eugene Onegin*:

> A village ball is a real exhibition of local dandies or (I will call them by the name which has not yet faded in the provincial lexicon) *petits maîtres*: here they distinguish themselves to the fullest. Those who are sedate and are not stupid do not exhibit them-

selves and remain unnoticed: they sit in a reserved manner in the corners and converse quietly. But the empty-headed fops gyrate through the rooms, often skipping, play the peacock, make a racket, and display completely all their petty pretensions to dexterity, gentility, intelligence and the like. . . .

I approached the musicians and ordered them to play a French quadrille. They unearthed an ancient one *du temps du roi Dagobert*—and the fiddles squeaked. I chose Nadezhda Sergeevna. She was timid and hesitant, but she accepted. Several of the most intrepid dandies flew to *bengage* [angezhirovat'] the ladies, as they say in their steppe dialect. . . . Ah, Alexander, would that you had been there!. . . With what sincere pleasure you would have heard the cries of amazement and rapture which resounded around me from the crowd of the spectators who arrived on the run from everywhere: "Devil take it! Wonderful! There's skill for you! That's real dancing!" Finally, how you would have rejoiced to see the district dandies trying to imitate my capers (for which, *par parenthèse*, I invented the most whimsical names: *pas de chamois, pas de gazelle, pas de bedouin*. How these fops, I say, tangled their feet, tripped and almost nosedived onto the floor. The evening was truly mine.

With respect to the evolution of Leon's prejudices, the story might aptly be called "The Education of a Young Snob." When he arrives in the country, Leon has a high opinion of himself fostered by his foreign education and his exposure to Petersburg society. The manner of life which he encounters at his uncle's estate is too routine and ordinary for his elevated tastes, and he cannot abide the studied sentimentalism of his young female cousin, who epitomizes his stereotype of provincial girls. The matrimonial plans which his aunt cherishes for him are immediately rejected, and he remains obdurate even after his accidental encounter with Nadezhda, who proves, in any case, not to be the ghastly fright he had imagined. At the ball he falls prey to his egotistical desire to flaunt his superior manners and accomplishments, and therefore gives himself no opportunity to become acquainted with Nadezhda's real personality and qualities. Only later does he realize that she is far from being the mousy and ignorant girl of his preconception, and he falls in love.

All the information about Nadezhda Sergeevna must originate with or be transmitted by our correspondent, Leon. In the course of the story a variety of means are used to acquaint us with her background, appearance, demeanor, and character, so that ultimately she emerges as a personality. Leon's aunt is an important source of information about the girl's education:

In our neighborhood, I think you won't find a girl who has been so well educated as Nadezhda Sergeevna. Why say it? Thanks to her parents and grandmother, nothing was spared for her education. Right up to now they pay a certain *madame*, a French woman, a thousand rubles a year, if not more. And for the piano teacher, a German gaffer, there's another salary of eight hundred rubles. I know this first hand, from my chum, Stefanida Vasilievna. How could she help but know, being Nadezhda Sergeevna's aunt and all. And what's there to say about the Russian teacher, a graduate of The Smolny Institute, who lived with your future bride since she was seven and taught her Russian and foreign languages and handiwork. . . . Yes. And there's more yet. I almost forgot to say that for the past two years the dancing master from Prince Dragolsky's has been going there every week, the same one that taught the princesses and charged not less than fifteen rubles an evening, and you still had to fetch him and take him back in your own carriage. You see, my friend, nothing was left out when it came to Nadezhda Sergeevna's education.

The girl's physical appearance is described in the second part of the first letter where Leon chronicles his meeting the Avdey. Following the rescue in the swamp, the two men proceed to Avdey's house:

Suddenly, from a path which crossed ours, there fluttered right at us, like a bird, a charming young girl in a chintz dress of *Robin-des-bois* color, her face aglow from running and with unruly locks, dark as pitch, black eyes and a keen glance. With a sly expression she turned her charming little face to my poor companion and her eyes fixed on his motley image. It was evident that the beauty recognized her village neighbor in my *bog boor*, and she was unable to restrain her laughter, displaying a row of pretty teeth, white and even, like a string of pearls.

Disposed by this sudden meeting to change his opinion of provincial girls, Leon is disappointed when he again encounters the girl at the ball, corseted, and wearing a dress which was poorly reproduced from a pattern appearing in a Moscow fashion journal. The girl's reticence and timidity destroy his positive first impression:

There wasn't a spark of animation in her, and my dream perished irrevocably. "That's a *well-educated* provincial girl for you!" I told myself.

But when he meets her at her own home, he finds her not at all as she had been at the ball:

What more is there to tell? I was charmed with her. I noted in her sparks of an original, at times even caustic, intelligence. I noted in her sincere sensitivity and yet another trait which I've sought for in women for a long time: a genuine candor lightly aroused by one in whom she begins to nourish confidence. Add to this a cheerful disposition, a lively imagination, and a sort of captivating, childlike good nature in her speech. Add to this a stature which is not tall but well-proportioned, beautiful features, a pleasant smile, large black eyes, with an animated, expressive glance. Wasn't this enough to make my head swim?
It is decided: I shall marry her!

And so he does, circumventing the tedium and rigamarole of a provincial courtship by eloping.

Somov's manifest interest in colorful types from his native Ukraine, is revealed here in the person of Avdey, the *bog boor*. This character is presented with certain dominant qualities emphasized to create an exaggerated image. Avdey's essence is elephantine oafishness, and everything about him, his appearance, his speech, his servants, his house and his actions reinforce this. One sees in this figure a precursor of the bizarre types in Nikolai Gogol's *Dead Souls*, who are, however, even more heavily stylized or conventionalized.

As we know, Leon first encounters Avdey in the bog into which he had lucklessly stumbled. Leon hastens to provide aid by tugging at the protruding head:

> Finally my strained efforts were crowned with the hoped for success: I dragged out a human figure of the most huge size—almost seven feet, with athletic limbs which under the thick layers of sticky slime seemed even more corpulent and crude.

When this monster finally is able to speak, his language is as lacking in elegance as his figure:

> "Although I don't have the honor to know you, guv'nor, I still thank you not the less respectfully for having freed me from this pool. What a misfortune! The Evil One led me into the bog. Lookee here, they was a snipe running and flapping from hummock to hummock, and me after it, and further and further. I got mad. Won't let him get away. I steal along, took a step, seems, to a firm place, and fell into the marsh. Ah, damn you! says I heartily, and bam from the gun at the snipe. He flew off, and under me the footing settled, and I sink to my waist. Well, struggle a bit, get out. I thought to reach the bottom with my gun, to push me out—where was it! And the gun went to blazes for the imps to enjoy. . . . Well, so I was sorry, and tried again to work out of the slime, but a fat lot of good! I'm for getting out, but it's like the wicked one is pulling my legs, and I'm deeper and deeper. If you hadn't showed up, I'd have disappeared completely."

They repair to Avdey's house, where in response to the master's shout, "Where are you, you monsters?" there appear three "gaping" peasants "with the most stupid mugs." The main room, which Leon describes in detail, is in keeping with the basic tone of the master:

> The furniture in it was of the most ancient style. The dust which lay thickly on the tables and cupboards testified that neatness had never been one of the domestic virtues of the master or his servants. In the room reigned the persistent odor of the rankest smoking tobacco. On one wall hung an oval mirror with wooden rosettes around the frame, which had once been gilded. On the other wall was nailed a large set of deer guns, rifles, hunting knives, powder horns and other armament of the Nimrods of our century.

In society, Avdey displays a lack of finesse and imagination which further underscores his crudity. However, at the story's end the image is somewhat softened when we learn that this oaf is essentially kind-hearted, and his self-effacing devotion to Nadezhda's welfare is touching without being cloying.

Somov departs radically from the sentimental tone which was typical of the epistolary form at that time; in fact, the work is anti-sentimental and displays a strong current of Realism, particularly in the evolution of the hero's *Weltanschauung*, the exposition of attitudes and way of life typical of the provincial gentry, and in the reproduction of individual modes of speech. The content of humor is satisfying without being hilarious, the characters are

187

nicely developed and sometimes colorful, and the plot is sufficiently engaging to keep the reader constantly involved. The warm sun of the Ukraine illuminates the action, and the gentle irony of the author, or his protagonist, smiles at the rustic foibles of the provincials, whose lives, though not idealized, are idyllic in their own contexts.

Matchmaking [Svatovstvo], published in *Northern Flowers for 1832*, like Somov's earlier *skaz* narrative *Kikimora*, is presented in a highly individualized style, and it gains much of its interest and aesthetic value from this special language. Subtitled "From the Memoirs of an Old Man About his Youth," it is an aging clerk's rambling account of his first and only love and the pathetic outcome of this attachment. The plot is really a vehicle for the conveyance of all sorts of facts and details regarding the lesser Ukrainian gentry, life in the village, food, raiment, diversions, with a long section devoted to a close description of the village engagement ritual. The clerk memoirist, Demid Kalistratovich, presents his tale in an informal manner which gives the impression of oral narration. The work opens, in fact, with a one-sided dialogue between the clerk and his anticipated readers:

Maybe, gentlemen, you are surprised, you are looking at one another and whispering among yourselves: "Who," you say, "is talking to us? And what's the use of one stranger irritating other strangers, and why should the inhabitant of a provincial hamlet speak with those who live in the capital and torment our ears, which are accustomed to choice expressions and involved greeting?" Permit me, gentlemen, to report everything about myself that is necessary. I remind you only that I myself was a learned person, and if it had not been for the damned school holidays, then it might have been that I would never have lost my knowledge of Latin.

The clerk's language is peppered with Russianized Latin terms, salted with regionalisms, seasoned with stilted and bookish expressions, and it is digressive throughout. The memoirist himself early talks of his predilection for digression, at the same time indulging in some Shandyan play by mixing narrative time and reader's time:

But it's been a long time since I set out from town for my father's place, and yet, as you deign to see, I haven't got there. The reason is the simplest: Slowness of motion. And why? You'll learn right now. We humble students of Philosophy or Theology did not fly on swift troikas like your town gentry. No, our parents didn't indulge us in that. Having taken my walking staff, I had thought to measure with my own legs and the sweat of my brow the distance from the seminary town to my native Krokhalievsk (a distance, I will note in passing, not less than eighty versts), but happily at the town market I met an inhabitant of Krokhailievsk, who had come there with three pair of oxen to sell wheat, wax, hemp, and hemp oil.

And this leads to another digression.

The tone changes perceptibly in the course of the story. When Demid is recalling his life at the time he returned from the seminary, his growing love for the pretty daughter of a widowed neighbor, their engagement, the

188

tone is facetious and buoyant. But when the narrative proceeds to the deception of the girl's mother, who marries her suddenly to a brutal officer, the bantering conversational tone gives way to one of pathos, and the language itself becomes heavy with Sentimentalist phraseology. This change in style is consistent with the modest education of the narrator and the sad events he recounts.

In the early portion of the story, the memoirist recalls with obvious pleasure all the details of that summer when he completed the seminary and returned home to the village to assist his father, an affluent and honest village priest. In a digressive manner, punctuated with continual apostrophes to his readers, he describes life in the hamlet, his mother's silent but salient role in family affairs, her domestic occupations and the preparation of her favorite dishes, behavior in church, peasant superstitions, and even such minor matters as how shoes were shined. Homely proverbs mingle with regional terms and Latin affectations. Demid speaks of his own activities with light-hearted self-deprecation, often combining situational and verbal humor. An example is his description of his debut in local society, a whole series of *faux pas*, the first of which is his vain attempt to attract admiration by his garish and outmoded attire. With high hopes of displaying sophistication, he attends a wedding reception:

The local worthies, some in black or dark blue dress coats, bared their teeth at my appearance. I was scared stiff. However, remembering the words of my mummy and quite conscious of my own dandified raiment, I said to myself, "It's envy, envy!" Probably some of them lacked the things which I had in my wardrobe. Others were arrayed in little dress coats which were dock-tailed in order to use less cloth. This thought gave me new confidence. I bowed to all sides and set about looking for the hostess. At that moment she herself carried in vodka for her guests. I thrust forward to kiss her hand, knocked my elbow against the tray—the decanter and glasses clashed together and were thrown to one side, the vodka spilled onto the floor and the hostess's dress. By good fortune she held on to the tray with her strong hands. However, the laughter of all the guests—a demonic, heartrending laughter—resounded around me. Having kissed the hostess's hand, I drew back quickly at the same time as she bent forward in order to respond to my kiss with one on the forehead. A new misfortune! My head knocked her in the face so hard that sparks flew from her eyes and she almost had a nose bleed. The hostess cried out involuntarily and pressed her left hand to her face, while a solicitous worthy supported her tray and thus prevented the potable supplies from complete destruction. I admit that at this point I became confounded from fright. I couldn't see where I stood and almost rushed headlong from the house.

The progress of the story, never very rapid, nearly comes to a complete halt when Demid describes the formalities connected with his engagement to Nastasia. Here Somov's particular interest in ethno-sociological matters is fully indulged, and the story thus serves, as Somov intended, to record the customs of his native land, customs which he felt were rapidly being abandoned and which deserved, if not preservation, at least inscription in the record of Ukrainian cultural traditions. At the same time, Somov creates an amusing portrait-caricature of the sly and artful marriage broker, Savely Dementievich Peresypchenko, a retired clerk from the chancery court. This "besoiled pedant" has his distinctive manner of speech, which is marked by archaic grammatical forms, extraneous "filler" words, and pompous and stilted phraseology. He is at his best when he represents Demid in the marriage negotiations with the widow:

The older match-maker, that is Savely Dementivich Peresypchenko, made his speech with all kinds of circumlocutions, almost starting from the creation of the world and he concluded with these remarkable words: "You can't escape from God's power. The old grow older and fall by the wayside, while the young blossom and appear youthful. Being an example of this, so to say, is your daughter. Thence thus a bride albeit. Such valuable goods will not lie for long on her mother's hands. And so a buyer is found among us. We bow to you and beg your indulgence to us and our bridegroom."
Matrona Yakimovna made a sort of ambiguous grimace with her lips and silently indicated chairs to us. We sat down.

Distinct speech patterns are characteristic of the other *personae* of this story, especially Demid's parents and the widow. In this respect, the work is a *tour de force* of individualized speech.

One of Somov's contributions to Russian fiction was his use of common or even lower class protagonists, a necessary step in the growth of Realist literature. Demid Kalistratovich Slastiona is one of the first of Russian literature's petty clerks, a victim of human malice and a hostile fate. The tragi-comic treatment of his fortunes, and misfortunes, was later imitated in other stories of brow-beaten, frustrated, and penniless quill-drivers.

Mommy and Sonny [Matushka i synok], a delightfully humorous work, was published in *Alcyone for* 1833.[1] In general terms it is a satire on the education or, actually, the ignorance of provincial gentry, exemplified by the absurd behavior of a *petit maître*. More specifically, the work describes the ludicrous program of modern education which a *nouveau riche* woman arranges for her milk-sop son and the preposterous consequences of his schooling. The work does not attack the gentry as such, but rather exposes those of that class whose pretentious ignorance leads to one folly after another. On a different level, the work satirizes Sentimentalism, which is mocked both as a personal attitude and as a manner of literary expression; the story also lampoons the egregious excesses of the Gothic tradition and its heir, *l'Ecole frénétique*. The man of sentiment is caricatured in the figure of the story's hero, and novels of terror and bloodshed are travestied through the figure of his mother.

Immediately following the satirical epigraph, "The child has promise," we are introduced to our "hero" and his parents.

Thirty years ago in the country, far from the county seat and almost two thousand versts from the capital, Valery Terentievich Vyshegliadov was born. His father was a conscientious judge, who in his time had unconscionably plundered the innocent and the guilty, and finally by this (albeit not entirely innocent) trade had accumulated for himself, as such gentlemen usually phrase it, a tidy little sum, and with this he bought a miserable hamlet with an annual income of less than ten thousand.

The name of this hamlet is Zakurikhino (beyond the hen house), and there the judge's wife, the daughter of a contractor, brings into the world their heir, Valery. His birth is commemorated by the village deacon with a poem, a masterpiece of rustic rhetoric, which elegantly concludes, "*Vale, Valeri.*"

The story is divided into two parts, the first concerned with the formative years and education of Valery, the last dealing with his travels and tribulations. But the author is not overly concerned with an even tempo of events, so Valery's biography is recounted with many digressions, halts for the presentation of dramatic scenes, inquiries into the background of peripheral characters, and discussions of provincial customs and activities. In fact, biography is merely a vehicle for satire, and the author indulges his taste for irony or comedy whenever it suits him.

The characters are creatures of a few exaggerated traits, among which ignorance and cupidity serve as common denominators. The mother embodies a number of dubious virtues, and, withal, is self-satisfied, self-confident, and self-centered. The father is predominantly stingy, to such a degree that he resists employing any tutors for Valery until his son has passed from childhood to youth. He finally acquiesces, and a Frenchman and a German are hired:

Finally from Moscow arrived a young and unconstrained Frenchman, once a valet's valet of some nobleman, and a German, who, owing to an affliction of his legs and yet another unmentionable weakness, had retired as a riding master and clown from a troupe of bareback riders and tightrope walkers.

These pedagogues are eminently qualified: the Frenchman has a diploma from the French Academy signed by Voltaire, Diderot, d'Alembert, La Harpe, and others who died before he was born, and the German boasts doctorates in all sciences from all German universities. Owing to their number, he has left these in Moscow.

There is yet another teacher, a young student from a nearby seminary. The mother's interview of this brilliant scholar is a charming example of the comedy of catalogue seasoned with unexpected absurdities caused by the disruption of logical order:

"Well, my friend, have you studied?" was her first question, following the polite seminarian's low bow and speech of greeting.
"I have studied, utterly dear madam!" he answered with a new bow.
"What did you study?"
"Everything, from *Infima* and *Synatasima* to Theology."
"Well! Good! I understand. Therefore you are acquainted with Zoology, Philology, Anthropology, Cosmology, Chronology, Etymology, Ornithology, Pathology,

Meteorology, Ideology, Mineralogy, and Mythology?"
The Seminarian answered only with a bow.
"Also Astronomy, Binomy, Agronomy, Anatomy, Metronomy, and Political Economy?"
A bow and not a word.
"And Logics, Physics, Heraldics, Grammatics, Hydraulics, Tactics, Poetics, Botanics, Materia-Medics, Rhetorics, Ethics and Arithmetics?"
Silence, and a new bow.
"Geography, Stenography, Orthography, Hydrography, Calligraphy, and Chorography?"
More silence and another bow.

He is hired with great satisfaction and anticipation.

Hyperbolic elements strengthen the humor: the exaggerated expectations of the mother, her unusual command of -ologies, -omies, -graphies, and -ics, the presumptuous agreement of the seminarian, who does not lie but continually bows in answer to her recitation of his supposed academic competancies.

Neither the mother, the seminarian, nor the two professors from abroad succeed in teaching Valery much. In fact, the French valet and the German horse-trainer "taught Valery almost as parrots are taught, and they boasted of the ease of their method of instruction. They rarely took to the books, preserving them, in Griboedov's expression, for important occasions." At eighteen his education is finished and his doting mother takes him into society. Valery is ready to consider himself the Eighth Wonder of the World, although he still preserves a certain courteousness, unlike, Somov informs us, Pushkin's Eugene Onegin.

The death of Valery's father initiated a mourning period during which the bereaved mother and son remain closeted at home, the youth continually reading Sentimental works and his mother avidly devouring Gothic novelists and stories by their French and Russian imitators. As the mother identifies with the drastic anti-heroes of her reading, she becomes increasingly domineering and intransigent, while the son becomes enslaved by the tender passions idealized in his favorite literature.

The stage is now set for the conflict which dominates the action of the second half of Mommy and Sonny, and in developing his plot the author exploits fully the opportunity to satirize the literary school responsible for Valery's post-adolescent personality. The mother insists that Valery spend four years travelling, and so in the company of a sly servant, who is much more perceptive than himself, he sets forth. His letter home is a parody not only of the Sentimentalist Weltanschauung, with its effusive love of nature, the natural man, and emotions, but it also satirizes the stylistic mannerisms typical of the movement: turgid phraseology, exclamations, hyperbole, periphrasis, and euphemisms. After speaking of his home as "that peaceful haven of my youth," he weeps copiously before continuing:

We departed from Zakurikhino under the most propitious of prognostications: the sun was gliding along its heavenly path, birdlets were singing in the groves, butterflies fluttered over the meadows. Along the road we encountered interesting peasant women in torn sarafans, like a crowd of Pharonites, with rakes on their shoulders and the loud sounds of folksongs, sweet in their wildness. Nature, immeasurably deep and eternally young! I venerate you!

Arriving in the country town for a brief sojourn, the impressionable and sensitive youth immediately discovers the object of his eternal affection, Malasha, the pretty but quite common daughter of a widowed wafer baker, who is also his landlady. An opportunity to declare his love occurs when he finds her alone in the kitchen garden:

He approached the beauty, he wanted to express to her everything that he felt—and suddenly he became agitated, faint-hearted, and he was only able to stammer: "You will have many cabbages: look at how many carrots, turnips, and onions there are."

This pathetic overture is followed by a dialogue in which the author intensifies his travesty of the Sentimental mode by presenting Valery's bookish declarations against the background of Malasha's unliterary responses and the mundane advice of her eavesdropping mother:

"Melania, dear, incomparable Melania! Angel of beauty and innocence!" exclaimed Valery, raising his voice higher and higher and almost losing his self-control.
"Be more quiet, sir, for the love of God, be more quiet! Mummy will hear you, or someone else. Then I'll be in trouble."
"What's that to me! Let the whole world hear me! Let Heaven itself attend my vows! I am yours, eternally yours!"
"And if you're really hers, honorable sir, then a priest and the holy church can take care of it," answered the wafer baker, who, having heard loud voices in the garden, had looked out there and sneaked up on the young people.

This scene is also witnessed by Valery's servant, who immediately writes to the boy's mother reporting that he has been bewitched. When she hears of her son's intended misalliance, the mother hastens to the village and tries to browbeat everyone into obeying her wishes. But Valery won't recant, and the landlady, sensing a good thing, refuses to be bribed. Left no alternative, the mother carts Valery home and incarcerates him in a tower which she has recently had built following a plan described in some novel. And there, we are told, he remains to this day, absorbed in thoughts of his beloved Melania.

For a mother to sentence her son to life imprisonment may be a reasonable way to resolve a domestic problem, but it is certainly not the sort of thing that happens frequently in life—or even in literature, where devotion, even misplaced, is rewarded, and misalliances are happily avoided by the poignant death of one of the lovers. But that which customarily happened in the world of contemporary literature was not so likely to happen in Somov's literary world, where cliches of plot development often became the victims of of his irony. Another example of this occurs in *Giant Mountains [Ispolinskie gory]*, when the knight Ratomir, who had sworn eternal fidelity to Liubusha, returns in glory to his homeland to learn that his beloved is the prisoner of a heinous giant—and he abandons her to her fate. There is a double irony in this story, though, for the presumably abused and forsaken Liubusha has become the doting spouse of her hideous companion.

And we may share the joke with Fate over the ironical lot of Valery, whose mother spared no expense and effort in his education to prepare him for a brilliant future, but ended up as his judge and jailer.

An Epigraph In Place of a Title [Epigraf vmesto zaglaviia], Somov's society tale which appeared in the almanac *Biela's Comet* in 1833, is a disappointing work. One of his longest stories, it lacks the colorful characters and humor found in other works of his final period. Further, it has a sentimental strain which is out of place in the mature works of this author.

The story opens in a promising manner with a lightly satirical description of the social activities of a provincial town, where a hussar regiment and an artillery company are stationed. The town boasts a theatre, hardly a remarkable one, but nevertheless "the best society frequented it in order to kill evenings, while the hussar and artillery officers did so to yawn at the farces." Then follows a description of what was called the *redoubt* [redut] ; here Somov makes full use of endearing diminutives and overstatement to strengthen the satirical flavor:

> They were much more attracted by the *redoubt*, or club of nobility, where twice weekly gathered the most illustrious and wealthy gentry and several members of the honorable mercantile class. Here staid mommies appeared with their sweet young daughters or tall, adolescent sonny-boys. Oldsters of both sexes played cards or chatted among themselves of those important matters which have been the topic of provincial conversation from time immemorial. Meanwhile, between dances, their daughters minced about or flirted with the officers; the adolescent sons sought to show their youthful valor, twisted their prospective moustaches, and gave vent to banal jokes which they considered extremely witty.

We are then introduced to the story's hero, Count Krinsky, a young man of twenty-one whose wealth, appearance, and talent seem more properly to have destined him for a fashionable Guards regiment than for an obscure provincial hussar regiment. From a discussion which takes place at a ball between two of Krinsky's comrades-in-arms, it appears that provincial society provides only two possible candidates for the Count's future spouse: the beautiful and wealthy Felitsiata Nelskaya, a General's widow in her mid-twenties, and the seventeen-year old Liubov Vishaeva, the daugher of well-to-do gentry. When the officers make a bet as to whom the Count will choose, an old gentleman standing nearby predicts that Krinsky will tire of Felitsiata's affectation and discover that Liubov has no soul. There is, the gentleman adds, only one woman worthy of Krinsky, but he refuses to name her because the officers might laugh.

Somov then details the vicissitudes of the Krinsky-Nelskaya relationship, the sub-theme here being "all that glitters is not gold." Just when the Count falls in love seriously, they quarrel and Nelskaya's true nature is revealed. His attention then shifts to Vishaeva, who, only moments before Krinsky is about to propose, displays the meanness which pervades her personality. The Count then flees to a nearby village, where he meets the Reyev family. The eighteen-year old daughter, Olga, is not pretty and lacks the brilliance of Felitsiata or Liubov, but she is sincere, charitable, modest, and, in fact, embodies all virtues. Not unexpectedly, her true worth becomes apparent to the Count, he proposes, and they are happily wed. The epilogue, which is superfluous, prolongs the story with the unnecessary resolution of Felitsiata's and Liubov's fates. The old gentleman who had predicted the Count's rejection of both women marries Felitsiata, and it is to this gentleman that the epigraph (in place of a title) applies: "It was written at his birth."

There is a goodly measure of amusing satire in the story connected with provincial society, its love of gossip, and pretensions of Felitsiata, and the mercenary speculations of Liubov's parents. But the satirical content is vitiated by the intrusion of a sentimental strain, which not only rings untrue in the story itself but seems out of place in view of the sophistication which Somov had earlier manifested in his mature works. Moreover, the sentimental content is introduced in unnatural and hyperbolic situations. For example, Liubov's lack of compassion is revealed when she is accosted by a hungry woman with two starving children. As if this were not enough, the beggar has recently been widowed, her husband having died when their hut burned down. The widow and the children cry piteously throughout the scene, while the heartless Liubov admonishes them to get to work and stop begging.

Sentimentalism also pervades the description of Krinsky's growing attachment to Olga: tormented by jealousy, one morning he follows Olga and the household physician. His worst fears are confirmed when he sees them enter a peasant hut together. As it turns out, predictably, they are engaged in an errand of mercy:

The spectacle which presented itself to him filled his soul with the most tender feelings. Opposite the door, on a bench covered with felt, sat an aged woman. From her right arm blood was being let. Olga, with a black apron over her morning dress, in one hand held a cup into which the blood poured, and with the other raised a phial of smelling salts to the nose of the sick woman. At the table, the doctor prepared bandages. . . . Krinsky was unable to bear this emotional crisis. His heart was compressed by the gnawing of conscience for his humiliating suspicions of Olga's pure and heavenly virtue. Almost out of his mind, he leaped onto the street and flew into the garden.

Despite its many obvious faults, a word must be said in defense of this story, or, rather, in defense of one or two significant features. The satirical content, as has been noted, is handled well, but that was nothing new for

Somov. What is important is the author's obvious concern for psychologizing his characters, for creating more involved and complex personalities then he hitherto had attempted, especially with respect to his female figures. Nelskaya and Vishaeva are more than stereotypes of selfish and cold personalities, though each possesses these qualities. They are also intelligent, using their intelligence further to satisfy their self-centeredness; they are amiable to a point, using their amiability to attract the attentions of Krinsky. They are also different, and their difference derives from inner qualities as well as from age and experience. Felitsiata's marriage to an older man, a general, was a calculated move to secure comfort, position, and wealth, and she is unwilling to sacrifice these to acquire control of Krinsky. Her essential interest in him is to have a pleasant and submissive page-boy, a companion-on-call who will demand nothing more than the privilege of catering to her whims. Liubov's coldness and calculation, perhaps qualities 'inherited from her *parvenu* parents, make her incapable of love, although she is not averse to a marriage which would provide material comforts and prestige.

In thus delineating these two women, Somov made a step in the direction of three dimensional characters. But he failed by utilizing artificial situations to display their characteristics. In his attempt to create a positive type (that is, Olga) to contrast with these two, he was less successful, for Olga emerges simply as a goody-goody devoid of faults which might have made her more human.

Although *An Epigraph in Place of a Title* is seriously anchored in Sentimentalist situations and style, it also provides one of the best examples of Somov's dramatic manner with respect to dialogue and exposition. In the scene describing the end of the relationship between Krinsky and Nelskaya, the language of the disillusioned lovers mirrors their inner states of anger and reflects as well certain basic qualities of character. The exposition is limited but quite adequately conveys a visual image which reinforces the verbal one. The scene creates a strong illusion of reality:

"You wanted to say something important to me?" Nelskaya asked after a certain silence, her feigned gaiety betraying the agitation reflected in her eyes and in the arch of her brows, which involuntarily frowned.

"How can I say it?. . . I must ask your pardon."

"For what?"

"For my rashness, for the fact that, not knowing my own heart, I thought to put it to a dangerous test."

"Ah, that's it!" Nelskaya broke in with a derisive tone. "This smacks of a drama, *et moi il faut que je l'avoue, j'aime la haute comedie*. . . continue."

"I know," said Krinsky, somewhat chagrined by her tone and expression. "More than once I heard from you yourself that you value your freedom above all, that you consider marriage an unbearably burdensome trial. . . ."

"Who told you I haven't changed my mind since then?"

"That rapid a change might also be followed by another change. It would be too late to repent."

"Listen to me, Count! she burst out, her face flushing from anger. "I am very grateful to you for your admission of a fault which until now I didn't suspect in you, namely rashness. Further explanations are superfluous. I can explain for myself anything more you might say to me. I see that you, as you yourself admitted, chose me in order to solve some sort of problem and that the experiment was unsuccessful. I am satisfied with this. For the rest, that is, your apologies etc., etc., I see no use or necessity: save them for another occasion. If you weren't so young, then maybe I'd really become angry. But one must forgive a great deal owing to your age. The playfulness of children, however impertinent, amuses rather than distresses adults."

During this speech her voice gradually rose, and toward the end became halting. The somewhat coarse sounds of breaking out in it echoed unpleasantly in the ears of Krinsky, who could not now recognize in them Nelskaya's pleasing voice, which but a little while before had soothed his ear.

Her face and bearing reflected the theatrical tension of Phaedra or Clytemnaestra. Everything in her betrayed her pretended indifference and quiet venomness of speech. Krinsky heard her to the end, looking at her more with curiosity than with any inner response.

"You didn't completely guess," he answered with indifferent acrimony, "My experiment wasn't a complete failure. Thanks to it, I now see on what a shaky foundation our mutual domestic happiness would have been based, had eternal, unseverable bonds tied us for our entire lives."

"Well, who said anything about domestic happiness or eternal bonds?" Nelskaya cried out in an almost hysterical voice. "You should have asked first if I had decided to throw my peace, the advantages of my freedom, onto these scales—to balance the pitiful bait of a pretty male baby-face? I say nothing about social distinctions: my late husband was a General, and it would be laughable to change my present title and place in society for some low dignity."

"Ah! Then I have understood you better than you have me!" interrupted Krinsky in the heat of his displeasure. "You wanted to find in me a devoted Rinaldo, who kisses his bewitched chains and doesn't think to escape them, a humble Celadon, an obedient servant of your capricious will. . . ."

And so the argument continues, becoming more bitter, until Nelskaya breaks into tears:

Her voice broke, and tears, the bitter tears of unavenged insult, poured in streams from her eyes.

The conclusion points up one of the major difficulties besetting the literary language during the period when fiction was coming of age in Russia: the conflict between naturalness of expression and cliché. In this particular example, the dialogue and exposition for the most part are straightforward, tense, muscular, but then the whole effect is vitiated by the "tears pouring in streams." But what is important, however, as the long quotation demonstrates, is that Somov, with some success, was striving to create dramatic dialogue devoid of artificial floridity, dialogue which would convey the reality of a strained emotional situation. In utilizing a language which had little tradition in this respect, it is natural that he should occasionally regress to the practice of Sentimentalist writers.

An Epigraph in Place of a Title was one of the last, perhaps *the* last tale from Somov's pen. He died in the spring of 1833, and to say that he passed into oblivion would almost be an understatement. With the exception of *A Novel in Two Letters*, reprinted in the Soviet Union in 1965, none of his works were reprinted until 1975, when *Orest Somov. Selected Prose in Russian*, containing nine of his works appeared in the *Michigan Slavic Materials* series, annotated by George Harjan and with my introduction. If Baron Rosen, Somov's friend, could chide the Petersburg literary clan for failing to attend Somov's funeral, then might we not with equal justification criticize both Russian and Soviet literary specialists for their failure to reprint or even recognize this author, who in my opinion, though less popular, was far more important than Bestuzhev-Marlinsky in the introduction of literary devices, the development of the prose literary language, the recording of social history, and the expansion of Russian literary horizons. As a teller of tales, Somov was perhaps the equal of Marlinsky.

XVII. *The Tales of Mikhail Pogodin.* The Family Chronicle— Begichev. The *Kuenstlernovellen* of Polevoy and Timofeev.

We have already met Mikhail Pogodin, the writer whose stories of the Moscow merchant class anticipated the plays of Alexander Ostrovsky. Reading through the three volumes of his collected works, published in 1832 with the title *The Tales of Mikhail Pogodin [Povesti Mikhaila Pogodina]*, we can distinguish a number of salient features: the social focus is quite broad, ranging from peasants to gentry, but the emphasis is upon the merchant class; the genres are varied and often hybridized; there is an abstract interest in psychology *per se* as distinct from the psychological interest inherent in characterization; the folklore content at times becomes almost ethnography; the author is a champion of persons coerced by forces over which they have no control; the quality of the works is very uneven, but generally his humorous works are more effective than those with sombre or tragic overtones.

Pogodin was in many respects a Muscovite counterpart to Petersburg's Orest Somov, and like Somov he has been largely overlooked since his death. Both were active in publishing affairs, both had ethnological interests, they both experimented with a variety of genres, their social range was broad, their works reveal an interest in the *argots* of various classes and profession, and both had an appreciation for the comic in life.

One collection of Pogodin's anecdotes is entitled simply *Psychological Phenomena [Psikhologicheskie iavleniia]*. These totally lack dramatic development. *The Murderer* is a study of the motivation for a young merchant's slaying of wife and mother-in-law. "Revenge" describes the strange imperatives of the conscience: a customs official steals and puts the blame on others, who are punished. Later he is falsely accused and sentenced for murder. When he is ultimately proved innocent and freed, he voluntarily confesses his real guilt.

On the same pattern, but much longer, is *The Malefactress [Prestupnitsa]*, which might be sub-titled "Blackmail Will Get you Burned." Again we have a story-confession, whose protagonist is a demented girl arrested for setting fire to a tavern. Enter Catherine the Great, enroute to Astrakhan, whose sympathetic interests in her subjects enables her to coax a confession from the girl. When the truth is out, we have learned that the girl had been viciously blackmailed and in desperation set fire to the tavern in which her enemy and his brutish cronies had drunk themselves to a stupor. Catherine sees to it that the girl can realize her childhood desire of becoming a nun.

Far more interesting, and nearly suspenseful, is *Saint Basil's Eve [Vasil'ev vecher]*, a tale of bandits, hatchet murders, abduction and other delights of *l'Ecole frénétique*, but whose plot is too involved to summarize here. The emphasis is upon the adventure content, the tension, the drastic nature of the events, and the triumph of virtue.

A most engaging, even delightful, tale is Pogodin's *The Deacon-Wizard* [*Diachek-koldun*] , which combines genuinely amusing situations with the comical conversations of his lower class characters. In this story an impoverished sexton is persuaded by a cunning and glib bell-ringer to connive with him by pretending to have second sight. When the sexton miraculously divines the location of some missing horses, which his friend had hidden, his reputation is firmly established, and others soon come to seek aid from his occult powers.

Soon there comes to the wizard a peasant woman, presenting on a plate ten eggs, three lace towels, and two copper rubles.

"Help a poor woman, Grigory Dmitrievich! There's no living from my husband. He goes to Peter to work and every time he returns he beats me, not on the belly but like on to death. Black and blue spots don't leave my back or my sides. I hardly rest up while he's gone for the year, but just let him come back and the thrashing starts again. Isn't there some way, benefactor, to bewitch him for me?"

"Tell me first why he beats you. Certainly not without reason."

"I don't know, deary, I guess such happiness was assigned to me at birth. For every trifle he begins to complain, and then I say something back at him, word follows word, and he goes after me with whatever's handy, a log, the oven-fork, even the poker, and then he always whirls it around so that I'm smacked down cold on the ground— finally they pour water on me. Well, if he'd beat me to death, then there'd be an end to it. A sinner I have sinned!"

"I ask again about this. Doesn't it happen that you shout louder than your husband before he starts beating you?"

"There's no way not to, Grigory Dmitrievich," answered the old woman, somewhat calmed , "I don't want my words to go for nothing."

"I'll help you, Yegorovna, you're a good woman and I'm sorry for you. Only don't forget your benefactor. You have a lot of cows, so when there's a little butter, a bit of sour cream, some cottage cheese, a drop of milk. . ."

"Gladly, gladly, benefactor, whatever you want, only that the villain wouldn't beat me quite so hard."

"I'll brew you something infused and charmed. As soon as your husband begins to complain, turn around and put into your mouth, how should I tell you, a spoonful and a half or two, and hold it in your mouth until your husband stops yelling. If my brew works, come to me again with respect and I'll give you some Ivan's grass for a new infusion. . . ."

The remedy works wonders!

Through lucky breaks and cunning the wizard and his accomplice acquire clients even among the gentry, but their success is ultimately their downfall. Word of their pagan activities reaches the church authorities, and they are banished to a monastery to do penance.

Hidden under the comic surface of this story are more than a few shoals of social protest raised on behalf of serfs who are the defenseless victims of unfair and brutal masters. In one episode they are commissioned to find a ring which the master's child lost while walking with its nurse. The luckless nurse has been told that not only will she be flayed but all the peasants will be beaten if the missing ornament cannot be located. The seers deduce that it has been picked up by a tom turkey, and a post mortem on the greedy fowl proves them right. Later they are offered five hundred rubles to locate a missing ten thousand rubles, amassed by a nobleman to buy a serf theatre from another wastrel gentryman. They locate the fortune and are given their reward, but the delighted master soon has second thoughts and pursues them to retrieve the five hundred. Being superstitious, he is afraid to rob them before testing their occult powers, so he picks up a large bug and hides it in his hand. He then gallops up to them, intending to ask them to tell him what he has hidden, but his approach is so frightening that one of them blurts out, "Little bugs [e.g., swindlers] have fallen into gentry hands!" ["Popalis' zhuchki v barskie ruchki!"] Amazed by this apparent clairvoyance, the Indian giver wishes them a good journey and rides off.

The sub-text here is very pointed, for even though the protagonists are themselves con men, they are innocuous and even to some extent useful. By contrast, the gentry appear rapacious and gratuitously vicious. In this peasant-master juxtaposition, Pogodin precedes N.F. Pavlov and, of course, Turgenev.

Ever popular from the days of Richardson and Rousseau (and Emin), the epistolary tale or novel found many practitioners—in some cases "mechanics"—among the Romantic fictionists. Pogodin's *Sokolnitsky Park [Sokolnitskii sad]* rates with the best of them, and from the point of view of its conception is more ingenious than most of the others. It is quite a charming story, full of sentiment without being sentimental, quietly engaging in the development of a restrained suspense. The characters are pleasing and at the distance of 1825 when the action takes place, can even seem believable.

The main correspondents are B.B., an educated young Muscovite well up on Romanticism, who falls in love with Luisa, a graduate of the Smolny Institute, who lives in opulent surroundings with her uncle, a retired officer named Winter. B.B. writes to his rather domineering schoolmate, Vsevolod, who has retired to the country to immerse himself in Roman history and authors of *die Aufklärung*. Vsevolod is outraged that his disciple has apparently abandoned his rationalistic attitudes and fallen prey to female charms, and while he admonishes his friend to snap out of it, B.B.'s letters increasingly show that Luisa has completely displaced Vsevolod as a force in the young man's life. For her part, Luisa writes to Katinka, a Smolny classmate, who is now in some remote backwater, telling her of her chance meeting with B.B., his visits to their house, how he entertains her uncle, and so forth. Katinka instantly sees through Luisa's efforts to screen her interest in B.B. and proves her point by analysing Luisa's letters line by line. The plot thickens when Luisa's uncle tries to marry her to the son of an old military acquaintance, a development paralleled by the meeting of Vsevolod and Katinka, who turn out to be neighbors. B.B. and Luisa overcome their obstacles, and misogynist Vsevolod softens towards Katinka, who finds him not quite the aloof Seneca which at first she had thought him to be.

201

Pogodin makes full use of the potentials of the epistolary form for characterization. The style of the individual letters is, of course, revealing. He has his correspondents comment upon the same event, thus reflecting their different perspectives. Luisa's dissimulations in her letter to Katinka are revelatory, and the basic contrast in the personalities of the two male correspondents and the two female ones reveals each of them more clearly. Personality traits are also revealed as the correspondents discuss their preferences in literature. Luisa provides Katinka with a complete inventory of her private library, and in discussing the furnishings of her study mentions the single portrait, that of Byron. B.B. teaches Luisa Italian, they read Ariosto and Dante, and for her birthday he translates the whole of Schiller's *Wallenstein's Camp*, a deed which seals their affection.

Best of all, though, are the tones of the letters themselves, especially those of B.B., which quietly and quite persuasively reveal the development of his love for Luisa. This is not the usual sentimental pap of the typical epistolary novel, but rather a chronicle of developing affection. The rapid series of notes which accompany B.B.'s knowledge that Luisa is in love with him quite nicely conveys the exuberance of the correspondent:

Letter XXI

From B.B. to S.S.

Happy, I am happy, Vsevolod! So that's what happiness is! I have now grasped this word, and I see that previously it was for me a sound, empty. She loves me, she loves *me*. Do you hear? This Angel, Luisa, loves *me*. She herself, just now , told me that. I heard and I felt her words.

Ah, what a kiss I planted on her lips! My whole life, my past, present, and future were together in that kiss. What a vital and broad life! Isn't this eternity? My God! My God! I thank you. I can die now—what's there to learn on earth? *Ich habe gelebt und geliebt.*

Several hours later.

This is how the discovery came about. With fear and trembling I went to Sokolnitsky after sending my letter to her. . . . Mr. Winter luckily wasn't home. Luisa appears. It is impossible, impossible to describe the confusion on our faces. We said several disjointed words to each other and were silent. I couldn't make a sound, and at the same time how I wanted to speak! Words swarmed on my tongue, they crowded one another, but not one could be pronounced. Finally, mustering up my courage, I said, "Are you feeling better? Ach, don't hide anything from me, I beg you." She broke into tears. "My uncle proposes. . . ." "Do you want to. . . ?" She looked at me. "Luisa, Luisa! I adore you. Life and death, even more, my happiness and misfortune depend on you. Will you be mine?" "I am yours," she said after a certain struggle and threw herself into my arms. Ach,Vsevolod! How can a person feel so much? Can this have been but a minute in my life?

I am going to her again now. We'll arrange things after my return.

I was at her house. My friend, my friend! My present life has become a delight. Something marvelous has become of me. Heavenly powers! Can I really be a person? It seems to me that I have gathered all nature in my soul and that I myself have become all nature.

Tomorrow Luisa will give her uncle a positive answer. I will go and ask for her hand. . . My friend! Pray for us at ten o'clock.

With its "Achs" and tears, and with its rather highfalutin' emotiveness, one might get the impression that this harks back to hard-core Sentimentalism, but that would be wrong. The protagonist who writes this letter is an impressionable young man, a devoté of Dante, Schiller, and the cult of high emotions, a lover of nature (he meets Luisa just because of having been attracted by the beauty of the garden-park behind her home), and this is his first love affair. We must remember that both language of emotions and the habits of expressing it vary with the times and with nationalities, and that a century and a half ago tears and swooning really were more common than today. One can believe (or at least try to) that B.B., constituted as he was, might have written such a letter, whereas, for example, Poor Liza, the artificial flower girl, could hardly have existed at any place at any time.

The inventory of Pogodin's works would not be complete without mentioning *Adele [Adel]* and *Happiness in Misfortune [Schastie v neschastii]*, although they might disappear without any great loss. Both consist of a series of notes or letters followed by an omniscient epilogue necessitated by the fact that each of the protagonists has perished. In the former case, the notes (purportedly gleaned from the author's papers) are an impassioned outpouring of the writer's love for Adele, including a whole imaginary life which is to follow their marriage. However, she dies. The epilogue tells us that at her funeral he broke from the restraints of his friends, cried "Wait" to the body of his beloved, flung himself upon the corpse, which seemed to smile as he covered it with kisses, and dropped dead.

Happiness in Misfortune is an epistolary record of a woman's gradual and total degradation followed by spiritual regeneration. An educated young woman chronicles her descent to the lower depths as she accompanies her drunken bully husband through dismissal from the service to life as a common thief, living in a Moscow cellar. A feeling of superiority animates her earliest letters, then despair and recrimination, then pride in her ability to withstand anything—her brutish companions, her sordid surroundings, her husband's indifference, even the death of her child—and finally humility, a recognition that the social dregs around her are people, that her husband is more unfortunate than evil, and that they all have real compassion for her as she dies of consumption.

Unfortunately, the psychological-philosophical development is much less interesting than the picture of the social milieux through which the family passes. The wife's description of her husband's hussar cronies, the gambling and drinking that typifies life at a provincial army post, the absence of all refinement suggests the exposes of military life to come from the pen of Kuprin at the turn of the century. The sopping, stinking basement which is her final dwelling, with its thieves, prostitutes, drunks, even her declassé husband, is right out of Levitov or Gorky.

The family chronicle by its very nature tends toward a circumstantial description of everyday life, and thus the calculated suspense, contrived plots, and bigger-than-life characters of the Romantic tale are absent from this form of fiction. Nonetheless, if one considers a typical example of the family chronicle or domestic novel, at least those produced during the thirties, one will still find authors relying upon many of the norms basic to the Romantic period of Russian prose, but against the background some new norms, later to be associated with canonical Realism, will stand out. Typical in this respect is *The Kholmsky Family. Certain Features of Manners and Images of Life, Familial and Individual, of the Russian Gentry [Semeistvo Kholmskikh. Nekotorye cherty nravov i obraza zhizni, semeinoi i odinokoi, Russkikh dvorian]*, the work of Dmitry Begichev (1786-1855), which appeared in three parts in 1832 and whose final sixth part came out in 1841.[1] The author's name does not appear on any of the first three volumes of this work because, as he explains in his unsigned introduction, he is afraid of what the critics might say. And with reason! since at that time literary criticism was particularly partisan, personal, and polemical. In fact, Begichev was so sensitive to the power of the critics that in his novel he even credits unfavorable reviews with the destruction of the domestic felicity of the would-be poet Aglaev and his wife Katerina, *née* Kholmskaya. This cruel breed of critics is admonished in a special apostrophe:

> . . . we will address ourselves to you, hard-hearted, implacable, mocker-reviewers. If you knew how much grief you cause and how it sometimes takes just once for your mockeries to destroy all hope, all the sweet dreams which had made the poet so happy. Don't you sense that in injuring the pride of a poet you give a fatal blow to the depths of his heart? And whom does he hurt with his poems? The good ones are read and bought out at once, the bad ones lie quietly on the booksellers' shelves. Let everyone play with his favorite toy.

The Kholmsky Family is far too long and involves too many characters—over one hundred—to give a synopsis of the plot. One need only know that it deals with the efforts of a widowed provincial gentrywoman to marry off her four daughters and one son. Into their stories are woven biographies of those with whom they come in contact, with special emphasis on the life style of the characters, their typical activities, their homes, and their marital problems. Both in his introduction and later in the novel itself, Begichev insists upon the true-to-life quality of his story: "In a word, my intention was to present not the ideal, but the real [sushchestvennye], that is, what we constantly see, what is before our eyes." This point is later expanded:

> Our narration will not present anything out of the ordinary. In it there are no novelistic [romanicheskie], unbelievable events. But we dare to hope that many husbands and wives will render us justice and agree that our tale includes truths which,

perhaps, they know from their own experience. They will also testify that in married life one must pay unceasing attention to his own actions, not to discount the slightest trifles, which, seeming insignificant nothings, sometimes have dire consequences.

So, his story is to be the truth plus a message, an object lesson. Today's reader will probably feel more comfortable with Begichev's efforts to render the quality of provincial gentry life than with his sermonizing on marital matters. He preaches quite directly , in the form of authorial digressions, and through certain characters, whose values and judgments are supposedly impeccable. One such character is Sofia Kholmskaya, the most level-headed of all the sisters, and it is she who literally coaches her thoughtlessly outspoken sister Elizaveta how to wangle new furniture—or whatever—out of her rich but stingy husband, Prince Ramirsky. My own sympathies are with Elizaveta, who can't stand the fatheaded complacency of her *poshliak* spouse, whose only concern (other than horses) is with appearances.

Whether one agrees or not with all that Begichev has to say about personal relations, one must credit him with providing an extensive and detailed picture of gentry life at all levels. Several of his concerns, such as the depiction of the interiors of many houses, their decoration and furnishings, are similar to those of Turgenev, but, quite unlike his, Begichev's work is consistently undramatic, it is a "told" story in which dialogue seldom appears. The characters do utter words, but they prefer to make speeches rather than converse. The description of Prince Ramirsky's country estate, *Nikolskoe* (which bears the same name as Odintsova's estate in *Fathers and Children*) is quite specific:

Everything in them [the rooms] remained in the same form and order as it had been during the life of his grandfather. Ancient trellises, perhaps the first product of the Petersburg Trellis Factory, adorned the walls of the large livingroom. The old fashioned, heavy armchairs, upholstered with raspberry-colored cloth, had stood more than half a century in the same place. The large mirror, in a carved gilded frame, and the floor, a checkerboard parquet of various colored woods, had been quite rare in their own time. The high, thick oak panels on the wall, blackened with age, completed the decoration of this room, which Prince Ramirsky admired greatly.

As with Turgenev and later Realists, such descriptions have a twofold purpose, providing a graphic image of the circumstances of life and a comment upon the taste of those who had decorated the rooms or, in this case, those who had preferred to leave them untouched. The long description of the family portrait in the billiard room is quite amusing—suffice it to say that the talentless artist had depicted the infant Prince Ramirsky in the guise of Cupid (reminiscent of a Chekhovian device), and the detailed description of the grotesque landscapes in Elizaveta's bedroom further reveal the master's insensitivity to ugliness and his cupidity in refusing to do over any of the room.

As the chronicle progresses, we go on excursions, visit neighbors, attend an at-home party for the newlyweds. A picture of Moscow life is interpolated by means of a long letter from sister Sofia to Katerina about a ball and other gentry diversions, and this picture is further developed at the end of the first volume when Sofia returns to Moscow to spend the winter with her Godmother, the wise and content spinster, Sviyazhka.

Begichev has a good facility for sketching out characters, and this stands him in good stead in a novel with so many figures. One particularly good example, at least in so far as the introduction of this character is concerned, is Countess Khlestova, who is determined to ruin the marriage of her brother, Prince Ramirsky:

> Countess Khlestova belonged to the *class* of malignant women, in the full power and extent of that word. She had already indomitably struggled more than fifty years in this area, and public opinion had decided that it would be impossible to find anywhere such a dissolute hypocrite, malignant gossip, and lover of slander and quarrels.
>
> In her youth she had been a beauty. Count Khlestov, a rich and well-known man, fell in love with her, offered his hand, and paid for his rashness all the rest of his life. His dissolute wife had no lack of lovers from the time of her youth. When she became older and her beauty faded, then it required large monetary offerings for her to hire adorers. She damaged her position and was shameless to the point that she didn't even hide her disgraceful behavior. At the same time she sought out every means to spite her husband both for the slightest trifles and for the most important matters, that is the marriage of their daughters. He had only to want something to meet the most stubborn resistance from his wife. Besides, not feeling any attachment to her husband, she constantly tortured him with jealousy, invented the most unlikely gossip, and complained to everyone, even trying to turn the children against him.

Needless to say, the husband is soon hen-pecked to death and the Countess left entirely free to do as she wishes. At the end of Book One she is desperately trying to ruin Sofia Kholmskaia's happiness.

The genre of family chronicle prospered in Russian literature, especially during the period of Realism, and one must credit Begichev with "having shown the way" to such recognized, though little read, authors as Sergey Aksakov, with his *Family Chronicle* and *Years of Childhood of Bagrov-Grandson.*

The year 1833 was marked by the appearance of Nikolay Polevoy's *The Artist [Zhivopisets]* , a work which was immediately imitated and which may be credited with establishing the formula for the typical *Kuenstlernovelle,* with its unrecognized hero, his unhappy love affair, his conflict with society, and his confession. Polevoi's story introduces us to Arkady, the son of a petty official, who has escaped a clerk's fate owing to the fortuitous recognition of his artistic potential by a patron. Arkady's talent gains him a toe-hold in society, but its indifference to anything artistic eventually arouses his hatred. Meanwhile, he has fallen in love with Verinka, but the girl's father sensibly plans to marry her to a more promising candidate. The deceived artist seeks revenge on canvas:

206

Now I will terrify them [society] with my brush. Now I will paint for them my enraged Prometheus. It will depict my soul, chained not to the Caucasus but to this ungrateful, unfeeling world. Oh God, they will not be human if they do not see the trace of my blood and my tears in the colors with which I will represent my Prometheus to them, if after this they do not return my Verinka to me.

But Verinka's wedding takes place, Arkady goes to Italy and dies, having first painted a picture of Christ, which symbolizes his resignation. For Verinka the thoughts of Arkady are soon displaced by her comfortable life as a rich lady.

Polevoy was back in 1834 with *Abbaddonna* [sic], a novel in four volumes which is basically an artist's story, but much longer than most and involves elements of the physiological sketch and the novel of manners. The element of satirical humor is particularly strong, but the reader's occasional amusement is poor recompense for the drudgery of reading this work.

The setting is a German principality in the early nineteenth century, and the story opens with the impoverished poet, Wilhelm Reichenbach, seeking to have his tragedy, *The Arminians*, staged by the royal theatre. Through the intercession of Elenora, an actress of bad reputation but good connections, the play is accepted. Meanwhile, Wilhelm has become engaged to Henrietta Schultz, the only daughter of a widowed bourgeoise. The play is an enormous success, and Wilhelm is swept off to Elenora's after-theatre party, which becomes a bacchanal. The poet discovers her in a secluded pavilion, *it* happens, and they declare their love. Elenora is prepared to fake her death and follow the poet, but he leaves town when news arrives of his mother's illness. Elenora suspects that Henrietta may still have some hold on Wilhelm's affections and schemes to have her married off while he is away. Then she goes to Wilhelm in the country and is just about to carry him away with her when he is saved by his mother's reading of Klopstock's *Messiah*: Abdiel saves the fallen angel Abaddon but perishes for his effort.[2]

It is easy to fault this novel, which is very long, owing to unconscionable digressiveness, and extremely tedious, since the characters are quite unattractive, with the possible exception of Eleanora. Once Wilhelm has left his garret, he loses his morals and we lose our concern for him. By rights he should be the victim, the artist misunderstood by the crowd, unhappy in love, but he does find acceptance and he is loved. Of course, we may view him as a victim of sorts, the unsuspecting thrall of the goose-like Frau Schultz, the epitome of bourgeois calculation and pretension, who sees Wilhelm as a potential son-in-law only after he has become recognized. But still, his rejection of the exciting Elenora for the virtuous and vapid Henrietta, with whom he will presumably live happily ever after in philistine *Gemütlichkeit,* makes him a poor candidate for our sympathies.

The novel has some redeeming features. Polevoy can be an amusing satirist, and his gibes at society are not limited to the *haut monde* alone:

the shortcomings of the bourgeoisie are also his target, and self-styled men of letters also get their comeuppance. In one digressive scene he presents a quite amusing vignette of an editor of encyclopedias of facts and figures, who proves mathematically to an astonished Reichenbach that Homer never existed. Reichenbach is then visited by a journalist and a publisher of almanacs, both of whom want a contribution. Scandalized by their cynicism and the stupidity of the compiler of encyclopedias (who has just left), Reichenbach threatens to cease writing.

"Stop, then," said Schpeier, "only before you do give me a tiny excerpt from your *Arminians* for my next edition.

"Ah, Mr. Schpeier! I'm so dissatisfied with it that I don't know what to select."

"Whatever you want to, dear poet! Don't worry. People will read it in the newspaper and forget it before you publish the complete version. When you do, rewrite it as much as you like."

"But I should like to give you something good as a sample. . . ."

"You'd better prepare it for my almanac, Mr. Reichenbach," said Weisse. "In two weeks I'm definitely starting to print it."

"Do you have so much material?"

"Lots and even more! There will be a portrait of Baron Kalkopf—that damn Steffens wants a lot for it, but there's no way out—an engraved title page. . . . the names of Hoffmann, Goethe, Schiller, Jean-Paul. . . ."

"Certainly not works that are unknown?"

"Yes, and until now never before published. A note from Goethe to Schiller when he sent him a cheese, five lines; Schiller's list of travelling underwear which he took on a trip from Jena to Weimar in 1798, Hoffmann's list of five bottles of wine drunk by him at a winecellar—a great joke, six verses; I myself paid two thalers for it? An extract of Jean-Paul's from the Augsburg's Newspaper, with a note. . . ."

"What kind of note?"

"He added at the end, 'What stupidity!' And then in his hand is written: 'A test of the pen,' and also, 'A fool, a simpleton.' It's evident that he was testing his pen. I'm adding a facsimile of this slip of paper."

"And that will be your almanac, Mr. Weisse?"

"Yes; But there's still room for verses and prose, isn't there? Give me something, dear poet, your collaboration is vital. Certainly you have a goodly supply of all sorts of things, I'm thinking. . . ."

An interesting feature of *Abbaddonna* is its connection with the physiological sketch in the style of Etiènne Jouy. The apartment where Henrietta lives is analysed floor by floor, with a depiction of the poverty residing in the basement and garret, with varying degrees of luxury in between. Wilhelm's attic is described in detail as well, but here Polevoy is also concerned with the room as an extension of the personality of its inhabitant:

Such were the cramped quarters of the stranger, who, late at night, in autumn, was sitting at a writing table in his room under the clouds. Wishing to acquaint our readers with him, we have made a detailed topographical description of his quarters. Now can you guess who this stranger was according to the saying. "Tell me how you live, and I will tell who you are?" But for a solution by this means our description of the stranger's quarters is not sufficient. It is necessary to complete it with several separate features.

The overt narrator-personality evident in this passage is a common feature of the exposition,

I want to describe to you the director's study, and to talk with you a bit in general about the physiognomy of studies, to tell you how one must abstract the character of a person from the character of his study.

Polevoy's range of styles is broad, at times reaching the heights of Marlinsky in his moments of grandiloquence, at times being simply reportorial. However, when he concerns himself with the depiction of Wilhelm's psychological condition, he adopts a method of metaphorical generalization which is extremely tedious. The interrogative form of the following passage is also typical:

Did not Wilhelm complain, did he not grieve, feeling the soullessness of his life, the banality of all sensations of social custom? Did he not call for a love and forgetfulness in a furious and mad love? But when a woman approached him with such a love, when the fire of the heart threatened to burn the poor hut of his social relationships to ashes, the entire petty economy of his life—then he became melancholy, he anguished unwillingly; his heart was oppressed with some foreboding of misfortune and unhappiness. He looked just like a man in whose soul some terrible fatal secret is hidden—and his glance became gloomy and dark, like the glance of a person engaged in some desperate undertaking which is to decide his entire life. . . .

The last chapter of the fourth volume is Wilhelm's autobiography-confession, a rambling account of his youth, his father's attitudes toward him, which range from indulgent to angry or indignant:

I was the youngest of four brothers and sisters. I was born weak, tender, and therefore became my mother's favorite from the cradle. My father, strict with the other children, considered me a weak, sick child, and spoiled me more than the others with his indulgence.

The father suffers business reverses, and Wilhelm is sent to an uncle to be raised, and there he learns, among other things, French, Italian, and English. When he returns home, his father is furious that he has no practical education.

"I shall remake you, Mr. Poet." The next day I was sent to the common school. This injured me more than any scolding. "Understand, stupid, that the guild of poets was destroyed long ago, so start studying to be whatever else you like, but not a poet!" my father said to me.

The father falls ill and Wilhelm leaves school to help him.

Good, intelligent, loving, he soon became convinced of this [Wilhelm's desire to satisfy him], he opened to me his entire life. I learned of the majesty of his mind and soul, of his high virtue. He even made peace with my poetry, he was a friend and not my father.

But Daddy has his bad moments too:

After some time the smallest irritation brought down his anger upon me, and he began to
scold me, to reproach me with the name of poet, and once, in an hour of anger, he threw
into the fire a pile of papers and some books which my uncle and Beatrice [Wilhelm's
first love] had given me.

And at last: "My father died. With tears he embraced and blessed me at that
very minute when everything was finished for him."

The arbitrariness of all this, not to mention the tediousness of the detail
and the undramatic narrative manner, remind one of Nikitenko. Only readers
with exceptional fortitude should consider attempting a personal acquaintance with Polevoy's grotesque creation.

Whether or not in emulation of Polevoy, the year *Abbaddonna* appeared
also saw the publication of another tale, *The Artist [Khudozhnik]*,[3] by
A. V. Timofeev (1812-1883). Timofeev does Polevoy one better, however, by
choosing a serf as his protagonist, all the better to exploit the theme of social
discrimination and to weight the scales even more heavily against the artist.

Signed simply "T.m.f.a.," the work is in three parts, and mercifully is
rather shorter than *Abbaddonna*. Still it shares with that work the undramatic
manner of narration, digressiveness, prolixity, and an indifference to logical
psychological motivation. The form is a first person *apologia* typical of the
"psychological novel." The story ends abruptly after having followed the protagonist's life from early youth to some time in his twenties:

Here the diary ends completely.
What became of its owner is unknown. Several of those who knew him say that
he is now in Italy; others say that he has already died, yet others that he lingers in
a madhouse.

In view of the unpredictability of the artist's behavior throughout the
three volumes of this work, the final possibility seems the most likely. Our
painter, who has no name until two-thirds of the way through the third
volume (he is named Ivan), is the illegitimate son of an estate owner and a
peasant girl, and his earliest memories are of his desperate loneliness: it is
as if he were a complete orphan, abandoned to fate, prey to starvation, privation, and human malice. His first friend is a hunting dog, which licks his
face, but then joins the pursuing pack when the huntsman sends the hounds
after the fleeing youth. Finally his father takes him into his house and makes
him his private servant, at the same time permitting him to be educated along
with his son and daughter, Mariya. The boy falls in love with the girl, not
realizing at that time that she is his half-sister. The waif's artistic ability is
noticed, and he is sent to study drawing in a provincial town. The retired
academic who is his mentor, not to mention his first real friend and benefactor, maintains Ivan at his own expense. Then occur some of those quite

puzzling examples of behavior which are typical of the story:

> Meanwhile, I had turned seventeen. Until this point I had lived entirely spiritually. . . . But nature finally had her way, the blood began to boil, passions flared up, and I, not being able to control myself, flew headlong into the abyss. At first my benefactor noticed nothing. Notwithstanding my youth, I was sufficiently circumspect so that for a time I was able to hide from him the change taking place within me. But my disorderly activities, the changed color of my face, the desire to avoid his presence, my acquaintance with people notorious for their immorality—these told him all—I heard nothing. He began to give me advice—the advice flew into thin air. He began to threaten me—I laughed at his threats. He began to plead with me, I saw his tears and—remorse gnawed at my heart. Still I did not reform. The false charm of debauchery drew me further and further. My pranks were related in all the servants' quarters, at each crossroads. On meeting me old ladies crossed themselves and ran off, maidens blushed at mention of my name. Scamps could not admire my daring deeds enough. I was feared, I was criticized, I was cursed—and I laughed at this.
>
> Finally my eyes were opened, the tinsel flew off, and I saw myself in all my nakedness—and I averted my eyes. Debauchery appeared before me in all its monstrous ugliness. . . . I controlled myself, remorse stung my soul. A fearful awakening!

Adolescence may explain the boiling of the blood, but brazen debauchery, the mockery of his benefactor, and finally, in view of his commitment to depravity, his very reform—all these are arbitrary. Meanwhile, the poor reader who has trudged down life's road in company with this dull companion is not even treated to a glimpse of his scandalous behavior.

At the age of twenty, Ivan's master-father dies, and he is called back to the estate, a summons which revitalizes his love for Mariya. He arrives on the night of her betrothal party, and determines to assassinate the bridegroom. However, his pistol misfires, and in fleeing the place of ambush he falls and seriously injures his head, which may explain some of his later problems and attitudes. His misery is further increased when his half-brother, who is now his master, subjects him to corporal punishment when he refuses to paint a portrait. He runs away, ultimately his freedom is purchased, and he ends up in Petersburg, where he starves for several years. Although his paintings attract attention—he does large canvasses, such as Prometheus being attacked by eagles—he acquires no reputation. Meanwhile he has befriended a beggar-woman, a drunkard and thief who wallows in her degradations. One day he encounters Mariya, who does not recognize him (!), and she introduces him to her husband and to her circle of friends. A few commissions improve his material situation, but essentially he remains unrecognized. Then he finds that his love for Mariya is more than platonic, and he eloquently expands on this theme in his diary:

> No, no, this still isn't right! I didn't seek a friend of this sort! What is there for me in this dry, vapid partnership, in this half love, half affectation! Give me life, fire, passions!. . . Fire, which would burn me, in which I would freeze, drown, be annihilated. . . . What is there for me in this consumptive, impotent love, which lacks the strength to

211

take a step by itself! What is there for me in this sugary tenderness, weighed on the scales of reason!. . . People, people! must your very dreams carry the stamp of cold calculation? If this is unavoidable, if you can't live without poison, at least poison me with something sweet! Mariya, be lightning. . . or better be a demon than an ordinary woman. Damnation, if I ever grow cold in your embraces!

. . . .
        Forgiveness, forgiveness! I insulted you, divine woman! You are right! One more step and we have perished! Woe if in your embraces the *man* in me awakens. . . . Then flee from me, Mariya. . . . Flee as from a scorpion!. . . One second, and—we will have perished!

To add to his many problems, the old beggarwoman turns out to be his mother, and she coincidentally turns up from time to time to embarrass him. Somewhere around this time Mariya's husband offers to advance the artist the money to go to Italy, but, as the conclusion indicates, we never learn whether he went or not.

Regardless of his pathetic youth, childhood, his talent, and his harrassment by a hostile fate, the protagonist remains an unsympathetic character, if, indeed, one can imagine a human being of this sort. His autobiography is one long complaint against life and people, interspersed with rather inane digressions of a quasi-philosphical nature. The narrator is long-winded, dull, and wallows in his misery to such an extent that the reader becomes indifferent and, ultimately, repelled. Presumably, that was not the effect that Mr. Timofeev had in mind.

The reader will better understand that the work is "undramatic" when he learns that in the first volume there are less than fifty words of dialogue, and those are pronounced by a demonic figure who appears to the artist in a dream. What little action occurs is incessantly interrupted with digressions which generalize about the human condition, human nature, or the narrator's *Weltanschauung.* Thus he voices his [Timofeev's?] indifference to society:

The longer I live in society, the more indifferent I become to it. Previously I experienced something similar in my soul, perhaps more from egoism, more from offended self-esteem than for a well-grounded reason. Then I used to see society from the window of my atelier, from a side view as on a stage, and it became unnoticed, it bored me and repelled me. Now I have left that lonely place, thrown myself into this society, looked behind the curtains, and played a role myself, and—without the slightest egoism I admit that society isn't worth being concerned about. With all its inflated qualities, it is so monotonous despite its variety. Don't people know how to build better wheels for this machine!

Timofeev's penchant for protagonists with bizarre patterns of behavior is reflected also in another work of 1834, *A Poet's Loves [Liubvi poeta]* . Here the poet rejects his beloved Mariya, preferring to remain alone and suffer rather than experience the inevitable disenchantment of married life. This withdrawal from the real world to the world of the "pure, sacred poetry of love" anticipates the withdrawal to a life of fantasy found in Odoevsky's

The Sylph [Sil'fida].

Timofeev's career continued unspectacularly through the thirties, and *The Library for Reading* published his society tales *Life and Death [Zhizn' i smert']* in 1834 and *The Last Day [Poslednii den']* the following year. In 1836 he co-authored with Osip Senkovsky a work entitled *Julio [Dzhulio]*.

Nikolay Grech

Osip Senkovsky

XVIII. The Picaresque-Supernatural Novel—Grech. Senkovsky and the Journal *The Library for Reading.*

A hundred years before the advent of the soap opera on American radio, Nikolay Grech (1787-1867) published the original tale of endless tribulation, machination, devastation, and resignation, *The Woman in Black [Chernaia zhenshchina]* (1834).

Today we remember Grech as one of that notorious triumvirate of monopolist publishers, including Faddey Bulgarin and Osip Senkovsky, who had such a powerful grip upon the Petersburg literary market. From 1812 to 1839 Grech was editor-publisher of *Son of the Fatherland*, which he shared with Faddey Bulgarin after 1825. These two also collaborated for almost thirty years in publishing *The Northern Bee*, a newspaper which enjoyed official approval. He was, moreover, a literary critic of some importance and the author of several grammars of the Russian language.

The Woman in Black was apparently a considerable success, probably because its combination of picaresque adventure, the supernatural, and social satire provided something for everyone. There is no possible way to convey the complexity of this story. The action ranges from Moscow to the Caucasus, Lombardy, Nice, Paris, Holland, Revel, and Petersburg. Events are not presented chronologically but in bits and pieces, with the adventures of the central figure continually set aside in favor of lengthy biographies of secondary characters. There is even an entire "psychological tale" interpolated into the work. The affairs of some of the characters reach back to the time of Peter the Great, stretching the temporal frame of the novel to almost a century.

The central figure is Prince Kemsky, a bastion of moral rectitude, whose fortune is coveted by his half-sister, Alevtina. Owing to her scheming, he has to take messages to General Suvorov in Italy, leaving behind his pregnant wife, and when the report of his demise proves to be false, the perfidious Alevtina does not tell Natasha that her husband is still alive. Natasha bravely gives birth to a daughter, which Alevtina has taken to an orphanage, telling the mother that the infant died shortly after birth. The distraught Natasha flees the house, and, when her cap is found along one of the Petersburg canals, it is presumed that she drowned herself. The news of the double tragedy is sent to Kemsky, who mourns his loss. Many years pass, Kemsky returns home to find that Alevtina and her three children, assisted by her second husband, Von Drach, have pillaged his estate and swindled him of his assets. Through a series of coincidences, each more extraordinary than the other, Kemsky discovers that his daughter is alive, that her beloved is the young officer, Vetlin, whom Kemsky had befriended, and in the final chapters, who should appear but the long lost Natasha. Convinced that her husband and child were dead, she had taken refuge all those years in a convent. The title refers to a woman clad in black whom the five-year-old Kemsky first saw in Moscow during the plague, when she threw herself from a balcony upon the body of her dead child. She later turns up as an unearthly vision which saves him during the Pugachev Uprising, and afterwards appears opportunely at critical moments in his life. As the years pass he more and more strongly identifies the woman in black with Natasha, his late wife. And, of course, when Natasha leaves the convent for Moscow, she goes to the same apartment from which the woman in black had jumped half a century before, an apartment just opposite the house where Kemsky and his daughter are staying.

> What was wrong with the prince? At that moment when Nadezhda, with the impulsiveness of youth, had touched the tenderest string of his heart, he looked out the window at the street. Something known, seen long ago, awoke in his soul. He began to look more closely, and he saw that he was in the former quarters of his parents, that he was sitting at the window, which with his childish curiosity he had opened during the terrible time of the plague, that opposite this window was the house with the balcony from which the woman in black had thrown herself upon the dead body. He stood up engrossed in thought, went onto the street, and approached the house with the balcony and looked up. Only the balcony, which in his childhood had seemed so high, now seemed quite low. The balustrade had been removed. . . .
> Suddenly the doors to the balcony opened. In them appeared a woman in a black dress, she looked at Kemsky, and threw herself at him with a loud cry.
> He seized her, looked at her face.
> In his embrace lay Natasha!

Such melodramatic scenes are common in this tale, which combines the most improbable adventures and coincidences with sententious disquisitions on virute, evil, and other abstractions.

The vicissitudes of the life of Kemsky's and Natasha's daughter are illustrative of the complexity of Grech's plot. At Nadezhda's birth, Alevtina forces a maid to take the infant to an orphanage, but the nurse, conscience-stricken at the sight of the pitiful orphans at the institution, places the baby in a basket sitting in an unoccupied cart. The basket's owner is an artist, Berilov, himself an orphan, who then raises Nadezhda to the age of five, at which point he permits her to be taken away by a wealthy lady, who can provide a good education and environment. The wealthy lady is afraid that the artist will reclaim his "daughter," and so she takes her to Estonia, ultimately sending Berilov a letter telling him that Nadezhda has died. Nadezhda herself believes that she is an orphan. Meanwhile, Kemsky has befriended Berilov, who gives him a painting of a beautiful young lady resembling the prince's wife, a portrait completed by the artist when he learned of his foundling's death in Estonia. Simultaneously, Vetlin, an officer that Kemsky had raised as an orphan, sees Nadezhda in Revel and falls madly in love with her, but his bad reputation as a brawler makes further contact impossible. Love initiates his reform, and, when Vetlin comes to Petersburg and visits Kemsky, he is astounded to see Nadezhda's portrait there. The errant Berilov soon returns and dies in Kemsky's arms. His effects show that he was in fact Kemsky's brother, lost during the Pugachev Uprising. Kemsky, who had learned from his sister's servant that his daughter had been left in an artist's basket, now knows that Nadezhda is his missing child. They are reunited, and in the final chapter we learn that she wed Vetlin.

All of these orphans, missing parents, and cases of mistaken identity, not to mention the interpolated biographies and confused chronology, remind one of Narezhny. However, the somewhat tedious involvements of *Bursak* or *The Two Ivans* are redeemed by the robust crudity of Narezhny's art, which, if not fancy, is at least lively. The same cannot be said of Grech's novel, which is simply dull, lifeless, and filled with cliches. This is even true of the dramatic scenes, such as the description by Kemsky's friend, Doctor Alimari, of the Lisbon earthquake:

"The 1st of November, 1755," Alimari continued, "I was the happiest man in the world. But some sort of tormenting agitation, a sort of foreboding of misfortune, agitated my breast. The air that day was unusually heavy. Thick clouds scudded over Lisbon. With their harsh croaking, ominous birds forecast a terrible storm. I went to bed in expectation of some unknown disaster. Terrible dreams soon aroused me. Awakening, I saw Antigone [his wife]. She was kneeling before the crucifix and, bathed in tears, was praying fervently.

'What is the matter, my friend,' I asked agitatedly.

'I am afraid!' she said, 'I want to fortify and calm myself with prayer!'

I was about to answer her, but suddenly a terrible rumble and crash on the street shocked and frightened me. 'What is that?' cried Antigone trembling, and flew to the sleeping children. I threw on my coat and hastened to leave the house. On the street, which was filled with frightened people, wails of terror and despair resounded. The earth rocked under my feet, the walls of huge buildings fell like houses of cards and crushed the people under them. The night was dark. Thunder in the heavens echoed the underground rumble. Each second lightning illuminated the picture of devastation. Having gone several steps along the street, I turned back towards my house, in numbed immobility, not knowing myself where I was and what was happening to me. Suddenly the lightning flashed: Antigone stood at the window holding the children in her arms. Catching sight of me, she cried out, 'Goodbye forever!' More lightning, and I saw my home disintegrate into the abyss."

Characterization in such a work is obviously at the service of the plot, and all of the figures in the novel are quite conventional. Nowhere is this truer than in the depiction of Alevtina's nasty children, who are even more callous in their quest for Kemsky's property than their mother. The oldest son, Plato, plots to have Kemsky declared insane, and when his plot is foiled, he salvages his fortune by marrying a merchant's daughter who has a dowry of 300,000 rubles and two houses. His pretentious sister, Kitty, affects English manners and publicly rebukes her mother for mispronouncing the name of her English bull, who is called "Sir." Needless to say these children are openly rude to Kemsky.

In the end, despite the moralizing which permeates this novel, the vicious Alevtina and her devil's brood are only forced to make restitution to the fleeced Kemsky, but they are free to continue their slander and calumny. The fiscal sanctions seem hardly sufficient punishment for the types of crimes they accomplished and contemplated.

Grech returned to literature in 1836 with a novel in letters entitled *A Trip to Germany [Poezdka v Germaniiu]*, a work which mercifully signalled the end of his efforts at major fiction.

Critical antipathy toward Osip Senkovsky (1800-1858) is owing in part to this association with Nikolai Grech and Faddey Bulgarin. In 1929 the Soviet critic V. Kaverin attempted to modify Senkovsky's image in his study *Baron Brambeus*, the title from Senkovsky's pseudonym.[1]

At the age of nineteen Senkovsky left the University of Wilno for the Near East to study its languages, history, and culture, and so successful were his efforts that the University of St. Petersburg appointed him full professor of Arabic and Turkish at the age of twenty-two. But his personality was a difficult one, and he was not successful as a professor. In 1834 there was immediate controversy when he became editor of the first "thick" [*tolstyi*] journal, *The Library for Reading [Biblioteka dlia chteniia]*, a monthly published by the book dealer, Smirdin. Many objected to a Pole receiving 15,000 rubles annually to edit a Russian periodical, others claimed that Senkovsky had played a role in fomenting the Polish Uprising of 1830-1831, and still others were irritated by his cavalier treatment of their manuscripts, which he altered without so much as by your leave. Before long some of the best writers of the period were boycotting *The Library for Reading*. Nonetheless, this journal played a dominant role in periodical publication, even after Pushkin began his quarterly, *The Contemporary [Sovremennik]*, in 1836.

Senkovsky first introduced himself to his Russian audience with translations of Eastern tales from Arabic, Tatar, and Persian, five of these appearing in *The Polar Star*. His popularity, however, was achieved under the pseudonym Baron Brambeus, his *porte parole* who wittingly and tellingly exposed the excesses of Romantic Literature. Senkovsky's antagonism, deriving from his classical education at the University of Wilno, was particularly strong in the case of German idealistic philosophy, Young France or *l'Ecole frénétique*, and its Russian imitators. His antipathy also extended to the historical novel, which he considered a bastard genre. In his monograph on Senkovsky, Louis Pedrotti has excerpted a number of the more violent declarations of Baron Brambeus in this regard:

> . . . There is no literary genre. . . more ridiculous, more false, more monstrous, more repugnant to art, to the beautiful and, consequently, to morality, than the modern novel. . . . It is a sewer of household gossip! What do men do in it? They eat, drink, stroll, play cards, look at furniture, quarrel without courage over trifles, fight duels without valor over nothing at all. What do the heroes do? The same as other men, ex-

cept that in addition these. . . nonentities cast terrible, fiery glances at each other, engage in love affairs senselessly and irresponsibly, become enflamed, kiss, sigh, weep, fall sometimes into fits of incandescent ecstasy and sometimes into fits of wild despair, perpetrate all possible kinds of stupidities and, finally, hurl themselves ingloriously into marriage or into the grave. This is imagination! This is what is called beautiful!. . .

Senkovsky parodied the cliches of Romantic fiction, and one must accede that he was an effective satirist. *The Entire Life of a Woman in Several Hours [Vsia zhizn' zhenshchiny v neskol'kikh chasakh]*, which appeared in 1833, recounts how Olinka, a naive young lady fresh from an institute, falls fatally in love with the blasé Count Alexander Sergeevich P_____ [a dig at Pushkin's Onegin], and, when he doesn't fulfill her anticipations, dies.[2]

Senkovsky's persistent carping against the immoral, the exaggerated, the indecent, and the gross in fiction at least had the virtue of irritating the opposition to the point of frenzy, and he was even accused of plagiarism by those insensitive to his parody. It must be said that there was considerable truth in his attacks against Romantic excesses, but, unfortunately, he was himself not destined to lead Romantic fiction out of the wilderness.

I. I. Panaev

Alexander Veltman

XIX. The Society Tale and Its Parodists—Pushkin, Panaev, Shibaev, Odoevsky, Veltman, and Senkovsky.

Pushkin's *The Queen of Spades [Pikovaia dama]* is one of world literature's most celebrated stories. It was Pushkin's last completed piece of short fiction, one of the fruits of the author's stay at the family estate of Boldino in the fall of 1833.

The history of the interpretation of the work is a good example of how people tend to see in a story what they wish to see and ignore the rest. When it first appeared in 1834 in *The Library for Reading*, the Romantic tradition of the supernatural tale was still alive, and so, understandably, many contemporaries saw the work in the context of that genre. And this misinterpretation exists even today, notwithstanding all the evidence within the text to the contrary. *The Queen of Spades* is not in the tradition of the supernatural tale, but in Pushkin's tradition of psychological analysis and irony.

From the facetious epigraph on gambling, which prefaces the first of the six chapters, to the epilogue, which sums up the fates of the main characters, *The Queen of Spades* is permeated with irony. On a literary level Pushkin is playing with the conventions and cliches of both the supernatural tale and the society tale.

The "hero," Hermann, is a Russified German, a colorless young officer committed to prudent behavior. But the cautious young man becomes obsessed with the idea that he can make his fortune by gambling if only he learns a certain winning sequence of three cards, a secret known only to an ancient Countess. The scheming Hermann feigns love for the Countess's ward, Lizaveta, to gain entrance to the old lady's mansion, but when he confronts her and pleads for the secret she tells him that the secret was a joke. He draws a pistol, at the sight of which the Countess expires. Our blundering Romantic hero becomes beset by superstitious fears of his victim, and, when he goes to her funeral to pay his last respects and beg forgiveness, it seems to him that the corpse winks. Later that night, after much wine, he is visited by the Countess's ghost, which conveys the secret and extracts his promise to marry Lizaveta in return for forgiveness. Armed with the winning sequence of three, seven, and ace, Hermann appears at the salon of the celebrated gambler Chekalinsky, where he stakes his nest-egg of forty-seven thousand on the three and wins. He doubles his stake the second night and again is successful. By the third night he is a celebrity, and a crowd is present to watch the contest. Somehow the ace which Hermann chooses turns out to be the queen of spades, so he loses. Dumbfounded, he sees the figure of the queen sneering at him, and in her features he recognizes the Countess. He goes mad.

Pushkin's variations on the theme of the psychological imposter finds its most developed prose treatment here (I say "prose variation," because it might be argued that Eugene Onegin or Boris Godunov, who are verse and dramatic embodiments of the type. are more defined). Indeed, it would be difficult to find in Russian fiction any predecessor of Hermann who was more psychologically complex unless it be Pushkin's own Sylvio.

The creation of Hermann reveals a conscious effort on the part of the author to provide a "mentality" for his character, not simply an exterior portrait animated by an arbitrary cluster of motivations. Hermann's initial prudence and self-control are not simply stereotypical features associated with the Russified German, for they are intimately bound up with his ego, his superiority complex, which itself is carefully masked by his typical caution.

When he first hears the story of the three winning cards, which is related by the Countess's grandson, Tomsky, he dismisses it as a fairy tale, but not for long:

> He had strong passions and a fiery imagination, but firmness had saved him from the usual mistakes of youth. So, for example, being a gambler in his soul, he never took cards in his hand, for he calculated that his wealth did not permit him (so he used to say) *to sacrifice what was necessary in hopes of winning the superfluous.* [Pushkin's italics.]

But the secret begins to obsess him, and he becomes convinced that he must acquire it, even if he has to become the old Countess's lover. The grotesqueness of this idea, since she is almost ninety, is an early indication of the expansiveness of Hermann's mind. However, prudence, his strong suit up to that point, wins out, and he resolves that "calculation, restraint, and industriousness, those are my three reliable cards, that is what will triple, make sevenfold my capital and acquire peace and independence for me." But the spark is in the powder keg, and when he finds himself inexplicably wandering in front of the Countess's house, he explodes into action.

Hermann's icy egotism makes it easy to use the susceptible Lizaveta, for to him she is just a thing, a part of the staircase leading to the Countess and her secret. The real depth of his venality and egregious egotism comes out in his confrontation with the old woman, when he insists that he alone is worthy of the wealth which the cards will insure:

> "For whom are you guarding your secret? For your grandchildren? They're rich enough as it is. They don't know the value of money. Your three cards won't help a wastrel. He who does not know how to preserve his patrimony, despite whatever demonic forces, will nonetheless die in poverty. I am not a wastrel, I know the value of money. Your three cards will not be wasted on me."

The statement about the preservation of patrimony reinforces the earlier formulaic and pedantic assertion about his not being in a position to sacrifice the necessary for the superfluous, and both assertions, not to mention his actions themselves, reveal a personality directed totally inward. But Hermann has another dimension as well—his superstition, the natural surrogate for his lack of religion or ethics.

Hermann's real problem—and here Pushkin has definitely gone beyond the typical features of Romantic characterization—is that he is essentially a weak personality and is himself unaware of this fact. The first indication of this occurs when he displays unexpected agitation while waiting in hiding for the Countess to return. Then he loses his self-control and frightens her to death. Subsequently, he is unable to bear the guilt for her murder:

> Though he felt no repentance, he nevertheless could not completely still the voice of conscience that kept repeating to him, "You are the murderer of the old woman!" Having but little real faith, he was hagridden by a host of superstitions.

When he attends the funeral, he hallucinates, thinking the corpse winks at him. Then he, "contrary to his habit, drank too much in hopes of silencing his internal agitation. But the wine even further agitated his imagination." This wine, of course, is the catalyst for his dream of the ghostly visitation by the Countess, a dream in which he is told that his guilt is to be expiated if he marries Lizaveta.

The dream itself is interesting. Pushkin often incorporated dreams into his work, the best known probably being the symbolic and/or Freudian dream of Tatiana in *Eugene Onegin*. In *The Queen of Spades* the dream is "realistic," since the naive reader must not be disabused of the idea that Hermann is really being visited by a ghost. However, the whole "visitation" is a product of his intoxication, superstition, and anxiety.

The content of the dream is thoroughly motivated. The spectre begins with a preamble stating that its appearance is against its will, a fact which Hermann must realize in view of his relationship with the late Countess. The sequence of the winning three cards which she reveals has already been partly established, since Hermann previously had mentioned "calculation, restraint, and industriousness" as the three cards which would *triple* and *make sevenfold* his capital. The ace as the third card is the natural choice of a person suffering from delusions of grandeur: would the great Hermann cap his triumph with a lowly ten or knave? No, the two magical cards, three and seven, are crowned by the ace, with which Hermann identifies personally— in Russian the word ace [tuz] refers to a person of particular importance and prestige. Finally, forgiveness is promised if he will marry Lizaveta, a dream admonition developing from his unconscious guilt at having treated Lizaveta in a base and cruel manner.

Lizaveta Ivanovna, the poor bedeviled ward of the captious old Countess, is Hermann's willing dupe. Again, like many of Pushkin's characters, and in particular Tatiana, Lizaveta's secret emotional life is a product of her

223

reading. She is waiting for a savior, a Prince Charming, and Hermann, who has the profile of Napoleon, is quite suitable for this role. Pushkin motivates her acquiescence to Hermann's "courtship" by detailing the misery and frustration which she faces as the "poor relative," the dependent of the petulant and childishly selfish Countess. This theme of "Bitter is another's bread" had already been sketched in Pushkin's earlier *A Novel in Letters*.

At the ball which precedes Lizaveta's hoped-for tryst with Hermann, her imagination is further excited when Tomsky, quite by accident, begins to tease her about a secret admirer:

> "This Hermann," Tomsky continued, "is truly a figure from a novel: he has the profile of Napoleon and the soul of Mephistopheles. I think he has at least three crimes on his conscience."

Lizaveta turns pale, but, as the narrator pointedly informs us,

> Tomsky's words were nothing but mazurka chitchat, but they deeply penetrated the soul of the young dreamer. The portrait sketched by Tomsky corresponded with the image which she herself had composed and, thanks to the latest novels, this already banal character frightened and captivated her imagination.

There are, of course, all kinds of ironies here. The rather pedestrian Hermann, who even copies his love letters from a German novel, accidentally acquires the intriguing aura of a novelistic hero—and then he does become responsible for a death. For her part, Lizaveta, in arranging Hermann's access to the Countess's chamber, becomes an accessory to the murder of her benefactress, but this accidental murder in fact frees her from virtual slavery as a ward. Thus, the bogus Prince Charming does bring about the release of Cinderella from her thraldom.

The title is enigmatic until the dénouement, at which point its relevance is finally revealed. At the very moment of the climax, when he thinks his third card has beaten Chekalinsky's, Hermann cries out, "The ace has won," a statement which refers to his own personal victory as well as that of his card. But this is countered by Chekalinsky's "Your queen is beaten" [*Dama vasha ubita*], which can in a different context have another meaning, one to which Hermann is unquestionably sensitive: "Your lady has been murdered."

The epilogue, which follows immediately after this scene, relates how fate apportioned the spoils. Hermann became a muttering lunatic, but Lizaveta married "a very nice young man. He serves somewhere and is rather well off: he is the son of the old Countess's manager." In view of what earlier had been said about the "domestics outdoing one another in fleecing their moribund mistress," one more than suspects that the harried ward has now gained through marriage the financial independence she craved as a maiden. We ponder the further significance of the apparently gratuitous remark that she is raising a poor relative.

To see this story as an example of supernatural forces impinging upon the phenomenal world is to deprive it of its significance as a harbinger of the novel of psychological Realism. If the supernatural is "real," then Hermann is simply a victim of forces beyond his control, and the story, despite its interest even on this level, remains in no way innovative. But if we see the supernatural as a manifestation of Hermann's anxieties, his superstitions, and his megalomania, then we have a psychological study of a would-be superman who becomes his own victim. Dostoevsky understood this perfectly, and in creating *Crime and Punishment* he depended heavily upon themes and motifs of *The Queen of Spades*. Raskolnikov is a more detailed and complex mutation of Pushkin's basic type, the weak man who aspires to power and position. The quest for easy riches, the Napoleon complex, and the ultimate collapse of the mind which proves too "human" to bear extraordinary stress, all these are found in Dostoevsky's novel. In addition, we have the innocent victim named Lizaveta, the unanticipated murder, mockery by the deceased, and the destructiveness of haunting dreams and unconscious guilt. If Pushkin's Sylvio is a grandfather of Dostoevsky's Underground Man (whose father is Turgenev's Chulkaturin, the "hero" of *Diary of a Superfluous Man*), Hermann is Raskolnikov's direct parent.

Notwithstanding Pushkin's advancement of the short story in the direction of Realism with his emphasis upon psychologization and his subordination of theme and incident to this purpose, the tale remains within the canon of Romantic fiction. Essentially, it is a "told" story, with our concept of Hermann based on judgments provided by the narrator. Hermann, therefore, remains a theoretical psychological type, not one of those flesh and blood personalities which Realist authors, somewhat later, were able to project by exposing their reader to the protagonist through a series of revelatory scenes and letting him evaluate the character for himself—as happens in life.

Pushkin's restrained and unornamented prose is typical of *The Queen of Spades*, which opens with a let's-get-on-with-the-story paragraph. The scene is set and the dominant theme, gambling, initiated in just forty-six words (in Russian):

They were playing cards at the home of Narumov, of the Horse Guards. The long winter night went by without being noticed. It was going on five in the morning when they sat down to supper. Those who had won at the game ate with considerable appetite. The others sat in abstraction before their empty plates. But when champagne appeared, the conversation grew more lively and everyone took part.

When Prosper Mérimée translated this work into French, he noted he could do so virtually word for word, and he also commented that Pushkin's phrase was not only French in essence but French of the eighteenth century. Although we know that Pushkin did much to advance the art of literary prose, his particular style was too terse, too devoid of emotional content to serve as a completely adequate vehicle for literary expression. It is Lermontov, Pushkin's disciple, who is the real father of modern Russian literary prose.

I.I. Panaev (1812-1862) was one of the recognized "masters" of the society tale, and his work of 1834, *The Boudoir of a Fashionable Lady. An Episode from the Life of a Poet in Society [Spal'nia svetskoi zhenshchiny. Epizod iz zhizni poeta v obshchestve]*, combines satire of Petersburg society with social protest on behalf of a poet who is society's victim. Generally unremarkable, this story does appear to have had some effect upon Lermontov's unfinished society tale of 1836, *Princess Ligovskaya*, particular with its *in medias res* opening with a scene of a poor clerk narrowly escaping being crushed by speeding horses, its emphasis upon class distinctions, and the theme of social "advancement."

Victor Gromsky, a poet steeped in German idealistic literature, prevails upon his sometime friend, Count Versky, to introduce him to the enchanting Princess Lydia Granatskaya, whose rich husband, a military man, is conveniently in the Caucasus. She is intrigued by her sensitive new friend, who proposes to teach her Russian literature. Ultimately, she withdraws from society to her *dacha*, they declare their love, and so forth. Meanwhile, it appears that the obliging Versky had introduced Gromsky to Lydia as a gesture of mockery and that he intends to regain her affections. When Victor learns that she and Versky had previously been lovers, he shoots himself. The deceived poet recovers, but Lydia, whose husband returns to discover her infidelity, is condemned to a life of joyless penitence far from the capital.

Panaev's story is interrupted by frequent authorial intrusions, rhetorical exclamations, and direct address to the reader.

> Whoever has lived and been in Petersburg knows how its society is endlessly divided, knows how the transition from one level to another is impossible.
> . . . .
> Indeed, God preserve you from having faith in a man of society. For him there is nothing lofty. . . . He is not a villain. . . he is a lowly slave of custom, he is a pitiful navvy of fashion. . . nothing more!

The characters are flaccid and uninteresting. The hero is described as follows:

> His rather baggy attire gave him a strange, even, if you will, comical appearance, and his hat with its broad brim threw a heavy shadow upon his face. His gait was rapid, which was connected with his clumsiness and absence of concern for fashion. But if you could look at him at that moment when he, having raced to his modest apartment. . . oh, you truly would be struck by his noble and attractive features, despite the fact that they expressed some sort of unusual agitation and were tense with fatigue.

His lament to Versky about his poverty is hardly likely to stimulate our sympathies, and his wants are hardly those we would associate with someone nourished on German Romantic idealism:

"You know that *I am poor*! I have no name in society. . . Alexander! I cannot think about rich dinners, nor of famous patrons, nor of brilliant friends. . ."

Panaev alternately satirizes the periphrastic locutions of the early Romantics and mocks their cliches of metaphor, but at the same time he himself is guilty of such equally shopworn expressions as "The minute of love struck on the clock of her life," or "Their lips flowed together! It was necessary to cast out this moment from the book of their life. At this moment they did not exist!"

Panaev returned in 1836 with *She Will Be Happy [Ona budet schastliva]*, and the following year saw the appearance of his *Today and Tomorrow [Segodnia i zavtra]*, which shows no improvement over his earlier works. In this Kremnin, a young *parvenu* official, aspires to a place in society and the love of Princess Olga, the betrothed of Count Bolgarsky. When Kremnin hears the Count mock him before Olga, he challenges him and a duel takes place. The Count never returns. The scene shifts to a Volga River estate where Olga, slightly demented, identifies an oak tree in the yard with her betrothed. To the accompaniment of a raging storm, she falls ill, and as she dies the oak is uprooted! At her funeral an anonymous stranger clothed in black appears and prays at length. Olga is soon forgotten.

Here again society is chastized for its meanness, its elitism, its vacuity, and allied weaknesses, but Olga and the Count, though members of this clique, are themselves not attacked. In fact, their love is presented in purely Sentimental terms, and the idea of love beyond the grave reinforces the idealization of their relationship

The story suffers from want of a hero. The Count is grudgingly admired for his bearing, good looks, and passionate eyes, but withal the narrator identifies him as "a man of society, *a man of the drawing room*." The poet Kremnin is not even a sympathetic type, for his avid desire to find a place in society is patently foolish, and it is his false goals and plebian indignation which lead to the death of the Count.

For the next three years this author continued to produce society tales, including *Twilight at the Hearth [Sumerki u kamina]*, *The Daughter of a High Official [Doch chinovnogo cheloveka]*, and *Delirium Tremins [Belaia goriachka]*. After 1840 Panaev is more properly considered a representative of the Natural School, that transitional "movement" which bridges Romanticism and Realism.

It is difficult to work up any enthusiasm for Panaev, for he seems, notwithstanding his productivity, to have done very little to advance Romantic fiction, and his exposés of the *haut monde* are at best only of moderate interest. One has the definite feeling that Panaev was a sort of journeyman writer, a manipulator of formulaic situations and stock types, no worse than many of his contemporaries, but totally lacking in originality or elan.

Worse than mediocre, however, was Boris Shibaev's *Can This Be?* *[Mozhet li eto byt'?]*, which appeared in 1834 in *The Library for Reading.* The plot involves the dastardly schemes of a certain Margin to seduce Dolskaya, the virtuous wife of a dull and unloved husband. Up to the point of their nocturnal rendezvous in an arbor, a climax of sorts , there is not a bit of dialogue. Shibaev closes with Dolskaya's three letters to Margin, in which she explains that the spiritual quality of their love can no longer be maintained and therefore she is parting from him.

The story is pedantic from beginning to end: "Parents used to forget and will forget that a marriage vow without love is a preface to a dirty novel," and "Oh, how happy I am that I can throw these letters as a reproach to anyone who, having forgotten that he had a mother, denies the possiblity of virtue in a woman." Banal similies mark the exposition: "The list was longer than the face of an arrested lieutenant." Worse yet is the effort to show a facetious authorial face to his readers when discussing the mechanics of his tale:

Enjoying the advantage of narrators to penetrate all secrets and to unlock all locks without keys, I shall conduct you into the Margin's study, unlock his bureau, and take from a secret drawer three letters of Dolskaya-read them.

In describing his heroine, Shibaev again intrudes as author, one who provides, unwittingly of course, what might serve as a parody of petrified Romantic locutions:

I shall not, as is the habit of narrators, enumerate her charms and praise in turn her bloom and paleness, her shapely waist and silken locks, but in order to give some idea of her I will say that it is difficult to find a face which along with regular features would have such a kind expression of modesty and simplicity. Her blue eyes, covered with mist, reflected the tenderness of a beautiful soul. Particularly captivating was her voice. It had none of those rude and squeaking sounds which from envy, haughtiness, mendacity, and other unpleasant traits, insinuate themselves into one's way of speaking. This was a voice as pure as childish joy, attractive as flattery, as touching as a prayer, a voice able to lull the suspicion of a man who had been led by experience beyond all the delusions of the heart.

This example of Shibaev's style suffices to prove that even by the mid-thirties there were still authors whose facility with the prose literary language was hardly better than that of mediocre Sentimentalist writers. The surprising thing is that they were still being published, but, in the inimitable words of Shibaev's own axiom, "No one can tear his page from the book of fate."

While concerned with a genre undistinguished by really first rate works, it is pleasant to find a society tale which does have some merits. Although

V.F. Odoevsky's two efforts in this line are considered the least of his works, they nonetheless are better than many we have seen. The better of the two, *Princess Mimi [Kniazhna Mimi]* was published in 1834 in *The Library for Reading.*

One of the unusual features of this tale is the place of the preface, which the author introduces in the middle of his story at a moment of tension. His purpose, he says, is to make certain it not be ignored. The preface is dedicated to the theme of the difficulty of writing a novel of manners in Russian, which the author feels has been caused by the fact that Russian ladies don't speak Russian:

Listen, dear mesdames. I am not a student, not a school boy, nor an editor, neither A nor B. I do not belong to any literary school and don't even believe in the existence of a Russian literature. I myself seldom speak Russian. I express myself in French almost without error. I roll my R's in the purest Parisian dialect. In a word, I am a gentleman. But I assure you that it is shameful and unconscionable not to speak Russian! Now I know that French is already beginning to fall from use, but what evil spirit whispered to us that we should replace it not with Russian but with Damned English, for which you have to break your tongue, clench your teeth, and shove your jaw forward?

Odoevsky goes on to comment more soberly that French has conventional formulas for the expression of various passions, but Russian equivalents are lacking. Pushkin, he notes, uses the English word *vulgar* because "This word sketches half a man's character, half of his fate, but in order to express this in Russian, one has to write two pages of explanation, and how could this be easy for a writer and how could it be pleasant for a reader?" Griboedov, author of the dramatic satire in verse, *Woe From Wit*, is the only author who, in Odoevsky's opinion, had fathomed the art of transferring Russian conversational language to paper.

So echoes of Pushkin's and Somov's complaints about the problems of a fully viable Russian prose language are still resounding in 1834. The matter is not insignificant, because until there existed a *bona fide* literary conversational language, there could be no true Realism in literature, a fact on which V. Vinogradov insisted during the polemics in the 1960's concerning the essence of Romanticism and Realism.

Princess Mimi concerns the spiteful efforts of the spinsterly title figure to blacken the reputation of Baroness Eliza Dauerthal, which she does by slander and some fortuitous (from Mimi's point of view) accidents. At the end we find the harmless Granitsky, a friend of the Dauerthals, killed by Baron Dauerthal's bullet and the Baroness dead, her loss of honor apparently confirmed by the fatal duel. Mimi rejoices.

While Odoevsky's society tale exhibits many features typical of Marlinsky's efforts in this genre, such as apostrophe to the reader, didactic generalizations, rhetorical exclamations, and authorial caprice, it also demonstrates concern with psychological motivation. The following explanation of

Mimi's antipathy toward Baroness Dauerthal is a step in the direction of Realism's psychological verisimilitude, albeit a rather tentative one:

> Do not suppose, however, dear readers, that the Princess's malice towards Eliza was the product of some momentary chagrin. No! Princess Mimi was a very prudent maid and a long time ago Eliza had done a grave injury to Mimi. In the final period of her attending balls, the Princess had been regarded as a sort of semi-betrothed to Eliza's first husband, that is, he wasn't repelled by her as were other men. The Princess was convinced that had it not been for Eliza that she would now have the pleasure of being married, or at least being a widow—which is no less pleasurable. But all was in vain! The Baroness appeared, the admirer was won over, married her, she worried him to death, married another, and still she pleases everyone, makes everyone fall in love with her, knows how to land on her feet, but Princess Mimi remains a spinster, while time really flies! Often at her toilette the Princess regarded her overripe charms with secret despair, she compared her tall figure, her broad shoulders, and masculine appearance with the scarcely worn face of the Baroness. Oh, if one might eavesdrop at what went on then in the Princess's heart! What her imagination conjured up, how inventive it was at that moment, what a wonderful model she might have served for an artist who wanted to depict a savage islander tearing to pieces the captive who had fallen her share! But one had to squeeze all this under a tight corset, under conventional phrases, under a polite exterior, to release the flame of all hell as a fine, unnoticeable threadlet!

We are still on firm Romantic ground here, as the style clearly indicates. But despite the rhetorical exclamations, the emphasis on telling rather than showing, the metaphorical content, the psychological basis for Mimi's efforts to destroy the Baroness is not arbitrary, and the author does more throughout the tale than was commonly done to avoid the unmotivated attribution of virtues and defects to his characters.

One could not expect the prolific Veltman to ignore the society tale, and he came forth in 1835 with an amusing parody of the genre entitled *Erotida*, published in *The Moscow Observer*. Brigadier Khoikhorov, a widowered proprietor, raises his daughter, Erotida, as if she were destined for "service in the dragoons." Nonetheless, she turns out charming and pretty. The father sees that all suitors are rejected, but the girl does not object, because they are all old or unattractive. However, when a uhlan officer, Lieutenant G., is billeted in their village, she instantly falls in love with him, and her attraction deepens after he rescues her from a bolting horse.

All this is related facetiously, and the fate of Erotida and her father is left unstated as we are abruptly conveyed to the beginning of Part II. It is 1814 and the now vacationing Captain G. is heading for Karlsbad:

> He had long ago heard of Karlsbad, he had long thirsted for Karlsbad: there the waters flow from gold faucets, and the banks of the Teppela and Eger are strewn with living flowers, there the waters and love are at a temperature of 165 degrees, there in addition to the waters one drinks the *beneficent breath* of those suffering from melancholy, insomnia, lack of appetite, all kinds of attacks for which one needs diversion and 165 degrees, strudel and love, love, which is the medicinal ailment of ailments, the opium of awakened activity of feelings, day amidst night, blessed suffering.

At the gambling tables, G. becomes acquainted with a youngman who offers to show him the sights. Stopping by the post office, he receives a letter which had been mailed in the middle of June, 1812. He scans it, laughs, and addresses his new acquaintance:

"Well, tell me, please, you be the judge. At the end of 1811 I was stationed with a platoon in the village of a certain brigadier, an eccentric of the old school, who had a daughter. At that time I was younger, more feather-brained, and I fell in love with the girl. There was no lack of reciprocation. It was impossible even to think of the old man letting me have his daughter, because I had nothing back of me other than *my honor*. I was prepared to carry her off, but she couldn't decide. 'How can I marry without Papa's permission?' Well, youth doesn't consider the consequences. In departing, I swore boundless love, by all that's holy, eternal faithfulness, I swore to write, to serve until the rank of brigadier and then to request her hand formally. Before the beginning of the war I used to write, but the war began and there was no time for love. In Germany, in France, victories! An endless supply of beauties, each better than the next, each more fiery than the other.

Victory after victory, and everyone puts down his weapons before the victors. And so three years passed, and so this letter of my dear Erotida has followed me to the edge of the world and has arrived late. It says that she is free, that Papa has died, that she is ready to give me her hand. She is too late! No, after three years I won't risk the stage fare! A lot of water has flowed since then, and girls don't like to wait for suitors, and moreover, I must admit, she doesn't know how to write."

The garrulous G. then confesses his preference for a certain Adeline, whose letter he translates for his young friend. They part. Shortly a new face appears in Karlsbad, Emilia Khoreva, a young and beautiful Russian widow, and the confident G., encouraged by his past victories, begins his discreet pursuit. They meet, become friends, she proposes they exchange rings, which they do. When questioned as to the inscription inside his ring, *Erotida, 1811,* he tells her it refers to his mother. She abruptly leaves and sends word that she is ill. That evening G. agains gambles, his young acquaintance appears, gambles and loses. The unlucky youth proposes G. take his ring for a stake, which G. accepts. When he notices the inscription, *Erotida, 1811,* he demands an explanation. The young man refuses and is challenged to a duel. They agree to meet within the hour, without seconds. The final scene ends surprisingly.

At the appointed time G. orders his horse to be saddled, takes his Kuechenreuther pistols, rides to Kirstensprung. The young man is already there.

"How many paces do you want? With a barrier."

"You challenged me to answer you at a distance of four paces, and I am ready, but not otherwise until one is mortally wounded."

The decisiveness of the young man shook the spirit of the captain.

"All right, all right!" he answered, "load the pistols."

The pistols were loaded, the paces measured off.

"I repeat to you, sir," says G., deign to answer the question put to you and the matter can be settled without blood."

"The answer is already in the muzzle, sir. Deign to repeat your question with your

231

shot!"

G. drew back the hammer, the young man did the same. He walked right up to the barrier, aimed slowly at the captain.

G. didn't wait. He released the hammer, and the bullet penetrated the breast of the young man. He fell to the ground, threw away his pistol, pressed his wound with his hand. "I killed him!" G. cried out involuntarily, running up to him.

The young man raised himself up, tore off his wig, and pronounced in a dying voice: "Leave me, your help is useless both for your rival and for my rival. . . ."

"Emilia!" cried out G., falling on his knees.

"It is also useless for Erotida. . . goodbye. . . ."

The corpse of Erotida-young-man-Emilia is flung into the Eger River, and the Captain returns to Karlsbad to continue his pursuit of Adelina. *Finita la commedia.*

Eternal love, true devotion, sworn fidelity, are shown to be figments. The would-be bride is rejected because her letter is late and ungrammatical. The officer turns out to be a cad, and his simultaneous slaying of his old love and his new love, not to mention his young friend, seems not to affect him. Rather than mourn his victim, he crassly commits her to the river. Is this the way a society-tale hero acts? Veltman also incorporates the cliche of mistaken identity, here developed egregiously, and the irony of a heroine raised like a dragoon who perishes while engaging in the recreation typical of military officers.

Russian Romantic fictionists, and Realists as well, were somehow unable to refrain from teasing their Teutonic brethren, whose punctiliousness, sobriety, attention to detail and phlegmaticness they found amusing. Somov's *A Command from the Other World* poked fun at a pompous and silly Bavarian innkeeper, and Veltman satirizes the Austrian border guards and the ambiance of Karlsbad:

And so captain G. is traveling thither [to Karlsbad].

Now he already sets foot on the Austrian pavement, for whose maintenance he is obliged to pay out money, he curses both *Geld* and *Trinkgeld*, and *deutsche Sprache,* which he doesn't understand.

But now he is entering Karlsbad. And now he hears *Halt!* and *Erlauben Sie!* The gatekeeper, unhurriedly blowing his horn, plays an advent salutation, and for his *Trompeterstückchen* demands money from G. He settles up. But there still remain twenty questions, twenty proposals and recommendations, printed and oral, from all the hotels and tables d'hote of Karlsbad: Where does he want to stay? For a long time or or short time? By the day, week, or month? Which waters does he want to drink? The questions irritated G. "It's all the same to me where you take me," he says.

"How is that possible," they answer him. "Here there are expensive tourist homes and cheap ones, *Gott weiss* which of the many to choose from will please you. Here we have the *Böhmische Saal* and *Rothen Ochsen*, you may stay under the *Gold Shield* or under the sign of the *Deer,* perhaps you like to play billiards. . . .

G. chooses the *Golden Shield.* He rented the rooms for a month. New emissaries and propositions appear. What waters will he use? Does he want his name printed in the *Badelist* for 30 kreutzers or not? Does he want to have the *Badelist* just to read or his own copy?

Towards evening at the door of his apartment appear the *Nachtmusik* crowd.

They play and demand money.

In the morning the owner appears with the proposal to take Karlsbad salts, a necessary means of cleansing before using the waters.

Finally all proposals are exhausted, G. is a Karlsbad patient.

Erotida is amusing as a spoof, but like most parodies it hardly bears rereading. Alas, this is true of most of Veltman's product, which generally lacks thematic significance or any humor deeper than surface wit.

In view of Senkovsky's attitudes toward German mystical philosophy, Young France, and the excesses of the society tale, it is quite possible that he was the anonymous author of another delightful parody of the society tale which appeared in *The Library for Reading*, entitled *The Muscovite European [Muskovskii Evropeets]* (1837). The title refers to our hero, Bornov, a civil servant of the lowest rank, who is convinced that his finer qualities have been scorned by an insensate society.

He is described as follows:

> His face had a strange expression. Pale, almost greenish, it expressed no trace of thought, no feeling. His dull, or better, turbid eyes had already completely lost the glitter which eyes usually have at this age. . . . But a strange smile, a mixture of epigram and derision, always lay upon his lips, and from it one could tell that this was a Muscovite "European," one of those young people, who, still in the fourteenth rank in the civil service, have already devoured all wisdom and all women.

Bornov cultivates a reputation as an iconoclast, a dangerous free-thinker, a dangerous foe. "The young ladies of Moscow, hearing his remarks about marriage, taken directly from the novels of Mme. Sand, feared him as they would a monster."

This young poseur seeks to impress naive young ladies, among them a certain Princess Liza:

> "You are afraid of me? Princess, I am a criminal in the eyes of the world, that is true. But you, do you want to hear my justification?. . . People. . . You do not yet know, Princess, what people are like!. . . You live in the future, but I. . . I have experienced the world and people. I have bought this knowledge with the bitter price of experience, I have exchanged innocence of soul for the pettiness of social conventions."

The narrator then intrudes:

> Whoever knew Bornov as we know him—I forgot to say that he was only twenty-four then—would have rocked with laughter, but the girl listened to these words of despair and torment with anxiety.

The satire extends also to another type, the philosophical speculator Apollon Mikhailovich Lutsky.

Bornov was a European. Apollon Mikhailovich a speculator. That is, a philosopher in the manner of the literature of Young France. That is, a desperate Schellingist. In Bornov's opinion the first writer in the world was M. Balzac, and in Apollon Mikhailovich's, Mr. P— —v.

Explain, if you can, two such deviations of the human mind from its normal state!

Zinaida, Bornov's mistress, irritated at his attentions to Princess Liza, convinces Apollon that he must duel with Bornov to protect the Princess's honor. To do this she has to persuade the philosopher that he is the Princess's betrothed:

"Yes, the betrothed," said Zinaida, smiling cunningly. "You may persuade yourself, speculatively, that she is your fiancée. Surely you yourself have explained to me that the idea of a thing and the thing itself are *one and the same.*"

"Identical," Apollon interrupted solemnly, correcting Zinaida's unphilosophical expression. "Yes, I could even be able to marry her speculatively, now, in front of you! From this moment she is my wife; I am her speculative husband. The idea and the action are identical. Oh, I am as convinced of this as I am of my existence. I shall tell Bornov that I am defending the honor of my wife against a vile seducer, who. . . . In one word, that she is my legal wife."

The final absurdity occurs when Apollon confronts Bornov, who convinces the philosopher that his intentions are honorable. Bornov is so impressed with Lutsky's magnanimity that he tearfully falls on his knees before him, which in turn brings the philosopher to his knees: "Their tears flowed in streams, their noses reddened from crying, their faces screwed up in the same amusing manner."

Whether or not this was the work of Senkovsky's pen, it certainly reflects his attitudes towards phony Romantics, Balzac, and Schelling.

XX. Veltman's Later Novels. N. Pavlov's *Three Tales* and *New Tales*.

Originality of concept, content, and expression are all hallmarks of Veltman's art, and these qualities are repeated in his novel, *The Sleepwalker. An Occurrence [Lunatik. Sluchai]*, which appeared in two parts in 1834. The division into two parts is not a casual function of the length, but is related to a basic structural feature. The first part by its style and content emphasizes the protagonist's totally unreal perception of the world and himself; the second part reveals a transformed protagonist, a hero who relates to the world around him. The action takes place during 1811-1814, and it centers around the invasion, occupation, and retreat of Napoleon's army. Military events gravely affect the lives of all the central characters, and in this respect, and in several others, the novel anticipates *War and Peace*.

Our "hero" is Aurelius Yuriergorsky, a doctoral candidate at the University of Moscow.

Aurelius was distinguished from his companions by his good looks, his mind, and strange behavior. He was reserved and modest, but he disliked women to the point of hatred. No one knew the reason.

In keeping with his father's admonition that knowledge alone is incapable of betrayal, he has become immersed so deeply in the study of mathematics and astronomy that he has lost touch with reality. One night he sleepwalks (or is it a trance?) and ends up in the room of a beautiful girl, Lydia, whose cries of frightened surprise snap him back to consciousness. He flees, carrying with him a vision of the ideal woman, whose face he has been able to see only momentarily. With the French beating on the gates of Moscow, his devoted servant, Pavel, leads him through crowds of rioters and looters to safety on the outskirts, but, as Moscow begins to burn, Aurelius, obsessed with the sight of a comet, runs back toward the University observatory. An apocalyptic atmosphere prevails over the events accompanying Moscow's fall, which is presented in kaleidoscopic fragments conveying the impression of Aurelius's disturbed perceptivity. Fire, smoke, and noise intensify the mad mood. A French soldier shoots at him, he is captured, he escapes, he saves Lydia from her burning house, takes her to a cemetery, is captured again and put in jail. Impressed by the patriotism of a fellow prisoner, the son of a merchant awaiting trial for larceny and other crimes, he escapes. The action then shifts to a band of guerrilla cavalry led by Aurelius, whose men, inspired by his call for sacrifice, overwhelm a vastly superior enemy force.

Projected into this plot are two other stories, one concerning Lydia and her parents, the other the circumstances which brought the merchant's son to a Moscow prison. A rather facetious sketch outlines how Lydia's father rose from the ranks to become a major. Having retired, he somehow captured the affections of a provincial landowner's wife, whom he persuaded to abandon her husband and infant son. The major and his "wife" settled on an estate near Smolensk, where their daughter Lydia was born. At the same time the French army crossed the Nieman, she had just finished her education in Moscow. The advancing troops force the major to retreat to Moscow, where he remains untroubled by the military situation, only regretting that he is too old to rid his country of the foreign dogs. The ridiculous over-confidence of the old veteran and the unreality of the whole situation are conveyed in the following satirical paragraphs:

> Mr. Major in no way believes the rumors that Moscow is in danger. He knows that in Vorontsok a balloon is being constructed, which will be armed with several weapons, filled with a whole detachment of soldiers and will fly against the enemy like a black cloud to drop thunder and lightning.
> Mr. Major now reads a poster that this balloon will fly over Moscow. Mr. Major sits on his balcony. Like an astronomer he scans the sky with his eyes. He waits. The day is clear. The balloon is not flying. Only the sun rolls from east to west.

The second interpolated tale, entitled "The Story of the Prison *Starosta*" [*Starosta* normally means village elder, but here refers to a prisoner selected by his mates as spokesman], is a *skaz* narrative related in the highly individualized idiom of the merchant's son. The translation cannot reproduce the qualities of the vernacular which convey the speaker's class and unique personality:

> In Makariev I saw a Frenchman. He lived with some gentleman, taught the children, taught everything. For his learning, he got two thousand. Well, I thinks to myself, it's not for devils to fire pottery, I'll go be a Frenchman.
> I heard that in the sticks there's a boyar and his young wife, they've got two brats. I go to them, speak some gibberish, and they're happy.

The enterprising merchant's son progressively becomes a trader, a German major, marries a Polish girl, loses her dowry at billiards, gets into a brawl, is arrested, indicted for theft, and sent to Moscow for trial. His desire to escape and fight the invaders inspires Aurelius to take part in the defense of his homeland.

The moon presides over Part I, appearing repeatedly to signal the reader that our hero, Aurelius, is under its influence. In Part II it discretely remains out of sight, its absence suggesting that Aurelius has recovered his senses. The astronomer-become-officer is severely wounded in battle and is taken by his friend, Beloselsky, to his family's estate on the Oka, Beloselsky's sixteen-year-old sister, Eugenia, falls in love with him as he convalesces, but he remains true to his vision of Lydia. When Moscow is liberated, Beloselsky's father is taken there for medical treatment and the family goes also. Old Beloselsky soon dies, and as he is being interred Aurelius is dumbfounded to see

236

Lydia among the mourners. She had stayed with the priest in charge of the cemetery to which Aurelius had carried her those many months before.

Having rediscovered his ideal, Aurelius virtually forgets Eugenia and plans to marry Lydia. His father arrives to bless their marriage, but before the wedding they all travel to her estate near Smolensk. Aurelius and Lydia wander in the garden, and the happy youth expresses lyrically his feelings for her:

> "Fate rewarded me abundantly for my suffering. Oh, how fine the world is when all its beauties are poured into one being, and that being is next to one's heart, when the whole purpose of my life is united with you, Lydia. Dare I fully trust my feelings? Is not this a new dream, a wondrous dream? Is this not a dream, but a dream which is better than life, flying from planet to planet? Your eyes, Lydia, look at me. Oh, that look which penetrates to the limits of the heavens is the very same which penetrates my heart."

This emotional outpouring is interrupted by his father, who embraces them and asks that they follow him:

> The old man led them onward. They entered the house. In the living room the old man stopped, again embraced Aurelius and Lydia, and, directing his gaze at the portrait of a woman which was hanging on the wall, he cried out: "Aurelius, Lydia, that is the portrait of your mother!"

The reader is likely to be as surprised as the young couple, since he has probably forgotten some critical information revealed early in the novel: Mr. Major, Lydia's father, had run off with his neighbor's wife, who abandoned her husband with an infant son. That child, of course, was Aurelius.[1]

At this point the action shifts to Paris in 1814, and we learn that Aurelius is there, crushed by a secret grief. One day he abruptly departs, having received a letter from Beloselsky urging him to return home and satisfy "little Lydia's" desire to see her uncle. A final scene completes the story with the information that Aurelius and Eugenia have married.

Many things in this novel suggest comparison with *War and Peace*. The civil disturbance which preceded the fall of Moscow, the burning of the city, scenes which reflect Veltman's own observations as a young Muscovite in 1812, the account of guerrilla warfare, the general description of the French invasion, all this suggests general comparison with Tolstoy's epic. But there are also some more striking parallels which are not derived from the history of the period as such. In both works there is a didactic insistence upon the role of simple Russians who rallied to the defense of their native land, the unsung heroes whose patriotism turned the tide:

> The first wounds received in time of victory are considered a misfortune only because they spoil the possibility of sharing new exploits with one's comrades. Ask any young soldier, shot through, slashed, maimed, what he feels more strongly, his pain

or his yearning for the new fame and dangers which his comrades in arms are experiencing? He is tormented by the need to be patient, by the thirst for battle, and he is ready to tear the bandages off his wounds in order to fly again to the ranks, to attack with the bayonet, to face bullets, the enemy host, the slashing sabres. The only thing he would ask God to spare him would be trenches and melancholy encampments under enemy forts. No, the Russian doesn't know how to attack furtively, how to dig like a mole in the ground, or how to be cunning, or how to hide his real self from the enemy, or to hatch victory by sitting on eggs. No, give him for leadership "Hurrah, my boys!" and he will overtake the echo of his voice, break into a fortress like a deluge, cut into the ranks of the enemy like a sharp bayonet between the ribs.

This spirit is exemplified in the novel in the scene of Cossack foragers who cause confusion to a whole regiment of the French by their daring diversions, or the Kalmyk who angrily rejects the idea that he should not attack a squadron of cavalry because there are thirty of the enemy. "You know I can't count," he declares and singlehandedly routs them all.

Veltman's Eugenia, the dynamic young tease of the Beloselsky household, in love with life, her brother, and, even Aurelius, sight unseen, seems an earlier version of Tolstoy's Natasha Rostova:

> And Eugenia, having just finished the pension and enjoying the same rights of freedom as any guest, as before, never sitting in one place, began to fly about like a butterfly through the rooms, to hop, laugh, sing, play on the piano, help her mamma knit a jacket, scramble Anfisa Gurievna's fortune-telling cards, secretly take the needle out of the sock her nurse was knitting, carry off the housekeeper's glasses, without which she couldn't find the keyholes in the locks, dress up in her uncle's caftan and hat.

This spontaneous little creature, hearing her uncle mention the wings on a windmill, cries out: "Oh give me wings. Oh, I shall fly right now!"[2] And she has the same sort of innocent reveries as Natasha. When the household begins to wonder if her brother is possibly bringing Aurelius as a potential suitor, she

> little by little began to make some logical conclusions from these considerations and to guess the answers. Certainly my brother would not have become friends with some sort of monster or with an old man. Certainly his friend also has a kind heart just like his own. Whoever loves my brother, I must also love, because I love my brother. And whoever loves my brother must love me. But. . . maybe my brother loves me only because of his kind heart. Will his friend like me?

Tolstoy may not have known of Eugenia Beloselskaya. Whether or not he did does not affect the fact that Veltman was perhaps the first Russian author to animate this particular type of female personality, and by so doing to demonstrate that Romantic heroines need not be abstractions of idealized virtues.

Lists and catalogues are associated with the exuberance of Gogol. In *The Sleepwalker* we also find many of them, all having a humorous or satirical effect. The generals under whom Mr. Major served with distinction are all fully named, the various kinds and qualities of household flies are presented in one long catalogue, and we are provided a full inventory of the books purchased by the resourceful Mr. Major as the most useful for domestic economy and bliss, including Engleman's *Handbook for the Construction of a Grain Storage Barn*, Christian Hermeshausen's *Master and Mistress, or the Duty of the Lord and Lady in All Ways and Places,* and Eugene Witzmann's *A Short Book of Easily Comprehended Rules on How to Handle People Who Have Drowned, Frozen, Suffocated, or Hanged Themselves.*

The Sleepwalker ends on a strong note of social protest, thus reinforcing a theme introduced originally in connection with Mr. Major's treatment of his serfs, whom he habitually called "You dogs." At the conclusion of Part II we are transported to the luxurious study of a Moscow nabob, who is in the process of having a postprandial slumber. A dwarf is on hand to whisk flies from the master's face, but one penetrates the defense and the nabob awakens. He calls a servant and, ignoring the dwarf's supplications, orders that the homunculous be put in the cupboard.

> The dwarf's face expressed exactly the same suffering as is expressed on the faces of normal people. Certainly he understood that a dwarf is also a person, certainly his heart, like his head, was too big for his size. But the master knew him only as a dwarf, something for his amusement, an ugly little child. But the dwarf was forty-five years old.

Having shelved his dissatisfaction, the master then goes to mingle with his guests in the salon. There he regales them with a scandalous anecdote, which turns out to be a completely fallacious account of the vicissitudes of Aurelius, Lydia, and Eugenia, with the principals depicted as base and vile people. A young man in the group, obviously either Beloselsky or Aurelius, gives the lie to the slanderer and storms out of the room. The nabob is irritated, and at that moment the dwarf's tiny wife arrives to intercede for her husband—and she, too, ends in the cupboard.

If the summary and quotations from *The Sleepwalker* create doubts about Veltman's ability to put it all together, such doubts are quite justified. His work is a hodge-podge of Mad Hatter material, skewed descriptions, improbabilities, coincidences, caricature, and farce, all combined with scenes of persuasive reality and characters (some, in any case) who seem to come to life. The mixture of the fantastic with the real is infelicitous, since the reader is uncertain as to how he should respond to the material. We never know beforehand whether Veltman is going to be facetious or not, for unlike Sterne, from whom we can confidently expect the plastic tear and hidden sneer, Veltman often seems in earnest.

Most of Veltman's longer fiction of the thirties belongs to the genre of historical novel or at least has a setting in the past. At the end of the decade, however, he began to write contemporary novels, but again, although there was a strong content of realism, the fantastic was still present. *Heart and Thought [Serdce i dumka]*, for example, which concerns the life of provincial clerks and Muscovite society, also involves demonic forces, and again, the combination of the mundane reality of provincial life with the fantastic is unsuitable. In the mid-forties he initiated his cycle, *Adventures Drawn from the Sea of Life [Prikliucheniia, pocherpnutie iz moria zhiteiskogo]*, of which the first, *Salome [Salomeia]* (1846), is generally considered the best. The focus is on the lower middle classes, officers of middling rank, middle-level officials, impoverished gentry, pensioners, and the action ranges from seedy Podolian taverns to once fashionable Moscow suburbs. The portraits are lively, as for example the insouciant officer-embezzler Dmitritsky, the scheming spinster Salome, the avaricious marriage broker Vasilisa Savishna, the *parvenu* clerk Lychkov, and others, but the strong satirical content, the emphasis on speech peculiarities deriving from class and occupation, and the absences of more than external psychological motivation (Salome is pushy because she's envious of her sister) indicate that this tale belongs rather to the Natural School than to Realism.

Veltman, having lost his popularity, published nothing during the fifties, but he returned briefly to literature in the early sixties with a third and fourth novel for the *Adventures* series. By the time of his death in 1870 he was virtually forgotten.

In 1835 a new voice was heard in the chorus, that of Nikolay Pavlov (1805-1864), whose *Three Tales [Tri povesti]* appeared that year. Two stories in that collection merit attention, *The Name Day Party [Imeniny]* and *Yataghan [Iatagan]*, both embodying vigorous social protest. The former is a *Kuenstlernovelle* whose protagonist is a serf musician. Pavlov himself was born a serf, freed while a child, and then trained as an actor, and thus was especially sensitive to the plight of the serf artist.

This story is complicated by having numerous narrators whose voices are indistinguishable, making transitions from one narrator to another not always obvious. The general verisimilitude is weakened by coincidence and eavesdropping, and the style displays a goodly amount of latent Sentimentalism. Still, Pavlov makes an effort to present a logical psychological portrait of the central figure, who is a victim of gentry indifference and a hostile fate.

The serf musician, a cousin to Timofeev's serf artist, is able, thanks to a good education, to circulate in provincial gentry society without disclosing his origins. He is forced to reveal his position when he falls in love with one of his students, Alexandrine, and his complete personal tragedy is realized when his master loses him at cards. So deep is his sense of betrayal that he contemplates murder, but instead runs away, enters the army, and through the heroism of desperation wins honors and promotion to an officer's rank. Returning home, he is befriended by a stranger at a country inn, and it is to him that he tells his unusual life story. At its conclusion, the stranger invites him

240

to attend his wife's name day party, and (you guessed it) the wife turns out to be the serf's first love, Alexandrine.

Yataghan, whose title refers to a Turkish sabre with a curved blade, is far more sophisticated. Here Pavlov demonstrates a continuing concern with human motivation, while exploring the psychological factors which affect social relationships. In so doing he is no Tolstoy, but his effort points in Tolstoy's direction.

The plot is simple: three officers, a fledgling cornet, whose name is Bronin, a worldly adjutant, and an unsophisticated colonel are in love with a princess who lives with her widowed father in a provincial garrison town. The cornet kills the adjutant in a duel and is reduced to the rank of common soldier. With his younger rivals out of the way, the colonel flatters himself that he may marry the princess, but he is reluctant to propose, fearing a refusal. When the demoted Bronin is assigned to his regiment, the colonel patronizes him by relieving him of duty, but he also intimates that Bronin should not visit the princess. Everyone is astonished when the colonel appeals to Bronin's mother to serve as matchmaker on his behalf. But the colonel's hopes are dashed when he discovers Bronin dallying with the Princess. In a vengeful mood he orders the soldier to full duty. At a drill the colonel takes out his ire on Bronin, who "talks back" and is then flogged for his insubbordination. Later, having realized his intemperance and unfairness, the colonel is ready to be reconciled with Bronin, and meanwhile word has arrived that Bronin has been pardoned for his part in the duel with the adjutant. However, Bronin has been so humiliated that he can think only of revenge, so he takes the Turkish yataghan, a gift from his mother at the time of his commision, and assassinates the colonel. For this deed he is sentenced "to walk the green street," that is, to pass between two files of soldiers equipped with fresh cut rods and be beaten to death.

The story is suspenseful and strangely powerful. The tragic conclusion is intimated from the first, when several characters comment on the unsuitability of the yataghan as a gift. But the real cause of the tragedy is not the weapon but rather the false values which motivate all the social relationships. The adjutant is insulted when Bronin is amused at his fall from a horse, and so they duel; the over-confident colonel aspires to the princess's hand owing to a desire for prestige and material comfort, and Bronin's revenge is the response of a person whose sense of honor has changed into something grotesque. And the final injustice is the cruel execution of the murderer.

Pavlov's concern with the inner states of his characters is nicely displayed in the scene describing the colonel's thoughts as to how he should propose to the princess. The method, a sort of rudimentary interior monologue, is weakened by the initial metaphor, which is much in the style of Marlinsky:

But this proposal, this explanation of his love, these were the colonel's tormenting furies, these were the ghosts which met him while in bed both morning and night, which stood in the soldier's ranks, which marched at drills and, like the regimental colors, never left him. How to offer his heart and hand? How to say, "I love you"? How to say this? How to get up the courage to say it, and to whom? To the Princess! She is so elegant, illustrious, so frightfully surrounded by all the majesty of decorum. "To fall at her feet," thought the colonel, "but this, it seems, isn't proper, this wouldn't suit my position and years. Simply to say it, not falling on my knees, is somehow cold, embarrassing. To write a letter, but one doesn't write to princesses in Russian. To declare myself to her father, but she would be angry that I had not asked her." In a word, whatever the colonel conceived, everything seemed clumsy.

The covert ploys, the games people play with others, are also a feature of human psychology incorporated into Pavlov's story. When the colonel first receives the demoted Bronin, to whom he feels somewhat socially inferior, he affects an informality which is intended to emphasize his generosity and condescension in treating Bronin other than as a common soldier. Notified of the soldier's arrival, he asks,

"Where is he? Bring him to me." The adjutant opened the door.
Without a necktie, in a coat without epaulets, in the disarray of power, the colonel took up his cup, regarded the door with triumphant unconcern, raised his pipe to his lips, straightened up—sat down. He recalled that the cornet had been considered the princess's betrothed, he remembered the cornet beside the princess, and her father's requests, his mother's tears, and personal advantage gave way to a flash of egotism. This was the minute when those in power wish to show thunder to the weak with the majestic calm of an ancient statue or insulting, indifferent languor,when one prepares to ask questions and to look askance, the minute when the colonel would say "thou."

A further indication of Pavlov's concern with the individualized personalities is his use of metonymic means in characterizing the colonel. A circumstantial description of his lodgings reveals a combination of ingrained military traditions and the newly acquired affectations of the civilian society in which he seeks to find a place.

One other device of Pavlov's for the revelation of inner states is the use of what might be called stage business, that is, the descriptions of actions that reflect anger or other emotional states. Already developed in *The Name Day Party*, this becomes widely used in *Yataghan*: the colonel's fiddling with the weapon when he feels out of place in the fashionable drawing room of the princess, or Bronin's pulling at his tie, which begins to choke him as he listens to the colonel's assertions of his intentions regarding the princess.

Although still somewhat in thrall to the traditions of Marlinsky's Romanticism, Pavlov's independence is asserted in the unexpected understatement which governs the story. Imagine what a hundred percent Romantic should have done with the duel, the assassination, the execution. Compare Pavlov's treatment. The duel itself is not described, although its imminence is suggested by the movements of Bronin and the adjutant, who are out of earshot of the princess. Some time later the colonel appears and "then he quickly approached the prince and to the question, 'Well, what happened there?' he answered in a whisper, "A small unpleasantness, your radiance."

The murder of the colonel is also kept under tight control:

> Then the colonel appeared. Leaving his quarters he turned back and said gloomily to someone,"Reconcile me with him." Then he set off for the church, but he had hardly taken any steps when the soldier overtook him. . . without a cap, uniform unbuttoned, face distorted. . . his left hand fell with gigantic strength on the colonel's shoulder. . .
> The edge of the yataghan flashed in the sun and disappeared. The bells were ringing for the service, but no one entered the church.

The laconicism of the execution scene makes it particularly graphic:

> After a certain time that same battalion which had followed the colonel's coffin was lined up on the drill field for another matter. In front of the ranks stood five soldiers. Among them one was without arms, in nonregulation dress. They saluted. The battalion adjutant read an order. The command was given, "Line up in two ranks, ground your arms."
> Fresh rods were quickly distributed to the ranks. Some soldiers grasped them expertly and swung them smartly through the air, and, bantering with their comrades, said under their breath, "You have to walk the green street."
> The drums rolled, and they led him to this street. . . .
> Several officers turned away. . . .
> Behind the ranks the doctor walked up and down, and nearby a cart was waiting. . .

For all of Pavlov's concern for psychological verities, his characters really do not come alive. In a sense they are abstractions, to some extent complex but without dimension: the dashing young cornet, the vain adjutant, the parvenu colonel, the princess with too many suitors, Bronin's doting mother. And although one may deplore the adjutant's death, the colonel's murder, Bronin's execution, and the grief of the princess and his mother, it is difficult to feel much sympathy for them, for one doesn't really know them. They are the bearers of psychological conditions, but not individualized to the point of reader empathy. Still, Pavlov must be credited with advancing the art of fiction in the direction of Realism with these two stories by introducing new means for getting at the inner man.

The same may not be said about Pavlov's *The Masquerade*, published in *The Moscow Observer [Moskovskii nabliudatel']* in 1835-1836. Against a setting which stresses the vacuity of society's activities, the author attempts to define the dynamics of love and death as they affect a young married couple. The story is "told" in a style which appears to be a combination of aged Marlinsky and prolix Balzac, the latter's *Eugénie Grandet* providing the epigraph. Among the society tales of the mid-thirties, this is one of the least interesting.

As the story opens, we are introduced to a young widowed countess, a woman of unusual sensibilities. She is fascinated by a certain Levin, a mysterious and attractive thirty-year-old newcomer to the Moscow social scene. At a masquerade ball, a doctor, a mutual acquaintance of the countess and Levin, tells her how Levin came to be the enigmatic and passionless shell that he now appears.

The doctor's narrative of Levin's marriage eight years earlier is tedious and hyperbolic and his characterization of Levin and his now deceased bride are totally lacking in interest. This is how he portrays Levin before his marriage:

> A huge fortune, a name, twenty-two years old, a fine education, an enlightened mind, and add to this moral purity, purity of heart! He never had an opportunity to touch life from the side which besmirches a person, he had no need to memorize mundane resourcefulness, to drive from his mind all of his own opinions in order to give way politely to other's opinion, constantly to ask others for patronage, advice, and permission to exist. He did not have to bear the yoke of being a vassal of society. He did not extend his hand in order to gain favor, and he did not smile in order to please. Society immediately senses an independent person and hastens to flatter the one who has the strength to resist abasement to the flatterer. Oh, how society received him! But Levin was not created to be carried away by the whirlwind of momentary impressions or to be satisfied with food for vanity alone. On the parquet floor he quietly refused the first role, he hid behind others, and did not try to assert his brilliant advantages.

Levin's ultimate marriage to a poor but exceptional (beautiful, modest, intelligent, generous) young woman precipitates a life of pure delight. But then she falls ill, and the doctor chronicles in detail Levin's reactions to the development of her illness, which ends in death. From the doctor's account the countess surmises that Levin's strange moods and moribund appearance are the result of tuberculosis. The tale ends, "Levin went off somewhere to die."

In 1839 Pavlov published a collection entitled *New Tales [Novye povesti]*, which included *The Masquerade*, another society tale *The Million [Million]*, and the rather unusual *The Demon [Demon]*.

The Demon is the story of Andrey Ivanovich, a poverty-stricken copying clerk who lives in a small flat in a Petersburg backwater. The middle-aged Andrey Ivanovich is married, his wife a young woman forced to the altar from poverty. The narrator implies that the marriage is little more than the sharing of quarters.

Pavlov's "high" style, evidenced earlier in *The Masquerade*, is given full rein here, notwithstanding the unexalted subject matter. Most of the story is exposition, the narrator wallowing in the bleakness and hopelessness of the clerk's miserable life. Andrey Ivanovich is acutely conscious of his depressed economic and social condition and thirsts for wealth and position to provide his wife the finer things of life, a carriage, a loge at the theatre. In an effort to ameliorate his lot, he requests an audience with his excellency, the head of his division, who treats him superciliously and even rudely.

Up to this point all these motifs of poverty and rejection immediately suggest that this work is prominent in the genealogy of Gogol's *The Overcoat [Shinel']*, a work of 1840, and probably this is true, though Gogol's mal-treated Akaky Akakievich would never have dared aspire to a real-life wife: the height of his ambition was a new greatcoat with a strong lining. However, Pavlov's story, unlike Gogol's, has a "happy" ending. At the conclusion of his interview, Andrey Ivanovich blurts out that his wife is infatuated with his excellency. This precipitates an angry demand that Andrey Ivanovich "Get out!" but the germ has been planted. Subsequent inquiries by his excellency reveal that the clerk has been recently married to a real beauty much younger than himself. The last chapter depicts a well-dressed and decorated Andrei Ivanovich in a fashionable new apartment with chic furnishings, his own study far removed from his wife's wing. He is receiving guests, and one of them mentions that his carriage is ready for him:

"No, brother, that's my wife's. She really lives to ride about. Did you see the horses?"

"I saw them, sir. Marvelous horses."

"And besides, brother, they cost a great deal."

"Well, for goodness sakes, why not have the satisfaction of paying money for something which pleases you," the guest noted with a sigh.

Andrey Ivanovich slapped him on the shoulder. "True, true, brother, where there's intelligence, there will be money."

Some others also appeared with congratulations, and in the meantime a person, a lackey or butler, handed over a ticket to a loge in the theater. Andrei Ivanovich raised his voice: "Well, why bring it to me? Take it to Marya Ivanovna's wing."

The cynical resolution of his problem denies Andrey Ivanovich the sym-pathy or compassion which his previous poverty had inspired.

Pavlov's other story from this collection, *The Million,* is devoted to extensive comment upon social relationships and is almost totally lacking in dialogue. Clearly, Pavlov never realized the potential indicated by his first tales, his initial interest in psychologization subverted by social minutia.

Nikolay Gogol, miniature by Vidal, 1838

XXI. Gogol's *Mirgorod* and Petersburg Tales.

Gogol's career as professor of history at the University of St. Petersburg began brilliantly in 1834 with a rhapsodic lecture but ended shortly with the professor, as if in imitation of his own grotesque fiction, passing around pictures of the Holy Places, his voice stilled by a black kerchief around his head and jaw, ostensibly necessitated by a toothache. Later he wrote to Pogodin that he had spit his goodbye to the university, thus terminating an academic "career" which lasted from the summer of 1834 until the end of 1835.

In 1835 two collections of Gogol's stories were published, one entitled *Mirgorod. Stories Which Serve as a Continuation of "Evenings on a Farm near Dikanka,"* the other *Arabesques.* Part I of *Mirgorod* contained the idyll of rural life, *Old World Landowners*, and the lyric historical novel, *Taras Bulba.* In Part II were the horror story *Viy*, which has ties with Narezhny's *Bursak* and which the author unreliably reports was based on a popular legend, and *The Tale of How Ivan Ivanovich Quarreled with Ivan Nikiforovich.*

The theme of *poshlust* inititated in *Shponka* is further developed in *Old World Landowners [Starosvetskie pomeshchiki]*. Here we meet the ever-loving old couple Afanasy Ivanovich and Pulkheria Ivanovna, whose tranquil and cozy life is religiously devoted to gourmandizing. With wistful recall, the narrator conjures up the ramshackle charm of the homestead, with its tumble-down manor house, the lush orchard of fruit trees, the overheated and cluttered rooms, the squeaking doors, the pregnant serving girls, and the flies which at night "covered the whole ceiling with a black cloud." Pulkheria Ivanovna's métier is the menu, and as she treats her ever-hungry husband or an honored guest to the products of her kitchen or distillery we are given a whole Ukrainian smorgasbord of vittles and liquors. The *poshlust* of vegetable life has never been recreated with such tender detail.

The conclusion destroys the idyl, for it recounts the death of the beloved Pulkheria Ivanovna, the subsequent deterioration of the bereft Afanasy Ivanovich, and the ruin of everything by their heir, a retired lieutenant: "The huts, which were almost lying on the ground, fell completely down. The peasants became drunkards and for the most part became runaways."

Poshlust is again the target in *The Tale of How Ivan Ivanovich Quarreled with Ivan Nikiforovich [Povest' o tom, kak possorilsia Ivan Ivanovich s Ivanom Nikiforovichem]*. The title immediately recalls Narezhny's *The Two Ivans, or A Passion for Litigation*, but notwithstanding some similarity in incident there is little connection between the two works. With Narezhny's story the authorial voice is clear, the moral is inescapable, and the characters, albeit one-dimensional, at least vaguely resemble humans with respect to motivation and attitudes. But in Gogol's *Mirgorod* we are confronted with the stage of a puppet show, whose puppeteer has many voices and who continually intrudes his sharp nose onto the stage to wink or grimace at the audience.[1]

Typical Gogolian ingredients abound: funny names, non sequiturs, absurdities, dirty details, hyperbole, irrelevancies, ludicrous comparisons. A somewhat abridged passage will demonstrate. Having outlined the (questionable) qualities of that "wonderful person," Ivan Ivanovich, the narrator turns to his neighbor:

> Ivan Nikiforovich is also a very fine person. His yard is next to Ivan Ivanovich's yard. They are also such friends as the world has yet to produce. Anton Prokofievich Pupopuz [Barebelly], who still goes about in a tawny coat with blue sleeves and who dines on Sundays with the judge, used to say usually that the devil himself tied Ivan Nikiforovich and Ivan Ivanovich together with a cord. Wherever one went, the other would turn up. Ivan Nikiforovich was never married. Although some people used to say that he had married, that was a total lie. I know Ivan Nikiforovich very well, and I can say that he never even had an intention of getting married. Where does this kind of gossip come from? In the same way it was rumored that Ivan Nikiforovich was born with a tail behind. But this fiction is so clumsy and at the same time so abominable and indelicate that I even don't think it's necessary to disprove it to my enlightened readers, who doubtless know that only witches, and very few of them, moreover, have tails behind, and they, besides, belong more to the female sex than to the male. Notwithstanding their great friendship, these rare friends did not at all resemble one another. One can learn their characters best from comparison: Ivan Ivanovich has the unusual gift of speaking extremely pleasantly. Lord, how he speaks! You can compare the sensation only with when someone is looking for lice in your hair or quietly draws a finger across your heel. . . . Ivan Nikiforovich, on the other hand, more often is silent, but still if he does spit out a word, then hold on: it will sever cleaner than any razor. Ivan Ivanovich is thin and tall; Ivan Nikiforovich is somewhat shorter, but on the other hand spreads out broader. Ivan Ivanovich's head resembles a radish tail down; Ivan Nikiforovich's head is like a radish tail up. . . . Ivan Ivanovich has a somewhat timid character. On the contrary, Ivan Nikiforovich has pants with such folds that if you blew them up you could put a whole courtyard with barns and outbuildings into them. Ivan Ivanovich has large expressive eyes of tobacco color and a mouth somewhat similar to the letter V; Ivan Nikiforovich has small, yellowish eyes and completely lost between his thick brows and puffy cheeks, and his nose looks like a ripe plum. . . .
>
> However, notwithstanding certain dissimilarities, both Ivan Ivanovich and Ivan Nikiforovich are wonderful people.

These two inestimable gentlemen unfortunately quarrel when Ivan Nikiforovich stubbornly refuses to give Ivan Ivanovich an antique gun which had taken the latter's fancy when he noticed his neighbor's ancient serving woman hanging it on the clothesline to air. Ivan Nikiforovich remains obdurate even when he is offered a sow and two bags of oats for the weapon. The scene is notable for the coarse language of Ivan Nikiforovich and the ridiculous turning of the conversation:

> "For God's sake, Ivan Ivanovich, you have to stuff on peas before talking with you. (That was nothing. Ivan Nikiforovich let off phrases worse than that.) "Where does it happen that anyone trades a gun for two sacks of oats? I bet you won't put up your

bekesha [short fur coat] ."

"But you have forgotten, Ivan Nikiforovich, that I'm giving you a sow in addition."

"How's that! Two bags of oats and a sow for a gun?"

"Well, what about it. Isn't that enough?"

"For a gun?"

"Of course, for a gun."

"Two sacks for a gun?"

"The two sacks are not empty but filled with oats; and have you forgotten the sow?"

"Go kiss your sow, and if you don't want to do that, then kiss the devil!"

When Ivan Nikiforovich calls Ivan Ivanovich a "perfect gander," the quarrel has progressed too far to be settled peacefully. Ivan Nikiforovich calls for his servants:

"Hey, old woman, lad!" At this there appeared from behind the door that same gaunt old woman and a boy of short stature wrapped up in a long and wide frock coat. "Take Ivan Ivanovich by the hand and lead him out the door!"

"What's that! To a member of the gentry?" Ivan Ivanovich cried out with a feeling of dignity and irritation. "Just you dare! Take one step! I'll annihilate you along with your stupid *pan*! A crow won't find a trace of you!" (Ivan Ivanovich spoke unusually forcefully when his soul was agitated.) The whole group presented a forceful picture: Ivan Nikiforovich standing in the middle of the room in his full beauty without any adornment! [He had been taking a nap naked when Ivan Ivanovich arrived.] The old woman with her mouth agape and the most vacuous and frightened look on her face!, Ivan Ivanovich with his arm raised, just as Roman tribunes are depicted! It was an extraordinary moment! A magnificent spectacle! And yet there was only one witness: that was the boy with the enormous frock coat, who stood quite calmly and picked his nose.

To spite Ivan Ivanovich, Ivan Nikiforovich builds a goose house on their mutual property line, the former clandestinely cuts it down and then lodges a formal complaint against his sometime friend, accusing him of plotting arson. The language of this complaint reminds one of the court order in Narezhny's *Two Ivans*, with its ponderous officialese and legalistic formulae. Ivan Nikiforovich also shows up at the court with his own petition, a defamatory document which not only refers to Ivan Ivanovich as a swindler and scoundrel and accuses him of premeditating murder but adds that his father and mother were total outlaws and unimaginable drunkards.

As if the breakdown of the long-standing friendship were not enough shock for one day, the court clerks are further astonished when Ivan Ivanovich's sow bursts into the courtroom, snatches Ivan Nikiforovich's petition in its snout, and escapes. The news of this outrage is enough to bring Ivan Nikiforovich to petition a higher court, but the wily court officials put it on a high shelf and forget about it. Two years later there is an almost successful attempt to reconcile the antagonists, but that too fails, and in fact leads to further litigation.

The comic tone is completely absent from the brief epilogue, in which our narrator very soberly recounts how he visited Mirgorod twelve years after the events he has reported. He was gloomy because of the foul weather:

> But notwithstanding that, when I began to approach Mirgorod, then I felt my heart was beating heavily. God, how many memories! Here had lived then in touching friendship two unique men, two unique friends. And how many remarkable people had died! The judge, Demyan Demyanovich, was already deceased by then. Ivan Ivanovich, the one with the crossed eye, had also died.

The narrator finds the two Ivans still clinging to life, each confident that the litigation will shortly be resolved in his favor. Leaving Mirgorod, he sighs, "It is melancholy on this earth, gentlemen."

This Gogolian change of mood and the narrator's fond memories of the two "unique" Ivans should not distract our attention from the true nature of our heroes. Ivan Ivanovich, who cohabitates with his servant Gapka, who solicitously questions the town beggars as to whether they would prefer meat or bread and then gives them nothing, who lives an existence of total spiritual vacuity; Ivan Nikiforovich, the coarse mannered glutton, shameless and Homerically slothful—these are "unique" and "wonderful" men.

Gogol is a master at sly innuendoes, and this story has its share, such as the passing reference to the hens on the courthouse stairs, which are attracted there by grains or other edibles dropped by careless litigants. Later the narrator speaks more openly of bribes, or at least of "various fowls, eggs, pies, rolls and other trifles brought by the petitioners." With matters of sex Gogol is less direct, and at times his narrators seem rather like sniggering adolescents. In *Old World Landowners* Pulkheria Ivanovna strictly observed the morals of her maids and was surprised when every few months "the waist of some maid or other would become fuller than usual; this was even more strange, because there were no bachelors in the household except a houseboy who went about barefoot in a grey tail coat and when not eating was certainly sleeping." As for Ivan Ivanovich, "He had no children. Gapka has children and they often run about the courtyard." "Gapka, a healthy wench, wears a *zapaska* [a skirt slit up the sides] and has fresh calves and cheeks." Later the passage of three years is chronicled: "a number of brides succeeded in getting married, a new street was built in Mirgorod, the judge lost a molar and two cuspids, more little children than before were running about Ivan Ivanovich's yard: God alone knows where they came from."

Taras Bulba is a curious work, the product of cross-breeding the Ukrainian popular historical song with the Scottian historical novel. It is a tale of Cossacks whose appetites are insatiable, be it for fighting, carousing, looting, or eating. An apotheosis of Cossackdom in the good old days, it celebrates the killing of Poles and Tatars as a noble duty, it demonstrates that skill in martial arts is the real evidence of manliness, and it postulates that the true faith, Orthodoxy, will sustain a believer even at the stake.

The skeleton is typical of the novel of Scott and his myriad imitators: two lovers of opposite "faiths" (political and/or religious) are separated by the forces of war, but the timely assistance of a servant reunites them. However, the bones are fleshed not with a love story against a circumstantially described historical background, because the love story is terminated suddenly long before the novel ends and the "historical" events do not relate to verifiable history. What we see here is a phantasmagoria of the clashes between Cossacks and Turks, Tatars, and Poles which filled the annals of the sixteenth and seventeenth centuries, and what takes place is largely the result of the awesome will of the title character. Ultimately this Slavic Titan causes the death of his two sons, Ostap and Andrey, and himself perishes at the stake.

Ostap and Andrey return to Taras's Cossack homestead having just graduated from the Kiev Academy. Their doughty father snatches them from their grieving mother and hustles them off to Sech, the "republic" of the Zaporozhian Cossacks situated past the rapids [za porogom] on the Dniepr River. But proof of manhood requires military exploits, so Taras welcomes news that rascally Catholic priests and scoundrelly Jews have conspired to persecute the Orthodox in Poland. A campaign is launched, towns and villages are given over to fire and sword, and finally Dubno is beseiged. Meanwhile Taras is delighted to observe the development of his sons, Ostap showing true signs of leadership and Andrey foremost among the courageous sons of Sech. However, one night Andrey learns that within the walls of the beseiged and starving city is his beloved, the daughter of the Voevode of Kovno, whom he had met briefly while in Kiev at school. Andrey steals into the city with food for her and shortly pledges eternal fidelity to his "queen." Subsequently, while leading a charge against the beseigers, Andrey is cut off from his troops and captured by his father. The terrible Taras shoots him dead.

Ultimately the Poles are reinforced and the Cossacks defeated. Ostap is taken prisoner and Taras, severely wounded, is hustled to safety in Sech. Although he ultimately recovers, he finds no joy in typical Cossack occupations, obsessed as he is by thought of Ostap. Finally, he bribes a Jew, Yankiel, to take him to Warsaw, and he is successfully smuggled through Poland and into the Warsaw ghetto under a load of bricks. Plans to see Ostap in prison are frustrated, but Taras is able to observe his son's torture and execution in the public square. Ostap silently endures the breaking of his bones, but as the end approaches he longs for the sight of just one familiar face.

And his strength failed him, and he cried in the agony of his soul, "Batko! Where are you? Do you hear me?" "I hear you!" rang through the universal silence, and the millions of people shuddered as one man.

Taras next appears on Polish soil as *ataman* of a regiment in the army of the Cossack nation, which had as a man:

251

arisen, for the people's patience was at an end. It had arisen to avenge the mockery of its rights, for their shameful humiliation; the profanation of the faith of its fathers and its holy rites; the desecration of its churches; the outrages of the foreign lords; its oppression; the Papal Union; the shameful domination by the Jewry on Christian soil—for everything that had so long brought about and increased the stern hatred of the Cossacks.

When his army makes peace with Hetman Potocki, Taras will have none of it, and he leads his regiment on a mission of vengeance in the name of the martyred Ostap. Ultimately Taras's force is surrounded and he is captured, but he dies happy, shouting a hearty farewell to his troops from his vantage point on a tree, to which he had been chained and nailed before being burned alive.

In the light of recent history, on the surface the novel reminds one of a eulogy to a fallen storm trooper, the unthinking exponent of perverted values, the dauntless persecutor of Jews, and the unhesitating executor of "enemies" of the state. Still, the lavish praise of Cossack exploits, the plaudits for Cossack bravery, the tributes to Ostap's and Taras's heroism do not still the wiggle of a tiny worm of doubt that Gogol, apologist though he appears to be, is himself not a convinced believer in the society he applauds. Can it be that our good Ukrainian author had no ironical intent as he praised the Cossack virtues: heedlessness, drunkenness, cruelty?

And often they suddenly appeared in those places where they least of all could have been expected—and everything then took leave of life. Fires embraced villages. The cattle and horses which were not herded after the army were slaughtered on the spot. It seemed that they were feasting rather than carrying on a military campaign. Today one's hair would stand up straight at the terrible signs of ferocity of that half savage age which the Zaporozhians exhibited everywhere. Slaughtered children, women's breasts severed, skin flayed from foot to knee of those set free—in a word, the Cossacks were paying their previous debts in hard cash.

The anti-Semitism which permeates this story does no credit to its author, and in this respect Gogol is in the gutter with Faddey Bulgarin, who also pandered to contemporary national prejudices of this sort. Had Gogol merely shown aspects of Jewish life with his usual focus upon sordid naturalistic detail, as he did when describing the garbage dump that was the Warsaw ghetto, we should not be offended, but he gratuitously provides pejorative generalizations which have no function in the story, as in the following example:

Taras stepped into a room with a large window. The Jew was praying, having covered his head with a rather dirty shroud, and he had turned to spit for the last time, as is the custom of his faith, when his eyes met Bulba, who was standing behind him. Instantly there flashed before his eyes the two thousand ducats offered for his head, but he was ashamed of his own greed and endeavored to smother within himself the eternal thought of gold, which, like a worm, coils around the Jewish soul.

Poles, of course, don't fare very well in this tale, and we are treated to a line-up of arrogant, egotistical peacocks, who are, however, courageous in battle. One quite amusing lampoon, essentially digressive, appears in the caricature of the Polish gentleman who has brought his girl friend to watch the execution of Ostap:

> In the foreground, next to the mustachioed men composing the city guard, stood a young gentleman, or so he appeared, in military dress, who had dressed himself with decidedly everything he owned, so that there remained in his apartment only a torn shirt and a pair of old boots. Two chains, one above the other, hung around his neck with some sort of ducat. He stood with his lovey, Josysia, and kept looking around so that no one would dirty her silk dress. He explained everything to her fully, so that there was decidedly nothing to add. "Now here, deary Josysia," he said, "all the people that you see have come in order to watch the criminals be executed. And here, deary, that person that you see holding an axe and other instruments in his hands, that person is the executioner, and he will perform the execution. And when he puts them on the wheel and does other tortures, the criminal will still be alive, but when he chops off his head, then he, deary, will die right then. At first he will cry out and make movements, but as soon as they chop off his head, then he will not be able to cry out, or to eat, or to drink, because, deary, he will no longer have a head." And Josysia listened to all this with horror and curiosity.

The lyricism which accompanies the narration of Cossack heroics, as when Gogol recounts the prowess of various warriors in hand to hand combat, is complemented in the passages devoted to the Ukrainian steppe. This type of description has been seen earlier in several stories of *Evenings*, but the landscapes in *Taras Bulba* are much less vague and unspecific:

> The further into the steppe, the more beautiful it became. Then the entire south, all that area which comprises present-day Novorossia, was a green, virgin wilderness clear to the Black Sea. No plow had ever passed over those boundless waves of wild plants. Only horses, hiding in them as in a forest, had trampled them. Nothing in nature could be better. The entire surface of the earth was a green-gold ocean, sprinkled with millions of different flowers. Through the slender, tall stems of grass glimmered azure, blue and lilac cornflowers, yellow broom shot upwards with its pyramidal summit, white clover with umbrella-like caps spotted the surface, an ear of wheat, God only knows from where it came, was ripening in the thicket. Partridges with outstretched necks slipped among the slender roots. The air was filled with a thousand different bird calls. In the heavens hawks hung motionlessly, having spread their wings and motionlessly fixed their eyes on the grass. The cry of a cloud of wild geese moving in the region was echoed from God knows what distant lake. From the grass a gull ascended with measured beat and luxuriously bathed in the blue waves of air. Now it sinks into the heights and shows only as a black speck. Now it turns on the wing and shines in the sun. Devil take you, you steppes, how grand you are!

The enthusiastic lyricism of this sort of passage seems much more justified than that accompanying the exploits of the Cossack troops.

Viy [Vii] has not attracted any coterie of partisans, and I find no reason not to respect public opinion in this matter. The story's title is equipped with the author's footnote, itself a bit of Gogolian whimsey:

* *Viy* is a colossal creation of the popular imagination. Such is the name given by the Russians to the leader of the gnomes, whose eyelids reach to the ground. This whole story is a national legend. I did not want to change anything in it, and I relate it almost with the same simplicity as I heard it.

Apparently the long-lidded gnome really arose in Gogol's imagination, because it is not found in Ukrainian folklore.

The story concerns the fatal adventure of Khoma Brut, a seminarian in the next to last year of study and thus ranked as "philosopher." The first part is largely concerned with seminary life, the details of which closely resemble those found earlier in Narezhny's novels. When the holidays arrived, the boys would scatter to their homes or wander about the countryside, singing for provincial audiences in exchange for something to eat. On one of these excursions, Khoma dreams of being accosted by a witch, whom he almost "rides" to death. Subsequently, he is hired to read prayers over the body of a wealthy Cossack landowner's daughter, who had mysteriously been given a fatal beating. The deceased turns out to be the witch. Isolated with the coffin in a remote chapel, for two nights Khoma is able to thwart the witch's attempts to penetrate his sacred circle. But on the third night the deceased produces Viy. Now this Viy is a very respectable type of spectre, but its walk-on part at the very climax hardly justifies the title slot of the tale. The finale is a rather vivid fantasy of fiends:

The last remnants of Khoma's intoxication left him. [The experiences of the previous two nights had unsettled him and led him to drink more than usual.] He only crossed himself and read whatever prayers he happened upon. And at the same time he heard how the demonic forces swept around him, almost touching him with the ends of their wings and repulsive tails. He didn't have the courage to look at them. He saw only how on an entire wall stood some sort of huge monster with tangled hair as in a forest. Through the net of hair looked two fearful eyes, whose brows were somewhat raised. Something like a huge bubble hovered over it in the air, with a thousand pincers and scorpion stingers protruding from the center. Black dirt hung on them in clumps. All were looking at him, seeking him, but without being able to see him, since he was surrounded by the secret circle.

"Bring Viy! Go for Viy!" resounded the words of the corpse. And suddenly silence descended on the church. The howling of wolves was heard in the distance, and soon heavy footsteps resounded, echoing in the church. Looking sideways, he saw them leading some sort of stubby, strong, colossal person. He was all covered with black dirt. His arms and legs, sprinkled with dirt, were like sinewy, strong roots. He walked heavily, constantly stopping. His long eyelids drooped to the very ground. Khoma noted with terror that his face was iron. They led him under the arms and stood him directly facing the place Khoma was standing.

"Raise my eyelids, I can't see!" said Viy in a subterranean voice, and the entire gang rushed to raise his eyelids.

"Don't look!" an inner voice whispered to the philosopher. But he couldn't resist and looked.

"There he is!" cried Viy, and he pointed to him with his iron finger. And everything there rushed at the philosopher. He fell breathless to the ground, and instantly his soul flew out of him from fear.

None of Gogol's early stories of the supernatural or fantastic are, in my opinion, of particular importance, and *Viy* is no exception. However, the rural-fantastic of the *Dikanka* and *Mirgorod* collections was shortly to be displaced by the urban-fantastic of *Arabesques* and other tales of the Petersburg cycle, which represent the Gogolian world view at its most intriguing.

Arabesques (1835) included, among other things, *Nevsky Prospect, The Portrait,* and *Notes of a Madman.* Here we find some vintage Gogol, stories which are as redolent of *poshlust* as the lives of old world landowners or the two Ivans.But the quality of *poshlust* in Petersburg is quite distinct from the treacly existence of the doting old couple or the fatuous campaigns of the worthy sons of Mirgorod. Petersburg is a city where rank has its privilege, where identity derives from status, where the feeble mortals who scramble towards the sun become victims of their pretense and end up in the madhouse, or die, or even lose their noses. This is a Petersburg quite unlike that of the typical society tale, with its balls, galas, receptions, officers and cards and duels, fast horses and pretty women, rich husbands and sentimental liaisons. Gogol's Petersburg is no "Venice of the North," but the squalid home of petty clerks, bullying officials, drunk artisans, stairways stinking of cabbage and garbage, billingsgate, envy, frustrations, and defeat. It is a town of hub-bub, scurrying crowds, and its heart is Nevsky Prospect, the main thoroughfare. At dawn it is sprinkled with beggars and muzhiks, noon finds it peopled with tutors, governesses, nurses, and their charges, and the fashionable set arrives at two. At four the avenue is deserted, but after dark the demi-monde arrives. This is the time of mystery, "when the lamps give everything some sort of alluring, wonderful light," an illumination which deceives and destroys, and which is the work of. . . . but of that later.

The tale *Nevsky Prospect [Nevskii Prospekt]* , which might be translated more meaningfully as *Neva River Prospect,* opens as a physiological sketch. In providing a typical sociological analysis of the crowds thronging the avenue at various times of day, the narrator untypically reduces them to synechdochic externals:

Here you will encounter unique mutton-chops, flowing with unusual and astonishing art under the necktie, mutton-chops which are velvet, agate, black as sable or coal, but, alas, belonging only to one Foreign Board. Those serving in other departments have been forbidden by providence to have black mutton-chops, and must, to their extreme distaste, have red ones. Here you will encounter miraculous moustaches, incapable of being described by any pen or brush, moustaches to which the better half of a lifetime has been sacrificed, the object of lengthy vigilance both day and night, moustaches on which have been decanted captivating scents and aromas and which have been annointed with every dearest and rarest sort of pomade, moustaches curled at night with thin vellum paper, moustaches which breathe with the most touching attachment of their possessors and which passers-by envy. A thousand sorts of hats, dresses, kerchieves motley, light, to which the attachment of their owners is maintained for the course of two whole days, dazzle even the people on Nevsky Prospect. A whole sea of butterflies seems suddenly to have flown up from a stem and to undulate like a flashing cloud under the black beetles of the male sex. Here you will meet waists such as you never saw in your dreams: thin, narrow waists no thicker than the neck of a bottle, which when encountering you respectfully move away from, lest you touch them carelessly with a rude elbow. Timidity and fear possess one's heart lest one carelessly break the most charming creation of nature and art. And what kind of ladies' sleeves does one encounter on Nevsky Prospect? Ach, how charming!

After a lengthy introduction in this mode, the narrator begins his tale, or rather his combination of two tales. One line of intrigue develops as a *Kuenstlernovelle*, and here we follow the adventures of the artistPiskaryov, an impressionable and sensitive man who, fooled by the deceiving street lamps of Nevsky Prospect, imagines a prostitute to be his ideal of femininity. When he realizes the brutal truth, he retreats to the bliss of opium-induced dreams, where his vision is untainted by harsh reality. Deciding to save her, he proposes marriage, but she crassly rejects his offer. The crushed artist slits his throat. The other plot is a parody of the typical anecdote involving the amorous adventures of the swashbuckling young officer. The protagonist, Lieutenant Pirogov, is a friend of the artist, but he has not an iota of poetry or idealism in his soul. The object of his amorous intentions is the pretty blonde wife of a German artisan, and one Sunday, when the husband is away, his plot for seduction is almost succesful. Alas, the smith, with his friends the cobbler and carpenter, all drunk, return unexpectedly, and they provide a humiliating chastisement. That an officer should be treated in this manner by mere German artisans is unthinkable, and the vengeful Pirogov contemplates protests and punishments. But in the end he does nothing, his practical nature concluding it wouldn't do to disturb his superior on Sunday. Thus, where the idealist Piskaryov is reality's victim, the *poshlyak* Pirogov makes his compromise with circumstances and survives.

The story of Piskaryov's transcendental pipe-dreams, which is marked by hyperbolized pathos, becomes somewhat tedious, but the companion piece involving Pirogov is quite lively and genuinely funny. The adventures of the militantly self-satisfied officer are prefaced by a long satirical digression on the middle-class society to which he belongs, a society whose philistinism permits no distinction among Pushkin, Bulgarin, and Grech.

> But Lieutenant Pirogov had a multitude of talents which belonged to him alone. He used to declaim quite excellently verses from *Dmitri Donskoi* and *Woe From Wit*, he had a special talent of blowing smoke rings from his pipe so successfully that he could string out about ten of them one after another. He was quite good at telling an anecdote about a cannon being a cannon and a unicorn being a unicorn. However, it is rather difficult to enumerate all the talents with which fate had rewarded Pirogov.

The comedy really gets under way when Pirogov first follows his blonde into her apartment, and there is greeted by an unusual sight:

> Before him was sitting Schiller, not that Schiller who wrote *William Tell* and *The*

History of the Thirty Years' War but the well-known Schiller, the journeyman tinsmith on Burgher Street. Next to Schiller was standing Hoffmann, not the writer Hoffmann but the rather good cobbler from Officers' Street, a great friend of Schiller's.

Both worthies are totally drunk, and Hoffmann is about to cut off Schiller's nose, because, as the latter complains, his nose costs him twenty rubles forty kopecks annually for snuff. "I am a Schwabian German. I have a king in Germany. I don't want my nose. Cut off my nose! There's my nose!" Pirogov's unexpected entrance happily interferes with the amputation, and when he realizes the degree of inebriation of the two, he wisely departs.

As the story develops, we learn more of Schiller's virtues, including his plan for wealth, from which he never departs, his rigid daily schedule, his punctuality, and his custom of getting drunk with friends every Sunday. Naturally, when the inebriated smith returns to his flat and finds Pirogov embracing his wife, he becomes righteously angry:

"You lout!" he cried out with extreme displeasure, "How do you dare to kiss my wife? You are a wretch and not a Russian officer. Devil take it, my friend Hoffmann, I am a German and not a Russian pig." Hoffmann answered affirmatively. "Oh, I don't want to have horns! Grab him, friend Hoffmann, by the collar. I don't want them," he continued, wildly waving his arms, while his face resembled the red cloth of his vest. "I have lived in Petersburg eight years, I have a mother in Schwabia, and my uncle is in Nurenburg, I am a German and not horned beef! Take everything off him, my friend Hoffmann! Hold him by the hands and feet, my comrade Kuntz."

In the original manuscript there followed a description of how Pirogov was soundly whipped, but the censors wouldn't permit one of the Tsar's officers to suffer such humiliation even in literature, so we are simply informed that the Germans acted so rudely and impolitely with him that no words can describe the sad occurrence. Pirogov's plans for violent revenge are rapidly dissipated by two cream puffs at a confectionary shop and a stroll along Nevsky Prospect, and he ends up dancing the mazurka at a friend's house.

The positioning of the officer's story is important, because it dispels the tragic overtones of the artist's tale which precedes it. The satirico-comic mood which is sustained through Pirogov's adventure and the officer's immediate acceptance of his comeuppance provide a comment upon the hectic Piskaryov's overreaction. In fact, not until the end do we become aware that Gogol has fooled us again, catering to our conventionalized literary expectations so skillfully that we take seriously what is really a parody of the *Kuenstlernovelle*.

Just who is Piskaryov?

He was an artist. A strange phenomenon, isn't it so? A Petersburg artist! An artist in the land of snows, an artist in the land of Finns, where everything is damp, level, pale, grey, foggy. These artists in no way resemble Italian artists, who are proud and burning, like Italy and its sky. Just the contrary, for the most part these are good, modest people, bashful, carefree, quietly loving their art, drinking tea with a couple of friends in a tiny room, modestly discussing their beloved subject and totally ignoring the superfluous. He forever calls some old beggar woman to his place and forces her to sit six long hours in order to transfer to the canvas her pitiful, impassive face. He sketches a picture of his room, in which all kinds of artistic rubbish appears: plaster hands and feet, coffee colored from age and dust, broken picture frames, an upset easel, a friend playing on a guitar, walls splashed with paints, with an open window through which one glimpses the pale Neva River and poor fishermen in red shirts. . . . To this species belong the young man we have described, the artist Piskaryov, bashful, timid, but bearing in his soul sparks of feeling ready to turn into flame at the proper occasion.

Albeit deluded by the infernal street lamps of Nevsky Prospect, Piskaryov should hardly have been deluded as to the true nature of his "Perugian Bianca" with the dark tresses, since, after his ecstatic discovery of her, the knowledgeable Pirogov makes it clear what she is:

"Why don't you go after the brunette, since she's so to your liking?"
"Oh, how could I," exclaimed the young man in the frock-coat, blushing. "As if she were one of those who walk Nevsky Prospect in the evening. This one has to be a very important lady," he continued, sighing, "Her cloak alone costs eighty rubles."
"Simpleton! cired Pirogov, pushing him forcibly in the direction where her bright cloak fluttered. "Go on, you ninny, wake up! And I'm going after the little blonde."

The description of the "very important lady" is presented in terms of Piskaryov's enthusiastic appreciation, but this kind of Sentimentalist effusiveness could hardly have been reproduced seriously by the mid-thirties, and definitely not by an author so sensitive to *poshlust*:

The unknown being, to which his eyes, thoughts, and feelings were so attached, turned her head and looked at him. O God, what divine features! The most charming forehead of dazzling whiteness was shaded by beautiful hair, like agate. They curled, these wondrous locks, and a part of them, falling from under her hat, touched the cheeks tinged with a subtle blush from the evening chill. Her lips were locked by a whole swarm of the most charming fancies. All that remains of childhood memories, that imagination and quiet inspiration give under the glimmer of the icon lamp, all this, it seemed, was united, combined, and reflected in her harmonious mouth.

Piskaryov's opium-induced dream world is sufficiently banal, with its visions of the bliss which would permeate the life of the artist and his "divine being," once he had redeemed her through marriage. Again, this is contrasted with the realities of life when he goes to propose. She greets him with the drowsy statement that she had arrived home completely drunk at seven that morning. He responds with a picture of their future life, an image of stereotypical roles which she pragmatically rejects:

"I will be sitting at my paintings, you will sit beside me inspiring my efforts, sewing or occupied with other kinds of handwork, and we will have need for nothing more."
"How's that?" she interrupted his speech with an expression of some sort of dis-

dain, "I am not an ironess and not a seamstress that I should start being busy with work."

Her insistent vulgarity destroys the idyl, and he flees to his room and the oblivion offered by his razor. Even then "one could see that his hand had been unfaithful and that he had suffered a long time before his sinful soul left his body."

Piskaryov can't do anything right. Where the artist ends as a suicide, Pirogov, who was also not only unsuccessful in love but got a thrashing as well, ends up dancing the mazurka: "There he spent a pleasurable evening and so distinguished himself in the mazurka that not only the ladies but even the cavaliers were in ecstasy."

Pirogov's mundane but sensible accommodation to his fate cannot but be appreciated in contrast with the pointless death of the silly Piskaryov, the victim of his own pompous idealizations. The Lieutenant's tale in itself erodes any residual sympathy for the artist, but there is a further "decompression" of his story in the penultimate paragraph of the frame, where the narrator muses upon fate.

"Our society is strangely constructed," thought I, walking along Nevsky Prospect day before yesterday and running through my memory of these two episodes. "How strange, how inconceivably our fate plays with us. Do we ever attain what we desire? Do we achieve that to which, it would seem, our powers have been expressly prepared. Everything turns out opposite. Fate gives this one the most beautiful horses, and he rides along with them, totally without noticing their beauty, while that one, whose heart burns with equine passion, goes afoot and has to be content with clicking his tongue when a racer is led past him. This one has an excellent cook, but unfortunately such a tiny mouth that he can't get more than two little bites through it, while another has a mouth the size of the ark at the General Staff, but, alas, he must be satisfied with some German potato dinner. How strange our fate plays with us."

So the descent is complete. From the heights of Piskaryov's Platonic fantasies we slip to Pirogov's singleminded pursuit of a *Hausfrau*, from there to fate's inexplicable doling out of pretty horses, and finally we end with German potato salad.

The story closes with generalizations on the unreliability of Nevsky Prospect, where "Everything is deception, everything a dream, everything is not what it seems. . . when the Devil himself lights the lamps only to reveal everything in an unreal form."

Notes of a Madman [Zapiski sumasshedshego] is the warm-up for Gogol's great feat of 1840, *The Overcoat*. The madman in question is a shabby clerk, Aksenty Ivanovich Poprishchin, who keeps a diary detailing his preposterous efforts to become the fiance of Sophie, the daughter of the director of his department. But when the upstart clerk is confronted with the realization that she is about to become the bride of a gentleman of the bedchamber, thus frustrating his efforts to become her husband, he shortly abandons his real identity and assumes the role of the King of Spain.

Poprishchin suffers from delusions of grandeur—on a Gogolian level, naturally. Thus he feels himself in the special good graces of the director, because he alone is employed for the ennobling task of cleaning pens, he prides himself on his ability to write, an indicator of gentry status, and he takes umbrage when a lackey offers him snuff without rising: "Yes, do you know, you stupid lout, that I am an official, that I am of noble origin!" When his division head chides him for setting his cap for the director's daughter, he heatedly asserts his feeling of self-esteem and his confidence in reaching a high rank:

> Devil take it, just because his face looks rather like a medicine bottle, and on his head there is some shock of hair curled into a tuft, and he holds it high, and he pomades it into some sort of rosette, so then he thinks that only he can do everything. I understand why he is angry with me. He's jealous. Maybe he saw the preferential signs of favor shown to me. Well, I spit on him! Am I from some sort of plebian background, from a family of tailors or the children of some petty officer? I am gentry. And even yet I may get somewhere. I'm only forty-two, a time of life at which, nowadays, one's service has just begun. Wait my friend, and even I will be a colonel, and, maybe, if God wills it, then something a bit higher.

In contrast to the stupid division head, Poprishchin is a man of intellectual pursuits and literary sensitivity:

> At home for the most part I lay on my bed. Then I copied out some very good little verses:

> > My darling for an hour was away,
> > I hadn't seen her for a year, I thought.
> > Since all this made me hate my lot,
> > I said, to go on living doesn't pay.

> This must have been written by Pushkin.

Fortuitously, the clerk learns that Sophie's lap dog, Madgi, not only can talk but has even been corresponding with another canine, Fidele. These gifted animals have been related correctly enough to Hoffmann's *Kater Murr*, but here we have a demonstration of Gogol's ability to make what he has appropriated uniquely his own. The clerk-narrator, having observed Sophie alighting from a carriage in front of a fashionable shop, notes that:

> Her nasty little dog, unable to jump through the door of the shop, remained on the street. I know this nasty little dog. Her name is Madgi. I hadn't been there a minute when suddenly I hear a tiny little voice: "Hello, Madgi!" How's that for something? Who said that? I looked about and I caught sight of two ladies walking under an umbrella. One was an old woman, the other quite young. But they had already gone by, and next to me again sounded, "It's too bad of you, Madgi!" What the devil! I saw that Madgi was sniffing around a nastly little dog which was following the ladies. "Aha!" I said to

myself, "that's enough, am I drunk? Only it seems that with me this seldom happens."
"No, Fidéle, you are wrong to think so." I myself saw that Madgi said, "I was, *arf, arf,*
I was, *arf, arf, arf,* very sick!" Ah you nasty little dog! I admit that I was very surprrised
hearing her speak as humans do. But later, when I had carefully considered all this,
then I ceased to be surprised. In fact, a large number of similar things occur in the
world. It is said that in England a fish swam up to shore which said two words in such a
strange language that for three years now scholars have been trying to determine what
they were and until the present time have discovered nothing. I also read in the papers
about two cows which went into a shop and ordered a pound of tea. But I admit that I
was far more surprised when Madgi said, "I wrote to you, Fidéle, probably Polkan didn't
deliver my letter." Let them strip me of my salary! I had never heard that a dog could
write. Only a member of the gentry can write correctly. Of course some merchant-
clerks and even serfs do write sometimes, but their writing is for the most part mechanical, without commas, periods, or style.

Curious about information contained in Madgi's letter to Fidéle, the
clerk contrives to steal the correspondence. The letter is a delightful parody
of late Sentimentalist epilostolary style, as well as a devastating satire on life
in the *beau monde.* The dog's eye view of human activities is an excellent
means for "making strange," that is, representing the commonplace in naive
terms.

"With great pleasure I am willing to inform you about things taking place in our
house. I have already said something about the chief gentleman, whom Sofy calls 'Papa.' This is a very strange person. He is silent for the most part. He speaks very seldom.
But a week ago he was constantly talking to himself. 'Will I get it or not get it?'He takes
a paper in one hand, he leaves the other empty and says, 'Will I get it or not get it?'
I was quite unable to comprehend, sniffed at his boots, and went away. Then, *ma chère,*
a week later Papa arrived in great joy. All morning people came to his house in uniforms
and congratulated him for something. At table Papa was happier than I had ever seen
him, he told anecdotes, and after dinner raised me up to his neck and said, 'Now look,
Madgi, at what this is.' I saw some ribbon. I sniffed it, but definitely didn't find any
aroma. Finally, surreptitiously, I licked it; slightly salty."

Learning of Sophie's impending marriage to the gentleman of the bedchamber, Poprishchin is precipitated into a fury. He simply can't understand
why he has been destined to be only a titular counselor. Therefore, when on
December 5 he learns that the throne of Spain is vacant, in itself an impossible and unheard of circumstance, he reasons that the real king must be
somewhere incognito. The entry of December 8 reports that, as was his habit,
he lay on his bed and thought about the situation in Spain, and the following
entry, "April 43, 2000," triumphantly reports that Spain has found its
king—he is that king.
The humor now becomes increasingly black as the clerk-king chronicles
the adventures which culminate in his being conveyed to "Spain" by a depu-
tation from that country. The brutal regime of the insane asylum is described from the point of view of the deranged and perplexed inmate, who
cannot reconcile his exalted rank with his being beaten and doused with cold

water. The final entry is actually pathetic, an anguished declaration that he can no longer endure the torture, a frantic plea to be saved, taken away, transported by a speeding troika to his home, to the arms of his mother, where he might be safe from persecution. And then the Gogolian puff of smoke with which everything disappears: "And do you know that the Bey of Algiers has a wen right under his nose?"

The Portrait [Portret] is the weakest link in the chain of Arabesques. Gogol reworked the piece for publication in 1842, but the 1835 version remains superior—because it is shorter. Somehow one hardly perceives this work as fiction, and certainly it is almost totally unlike the other stories of the Petersburg cycle. One might define it as a moralistic tract on the subject of artistic integrity, with a liberal seasoning of the value-of-prayer theme. Its relentless sermonizing is practically unrelieved by dialogue. It is all *utile* and no *dulce*.

A poor but promising artist, Chertkov, buys the forbidding portrait of an Asiatic usurer, notable for its life-like eyes. The first night the portrayed figure leaves the frame, much in the style of Washington Irving's *The Adventures of the Mysterious Picture,* Charles Maturin's *Melmoth the Wanderer,* or Orest Somov's *The Frightening Guest.* The following day the artist accidentally discovers 1,000 ducats which had been concealed in the frame, and from that moment he prospers. An elegant wardrobe and fashionable address combine with purchased publicity to ensure his success, and he becomes truly rich. However, in catering to the whims of his customers he loses his touch, and becomes incapable of producing anything of real artistic value. Envious of those who have remained true to their calling, he exhausts his fortune buying up paintings and slashing them to ribbons. Finally, he dies insane.

The second part of the story is retrospective and recounts how the fearsome painting had come to be painted and how it destroyed the lives of all those who kept it in their possession. When the artist who had painted it learned of its pernicious effect, he went to a monastery and thence to the wilderness, where he performed feats of asceticism worthy of a saint. Ultimately he was purified and able to resume his brush and palette to paint The Birth of Jesus.

> For a whole year he sat over it, not leaving his cell, scarcely supporting himself with a coarse diet, praying incessantly. At the end of a year the painting was ready. This was simply a miracle of the brush. . . a feeling of divine peace and humility on the face of the virgin mother bending over her child, the deep wisdom in the eyes of the divine child, as if already seeing something in the distance, the triumphant silence of the Magi, amazed by the divine miracle, as they bowed at his feet, and, finally, the whole picture, all this was presented in such a harmonious power and strength of beauty that the impression was magical. All of the monks fell on their knees before the new icon. . . .

All of this is very praiseworthy, and many commentators have pointed to the moral exemplified by Chertkov, who ostensibly yielded to the blandishments of cheap fame. Still, Gogol and his commentators have forgotten a vital fact: Chertkov was powerless, since he was under the spell of the fatal painting. Such being the case, he has been unjustly portrayed and interpreted as an object-lesson on the immiscibility of venality and true art.

In one of Poprishchin's ravings, he predicts that the earth will sit on the moon, a dainty sphere inhabited by noses (that is why we cannot see our own), and he fears that the weight of the earth will grind the noses into flour. This disgusting apprehension is "realized" in The Nose[Nos], where a loaf of bread is found to contain the olfactory organ of a certain Major Kovalyov,

Some commentators have been so dazzled or bewitched by Gogol that they fail to distinguish between his finer flights into the absurd and his occasional crash landing. Of his tales set in Petersburg, The Nose and The Portrait seem to me to fall into the latter category. The Nose was first sent to the Moscow Observer in 1835, which rejected it as being banal and foul [poshlaia i graznaia], then it was revised and published in Pushkin's Contemporary in 1836. An introductory comment was provided:

N.V. Gogol for some time did not agree to the printing of this piece, but we found in it so much of the unexpected, fantastic, light-hearted, and original that we persuaded him to permit us to share with the public the pleasure which his manuscript afforded us.

Far be it from me to gainsay Pushkin, whose critical acumen was more developed than that of any of his contemporaries. Still, there may have been other reasons for Pushkin to publish the story, such as the previous success of Gogol's The Calash [Koliaska], which appeared in an earlier number of the periodical. The suspicion also occurs that the statement was not made by Pushkin but rather by Gogol, for it somehow seems uncharacteristic of the former but quite in the manner of the latter.

The Nose is totally absurd, but that is not its weakness. It is that the absurdity is forced, and the whole story seems haphazard and more silly than comic. It opens with a barber, Ivan Yakovlevich, discovering a nose baked into the middle of his breakfast loaf. He immediately identifies the item as belonging to the collegiate assessor Kovalyov, whom he shaves twice weekly. His wife's wild accusations and threats of denunciation drive him from the house with the breakfast surprise concealed in a cloth. After a number of unsuccessful efforts to rid himself of the unwanted object, the barber surreptitiously drops it off the Isaak bridge. In so doing, he attracts the attention of a policeman, who demands an explanation. At this point the story breaks abruptly to Major Kovalyov, a pretentious gentleman who has assumed the military title of major although he is actually a civil servant. His discovery that his nose is missing is more than dismaying, since its absence cannot but hinder his quest for a vice-governorship and a wife with a dowry of two thousand rubles. Imagine his chagrin when he discovers his nose masquerading as a state counselor, a rank higher than the major's own, but even worse the miscreant organ cuts the poor major cold when approached in the Kazan cathedral. The snobbish facial appendage absolutely refuses to have anything to do with the socially inferior major, and walks away, leaving him baffled and helpless. Efforts to advertise for the runaway are frustrated, and the police prove uncooperative. The naughty nose is finally apprehended on its way to Riga, and somehow it ultimately returns to its proper station. Hardly high comedy, and a bit too confusing for parody.

Those who find Gogol a rich lode for the mining of Freudian elements have naturally suggested that in Gogol's topsy-turvy world Major Kovalyov's nose is really something else, and that his loss of that appendage is the manifestation of some *Ur*-fear common to males. The inverted approach also transfers nose envy to envy of another organ, which certainly adds further interest to the tale. Romantics, following Sterne, whose story of Swackenburgius's nose in *Tristram Shandy* may also be variously interpreted, were quite excited by noseology, and Gogol was not the first in Russian fiction to detach a nose.[2] In fact, there is a suggestion at the conclusion of his story that *The Nose* is a parody of such stories, which are "of no advantage to the fatherland." The double theme is also derivative, as any connoisseur of Hoffmann and the *Doppelgaenger* recognizes.

The story is original, however, in certain scenes where officialdom is satirized—mocked is a better word. Kovalyov's failure to have the newspaper accept his advertisement about his runaway organ is quite amusing, but funnier still are the gibes at the police. The police inspector to whom Kovalyov turns for aid is exceedingly fond of sugar loaves:

In his house the entire entry, it and the dining room, were stacked with sugar loaves, which merchants had brought to him out of friendship. At that time the cook was pulling the government jack-boots off the police inspector. His sword and all his military armor were peacefully hanging in the corners, his three year old son had already dragged off his terrifying three cornered hat, and he, after his martial, military life was ready to taste the pleasure of peace.

Kovalyov went into him at the time when he had just stretched, croaked, and said, "Ech, I'll sleep a couple of wee hours!" And therefore one can anticipate that the arrival of the collegiate assessor was totally inopportune. And I don't know even if he had brought to him at that time several pounds of tea or cloth he would have been received too joyously. The inspector approved greatly of all arts and manufactured goods, but he preferred above everything government paper money. "That's the thing," he used to say, "there's just nothing better than that thing: it doesn't ask to eat, it takes up little space, it always fits in the pocket, and if you drop it, it doesn't break."

The inspector received Kovalyov rather dryly and said that after dinner was not the time to carry out an investigation, that nature herself had ordained that having eaten one should rest a bit (from this the collegiate assessor could see that the police inspector was not unacquainted with the pronouncements of ancient sages), that noses are not torn off gentlemen, and that there are all kinds of majors on the earth who don't have even their underpants in decent condition and hang around all kinds of improper places.

That is, not on the brow but right in the eye! One should note that Kovalyov was an excessively touchy person. He could pardon whatever was said about himself, but he in no way could forgive anything relating to his rank or calling. He even proposed that in theatrical plays one would allow everything relating to *ober*-officers, but that it would be forbidden to attack staff-officers. The inspector's reception so confused him that he shook his head and having spread his arms somewhat, said with a feeling of dignity,"I admit that after such offensive remarks on your part, I have nothing to add." And he left.

The story concludes with the narrator's bumbling and confusing efforts to justify his story and also express his puzzlement over some of the events. And before the reader knows it, our squirming raconteur has slipped out the side door and left us with a bag empty of explanations:

That's the kind of story which took place in the northern capital of our vast state! Only now, after thinking it all over, do we see that there is a great deal of the improbable in it. Not speaking of the fact that the supernatural separation of the nose and its appearance in various places in the form of a state counselor is simply strange, how is it that Kovalyov did not understand that you can't advertise about a nose in a newspaper? I am not speaking here in the sense that it would seem to me to be expensive for an advertisement; that's nonsense, and I do not number myself among the penurious. But it is improper, inept and wrong. And then also—how did the nose find itself in the baked loaf, and did Ivan Yakovlevich. . . ? No, I don't understand this at all, I decidedly don't understand. But what is stranger, what is least of all understandable, is how an author can choose such subjects. I admit that this is quite inconceivable, this is just. . . no, no, I just don't understand. In the first place, there is decidedly no advantage to the fatherland, and in the second. . . but even in the second place there is no advantage. I simply don't know what this is. . . .

Nonetheless, with all this, although, naturally, it would be possible to permit this, that, and a third, maybe even. . . well, and where are there not contradictions? And yet still, when you think about it, there is indeed something in all this. Whatever you say, similar events do happen in the world, seldom, but they happen.

We shall return to Gogol for a discussion of his *Overcoat* (1840) and a brief treatment of *Dead Souls*, his picaresque fantasy of 1842.

СОВРЕМЕННИКЪ,

ЛИТТЕРАТУРНЫЙ ЖУРНАЛЪ,

ИЗДАВАЕМЫЙ

АЛЕКСАНДРОМЪ ПУШКИНЫМЪ.

ПЕРВЫЙ ТОМЪ.

САНКТПЕТЕРБУРГЪ.

ВЪ ГУТТЕНБЕРГОВОЙ ТИПОГРАФІИ.

1836.

Title page of the first issue of Pushkin's *The Contemporary*, St. Petersburg, 1836.

XXII. The Justly Forgotten—P. Mashkov and A. Pavlov.

Among the writers of the thirties were several who have quite rightly been forgotten, the Charity Sisters of Russian Romanticism, whose fiction is so incondite that by comparison even a Marlinsky emerges as a Shakespeare. Who read these authors? Probably provincial girls, old maids, and literate house serfs. Their stories are marked by preposterous situations, coincidences, insufficient characterizations, total absence of continuity in character behavior, authorial sententiousness, strained comparisons, periphrasic cliches, and general dullness. To read them is a tedious exercise, relieved only by an occasional guffaw as one encounters an unexpected egregious example of technical clumsiness. A few representative examples are provided, if only to provide a full spectrum of Romantic fiction.

Among these is Pyotr Mashkov, whose imagination, it must be said, was more facile than his writing skill. Included in his *Tales and Dreams [Povesti i mechty]*, published in 1833, is *The Institute Girl [Institutka]*, an example of petrified Sentimentalism from the linguistic point of view and improbable freneticism as far as the plot goes. There are two confessions, the first of Alexander, a gypsy orphan, who falls in love with Elizaveta, the daughter of his benefactress. This leads to a duel with her brother, whose death forces Alexander to part forever from his beloved. Somehow in his travels in the prairies of America he receives a notebook with the confession of Count Bronsky, an old confidant of the benefactress's family, who details the deception of his first wife, the death of their child, his later clandestine affair with Elizaveta while she was in a Petersburg institute, and finally his first wife's death and ultimate marriage to Elizaveta. Bronsky concludes by urging Alexander to forget his Elizaveta, and an epilogue reports the young man's funeral.

The only thing out of the ordinary here is the gypsy origin of Alexander, which causes his sense of social inferiority. Otherwise, we have two rather arbitrarily interwoven "psychological" tales, presented as usual with virtually no dialogue, minimal dramatization of critical events, and overly generous remarks about the frailties of human nature. Physical nature is employed for intensification, as in the opening description of the death of Alexander's gypsy father:

A fall evening. Black clouds, like crowds of criminal angels which had fled from heaven, flew quickly through the air. We camped for the night in a forest. A gusty wind whistled among the faded trees, the sounds of distant thunder and constant lightning presaged all the terrors of approaching night. I sat silently in the tattered tent, through the holes of which penetrated the cold wind. Next to me, on the straw, lay my pale, sick father. My mother sat at his pillow and quietly whispered to me that I should be quiet and not prolong the sufferer's death with sudden cries. "He is dying," she said quietly,

and tears flowed from her eyes. . . . At each flash of lightning he shuddered, opened his dull eyes, looked at my mother, at me, stretched his trembling hands to us and fell again into some sort of deep insensibility. His breath became less frequent, less frequent. . . he opened his dull glance once more, sighed, and that sigh was—the last. "He has died!" cried my mother, "your father has died!," and she began to give vent to cries of despair, she beat herself on the breast with her hands and kissed the corpse. . . .
The night was dark, thunder roared above me, lightning flashed, and rain began to fall. All the gypsies slept, except an old man, who quietly sang out his sorrow in front of a dying fire. The wind dried the tears of the orphan child. Suddenly I heard the voice of my mother, she calls me, I run to her, she bids me to go to bed, and I lie down on the mat next to my father, embrace his unfeeling corpse, and fall asleep.

This final touch, sharing the mat with a corpse, suggests Mashkov's familiarity with the excesses of Monk Lewis or Charles Maturin and his disciples of *l'Ecole frénétique.*

The plot of *Perfidy [Verolomstvo]* is entirely too involved to summarize here, but a general idea will be conveyed when we know that it involves a charming institute graduate, a misanthropic but handsome young man, a hideous wizard, a false friend, and a treacherous gypsy girl. We are treated to pursuit by a poisonous snake, blackmail, murder, necrophilia, two suicides, and the heroine, understandably demented by these occurrences, burns to death.

In 1835, Mashkov was back with his novel *The Fearful Marriage. An Event from the 17th Century. Taken from the Notes of a Certain English Traveler [Uzhasnyi brak, sobytie XVII veka. Pocherpnutoe iz zapisok odnogo Angliiskogo puteshestvennika].* Spain, an inexhaustible source of inspiration for disciples of freneticism, provides our setting:

At the time we have chosen for our narrative, in the vicinity of the town of Valencia roamed a most dangerous band of cutthroats known as the Bloody League. A certain Lorenzo, condemned to death by the government for the murder of a nobleman, accidentally had escaped execution and hidden himself from the searches of the police. Having lost his property, his honor, and his rights, and with his name disgraced, he had taken a fatal oath to dedicate his life to implacable vengeance against the government, which in defending unjustly the rights of the strong had rejected all the complaints which Lorenzo had brought before it against his powerful adversary, while the latter, making use of his power, increased his oppression and daring to the point that the despairing Lorenzo had decided to become a murderer. . . . Having gathered together bold vagabonds, as embittered by fate as himself, he impetuously gave himself to murdering, and with hellish joy he heard the cries of his victims. He thirsted for blood, and his firm hand was tireless in spilling it.

In order that his men not fall prey to the wiles of women who might betray them, Lorenzo has them all, himself included, take an oath to avoid women on pain of death. Then he himself falls in love with the comely Isabella, a girl of seventeen. With great rectitude he admits his passion to his henchmen and condemns himself to death, but they will have none of it. As a compromise, Francisc (not Francisco), also known as "Bear Paw," proposes that Lorenzo marry the girl and kill her after thirty days. Adopting the name Don Lerma—shades of Lermontov's Spanish period[1]—Lorenzo gains the permission of Isabella's father and marries the girl. His initial conjugal happiness gives way to gloom as the fateful deadline approaches, and on the final day he learns to his horror that he is to be a father. But he is a man of his word. He leaves the house and returns undetected that night, enters his bedroom, and raises his weapon over the sleeping figure. Connoisseurs of the macabre had nothing to complain about in the description of what followed:

> Then again the twisting steel sketched the design of death in the air and with the speed of lightning fell on its victim. . . a second blow followed the first, and the Spanish girl's head, severed from the torso, fell on the floor with open eyes. . . the tongue muttered several mute sounds and several violent spasms racked the nerves of the beheaded woman. . . one of her hands struck Lorenzo on the breast.

All of this is too much even for a virtuous monster such as Lorenzo, so he disbands his Bloody League and retires to the seclusion of Livorno, there to suffer remorse for seven long years. Caught in a storm one night, he sees the ghost of Isabella, but the phantom remains silent. Taking refuge in a nearby house, he encounters a little girl of six, who brings him wine and seeks to comfort him. Unconsoled, he takes poison, and imagine his shock when the girl's mother, who had gone away on a mission of mercy, returns and proves to be Isabella in the flesh! She explains that on the night of her "death" she had given her bed to a servant and had retired to another room. He dies, forgiven by his wife and child.

Although this story exemplifies Mashkov's usual inanity of plot and incomprehensibility of character motivation, it is superior to his other works owing to the absence of overt sententiousness and digressiveness. For what it is worth, he sticks to his story, and his prose style, while hardly exemplary, is not overly weighted with his usual metaphorical cliches, asides to the reader, and ponderous nature descriptions. One might even say that his work was almost on a par with that of the young military cadet, Mikhail Lermontov, who in 1832-1834 was trying his hand at a historical novel, *Vadim*, in the style of *l'Ecole frénétique*, a work also embodying an outcast hero, beheading, and violence for its own sake. Lermontov begins where Mashkov ends.

Another minor "talent" of Romantic fiction is A. A. Pavlov, whose *Kasimov Tales and Legends [Kasimovskie povesti i predaniia]* appeared in 1836. A brief introduction, dated 1833, explains that the author, while spending his summer on an estate near Kasimov (300 versts east of Moscow), thought to collect legends and beliefs retained by the descendants of the Kasimov Tatars, and he concludes:

> This is my first attempt, the first work of a young imagination, and therefore I ask that my readers not be severe judges. . . . If fate allows me to live to a ripe old

age, then with what pleasure will I open my composition, written in the 17th year of my life.

The young Mr. Pavlov quite correctly requested the indulgence of his readers, because his work, despite its rather unusual focus upon the lore of Kasimov, rarely breaks the boredom barrier. The initial thirty-five pages are not fiction but rather a most circumstantial and somewhat interesting description of Kasimov, a half-Russian and half-Tatar manufacturing town on the Oka River with many rich merchants and a sprinkling of gentry.

The first "legend," *Amin*, takes its title from the name of the youngest of three Moslem brothers, whose rectitude and adherence to his father's deathbed admonitions lead him to wealth, while his wastrel brothers are led to penury.

Pigich has momentary promise. It is the story of a legendary Kasimov robber, Pigich, who lives in a remote swamp with his grotesque and gigantic sister-in-law. They travel together on their criminal conspiracies in a cart pulled by a shaggy bear. The villain is indeed hideous:

> The oldster was more than fifty. His face was sprinkled with ulcerous reddish pimples, which came together on his nose into one putrid spot. On his face alone there were as many wrinkles as on fifty men of his age. His eyes—but how can one describe these muddy eyes! Now they would bulge out from his forehead at the sight of profitable things, now they would hide under his thick, grey lashes when the oldster was occupied by any thought. His height was the smallest. His back was ornamented, as with a camel, by two humps. From his knees his legs went in opposite directions, and they seemed momentarily ready to break under the weight of his body. His arms were disproportionately long, and three fingers on each of his hands did not bend.
>
> That is the portrait of this honorable old man! But who is this handsome fellow? The cutthroat and thief Pigich.

Pigich and his accomplice set fire to a village in the course of robbing a rich peasant, and the villagers besiege their hideout. The shaggy bear perishes in a hail of bullets as it attacks the avengers, the sister-in-law is shot and axed to death, and Pigich is captured and taken to Kasimov for trial. He repents his three hundred murders, his robbery of churches, his desecration of graves, and pleads with his captors for a speedy execution. His wish is their command.

The author's inexperience is evident in the story's lack of proportion, its long-windedness, its cliches, and its sententiousness. After all, how are we to take seriously the crimes of a brigand whose nose is one huge pimple and who rides in a cart drawn by a shaggy, albeit loyal, bear? Pavlov's collection includes other tales, such as *The Miller-Wizard [Mel'nik Koldun]*, *The Tomb of the Mad Woman [Mogila bezumnoi]* and *The Secret Defender [Tainstvennyi zashchitnik]*. This latter is a tale about Kasimov merchants and the supernatural intervention of a deceased son to save his wounded father, but once again the author fails to exploit successfully the potentials of his plot.

270

XXIII. Pushkin's *The Captain's Daughter.*

In 1836 Pushkin published *The Captain's Daughter [Kapitanskaia dochka]*, a historical novel whose superiority to more typical works of that genre is owing largely to an element not normally developed—psychological analysis. In his earlier works, especially in *Boris Godunov, Mozart and Salieri, The Shot,* and *The Queen of Spades,* Pushkin was engaged in the study of a personality type, the psychological imposter. In this work he probes the personality and motivation of Emilian Pugachev, the renegade Cossack posing as the deceased Peter III, who led a massive popular uprising which raged over south-eastern Russia from September 1773 until the pretender's capture the following fall. The history of Pugachev's meteoric success and fall are chronicled in the memoirs of a fictional character, Pyotr Grinyov, a junior army officer, who witnessed the deeds of the rebel leader. In a brief afterword, the publication of Grinyov's tale is motivated:

The manuscript of Pyotr Andreevich Grinyov was presented to us by one of his grandsons, who had learned that we were engaged in a work relating to the times described by his grandfather. We decided, with the permission of his relatives, to publish it as a separate work, having found a proper epigraph for each chapter and taking it upon ourselves to change certain personal names.

The Editor

The influence of Walter Scott has been discussed in the critical literature on this work. Suffice it to say that in the tradition of Scott Pushkin's novel involves historical personages and events mixed with the lives of fictional characters, a virtuous heroine and brave hero separated by the fortunes of war, a faithful servant willing to die for his master, and numerous vividly portrayed minor characters. But Pushkin's work reflects little of Scott's love of legend or historical paraphernalia—detailed descriptions of towns, houses, clothes, arms, food. In place of that, it concerns itself with the nature of the dominant historical figure.

The novel was begun in 1833 during Pushkin's research into the Pugachev Uprising, about which he also published a purely historical account entitled *The History of the Pugachev Rebellion [Istorii pugachevskogo bunta]* (1834). The history is a straightforward, totally reportorial exposition of facts. Such a scholarly approach probably did not satisfy Pushkin's interest in the personality behind the revolution, and to explore this he turned to fiction. Obviously, Pushkin was fascinated by the charismatic quality of Pugachev, an illiterate with the powers of a Pied Piper to attract followers, a man of studied cruelty and gross conduct but also capable of disinterested generosity and true dignity.

In a letter to his friend Korsakov (25 October, 1836), Pushkin explain-

271

ed the origin of his plot:

> My novel is based on a legend which I once heard about how one of those officers who had betrayed his duty and gone over to Pugachov's bands was pardoned by the empress at the request of his aged father, who threw himself at her feet. The novel, as you have deigned to note, has departed considerably from the facts.

The style is pure Pushkin, laconic and tinged with humor. In the *Vorgeschichte* the narrator describes his provincial gentry family and the circumstances of his formative years, when he was tutored first by a servant named Savelyich and then by a Frenchman:

> Beaupré had been a barber in his fatherland, next a soldier in Prussia, and then he had come to Russia *pour être outchitel*, hardly understanding the meaning of the word. He was a good fellow, but thoughtless and dissolute to the extreme. His chief weakness was a passion for the fair sex, and for his affections he more than once received blows from which he groaned for days at a time. Moreover, he was not (in his own words) *an enemy of the bottle*, that is, (speaking in Russian) he liked to guzzle a bit. . . . We immediately got along, and although his contract obliged him to teach me *French and German and all learning*, he preferred to learn as quickly as possible from me to chatter in Russian, and then each of us did what he wanted to. We lived in harmony. I had no desire for any other mentor.

The intrigue begins when the seventeen-year-old Grinyov, accompanied by Savelyich, is sent by his father to Orenburg to begin his military career. The protective servant is greatly distressed when the trusting youth is first fleeced at billiards in a country inn by a hussar, Ivan Zurin, and then gives his hare-skin coat to a ragged peasant who guided them to shelter during a blizzard. After reaching Orenburg, Grinyov is posted to Belogor fortress, one of many small posts scattered about the steppe to keep order among the nomadic tribes. There he is welcomed by the eccentric commandant, Captain Mironov, and his garrulous wife, Vasilisa Yegorovna, who really gives the orders. Grinyov soon falls in love with the Captain's daughter, Masha, a girl of many virtues, and this leads him to duel with Shvabrin, a young officer whom Masha had previously rejected. Grinyov is wounded, recovers, proposes, but his father will not bless the marriage. Meanwhile, Pugachev gathers his initial band and, supported by rebellious Yaik Cossacks, begins to plunder villages and capture fortresses. Belogor is attacked, the Cossacks defect, and the fort is overwhelmed. Shvabrin immediately joins the rebels. Captain Mironov refuses to acknowledge Pugachev as Peter III and is summarily hanged. Vasilisa Yegorovna is slaughtered when she protests. Grinyov, too, refuses to swear allegiance to Pugachev, but he is spared and sent to Orenburg to transmit Pugachov's demand for surrender.

The rest of the novel, typical of the genre, concerns Grinyov's efforts to find Masha, which he does after many suspenseful episodes, receiving Pugachev's help in thwarting the plans of the traitorous Shvabrin. Masha is sent to the protection of Grinyov's parents, who come to love her, while he joins the hussar Zurin's forces in putting down the rebellion. The story goes on to chronicle Pugachev's ultimate defeat, the reunion of Masha and Grinyov, and later his unexpected arrest for collaboration with Pugachev, the result of Shvabrin's denunciation. Grinyov is found guilty and faces severe punishment, but all turns out well when Masha tells the true facts to the Empress, Catherine II.

Despite the thematic and structural elements typical of the historical novel, *The Captain's Daughter* is unique for the period. It is a *sui generis* psychological study, and matters of setting are quite incidental. Pushkin is little concerned with historical *realia*, and so we have merely a general impression of Orenburg as a large, fortified town, and only a very sketchy idea of what Belogor fortress looks like. When the heroine goes to Tsarskoe Selo and encounters Catherine, we are provided a few scant details about the park but virtually nothing about the palace itself. Can one imagine Lazhechnikov omitting an opportunity for a long and circumstantial description of Orenburg in the 1770's? And certainly neither he, nor any other historical novelist, would have placed a character in the Summer Palace without a lengthy set piece on its plan, decor, ornamentation. But this is how Pushkin treats the scene:

After several minutes the carriage stopped at the palace. Trembling, Marya Ivanovna went up the stairs. The doors in front of her opened wide. She passed through a long series of empty, elegant rooms. A chamber lackey showed the way. Finally, having arrived at locked doors, he declared that he would announce her at once, and he left her alone.

Historical novels are traditionally filled with minor figures, whose comic stereotyped speech and eccentricities rapidly become predictable, and often wearisome. In *The Captain's Daughter,* however, the minor characters are lively and attractive, similar to some of those odd types found in Somov's tales. Especially noteworthy is Vasilisa Yegorovna Mironova, the wife of the commander of Belogor fortress. Outspoken and domineering, she is also good-natured and generous. When the first attempt of Grinyov and Shvabrin to duel is discovered, the two antagonists are brought before her:

Vasilisa Yegorovna met us."Ach, my fine fellows! What's going on here? How's that? What? To drag murder into our fortress! Ivan Kuzmich, put them under arrest immediately! Pyotr Andreich! Alexey Ivanych! Hand over your swords here, hand them over, hand them over. Palashka, take these swords to the storeroom. Pyotr Andreich! I didn't expect this of you. Aren't you ashamed? It's all right for Alexey Ivanych. He was read out of the Guards for murder, he doesn't believe in the Lord, but why you? Are you coming to that?"

When word is received that Pugachev's attack is imminent, Grinyov suggests that Vasilisa and Masha be sent to a safer place:

Ivan Kuzmich turned to his wife and said to her, "Do you hear that, my dear, and indeed, won't you both go a little ways away until we have dealt with the rebels?"

"That's just useless," said the commandant's wife. "where is there a fortress that bullets won't reach? Why is Belogor dangerous? Praise the Lord, this is the twenty-second year we've lived here. We've seen Bashkirs and Kirghiz. Maybe we'll even sit out Pugachev."

Captain Mironov, who lets his wife run the garrison while he drills his soldiers in his dressing gown, is the prototype for a number of similar characters found in Russian fiction, modest and simple soldiers whose long and faithful service has raised them to officer's rank, intensely loyal, revered by their subordinates, innately brave, the embodiment of natural Russian virtues. Lermontov's Maxim Maximych and Tolstoy's Captain Mironov are descendants.

Another marvelous characterization in this story is that of Grinyov's parsiminious servant, Savelyich, who is ready to sacrifice his life for his master but whose devotion often causes Grinyov anxiety and sometimes is so inopportune as to precipitate disaster, as when he self-righteously presents Pugachev with a demand for compensation for articles looted from Grinyov's apartment. Savelyich, however, is not the first such character in Russian literature, for he is preceded by Orest Somov's Sysoyevich Chuchin, the mentor-servant of Valery Vyshegliadov in *Mommy and Sonny [Matiushka i synok]*, published in 1833.

Pushkin does not provide any developed portrait of Masha, the captain's daughter, who is merely presented as a pretty, simple, but sensible young lady, a proper match for the uncomplicated Grinyov. But she is sufficiently characterized to serve the plot without causing the reader to become perplexed regarding her motivations or actions. Pushkin most likely chose such a minor character as the title figure to avoid problems with the censorship, for there was still a lingering fear in court circles connected with the name of Pugachev. The title proposed by Pushkin for his history of the rebel was changed by Nicholas I from *The History of Pugachev* to *The History of Pugachev's Rebellion.* Earlier Catherine II had proscribed any mention of his name at all, his house had been razed, his native village had been moved to a new location, and the Yaik Cossacks, who had supported him, had been renamed Ural Cossacks.

Pugachev is the real "hero" of this novel, for he affects the destinies of all the characters. And it is his personality that Pushkin seeks to explain, if not to excuse. Of course, Pushkin's sympathy is that of comprehension, not approbation. The litany of atrocities presented in Pushkin's history is paralleled in the novel, and in recording the end of the war Grinyov remarks, "God forbid we ever see a Russian rebellion, senseless and merciless."

Pugachev first appears as the peasant guide who confidently leads the lost Grinyov and his entourage to safety in the blizzard. Once at the inn, Grinyov is able to observe the man more closely.

His appearance seemed striking to me. He was about forty, of medium height, lean, and broad-shouldered. In his black beard grey hairs were already showing. His large, lively eyes were always in motion. His face had an expression which was rather pleasant but roguish. His hair was cut in a circle, and he was wearing a tattered smock and Tatar pantaloons. I offered him a cup of tea. He tried it and frowned. "Your honor, do me a favor. Order them to bring a glass of liquor. Tea is not a drink for Cossacks."

The man and the innkeeper then converse in thieves' cant, which mystifies Grinyov. The next morning when Grinyov presents the peasant with his hare-skin coat, the man responds with a low bow and "Thank you, your honor! God reward you for your charity. I will always remember your kindness."

After the fall of Belogor, Pugachev indifferently orders the execution of those who refuse to recognize him as Peter III, including Grinyov. However, Savelych's impassioned pleas on behalf of his master have their effect, and Pugachev spares the young officer. Later Savelyich identifies Pugachev to Grinyov as the peasant to whom he had given his coat:

I was greatly surprised. Indeed, the resemblance of Pugachov to my guide was striking. I was convinced that Pugachev and he were the same person, and then I understood the reason for the mercy he had shown me. I couldn't but wonder at the strange series of circumstances: A child's coat given to a tramp had saved me from the noose, and a drunkard staggering from one inn to another was beseiging fortresses and shaking the empire to its foundations.

Grinyov's forthright refusal to accede to Pugachev's demand that he serve him, or at least give his word not to oppose him, impresses the pretender, and throughout the rest of their relationship Grinyov's fearless refusal to compromise his loyalty actually works to secure Pugachev's admiration. The pretender's forbearance with Grinyov and his assistance in freeing Masha cause the youth to have mixed emotions about him. At times he sees real nobility of spirit in the man, at times he is dismayed by Pugachev's ugly insistence on his identity as a royal sovereign and his repulsive coarseness and self-indulgence.

Grinyov comes closest to Pugachev as they are traveling to Belogor to free Masha. The officer comments upon the strangeness of his situation, since only yesterday he was fighting against the rebel and today his whole happiness depends upon him. Pugachev obviously enjoys his role of patron and insists he is not so blood-thirsty as most people think. Grinyov, remembering the sack of Belogor, refrains from comment. Pugachev then asks what is said about him in Orenburg:

"There's no denying it. You've made yourself known." The face of the pretender expressed satisfied vanity. "Yes!" he said with a happy look, I wage war wherever I like. Do they know in Orenburg about the battle at Yuzeeva? Forty henerals [sic] were killed, four armies taken prisner [sic]. What do you think, would the Prussian king compete with me?" The cutthroat's boasting amused me. "What do you yourself think?" I said to him, "Could you master Frederick?"

275

"Fyodor Fyodorovich? Why not! I've already mastered your henerals, and they used to beat him. Up to now my arms have been successful. Give me time and I'll get to Moscow."

"You plan to attack Moscow?"

The pretender thought a bit and said in a low voice: "God knows. My road is narrow. I have little choice. My boys think they're so smart. They are thieves. I have to keep a sharp ear. At the first defeat they will ransom their own necks with my head."

Pugachev's awareness of the precariousness of his position, despite continuing victories, reveals an unexpected thoughtfulness. When Grinyov suggests he give himself up, Pugachev declares it is too late. He then tells Grinyov a Kalmyk fable: an eagle once asked a raven why the raven lived three hundred years and he only thirty years, to which the raven replied that he lived on carrion while the eagle drank living blood. But when the eagle tried carrion, he decided to drink blood and take his chances.

When Grinyov learns of Pugachev's capture, his happiness at the possibility of marrying Masha is spoiled by his thoughts of what will happen to the pretender.

At the same time a strange feeling poisoned my happiness. The thought of the criminal spattered with the blood of so many innocent victims and of the execution awaiting him involuntarily agitated me. "Emilian, Emilian!" I thought with chagrin, "Why didn't you throw yourself on a bayonet and expose yourself to grapeshot? You couldn't have thought of anything better." Well, what would you have done? My thoughts of him were inseparable in me from thoughts of the mercy he had showed me at one of the awful moments of his life and of the freeing of my fiancée from the hands of the repulsive Shvabrin.

The reasons for Pushkin's choice of an unsophisticated man as narrator for this story become more clear as Pugachev's portrait emerges from the incidents of plot and Grinyov's evaluation of them. The particular effectiveness of the naive observer has already been seen in Pushkin's *The Shot* and *The Station Master*, but the device is especially useful in this novel, where any evidence of authorial sympathy for Pugachev would have made the work unpublishable. As Grinyov's account proceeds, the reader is gradually able to construct his own portrait of the pretender, one which, if not significantly different from that of Grinyov, is rather more subtle. This is a case study of the dictator, vain, ruthless, opportunistic, at the same time brave, generous, and even merciful, capable of revelling in the adulation of sycophants while also admiring those few who dare to tell him the truth. Pushkin also shows the lonely road of such a pretender, who realizes that his future is precarious, since he can trust no one. The real Pugachev, in fact, was betrayed by his subordinates.

The challenge of Fate was a favorite theme of Russian Romantic authors, and Fate punished the best of them for meddling in her secrets. Many died prematurely, some violently. In the early morning chill of January, 1837, Alexander Pushkin and Baron Georges d'Anthès faced each other from opposite ends of a path trampled in the snow beside the frozen Black River. The seconds gave the signal, the duelists moved toward each other, and d'Anthès fired. Pushkin fell, bloodied the snow, sat up, took aim, and fired. D'Anthès fell, Pushkin cried "Bravo," and fainted. Three days later he was dead. The Tsar, fearing riots at his funeral, had him spirited out of Petersburg to a secret burial.

A young officer of the Guards, confined to his grandmother's Petersburg residence as the result of a riding accident, penned an angry elegy on Pushkin's death, and this was quickly circulated through town in handwritten copies. Then word was brought to the young poet that many felt that Pushkin, who had never been popular in aristocratic circles, had received his just desserts. A sixteen-line supplement was added to the elegy, this time excoriating the members of court society for having provoked the duel between Pushkin and d'Anthès and prophesying divine retribution. A copy was sent to the Tsar with the notation, "A call to revolution." The officer-poet was arrested, and within weeks was exiled to the Caucasus. Thus did Mikhail Lermontov become famous overnight.

Summer arrived. Alexander Bestuzhev, recently promoted to officer's rank, jumped from a small boat as a Russian landing party assaulted the beach at Cape Adler, south of Sochi on the Black Sea. He charged forward and disappeared into the almost tropical vegetation. Shouts, shots, the cries of the native tribesmen, and the Russians were driven back. Lieutenant Bestuzhev was missing, reported by some to have been hacked to death, by others to have been last seen still alive. But he was gone—forever. Years later rumor had it that Bestuzhev was living in a remote Caucasian *aul*, safe from official persecution. Given the longevity attributed to denizens of the Caucasus, he may still be alive and well at a spritely century and four score.

Vladimir Dal

V. Sollogub

XXIV. A Russian George Sand—Countess Rostopchina. Other Women Fictionists: "The Cavalryman-Maiden," Durova, Zhukova, Gan. Picaresque Satire—Kvitka-Osnovianenko and Sollogub. Dal's Fiction.

Countess Evdokia Rostopchina (1811-1858), *née* Sushkova, early dispayed a talent for poetry, but it was only after her marriage in 1833 to the son of the Governor of Moscow, Andrey Rostopchin, that she began to publish actively. Her marriage was not particularly happy, for her husband was several years her junior and preferred horses to literature. In 1836 she settled in Petersburg and quickly established a reputation as an intelligent and talented woman. Pushkin and others dedicated poems to her, and she was particularly close to Lermontov during his last sojourn in Petersburg in 1841.

She has been called the Russian George Sand, and it is certainly true that she followed Mme Dudevant's example in championing women's rights. She was also the only woman fictionist of the period of any great popularity. On purely literary grounds, it is difficult to understand her success, for her plots are banal, her characters ridiculous, and her style inflated Marlinskian rhetoric.

Her first two contributions to the society tale were published in 1838 under the pseudonym *Clairvoyant* [*Iasnovidiashchaia*]. *Rank and Money* [*Chiny i den'gi*] is an exposé of the abuse of position and wealth. This rather brief work has three parts, the first a letter from Vadim Svirsky to his sister, Katerina, then excerpts from his diary, and finally omniscient narration. In all three sections dialogue is almost completely absent, the dramatic potential sacrificed to emotional outpourings.

Vadim Svirsky, a handsome but poor officer, goes to Moscow and falls instantly in love with Vera Klirmova. With the help of her sister, who had been forced into a marriage of convenience, she attempts to find out if there is any chance of persuading her parents to accept Vadim as her husband, but her mother's violent antipathy to any suitor without rank and money provides a clear answer. Vera and Vadim, swearing eternal love, decide to part for a year, during which period the girl hopes to change her mother's attitude.

The diary entries begin with Vadim's ecstatic return to Moscow at the end of a year, but his tone changes when Vera receives him coolly. An omniscient narrator then relates how Vera's mother triumphantly announced to the stunned Svirsky that Vera was engaged to Baron Hochberg, an old general of reputation and wealth. Vadim dies suddenly. Several months later his sister, Katerina, is visiting his grave when she notices an elaborate procession entering the cemetery, obviously the funeral of a wealthy person. Her inquiry reveals they are burying Baroness Hochberg, the General's wife.

The story concludes with a brief epilogue reiterating the point:

Katerina lives in solitude with only the widow of a poor nobleman, whom she took in for propriety's sake. She has never married. And no wonder! She is not pretty, she has no dowry, she is without important parents. Whose business is it to know that within her, with her excellent female mind and character, the soul of an angel and a loving heart are pining away. In society beauty is pleasing and gold necessary!

Whatever may be said for the Countess's efforts on behalf of women's rights, she did nothing to advance the prose literary language. In Svirsky's first letter to his sister, he describes his new found love, Vera, in the following manner:

Joyous, unconstrained, from our first words my enchantress treated me without artifice, and in a quarter of an hour we were completely acquainted. Her conversation, sparkling with wit and intelligence, revealed to me both an excellent education and rare natural gifts. Childish mischievousness united in her with charming modesty, and at the same time, her eyes, without her knowing it, promised whole treasures of feeling and bespoke an unusual soul. I cannot explain why, but we drew together in reveries, as if prophetic dreams had accustomed me to her beforehand, as if her soul, like mine, awaited, sought, and found. At the end of the ball I was wildly in love, and I will tell you sincerely that I had reason to hope that Vera also was not entirely indifferent to me.

But our authoress is able to outdo even Marlinsky in tearing passions to tatters and indulging in nonstop emotional outpourings. In the first diary entry, just before his reunion with Vera after their year's separation, Svirsky writes:

Vera! Vera! In the agitated sorrows of my soul the thought of you alone remains bright, distinct, unchanged, enchanting. I ceaselessly repeat your name, your dear, sacred name. I find in it all the harmony of the Italian, all the expressiveness of my native tongue. For me this name is an echo of heaven, a pledge of all earthly joys, for me it is a secret, all powerful, magical word, revealing paradise! How sweetly it will tremble on my lips, when in a whisper it will be said to her herself. . . . And to think that she, by her inclination, gave me the right to call her that, that this right belongs to me exclusively, that I, I *alone* can pronounce "Vera," and add, *my own*, not fearing her denial.

The Duel [Poedinok], a companion piece to *Rank and Money*, must objectively be described as ludicrous and inane. Unfortunately, it is considerably longer than the previous work. The first third of the story is devoted to acquainting the reader with Colonel Valevich, whose quarters are always draped in black, on whose table is a lamp made from a skull, and on whose wall hangs a pistol along with a tarnished bullet on a string. Standing behind the lamp is the picture of a youth of exceptional beauty, but the position and the coloring indicate that the model must have been a corpse. These intriguing details are followed by a lengthy development of Valevich's habits of isolation, estrangement, and seclusion.

The second part of the story provides an explanation for Valevich's eccentric behavior and the unusual decor of his quarters. This first person account takes us back several years to a period when Valevich first met Dolsky, an officer of truly incredible virtues:

"He had still not experienced anything, but dreamed about everything. He believed in lofty, endless friendship, in self discipline, in virtue without pretension. He believed even more passionately in women and sacred, elevated love. He was *with us*, but not *of us*."

When Dolsky, who becomes Valevich's friend, first falls in love, it is with Julia, a married woman, but their love is pure as driven snow, Platonic, ennobling. Valevich is not in love with Julia, but he is jealous of her attention to Dolsky, and so he provokes Dolsky to a duel, in which the latter is killed. Valevich is then given a letter written by Dolsky on the eve of the duel, and in this letter the victim forgives his murderer, having foreseen his death owing to a prediction made by a gypsy when he was a youth. Although he had given his mother a sacred oath not to duel, he is ready to die, since he knows that the love he and Julia share must eventually become exposed if he lives.

All of Valevich's auditors are reduced to tears by this sad tale, but the story is not over. The regimental doctor then discloses that he knows the true identity of Julia, who had, shortly after Dolsky's death, been crippled for life in a fall at a ball. Actually, he reports, she was not crippled but had only pretended to be, in order to leave society and thus prevent herself from disclosing the secret of her relationship to Dolsky.

Like *Rank and Money*, *The Duel* is lacking in dialogue, and despite the fact that it is an extreme example of the "told" tale, the action advances creepingly. Countess Rostopchina had a talent, uncommon for her time, for squeezing each idea completely dry, for repeating herself almost endlessly, for creating countless variations on a theme:

And so, everywhere, in solitude, in a crowd, with comrades, in the presence of women, Colonel Valevich preserved his unconquerable coolness, his profound aloofness. Neither the sympathy of people ready to become his true friend nor the attraction of feminine wiles were able to rock his tempered indifference. Does some secret lie in his soul, is he unhappy with an unhappy heart, cannot the future cure him, or the past carry into the abyss of years the fateful event forever crushing his destiny?

But this is just the beginning. The obvious declaration, "Yes, Valevich is unhappy," is followed by two questions—"But with what is his soul ill? What feeling suffers within him?"—and a series of paragraphs which expand them. Each of these is introduced by another query—"Has not satiation, misuse of all the blessings of life led him to premature insensitivity. . . . ?" "Has not his self-esteem been damaged?" And after all this prolixity, we are told, "No, no. It wasn't that at all." And then we reverse direction in another series of long paragraphs—"No! No woman ever dominated this unbridled being. . . ."

"He never understood *disillusionment*, that plague of all times. . . ."

Nothing further need be said about this work, other than that it was reprinted in 1839, along with *Rank and Money*, as a separate book under the title *Sketches of High Society [Ocherki bolshogo sveta]*.

Countess Rostopchina wrote little during the forties. The last decade of her life was her most active period, her works appearing primarily in *The Muscovite* and *The Library for Reading*. Among these were *The Family Secret [Semeinaia taina]* (1851), a drama in five acts written in free verse, *The Happy Woman [Schastlivaia zhenshchina]* (1851-1852), a novel, *Flori Pallacio* (1854), a novel and *At the Wharf [U pristani]* (1857), a novel printed in ten small volumes for the convenience of those travelling by steamer or rail. All these works happily lie beyond the limits of this study.

For women to play an active role in Russian literary life at this time was in itself sufficiently unusual, and among the most unusual of this group was Nadezhda Durova (1783-1866), known as the "cavalry-maiden" (*kavelerist-devitsa*). A few biographical details will explain her sobriquet and provide a glimpse of her colorful history.

Her mother was from the Ukrainian gentry and eloped with a Russian hussar officer, thereby bringing down her father's curse. The couple's hopes to placate him with a grandson were dashed by the birth in 1783 of Nadezhda, whose mother resented her even to the point of flinging the infant from the window of a moving carriage on one occasion when its crying annoyed her. As a young girl Nadezhda led a dual life, resisting her mother's efforts to teach her domestic skills while clandestinely training her father' s unbroken Circassian stallion, Alcides. Pressured into marrying a petty civil servant at the age of eighteen, she bore him a son, but soon parted from both husband and child. In 1806, having cut her hair and donned male apparel, she fled from home with Alcides and joined a Cossack regiment.

Assuming the name Sokolov, and later Alexandrov, she played a hero's role in the battle of Gutstadt in the spring of 1807 and continued to see action until the battle of Friedland, when she was removed from the front lines by her general for being excessively zealous. On the conclusion of that campaign, she was called to Petersburg by Alexander I and presented a medal for valor. Following a furlough of several years, in 1811 she returned to active duty, seeing continuous action during the retreat of the Russian army. Wounded in the battle of Borodino, she later served as adjutant to General Kutuzov and took part in the invasion of Bohemia and Prussia. Throughout her military career she maintained the appearance and demeanor of a man, insisting that she be treated as Officer Alexandrov. She retired from the service in 1816 with the rank of Junior Cavalry Captain.

Durova's literary efforts were apparently inspired, at least in part, by the need to supplement her paltry military pension. In 1835 her brother wrote to Alexander Pushkin, whom he knew slightly, proposing that Pushkin edit his sister's memoirs. The poet responded very affirmatively, providing a prescription for the proper prose style:

As far as style is concerned, the simpler the better. The chief thing: truth, sincerity. The subject itself is so engaging that no ornamentation is needed. It would even spoil it.

In the spring of 1836 Durova set off from Kazan by carriage on a six weeks' journey to Petersburg, carrying her completed manuscript with her. Pushkin was charmed with it, and a selection was printed in his *Contemporary* with the title *Notes of a Cavalry-Maiden [Zapiski kavalerist-devitsy]*. This sampler was introduced by Pushkin's remarks lauding "the charm of this informal tale, so removed from authorial pretense, and the simplicity with which the ardent heroine describes the most unusual circumstances."

Her autobiography is a somewhat strange work, because of the arbitrary nature of what she chooses to relate. Her account opens with details of her family background and early years, with emphasis upon her mother's relentless dissatisfaction with everything she did. Mention is made of a short-lived attraction for a young Ukrainian, Kiriyak, effectively frustrated by her lack of a suitable dowry, but there is not a word about her subsequent marriage to Durov and the birth of her son. Nor does she tell us about her audience with Alexander I, and she passes over in silence all details of her adventures during the retreat from the Nieman, the Battle of Borodino, or her later service under Kutuzov.

There is little dramatic content, even in the descriptions of battle. Mostly she seems to have been constantly fatigued, hungry, wet and cold, but very proud to fight for tsar and country. Her account gives one the impression of a most determined and single-minded young lady, not overly intelligent but with a strong moral sense and kind heart. The description of the death of her beloved Alcides, who miraculously survived in battle only to die in an accident, is quite moving.

Humor, when it appears, centers around her failures of omission and commision, usually the result of poor judgement or excessive zeal. Her situation as a woman in a man's cavalry occasioned many problems:

They gave me an officer's coat, a sabre, a lance so heavy that it seems like a beam. They gave me woolen epaulets, a helmet with a plume, a white bandoleer with a cartridge belt. All of this is very clean, very pretty, and very heavy. However, I hope to become used to it. But what is impossible to become used to are these tormenting government boots, which are like iron! Until then I had worn soft and properly sewed footwear, and my feet were free and light, but now! My God! I am as if chained to the ground with the weight of these boots and huge rattling spurs.

Later she did become accustomed to her cavalry boots and learned to wield her lance effectively, even to the point of routing a group of French cavalry which was about to dispatch a fallen Russian officer.

May 22, 1807. Gutstadt. I saw battle for the first time and took part in it. How much nonsense had they harangued me about one's first battle, about fear, courage, and finally, about desperate manliness! Rubbish! Our regiment attacked several times, not all together, but by squadrons. I was dressed down for having attacked with each squadron. But this was not from excessive bravery but simply from ignorance. I thought I was supposed to and was very surprised when the sergeant of a different squadron, next to whom I was riding like the wind, cried out: "Get out of here!. . . . I almost lost my invaluable Alcides. Riding about, as I have said, near our squadron and observing the interesting picture of battle, I saw several enemy dragoons who, having encircled a Russian officer, had shot him off his horse with a pistol. He had fallen, and they wanted to slash him as he lay on the ground. At the moment I flew up to him, holding my lance at the ready. I suppose that this insane daring frightened them, because in an instant they left the officer and scattered. I galloped up to the wounded man and stopped over him. For two minutes I looked at him without saying anything. He lay with closed eyes, probably thinking that the enemy was standing over him. Finally he decided to look, and I immediately asked if he wanted to mount my horse.

The wounded man was led away on Alcides, and Durova was lucky to find her mount later after some enterprising Cossacks had stripped him of saddle and bridle and sold him to another officer.

Durova described her experiences in the capital in the largely autobiographical "A Year of Life in Petersburg, or Disadvantages of a Third Visit" [*God zhizni v Peterburge, ili nevygody tret'ego poseshcheniia*], a rather sardonic work which provides a dozen or more vignettes of her typical reception in society: on the first visit she is lionized, an object of general interest and admiration; on the second visit she is politely received but no special attention is paid her; on the third visit she is ignored or even rebuffed. Society is seen as frivolous, vacuous, egomaniacal.

Of some historical interest are the passages which concern her acquaintance with Pushkin, who was very solicitous and made an effort to assuage the apprehensions of this strange visitor to Russia's cultural center. While in Petersburg Durova continued to wear a frock coat, refer to herself in the male gender, and was addressed as Alexander Andreevich. This led to a number of anecdotes, one of which concerns dinner at Pushkin's.

At dinner, I had occasion to notice something strange in my kind host. He had four children, and the oldest, a girl who seemed about five, sat with us at the table. A friend of Pushkin's began to talk to her, asking if she had changed her mind about marrying him. "No," the child answered, "I haven't changed my mind." "And who would you rather marry, me or Daddy?" "Both you and Daddy." "Whom do you love more, me or Daddy?" "I love you more and I love Daddy more." "And do you love this guest," asked Alexander Sergeevich [Pushkin], indicating me, do you want to marry him?" The girl immediately answered, "No, no!" At this answer I saw that Pushkin blushed. Could he have thought that I would take offense at the words of a child? I began to talk in order to break the silence which inappropriately followed the girl's words of "No, no!" and asked her: "How can this be! One must love a guest more." The child regarded me suspiciously and finally began to eat. With that this little intermezzo ended. But Alexander Sergeevich! Why did he blush? Either this was the height of tact for not wanting me to hear anything not quite polite even as a joke or from a child, or did he have a strange concept about all those living in provincial towns?

Durova seems to have missed the point. Pushkin blushed because he had unthinkingly involved his daughter in Durova's masquerade as a man, a situation made even more embarrassing by the child's hostile rejection.

Although Durova's *Notes* were enthusiastically received everywhere, and Belinsky himself lauded them, the copies did not sell well, and she found herself with nine hundred unsold volumes and no funds to return home. Eventually she did find a purchaser and without regret quit Petersburg forever.

Immediately following the appearance of her *Notes*, Durova published in *Library for Reading* a largely autobiographical tale, *The Beauty from T., or The Game of Fate* [*T-skaia krasavitsa, ili Igra sud'by*], which strongly protests the treatment afforded women, such as the indifference to her feelings which led to her unhappy marriage. Perhaps her most successful story was "The Pavillion" [*Pavil'on*], published in *Notes of the Fatherland* and receiving an extensive review by Belinsky.

The Sulphur Spring [*Sernyi kliuch*], which appeared in 1839 in *One Hundred Russian Writers* [*Sto russkikh literatorov*], is noteworthy for two reasons, the straightforward and unembellished diction of the frame and the ethnographic information about the Cheremiss, a Finnic people of the Kazan region. The framed story is about two Cheremiss orphans, the beautiful Zeila and the handsome Dukmor, whose happiness is destroyed when the intrepid Dukmor is killed while combatting a bear. The Chermiss are depicted as simple and solitary people, ostensibly Christians but retaining pagan beliefs, whose closeness to nature makes them natural poets. Durova had previously presented an "ethnographic" tale in her *Notes*, where she interpolated a tale heard from an old Tatar about the unhappy fate of two Tatars whose marriage was forbidden owing to social prejudice.

Durova's pen produced several more works in 1839, including a novel in four parts, *Gudishki,* and in 1840 three more tales, a productivity which caused Belinsky to remark that "Mr. Alexandrov has apparently decided to give us a tale a month." However, he was wrong, for she stopped writing completely in 1840, thus ending a career which was as meteoric as it was prolific. No explanation has been given for this unexpected turn of events. One may surmise, however, that since Durova's works were essentially grounded in her own biography that, having reached the age of fifty-seven and living in a remote province of Russia, she had simply exhausted that store of personal experience which she regarded as suitable for literary adaptation.

Mariya Zhukova (1804-1855) made occasional appearances with her novellas, stories, and travel accounts from the mid-thirties to the mid-forties, her efforts revealing a tourist's acquaintance with provincial Russia and Western Europe, as well as a strong sense of self-confidence in herself and women in general. Her writing is marginally interesting as an example of prose written by an educated woman of the Romantic period. In the context of its own time, it was not inferior to much that appeared on the pages of contemporary periodicals.

Zhukova's lengthy *Judgment of the Heart* [*Sud serdtsa*] appeared in *Library for Reading* in 1837, prior to its publication in *The Tales of Mariya Zhukova* in 1840.

The insipidity of this work is difficult to convey without lengthy quotations, which would be inappropriate. A dutiful fourteen-year-old songstress, Francesca, and her younger guitarist brother, Rudolfo, return home from a daily tour of Geneva restaurants, where they perform for handouts, to find their mother dying.

"May the Lord God bless you, Francesca! Child, don't forget your confessor, pray and obey him. . . most of all. . . Francesca. Where is Rudolfo?". . . The young boy threw himself to his knees next to the bed. The child understood that the fateful minute had arrived. Francesca did not cry. Fixing her glance on the dying woman she seized each moment of the waning life. At that moment the confessor entered.

"Bless me. . . my father. . ," the dying woman pronounced in a weak voice. "Lord. . . to you. . . my children. . . Rudolfo," she said, suddenly coming to life raising herself off the pillow. "You are responsible for her to God. . . Oh Lord!. . ."

And she was no more.

A witness to this heartrending scene is Paolo Franki, a thirty-five year old political emigre from Italy, who had previously befriended the children and saved Francesca from assault by a stranger. Subsequently, Paolo renders timely assistance to Count Maurice Senmars (Cinq Mars?), with whom he becomes fast friends.

After testing Francesca for three years, the now almost forty-year old Paolo is sufficiently confident of her virtue to marry her. With his political problem (inexplicably) behind him, Paolo and Francesca move to Rome. The necessity of a long trip, also unexplained, causes Paolo to summon Maurice to watch over Francesca, who, although now a mother, is still being stalked by the malefactor who had tried to assault her in Geneva. Francesca, although in love with Paolo, whom she reveres, also feels herself attracted to Maurice, a feeling which he reciprocates. She tries to protect herself by going to confession:

Uncovering all the convolutions of her heart, she pronounced the name Maurice and the word *sin* stabbed her soul. "Beware of guilty passion, my daughter," said the confessor. "I see its frightening seed. Beware!"

What terror embraced Francesca's soul! Could guilty passion torment her, her? But she loves, she idolizes Paolo. True she also loves Maurice, but this is an attraction, a quiet and calm feeling. Until now it was a comfort to her in momentary grief, nothing more, and this feeling is a crime? She heard the word *hell*. In tears, on her knees, she begged forgiveness. She swore to avoid Maurice and actually began to avoid him. Unfortunately, there was no experienced friend who might tell her that half measures will not destroy evil, but increase it. Maurice came at the usual time. Francesca locked herself in her room. She wanted to read, to pray, but she thought about Maurice. He returned with Paolo. Answering this greeting coldly, she lavished affection upon Paolo and leaning against his shoulder, she thought: "What will Maurice say about me?" Constraint was burdensome to this simple, open soul. Her heart flew to meet the being with whom she was accustomed to share every movement, but wisdom said, "Stop." Oh, this was unendurable! The very attempt not to think about Maurice brought back the thought of him. Close to Paolo she sought protection from herself. At the altar she implored for strength to forget him. She spent whole hours at her son's cradle, but even there she found tormenting memory.

The relentless malefactor gives Paolo a letter which excites his suspicions, and he informs Francesca and Maurice that he must be away for three days. Maurice decides to part forever, but his farewell with Francesca ends in a passionate embrace—witnessed by the eavesdropping Paolo. Maurice does depart, Francesca dies, and Paolo's desire for revenge is assuaged when he discovers Maurice's letter indicating his plan to remove himself from their lives.

Quite unlike *Judgment of the Heart,* where the Italian setting is described only briefly and in conventional manner, the authoress takes particular pains in *Self Sacrifice* (*Samopozhertvovanie*) to provide very circumstantial details of her locale, Baden-Baden. Accordingly, we are taken to the ruins overlooking the town for a panoramic view of the environs. We are privy to the catty chatter of local denizens as they comment upon the tourists who promenade along the main street. We enter the salon for glimpses of life in high society.

The story itself has an exterior frame in which the narrator recounts her initial meeting with the beautiful Liza in Baden, and a second coincidental meeting with her, two years later, in provincial Russia, where Liza was teaching in a small pension.

I stayed in K. . .k [Kursk? J. M.] a whole week. Every day I saw my new acquaintance. Here is the tale of her life, or, to put it better, her heart. I regret that I cannot render it for you in the words of the heroine herself. Be content with my story.

The didactic and somewhat sententious tone of the frame is now replaced by didactic sentimentalism as we are transported to the remote country estate of the kind but bankrupt Pavel Vasilievich and his wife, Agafiya Ivanovna, who with their precious little Liza are on the eve of suffering foreclosure. The sound of the carriage bells does not signal disaster but salvation, for an Angel of God appeared:

And suddenly the Angel of God produces a document, and Pavel Vasilievich reads— all the tax arrears have been paid off. Lord! Great is Thy mercy! Oh, how he cried! How hotly he kissed the hand of the Guardian Angel! How eloquent was the mute expression of his gratitude! And Liza? She had awakened and, wearing only a shirtlet, had arisen, on tiptoes reached the half-opened door and with curiosity had pushed her wonderous little curly head through the opening. Agafiya Ivanovna stood at a distance and through her tears says: "Your Radiance!" The comforting angel who had appeared to our old couple was the young spouse of Count S., the son of that old countess, the proprietess of a beautiful settlement with a manor house at half a verst from U. . . , for whom Pavel Vasilievich had so much solicitude.

The countess S. takes little Liza in tutelage, raises her in patrician fashion, and ultimately takes her off to Baden-Baden as a fashionable young lady (where the narrator first meets her). There Liza falls in love with a certain Dmitry, while her benefactress favors the charming Frenchman de Nolde. Liza pretends to have accepted a tryst with de Nolde in order to protect the Countess, whose clandestine meeting with him is discovered and interrupted by her husband; de Nolde offers to marry Liza to protect her name, but the honorable young lady will have none of that. They all leave Baden. Liza returns home to nurse and then bury her father, and finally ends up a teacher in the small provincial pension.

Echoes of George Sand and her "school" are sounded here from time to time in remarks about the heartlessness of society toward those lacking the proper credentials of birth and wealth, and more particularly in Liza's insistence at the end of the story that despite her straitened circumstances, her ailing mother, the absence of accustomed luxuries, she will remain independent and accept help from no one. As a demonstration of her firmness, she has refused to spend the money sent anonymously to her by the Count:

> The Count has never written to me, but I received a significant sum of money from an unknown person—and it is from him, I know that. I accepted it, and there it is, in this coffer. I will never touch it. No! I will not spoil the single pleasure left me by fate: the conviction that I might pay the debt of gratitude. Moreover, if you know how much the thought—to be indebted only to myself for everything—makes me happy! Boldly I raise my eyes to heaven. The feeling of my independence inspires me with firmness which is comforting in moments of sadness. How satisfied I am when I succeed in doing something nice for my mother! That is my greatest happiness. It seems to me that I would almost be happy if I were. . . to lose my memory of the past.

My Kursk Acquaintances [Moi Kurkskie znakomstsy] is a special form of travel notes, incorporating historical background and contemporary description of Kursk with sketches of those people whom Madam Zhukova met while there on business. The principal objects of her attention are a certain Alexander Almov, a bachelor of some thirty years, and Nadenka Pritschenko, an unassuming but charming girl of twenty-eight who strangely seems destined for spinsterhood. With a great deal of unnecessary detail infused with trite commentary on love and duty, the author reveals that Alexander and Nadenka have been in love for many years, but that Alexander rejected marriage on the grounds that it might interfere with his support of his (spoiled) mother, a decision accepted by Nadenka, who has vowed to devote herself to the service of others.

This work contains a very strong and passionate defense of women who, for whatever reasons, find themselves categorized as "old maids." Zhukova musters a number of arguments to support the potential utility to society and others of this ridiculed caste, which is accused of not fulfilling its womanly destiny of serving a husband and bearing children. Her protestation, although perhaps overstated, has its persuasive qualities, as the following excerpt demonstrates:

Let women have moral rights equal to your own, gentlemen males! To avoid misunderstanding, I shall declare that we have no pretenses 'or epaulettes, nor for judicial chairs, nor. . . nor even for the authors' spectacles. Only permit us not to limit our goal to marriage alone, with all its consequences. Permit us to believe that one may not be a useless plant if one remains without bearing fruit, that with honor and with a right to your respect one may devote her life to her father, mother, brothers, male and female relatives, endeavoring to achieve self-perfection doing all that one may do for the general good, and then we, we old maids will not consider ourselves a class of intolerable amphibians.

Zhukova's last published works were *Evenings in Karpovka [Vechera na Karpovke]* and *Sketches of Southern France and Nice [Ocherki iuzhnoi Frantsii i Nitstsi]*, published in 1838 and 1844 respectively.

Elena Gan (1814-1842), *née* Fadeeva, married her artillery officer husband (G. Hahn) at sixteen and soon learned the worst about the stultifying routine of life in provincial Ukrainian garrison towns. Her own innate intelligence, and her obvious esthetic superiority to the masculine- military society which she was forced to accept, led her to protest against the *poshlust* of her circumstances and the intellectual suffocation she was experiencing. Her reading of George Sand doubtless was also a stimulus for her defense of women, who often found themselves powerless to overcome, or even criticize, the roles which society forced them to play.

In 1836 she and her husband spent some time in Petersburg, where she reveled in the cultural and social contacts for which she longed. When her husband was ordered back to the Ukraine, she went with her father to Astrakhan, whence she sent her first work, *The Ideal [Ideal]*, which appeared in 1837 in *The Library for Reading* over the pseudonym Zinaida R—va. This is a highly sentimentalized tale about the plight of Olga Holzberg, an imaginative and idealistic young woman unhappily married to a kind but utterly mundane artillery officer. To compensate for the emptiness of her life, she submerges herself in the poetry of the popular poet, Anatoly T. Fate happily rescues her from the mud and gossip of the wretched garrison town, and in Petersburg she finally meets the man whose poetry had sustained her during her spiritual and intellectual isolation. Anatoly dallies with her, but he loses interest when she resists his efforts at seduction. A long separation ensues, during which she thinks only of him. Learning that he is near death, she flies to his apartment, which she finds empty, but there she discovers a letter written by Anatoly to a friend disclosing his indifference to her. Olga flees, falls ill, and seems unable to recover from her inner malaise. One day she aimlessly enters a small chapel, and there she finds new and salutory strength in the image of Christ.

The salient features of this author's style are extended metaphors, sententious remarks addressed to the reader, and lengthy expression of how bitter life is for women of intelligence and feeling.

There are people who do not know why they have been born on earth, because bringing to this world full of cold rationalization and calculation a soul thirsting for deep and true feelings and a mind which sees all the baseness and the false mask of propriety, they are never able to make their behavior conform to the opinion of that despot, society, and most of all they bring confidence in their share of happiness! Such people are forced to follow the general path, and must, like the enamored *duc du Lorraine*, holding hot coals in his fist, never open it, even though their bodies turn to ashes along with the coals—unless they want to become the object of ridicule. They will never become accustomed to the conditions set by society, and they will be a burden to themselves and others, and even their voice is so strange to the world that it will nowhere find an echo.

Of some intrinsic interest, however, are those expository passages detailing the occupations and habits of the military in provincial towns. The author obviously speaks here from personal knowledge and with no little rancor:

Do you know what is the life of a so-called *military lady*? Olga married and several days later their carriage entered the filthy streets of a Jewish settlement. Ragged, half-naked, squealing little Jews surrounded the rare spectacle. Along both sides of the street stretched the pitiful and dirty shacks of the peasants and the sons of Judas. At every step disgusting filth met the eye. The carriage stopped at the doors of one of these shacks, newly whitewashed and surrounded with a new fence. These were the colonel's quarters. A sentry walked with measured steps next to a green sentry box, and Colonel Holzberg led his young wife past it into a low room ornamented with rugs. On the walls hung sabres and pistols, and in all the corners were pipes of various sizes and quality, and tobacco pouches jeweled and silken, sewed for the then bachelor colonel by kind neighbors, proudly displayed themselves. Three such rooms constituted their residence.

The description of the daily activities of Olga's husband concludes with a sketch of a typical evening:

Dusk arrives, and the officers, having nothing else to do, again congregate at their superior's, smoke pipes and sit around the samovar. . . and they talk about drills, horses, dogs, pistols, harness, they analyze military regulations, complain about the slowness of promotions, and meanwhile the smoke from their pipes grows thicker, a dense cloud is formed filling the whole room, the candles glimmer weakly in the smoky atmosphere. Now card tables are set up, and in the small room are heard only the technical expressions of the game, which are unintelligible to Olga, who is not initiated into these hieroglyphs, originally invented for the stupid but now occupying the greater part of all intelligent people.

Elena's experiences in Astrakhan, where her father was an official overseer of Kalmyk affairs, provided material for her next published work, *Utballa*, a story filled with Kalmyk lore. The heroine, Utballa, the illegitimate daughter of a Kalmyk woman and a rich Russian merchant, is portrayed as a victim of prejudice but capable of incredible sacrifice for love. Another exotic setting, the Crimea, figures in *Dzhelaledin*, a love story involving a young Russian girl and a Tatar prince.

290

The Medallion [Medal'on] [1839), subtitled *Notes of a Certain Patient at a Hot Springs, [Zapiski odnoi bol'noi na goriachikh vodakh]* is a framed tale lacking, strangely, the form of notes; it concerns the frivolous love of a prince for an inexperienced young girl. *The Judgement of Society [Sud sveta]* and *The Judgment of God [Sud Bozhii]* came out in 1840, the former again about garrison life.

This authoress' most artistic work, according to some, was *Teofania Abbiagio*, which depicts the tragedy overtaking Teofania when her husband, Dolini, whom she married to save her family from bankruptcy but came to love, gives her up in favor of his first inamorata, Olga.

Elena Gan has been called "a female Lermontov," the appellation probably suggested by her concern with the exotic, her frequent travels, and their brief and almost coincident life spans. However, further comparison would not be to her advantage, for despite some contributions in the area of local color or exoticism, she did not rise above the standards typical of the second rank Romantic fictionists.

Grigory Kvitka (1778-1843) was well established as a Ukrainian belletrist before 1832, when he made his first appearance in Russian with a story translated for *The Telescope*. His reputation in Russian literature is connected with his pseudonym, Osnovianenko, first used in 1833. Many of his works were composed in Ukrainian and then translated into Russian, often by himself, but he also wrote original works in Russian, and if only on the basis of these he deserves a modest place in the pantheon of Russian Romantic fictionists.

Kvitka's early stories had a discernible influence upon the Ukrainian tales of both Somov and Gogol, and we know that the plot of Gogol's comedy, *The Inspector General*, derives from Kvitka's play of 1827, *The Arrival from the Capital, or Confusion in a Provincial Town [Priezzhii iz stolitsy, ili sumatokha v uezdnom gorode]*. One may also see *Pan Khalyavsky [Pan Khaliavskii]* contributing something to Gogol's masterpiece, *Dead Souls*, which shares with Kvitka's work the picaresque form and the comic exposure of human foibles and vices embodied in exclusively negative characters.

Pan Khalyavsky was written originally in Russian and appeared in *Notes of the Fatherland* in 1839. It is a satire on the *poshlust* of the petty Ukrainian gentry, whose concerns focus largely on matters of rank, tradition, food and drink. The narrator, Trofim Khalyavsky, one of ten children of a well-off landowner, is seventy-six when he decides to chronicle his life from childhood through marriage. He is a conservative of the old school, a staunch defender of the age when illiteracy, corporal punishment, gentry privilege, and gluttony enjoyed popular acceptance. Much of his tale parallels the content of Vasily Narezhny's *Two Ivans* or *Bursak*, but, unlike Narezhny, Kvitka presents no positive characters and does not moralize.

As a narrator Trofim spares no details, his memory of the past being total, even to the kind of roll or pastry which his mother gave to him on whatever occasion. His tale is rambling, digressive, and his manner is that of a garrulous old raconteur reminiscing about his youth in the presence of an attentive listener. His story is full of absurd, farcical, comic, and pathetic incidents, the satire deriving from the fact that Trofim is largely oblivious to the import of his account.

Most of Part I concerns the exploits of Trofim and his two older brothers, the intrepid Petrus and the clever Pavlus, a hunchback. Their tutor, Domine Galushkinsky, a seminarian of hedonistic bent, conspires with his charges to spend much of their time in clandestine recreation, especially at the "little parties" which take place in one of the peasant households. Their presence is ultimately resented, and some of the peasant youths administer a sound beating to Petrus, Pavlus, and Galushkinsky, an object lesson from which Pavlus never recovers:

> After Petrus's departure brother Pavlus did not suffer for long. He died, to Daddy's and Mommy's grief. Have what you will, he was their progeny all the same. . . .
> At my parents' behest I, having lined a paper, wrote to Petrus: "Do you know what, brother? Brother Pavlus bids you long life!" Mommy listened to this and, having said that it was very piteously written, cried in earnest. In response Petrus extensively described—and entirely in a high style—all the excellent qualities of the deceased and in conclusion, consoling himself and me, added: "Now when Daddy and Mommy die the estate must be divided not among us six but among five brothers—if another one doesn't die."
> I say to you that this was a person of unusual intelligence!

Kvitka has created rather amusing caricatures in the narrator's parents. His father maintains respect by using his fists freely on the entire household, and his mother, a militant illiterate, swoons, wails, and carries on to shelter her sons from life's hardships, especially from the rigors of formal education. Trofim, her favorite, praises her lavishly, but he is not unaware of some shortcomings:

> One must say that my mommy didn't master running the household all at once, and at first she had a number of funny things happen. I will relate one painful anecdote. Shortly after her marriage to Daddy a neighboring family arrived at their house for dinner. In order to regale them very nicely, Mommy called the domestic cook and ordered him to butcher a ram and prepare what was needed. The cook, a zealous person when it came to his master's welfare, began to present the reasons that, so to say, if we butcher a ram and it's not all needed at table, then half will remain, and since it's summer, will spoil and have to be thrown out. "Well, then you do this," said Mommy, without thinking very much, "use the hind quarters of the ram for the table and let the front quarters of the ram live and graze the field until it's needed." The cook burst right out laughing. And Mommy set about thinking what was so funny to him. Then she thought it out and saw that she had said something foolish and amusing, so she waved her hand. blushed red as cherry brandy, and walked away from the cook. After that there was no way to keep him: he was let go to the village and a woman cook was designated.

The narrator's preoccupation with food is evident from the very first pages of his chronicle, which, in fact, might be considered an apotheosis of Ukrainian provincial cuisine. The description of the banquet for the regimental colonel provides a course-by-course presentation of the menu, which includes various borshchs, then soups, followed by "sweets," such as roast duck in cherry sauce, with a final offering consisting of roast fowl, suckling pig, roast rabbit, each course washed down with various vodkas, beers, and meads. Such gourmandizing is one of the major reasons why Trofim prefers the good old days to the present:

Ach, how I ate! Tastily, richly, abundantly, picturesquely, and, moreover, in sovereign style, not obliged to hurry from fear that a comrade would snatch the best morsels. To some people all this might seem insignificant, not worthy of attention, not to mention a story. But I am writing of that age when people "lived," that is when the single concern, the solitary care, the one thought, all stories and opinions were about food: when to eat, what to eat, how to eat, how much to eat. Everything was to eat, to eat, and to eat.
And they lived in order to eat.

Praise of the past, when things were as they should be, and condemnation of the present, when the younger generation fails to appreciate the old traditions and attitudes, account for numerous digressions, often with an emotional depth suggesting that despite his satire Kvitka retained more than a little appreciation for the unabashed self-indulgence of the past:

I am entering into details which are superfluous for the young people of today. They smile and don't believe my story, but my contemporaries experience, probably, a pleasure equal to mine and forgive the trivia of my memories of that happy, enviable life. Often I look upon the young people of today and with sad heart turn to my constant thought, "How the world changes!" Will they pass their best, golden, youthful years as we did? No way! They are slaves to the rules which they have invented for themselves. Without having lived, without having experienced life, they are oppressed by it! Not having seen real people in their own age, they have already withdrawn from them, and without having taken pleasure in anything, they grieve for the *past*, are bored with the present, and mournfully gaze at the future. It seems to them that in the distance, in the gloom, their star is glimmering, that it promises something ethereal, and until that time, like dried leaves fallen from the trees, they are carried hither and yon against their aims and wishes! . . . Did we live that way? We lived and enjoyed ourselves, and they do not live and are sad!. . . Well, be off with them, let's concern ourselves with our own.[1]

Pan Khalyavsky becomes a picaresque novel as Trofim, who in Part II unaccountably regresses from an ignoramus into an absolute simpleton, details his parents' deaths, his unwilling enlistment in the army, his fruitless quest for a wife, conflict with his brother Petrus over their inheritance, and the resulting lawsuit which necessitates his trip to Petersburg. There all of the adventures reserved for the provincial yokel in the big city befall Trofim, who is constantly gulled and deceived. Many of these episodes are predictable: his first visit to the theatre, for example, when he confuses life on the stage with reality and makes a fool of himself, or when he mistakes passersby mockery of his carriage or himself for friendly admiration. Ultimately he returns home, finds a bride, marries, and lives unhappily ever after. At this point the reader is quite weary of Trofim.

The problem with this story is that the exuberance with which it begins is not sustained. Kvitka assembled an impressive number of anecdotes to fill out the life of his narrator, but the rather innocent pranks of the first part of the story are replaced by acts of maliciousness and venality. All the characters are negative, and there is not one positive act in the entire second part. Petrus becomes a greedy schemer who defrauds his brothers, Trofim's bride is motivated solely by money, and Trofim's egregious seflfishness and self-indulgence make him more repulsive than comic. The same may be said for the minor characters. Of course, Gogol also presents many negative types, but they operate in a make-believe world which we recognize as artificial. Kvitka, however, presents characters who appear to belong to the phenomenal world, and the reader, generously disposed to laugh at their antics early in the story, gradually becomes intolerant of their behavior. At this point, the author has lost his audience.

Vladimir Sollogub (1814-1882) graduated from the University of Dorpat at the age of twenty and subsequently served in various departments of the civil service. He started publishing his stories in the late thirties. The first seven chapters of the work considered here, *The Tarantas [Tarantas]*, appeared initially in *Notes of the Fatherland* in 1840, but the entire work, which runs to twenty chapters, was not published until 1845. *The Tarantas*, therefore, really belongs to the period of Romanticism's wane.

The Tarantas is not so much a story as a survey of Russia's economic and social circumstances as evidenced in all classes from the gentry to the peasantry. Borrowing his format from Radishchev, whose *Journey from Petersburg to Moscow* (1790) had exposed the worst aspects of serfdom, Sollogub presents a string of vignettes and interpolated stories connected with a trip from Moscow to Kazan. Two travelers, Vasily Ivanovich, a gross and shaggy Kazan landowner, who although uneducated is far from stupid, and Ivan Vasilievich, an impecunious gentry youth just returned from Europe, set out in Vasily's tarantas, a primitive conveyance notable for its dependability and rough but stable ride. The youth has a large notebook which he intends to fill with travel notes, his main purpose being to understand Russia's past and its people. But nothing remarkable or picturesque appears:

> The tarantas stopped at a miserable low hut, before which a motley four-cornered pillar designated the habitation of the station master. It was already dark outside. A dull lantern scarcely lit an external stairway, which was shaking under its roof. Behind the hut stretched a three-sided shed, covered with straw, from which horses, cows, pigs and chicks peered out. In the middle of the soft damp courtyard stood a half ruined, four-sided timbered well. At the entrance itself thronged ugly beggars who had run up from all sides, legless, dumb, blind, with withered hands and repulsive sores, in rags, with

294

matted beards. Here were also drunken old hags and pale women and children in only ragged little shirts, whose hands were pulled from their sleeves and crossed on their chests against the cold.

The further they go, the more the would-be writer, Ivan Vasilievich, is aware of the truth of his older companion's statement that the word *journey*, in the sense of travel for pleasure, simply is not applicable in Russia. Provincial towns are all the same, the hotels and inns invariably dirty, infested and uncomfortable, the station masters predictably swear that all the horses are in use elsewhere, and the roads are rough and uninteresting.

Criticism of the gentry class dominates this story. It begins when Ivan Vasilievich encounters a school-mate who has been exiled to the provinces for his debts. He recounts how living beyond his means had reduced him to penury and caused his wife to leave him. They meet a Russian prince who has returned from abroad for the express purpose of squeezing arrears from his peasants, despite three years of crop failures. In his continuing contrast of Vasily Ivanovich and Ivan Vasilievich, the former a landowner of the old school regarded as a father by his serfs, the younger man a well-meaning but inept youth whose capacity for productive work was destroyed by his frivolous education, Sollogub makes this point: Russia has its faults, but its people have enormous potential given concerned and moral leadership by the gentry.

As the seamy side of Russian life is exposed, Ivan Vasilievich puts his companion to sleep with lengthy disquisitions on the state of affairs in Europe. Ivan Vasilievich feels that travel abroad provides valuable comparisons and provides an indication of what Russia should emulate in Europe and what it should guard against:

"What in your opinion should we take over?" asks the curious Vasily Ivanovich.

"Unfortunately, a great deal. In the first place, a sense of citizenship, of civic duty, which we do not have. . . . With a sense of citizenship we will acquire a desire for physical and mental perfection, we will understand the sacredness of a sound education, the full benefit of science and art, all that improves and ennobles a person. Germany will give us its sense of family, France its ardor for science, England its knowledge of trade and feeling of governmental responsibility, even Italy will transfer to our frosty land its divine arts.

"So that's how it is!" said Vasily Ivanovich, and what should we guard against?"

"That which is destroying Europe. . . . Its spirit of self-confidence, conceit, and pride. Its spirit of doubt and lack of faith, without which movement forward is impossible. Its spirit of dissension and unrest, which destroys everything. We should guard against German arrogance, English egotism, French dissipation and Italian laziness, and then such a path will be opened before us as has never been opened to any people."

The work is both tedious and illogical when the naive Ivan Vasilievich holds forth in this manner. However, the story acquires interest when the lumpish Vasily Ivanovich outlines the proper way to organize one's estate and support one's peasants. His rules are simple but effective, and he is confident that the Russian peasant is better off than his counterpart in Europe.

In two lengthy chapters near the end of *The Tarantas*, Sollogub provides the biographies of his travelers. While Vasily Ivanovich received no education to speak of, his diligence and confidence in tradition ultimately make him an established landowner with prosperous serfs. The education of Ivan Vasilievich, based on French rhetoric taught by an ex-Parisian tobacconist, proves worthless. He turns out fit for nothing, and although he perceives his need for true learning and accomplishment, he is without willpower.

And not he alone. Many of our young people suffer with him from a similar disease. Many of our young people languish under the burden of their impotence and feel that their lives are forever spoiled by their defective, insufficient semi-education. It is true that they console their egos with a mask of feigned disenchantment, of weariness with life, of deceived hopes. But indeed they are merely insignificant only by half, since they are unable to sense their own insignificance. Perhaps there lies hidden in them an inclination to activity, love for the beautiful and the true, but they have never acquired the strength to accomplish their inner desire. They have feeling, but no will. . . . A pitiful generation, poor youth! A fruit spoiled in the blossom!

In the concluding chapter, entitled "The Dream," Ivan Vasilievich, borne on the wings of the tarantas, which has somehow changed into a huge bird, is given a tour of an ideal Russia, with fertile fields, tidy villages, boat-filled rivers. His odd conveyance changes again into a sensible but attractive carriage, and he meets his old acquaintances. The prince now wears pre-Petrine dress, lives on his estate rather than in the capital, in a house built according to the Arzamas school of architecture rather than the Italian. He encounters his old schoolmate, who introduces him to his beautiful wife:

She smiled at the entering guest, and two rosy and exuberant children, embarrassed at the sight of the stranger, pressed their curly little heads to her knees. Ivan Vasilievich looked at this picture as at a shrine, and it seemed to him that in it he was seeing the bright embodiment of a tranquil sense of family, that high reward for all labors, for all of man's grief. And whether he stood for a short time or a long time before this wondrous picture, he did not notice. He did not remember what he heard, what he said, only his soul became broader and broader, his feelings calm in quiet bliss, and his thoughts fused in prayer.

Then in a sudden Gogolian shift of mood, Ivan Vasilievich awakens to find himself pinned under the overturned tarantas. With this the story ends, and the reader must decide if Ivan Vasilievich's utopia should be seen as a vision of Russia's bright future or a fatuous pipe-dream. The upsetting of the dependable and stable tarantas, a metaphor for the patriarchal Vasily Ivanovich, seems completely out of context.

Vladimir Dal (1801-1872) is remembered today for the two monumental works which crowned the final decade of his career as ethnographer and lexicographer, *Proverbs of the Russian People* and *Explanatory Dictionary of the Living Russian Language*. These were the result of Dal's lifelong interest in popular speech and traditions, beginning while he was still a naval cadet and continuing as he moved from profession to profession, first as an officer in the Black Sea fleet, then as a medical student at Dorpat, subsequently as a military surgeon, and then, after 1833, as a civil servant until his retirement in 1856.

His literary career began in 1830 in *The Moscow Telegraph* with a piece entitled *The Gypsy Girl [Tsyganka]*. Here a plot of sorts is roughly woven into the frame of a travelogue, the narrator-traveler meeting various distinctive types, Greeks, Gypsies, Moldavians, Jews, etc. as he journeys towards Jassy, where he rents an apartment from a picturesque Moldavian landlady. The style is lively and conversational, with the speech of the various types distinguished on the basis of ethnic peculiarities. Sketches alternate with Baedeker type information typical of travelogues:

> At the inn (Jassy) I paid 3 leva (120 kopecks) a day for my room, 30 k. for a serving of coffee, tea, borshch, roast meat, salad or sauce, and 15 k. for a carafe of excellent local wine. Jews, on their tiny feet and in black dressing gowns, *serve* and *regale*. The owner, a Moldavian boyar, with a grey beard (a distinction for which Turks pay a special tax), sits on a sofa the entire day from early morning until late at night in the Turkish manner, his legs folded, with a chibouk, a cup of Turkish coffee, and with bills in his hands. Thus he commands and directs the entire enterprise and has the reputation of a man of parts, a good proprietor.

It is, in fact, the "inessential" details connected with various ethnic types and their customs which provide the focus of interest, since the plot is insignificant. The narrator buys the freedom of a gypsy maid, Cassandra, to prevent her mistress, his Moldavian landlady, from selling the girl to a wealthy relative. Later it develops that Cassandra's gypsy fiancé is the man who had providentially appeared to repair the narrator-traveler's carriage when it broke down in a remote district.

In 1832, using the pseudonym the Cossack Lugansky, Dal published his *Russian Fairy Tales [Russkie skazki]*, the aim of which was to "acquaint his countrymen with popular language and dialect, to provide an example of popular words. . . ." Apparently some of his popular speech was too earthy, for Dal was arrested and his work confiscated. Throughout the thirties he published a number of works under the title *True Stories and Fictions of the Cossack Lugansky*, and at the same time he was publishing other tales, among them the very popular *Schlemiel [Bedovik]*, which came out in 1839 in *Notes of the Fatherland.*[2]

Dal's continuing conviction that popular conversational speech should be legitimized as a literary vehicle is clearly evident in the style of this tale, whose narrator uses a language which is apparently unstructured, rambling, digressive, peppered with comments to the reader, filled with colloquial expressions and proverbs. Our hero, Evsei Lirov, the ill-fated clerk whose adventures are the subject of this story, is introduced in a style typical of the work:

In one of our provincial towns, let's say Malinov, Sunday arrived. Evsei Stakheevich Lirov, a pleasant looking but not too adroit young man, by rank and occupation a bird of low flight, having stood through mass in the five-cupolaed cathedral, set off, in accordance with the invariable local custom, in a circuit of all servants' rooms and anterooms, that is, he set off to distribute visiting cards in his own hand-written signature and to sign in at the homes of all the directors and senior clerks on a greasy sheet of paper.

Evsei is a thinker, or rather day-dreamer, who talks to himself and has the reputation of an eccentric. We are treated to a long exposition of his thoughts on the social niceties of those Sunday and holiday visits, whose grating tediousness combines with the unexpected loss of his modest clerkship to cause him to try for a position in Moscow or Petersburg. In a Gogolian scene replete with suckling pigs, farce, and comic names, Evsei takes leave of Malinov:

He said goodbye to everyone and thanked them all sincerely and from his heart, and in saying goodbye with his superior he bit himself from trying so hard and squeezed out a stubborn tearlet. It is true, indeed, that his goodbyes concluded somehow lamentably. The superior had deigned to take tea on the porch where it was cool, and Evsei, in starting to get up, moved backwards with his chair until finally he flew right over backwards off the porch, crushing some half-dozen suckling pigs, which in Malinov enjoy full freedom and content themselves with green fodder. The superior's wife, however, calmed the frightened Evsei at once, saying: "It's nothing, it's nothing, they aren't ours but Pelageia Ivanovna's, and I told her long ago not to let her suckling pigs run through yards all over town, and I ordered the kids around the yard to pasture them in the vacant lots." Perepetuia Epidiforovna, whom we have mentioned above, was also there as a guest, and for her part also did everything possible to help our schlemiel.

The balance of the story details Evsei's adventures—and idle thoughts—as he, having left Malinov, shuttles between Moscow and Petersburg without ever reaching either. He finds himself in the wrong diligences, continually "misses the bus," is victimized by others, and even left penniless when absent-mindedness parts him from his fuss-budget servant, Kornei Goriunov, a later variant of Somov's Sysoevich (*Mommy and Sonny*) and Pushkin's Savelich (*The Captain's Daughter*). Ultimately he is rescued from his fruitless peregrinations by a widow from his home town, who marries him off to her pretty daughter. All's well that ends well.

For a tale published in 1839, virtually at the end of the Romantic period, this work has a striking degree of authorial presence. This is evident, certainly, in the constant, and often gratuitous, introduction of folklore material, which accords with Dal's ethnographic interests, but we also find a more direct presence in the deliberate confusion of the fictional world with that of narrator and reader, a trick borrowed from Sterne by many Russian authors, especially Veltman and Gogol.

Let us hasten after Lirov. He is galloping off at breakneck speed, and if we get too far

298

behind him, then maybe it will be as difficult for us to overtake him as it is for him to overtake the mysterious diligence which left him behind.

Or, another example, demonstrating Dal's ethnographic interest and his Shandyan temperament:

"A dog has no soul, but only steam," said Kornei Goriunov, reasoning with someone, and Evsei, having let himself go, as we have seen, into meditation and argumentation, from nothing better to do, began to analyze for himself what sort of a thing a soul was. He was already close to a final conclusion when Vlasov posed another riddle to the coachman: "Ten shoulders, five heads, but four souls, ten hands, ten feet, a hundred fingers, and it moves lying down, on eight legs. Five go out, four return. What sort of beast is it?

This riddle tormented and rasped at Evsei. . . but he didn't want to ask for an explanation from Kornei, who would have told him that this was a corpse carried to the grave by four persons. We can leave Evsei in this position for a time, since Stakheevich's [Evsei's] thoughts are sometimes rather fertile and it's quite a while to wait for them to end. So, let us move the setting forward to Malinov by an hour. It must be admitted, at first I caused Kornei to ask his master the religious question and then the riddle: the reader will see from this how easily Evsei has been able to carry us away in any direction with his thoughts and how stubbornly he wrapped himself up in every matter to which he abandoned his domineering imagination.

In the forties Dal became part of the Natural School, that movement which bridged Romanticism and Realism, but at the same time had its own existence outside of their continuum. The Natural School's interest in generalized types, often categorized by occupation, the desire to reproduce authentically distinctive features of speech according to class or trade, its sociological interest in modes of behavior, its concern with the "socially disadvantaged" and the sordid details of their surroundings, set this school apart from Romanticism. Certainly, all of these features of the Natural School can be found in Romantic fiction but they are not normally emphasized. Dal's writing in the forties, therefore, lies outside both the normative and temporal limits of Romanticism.

Nikolay Gogol (by A. Gibal, 1830s)

XXV. Gogol's *Overcoat.*

Gogol's *The Overcoat [Shinel']* (1840) seems destined to dupe each new generation of readers, a good portion of whom are invariably convinced that the author *intended* to show us a pathetic clerk victimized by a crass and brutal establishment. The sociological interpretation will doubtless continue despite the efforts of Eichenbaum, Chizhevski, Nabokov, Erlich, and others to debunk it.[1]

The bare bones of plot might seem to support a sentimental approach. A humble Petersburg copyist, Akaky Akakievich, scrimps and saves to have a new overcoat made, but it is stolen the very day it is delivered. The despondent victim appeals to a "certain important personage," but the official responds with a tongue-lashing so demoralizing that the clerk falls ill and shortly dies. Later, it is reported that his ghost confronts the "important personage" and takes his coat from him, an experience which considerably moderates the bureaucrat's future dealings with subordinates.

However, throughout the tale the extravagant rhetoric and numerous comic and grotesque details completely override any possible "message" and are clearly unsuitable for a purely compassionate view of the protagonist; they would suggest in fact, just the opposite:

> And so, *in a certain department* there served *a certain* clerk—a clerk, about whom it is impossible to say that he was very remarkable: rather shortish, somewhat pockmarked, somewhat red-haired, even somewhat shortsighted, with a small bald spot on his head, with wrinkles on both sides of his cheeks and with a face of the color which is called hemorrhoidal. . . . What can one do! The Petersburg climate is guilty.[2]

Then:

> The surname of the clerk was Bashmachkin. One can already see from that name it derived from shoe, but when, at what time, and how it came from shoe, none of this is known. Both his father and his grandfather and even his brother-in-law went about in boots, changing the soles only three times a year.

At the christening of the future clerk, his godmother, "a woman of rare virtues, Arina Semyonovna Belobryushkova (Whitebelly), presents the mother with the choice of names from the saints' calendar—Mokkiya, Sossiya, or Khozdazat, then Trifily, Dula, and Varakhasy, and finally Pavsikakhy and Vikhitsy, at which point the good woman yields to fate and gives the child his father's name, explaining how it "happened absolutely from necessity" that the babe acquired the name Akaky Akakievich.

The concentrated absurdity of the opening pages scarcely deters critics who insist on finding a philanthropic message. Their reading relies heavily upon two passages, the first of which relates how poor Akaky patiently endures the teasing of his fellow clerks until their pranks interfere with his copying:

"Leave me alone! Why do you insult me?" And there was something strange in the words and in the voice in which they were pronounced. In it was heard something inclining one to pity, so that a certain young man, recently appointed, who, following the example of the others had permitted himself to mock him, suddenly stopped as if transfixed, and from that time everything was, as it were, changed before him and seemed to have a different appearance. Some supernatural power thrust him from his comrades, with whom he had become acquainted having taken them for decent, well-bred persons. And long afterwards, at the most happy moments, the short clerk with the bald spot appeared to him with his penetrating words: "Leave me alone! Why do you insult me?" And in these penetrating words rang other words: "I am your brother," and the poor young man would bury his face in his hands, and many times afterwards he shuddered at his age, seeing how much inhumanity there is in man, and how much hidden, savage coarseness there is in refined, educated manners and, "Oh God! even in that man whom society considers noble and honorable. . ."[3]

Immediately following this rhetorical arabesque on the inhumanity of man, we drop to the narrow world of Akaky:

There, in his copying, he visualized some varied and pleasant world. Pleasure was expressed on his face; several letters were his favorites and when he got to them he was beside himself, and he laughed and grimaced and helped with his lips, so that it seemed on his face one could read each letter formed by his pen.

A master of verbal acrobatics, Gogol's agile narrator has vaulted from Akaky's pathetic "Leave me alone! Why do you insult me?" to his colleague's lofty misinterpretation, "I am your brother," to sentimental commonplaces, "Oh God! even in that man whom society considers noble and honorable. . ." and finally to our clerk's grotesque grimacing and chuckling.

Consider the underlying logic of "I am your brother" developing from "Leave me alone!" Can Akaky Akakievich be brother to anyone, since brotherhood implies some capacity for reciprocal feelings? Akaky Akakievich never shows the slightest interest in anyone, concern for anyone, or willingness to make the slightest sacrifice on anyone's behalf. He is like a sea anemone, a solitary polyp attached to a rock and mechanically waving its tenacles, accepting what fortune provides but closing upon itself when touched by beings intruding into its world. He sits glued to his desk, copying and chuckling, and once home, he gulps down soup, tasting nothing, until he notices his tummy beginning to swell, the signal for a return to his copying.

The second "philanthropic" passage is not nearly so dazzling as the first:

Akaky Akakievich was taken away and buried. And Petersburg remained without Akaky Akakievich as if he had never been there. There disappeared and was hidden a being [sushchestvo], defended by no one, not even attracting the attention of a naturalist, who never misses an opportunity to impale an ordinary fly on a pin and to inspect it under a microscope,—a being who meekly endured the office jokes and who went to his grave without any excessive fuss, but for whom, all the same, although just before the very end of his life, there flashed a radiant messenger in the form of an overcoat, which animated for a moment a poor life, and on whom misfortune then had fallen unbearably, as it falls on the heads of the powerful ones of the earth.

In this "eulogy" our protagonist has been demoted from "a person" [chelovek] to "being" [sushchestvo], while the overcoat, which previously had been a fiancée for Akaky, is now elevated to the status of radiant messenger. Further, the passage is *framed* by comic material. One searches in vain for sympathetic tones in the words preceding this passage:

> Finally, poor Akaky Akakievich gave up the ghost. Neither his room nor his things were put under seal, for in the first place there were no heirs and in the second place very little inheritance was left, namely: a bunch of goose quills, a quire of white official paper, three pairs of socks, two or three buttons torn off pants, and the bathrobe, about which the reader already knows. Who got all this, God knows. As far as that goes, it must be admitted that the person relating this story was not even interested.

The "radiant messenger" passage is followed by a marvellous scene in which the doorman sent to investigate Akaky's absence from the office reports back with classic understatement that Akaky cannot come any more. Only when questioned further does the true extent of Akaky's incapacity for copying become evident:

> Several days after his death there was sent to his apartment a doorman from his department with orders for him to appear at once, the chief demands it, so to say. But the doorman had to return without anything, giving the answer that he can't come anymore, and at the question, "Why?" he expressed himself with these words: "That's the way it is, he's already died. He was buried three days ago." That is how they learned of Akaky Akakievich's death in his department, and already by the next day at his place was sitting a new clerk, quite a bit taller and forming his letters not in that upright hand but quite more sloping and slanting.

Of course, the new clerk's stature and handwriting, or even his existence, are all beautifully irrelevant.

The conclusion of Gogol's tale reports the appearance of a corpse resembling Akaky Akakievich who wantonly snatches overcoats from one and all, regardless of trimmings of the rank of the wearer. The important personage is himself accosted by Akaky's ghost, wafting of the grave, and rudely ordered to surrender his coat. Terrified, the important personage divests himself of that garment and flees home.

> This event made a strong impression upon him, and he even much more rarely started speaking to his subordinates: "How dare you? Do you know who is in front of you?" and if in fact he did pronounce these words, then not before he had heard first what the matter was about.

Critics of sociological bent see Akaky Akakievich's revenge on the important personage as the triumph of the oppressed underdog. This interpretation, however, ignores the final details of the story, where we are told that "from this time on the appearance of the clerk-corpse ceased entirely":

> However, many involved and solicitous people just didn't want to calm down and kept on saying that in distant parts of the town the clerk-corpse still kept on appearing. And just so, a certain Kolomna policeman saw with his own eyes a ghost appear from behind a certain house, but being by nature somewhat a weakling—so that one time an ordinary full-grown suckling pig, which dashed from a private house, knocked him off his feet, to the great amusement of some coachmen who were standing around, from whom he demanded a penny each for tobacco because they had mocked him—so, being a weakling, he did not dare to stop him, and so walked after him in the darkness until finally the ghost suddenly looked around and stopping, asked, "Whadda ya want?" and showed him such a fist as you won't find among the living. The ghost, however, was already quite taller, wore huge mustachios, and directing its steps, so it seemed, towards Obukhov bridge, disappeared completely in the nocturnal darkness."[4]

Nabokov insists that the policeman mistook for Akaky's ghost the mustachioed bandit who stole Akaky's coat in the first place. This final paradox in the grotesque confusion of irrelevancies at the denouement, with its ghosts, puny policeman and the "ordinary full-grown suckling pig," completely distracts us from the defunct clerk. The less than insignificant Akaky, who scarcely qualifies for a spot in the naturalist's collection, is replaced by a more prestigious zoological manifestation, the full-grown suckling pig.

What's more, many parallels between Akaky Akakievich and the important personage suggest that the two reflect but differing degrees of emptiness, evil, and pretension. While Akaky speaks in meaningless agglomerations of prepositions, adverbs, and particles, the important personage seems limited to his three stock phrases: "How dare you?" "Do you know to whom you are talking?" and "Do you understand who is standing before you?" When Akaky Akakievich makes a copy of an official paper at home for his own pleasure, he chooses a paper "notable not for its beauty of style but for its being addressed to some new or important person." Akaky's consciousness of rank allows him to fulfill his menial tasks, just as the important personage's overdeveloped sense of position (a major factor in his characterization) permits him to stay in the graces of his superiors and properly terrify his subordinates.

Most important, there are the major parallels of incident at the end of the tale. At the party celebrating the new coat, Akaky Akakievich has a couple of glasses of champagne, and, starting home "in a cheerful mood, he even was suddenly, no one knows why, about to run after some lady, who flashed by like lightning, every part of her body full of extraordinary movement." This libidinous outburst is followed by the loss of his coat. The second "philanthropic" passage concludes by noting that misfortune had fallen upon Akaky "as it falls upon the heads of the powerful of this earth!" This is a transition to the story of the important personage's misfortune. The important personage also attends a gathering and at supper "drank a couple of glasses of champagne, a means, as is known, not acting badly as regards cheerfulness." "The champagne imparted in him a disposition for various special things," namely a visit to his mistress, but his intentions are thwarted when he is accosted by the ghost which takes his overcoat. He flees home, where he "spends the night in quite great distress," just as on the night of his tragic loss Akaky Akakievich "saddened, dragged himself to his room, and how he passed the night there—it will be left for the person to judge who is able somehow to imagine someone else's position."

We have already seen how Gogol exploits the use of false scents to undercut his readers' expectations, or lead them astray. In fact, we must see the entire story as an expansion of the same kind of authorial game, in which the reader is lured further and further and rewarded with a bursting bubble. Counting on his readers' acquaintance with the philanthropic tale, a genre which enabled the author and reader to enjoy a teary communion as they contemplated the miseries of the downtrodden,[5] Gogol could quite rightly anticipate that his audience would expect a traditionally sympathetic treatment of a humble clerk. The facetious nonsense of the opening paragraphs, is of course, somewhat puzzling, but we can relax and feel more at home on learning that Akaky is desperately poor and in need of a coat—a comfortably sentimental situation. At that point the author regales the reader with sour odors and billows of smoke pouring from the kitchen where Petrovich's wife is cooking fish—the sordid details of the tailor's household are rather difficult to reconcile with the conventions of the philanthropic genre. Still, Akaky's subsequent triumph and disaster portend a lachrymose conclusion, but this too is undercut when Akaky returns as a vengeful ghost. Yet no sooner is retribution against the important personage accomplished than the reader is led off to Kolomna, where full-grown suckling pigs run out of private houses to torment puny policemen. . . an odd way to confirm the compassion of the gullible reader.

At most Gogol's Akaky Akakievich is a worm which raises its head, is stepped on and crushed. This would be somewhat pathetic, perhaps, if we were talking about a worm with ambition, or lofty visions, a worm who dies seeking an ideal. But if a *man* is no better than a worm, his aspirations are clearly lacking nobility. Akaky Akakievich is passionless, a happily purring Xerox machine, and when he becomes "human" to the extent that he does, his human passion is not only ludicrous but banal. Instead of seeking a wife of flesh and blood, he fixes on an overcoat, with a "strong lining," to be the object of his love. The romantic theme of a spiritually elevating love has been grotesquely distorted.

For those who insist upon finding some moral, Gogol provides one, but nothing so saccharine as the sociological critics have imposed. The point is that the mundane is all-pervasive, that *poshlust* can be found in sub-human ciphers as well as in the important personages of this world. But perhaps it would be best to forego the luxury of a moral and simply enjoy the ludicrous dance of Gogol's preposterous puppets.

XXVI. Lermontov's Fiction and Psychological Realism.

With certain reservations, Lermontov's prose development mirrors that of the Romantic Movement in general, since he assayed almost all of the genres available to fiction in his time, while his style simultaneously developed from that typical of late Sentimentalism to that of early Realism. Lermonotov completed only one major work of prose, *A Hero of Our Times [Geroi nashego vremeni]*, first published in 1840, and this novel, despite its significant debt to Romanticism, must be considered the first fully developed example of psychological Realism in Russian fiction.

It is not the purpose of this study to detail Lermontov's career as a poet or playwright, but it is interesting that his development in those areas paralleled that of his prose. He began as a very subjective and derivative author, only gradually creating his own manner. His first prose effort, *Vadim*, was written, as far as we can tell, while he was a cadet at the Guards School in Petersburg, sometime between 1832 and 1834. This was just the period of the triumph of the historical novel, and it is scarcely surprising that an imitative young author would attempt this genre.[1]

Vadim was never finished, and properly so, for it has an inner flaw which could not be corrected—the hero turns into a villain. The story is set against the background of the Pugachev Uprising (Lermontov preceded Pushkin in this respect), and the protagonist, Vadim, a hunchbacked genius with magnetic eyes, seeks to capitalize upon the civil unrest to avenge the death of his father, the victim of Palitsyn, the usurper of his property.

Lermontov's acquaintance with Walter Scott, particularly his *The Black Dwarf*, and the classics of *l'Ecole frénétique*'s historical fiction, Balzac's *Les Chouans* and Hugo's *Notre Dame de Paris*, is evident in the structure of *Vadim*, its character types, its emphasis, and the typical cliches of situation. At first the protagonist is justified in seeking retribution against the odious Palitsyn, especially since the old voluptuary has his eye on Vadim's beautiful sister, Olga. But Vadim himself becomes reprehensible, first revealing his incestuous love for his sister, then wantonly inciting rebellious Cossacks to murder their innocent prisoners, killing a servant loyal to Olga, and finally seeking to destroy his sister, along with Palitsyn and his son Yury, whom Olga loves.

If Lermontov's older European colleagues influenced the external form and details of this novel, its style was influenced most directly by the language of Bestuzhev-Marlinsky, especially that of historical tales such as *Roman and Olga* or the later *The Frigate "Hope."* Marlinsky's pathetic high style, in which his heroes comment upon their psychic states, his striking metaphors, his anaphoras, his frozen epithets, all are echoed here.

"No, no! thought Vadim, drawing away from them. "This is my victim. I alone shall lay hands upon him, I alone shall hear his last cry, I alone shall have engraved upon my memory the final sight of him, his last convulsive movement. He is mine. I have bought him from heaven and hell. I paid for him with bloody tears, with terrible days during which I deliberately devoured all possible feelings, so that there finally would remain in my breast only feelings of malice and revenge. Oh, I'm not one to indifferently let my prey out of my grasp and leave him to you, you base slaves!"

Until Lermontov could overcome his taste for Marlinsky's style, he was anchored firmly to Romanticism.

Lermontov's second prose effort, *Princess Lygovskaya [Kniaginia Ligovskaia]*, was a society tale which he began, probably in late 1835, in collaboration with a cousin, Svyatoslav Raevsky, and this, too, remained unfinished. Like many examples of this genre, it is a satirical *roman à clef* incorporating various incidents from Lermontov's life, principally his relationship with Varvara Lopukhina-Bakhmeteva, the prototype for the title figure. The tale has several lines of intrigue—the efforts of the protagonist, Grigory Pechorin, a young officer, to acquire a reputation in society as a Don Juan, his quest for revenge against the princess, who, despite an earlier pledge of eternal love, has married a stupid but rich old man, and Pechorin's confrontation with a noble but impoverished clerk, Krasiński, who seeks revenge for Pechorin's indifference and chaffs from a feeling of social inferiority. It has been supposed that the figure of the clerk was created by Lermontov's collaborator, Raevsky, himself a civil servant, but nothing about the character or the style associated with those scenes in which Krasiński appears indicates Raevsky's particular participation. Furthermore, Krasiński, who is of Polish descent, reflects qualities of nobility and decency which Lermontov found in his Polish friends, the Branicki brothers.

Were this tale completed, were some of the vestiges of Romantic style purged and the narrative perspective stabilized, this might well have become one of the very best society tales. Even as it stands the work shows a concern with psychologization far beyond the norms for the genre, even for such authors as Odoevsky. Lermontov is on the threshhold of Realism, moving away from metaphor to metonymy, from characterization by comparison to characterization by contiguity, from "telling" to "showing." The work reveals an authorial concern not with detail or plot for their own sakes, but with the use of these elements to synthesize psychologal portraits of the central characters, especially of Pechorin. We learn of his occupations, his interests, his tastes, his friends, and his past, and these combine to suggest a real-life person who acts differently in different milieux, whose voice and gestures betray his inner states, whose actions speak louder than his words. All of the scenes are revelatory, and, while interesting in themselves, they serve the ultimate purpose, to expose character.[2]

Lermontov never finished the story, perhaps because his own attitude toward his relationship to Varvara Lopukhina-Bakhmeteva underwent some reassessment. In any case, he wrote to Raevsky in June, 1836 that "the novel I began with you [or, "at your place"] has bogged down and will probably never be finished." Nonetheless, as a fictionist he had matured from the effort, and his attempt at creating a Pechorin was highly successful.

Much has been said about *A Hero of Our Times [Geroi nashego vremeni]* not being a novel at all but simply a series of tales united by the person of Grigory Pechorin, the hero, or anti-hero, whose adventures constitute the various tales. But as Boris Eichenbaum first showed, the tales are arranged without regard to chronology to provide a gradually more intimate acquaintance with the protagonist. Setting and incident are fully subordinated to characterization.

The lead story, *Bela [Bela]*, has an exterior frame of travel notes in which a peregrinating author details his journey northward across the Caucasus. The following description of one of the breath-taking panoramas is typical:

A wonderful place is this valley! On all sides are inaccessible mountains, reddish cliffs hung with clusters of plane trees, yellow precipices lined by torrents, and there, high, high above is a golden fringe of snow, and below the Aragva River, having embraced another nameless stream which breaks noisily out of a mist-filled gorge, stretches in a silver thread and glistens like the scales on a snake.

In the course of his trip along the Georgian military road (in those days a dangerous mountain path), he encounters a colorful "Kavkazets," a Russian junior captain named Maxim Maximych.

Behind [the cart] walked its master, smoking a small Kabardian pipe inlaid with silver. He was wearing an officer's coat without epaulettes and a shaggy Circassian hat. He appeared about fifty. The swarthy hue of his face showed a long acquaintance with the Trans-Caucasian sun, and his prematurely greyed moustache did not harmonize with his firm gait and vigorous appearance.

The depiction here and later follows patterns typical of the physiological sketch, which in the later thirties was just coming into its own. Interestingly, Lermontov also wrote a short physiological sketch entitled *Kavkazets*, which outlined a similar character type.

The travelling author encourages Maxim to tell him a story, and the latter obliges with the tale of an incident when he was in command of a remote Caucasian fortress. This is retold word for word by the author. Maxim recounts how five years previously there was posted to him a young officer, Grigory Pechorin, handsome, fearless, and quite indifferent to military protocol. Bela, a Chechen princess from a neighboring village, soon caught Pechorin's eye, and he had her kidnapped and brought to his quarters. Gradually she accepted him, and they were happy. Subsequently, however, Pechorin grew bored with her and spent more and more time hunting. Ultimate-

309

ly Bela wandered beyond the ramparts of the fort and was stabbed to death by a *dzigit*, Kazbich, in revenge for her brother's complicity in the theft of Kazbich's fabulous horse, Karagyoz. Pechorin's apparent indifference to Bela's death puzzles Maxim Maximych, for whom Pechorin has remained an enigma. *Bela* concludes with more travel details and an indication that the traveling author was to meet again with the old officer.

What Lermontov did here was to take the then nearly exhausted genre of travel notes and combine it with the equally tired story of the love of a Byronic hero from civilization for an "exotic" native. But Lermontov infused new vitality by putting the tale into the mouth of an old veteran who had never heard of Romanticism or Byron, a narrator who, moreover, has his own distinctive manner of speech, an idiom seasoned with colloquialisms and Caucasian words. All of this was enclosed in the attractive packaging of the spectacular scenery described by the traveling author in the course of his journey.

The second story of the novel is called simply *Maxim Maximych*, and in it the traveling author tells of a later meeting with the old junior captain at Vladikavkaz, a rustic posting station on the northern flank of the Caucasus. Word is received that Pechorin himself is expected, and Maxim Maximych cannot contain his elation at the chance to show off his old friend to the traveling author. What happens, however, is that Pechorin ignores Maxim Maximych's presence, and they meet only accidentally the next morning. Pechorin's reserve totally undercuts the captain's expectations, and the long anticipated reunion turns completely sour. Later Maxim Maximych petulently unburdens his disappointment upon the traveling author:

"What am I to him? I'm not rich, I have no rank, and besides, our ages are completely different. See what a dandy he's become. . . . It's funny, by God, it's funny! I always knew he was a flighty fellow and couldn't be counted on. True, it's too bad he's going to end up badly—and that's for sure! I've said many times that there's no use in a person who forgets his old friends!"

The traveling author, of course, has observed the meeting, and, as a professional writer, he indulges in some speculations about Pechorin's character on the basis of his dress, actions, and behavior.

. . . his dusty velvet frock-coat, fastened only by the two lower buttons, permitted a glimpse of dazzlingly clean linen, which betrayed the habits of a gentleman. . . . His gait was careless and lazy, but I noticed that he did not swing his arms—a true sign of a certain secretiveness of character. . . . To finish the portrait, I shall say that he had a slightly turned-up nose, teeth of dazzling whiteness, and hazel eyes. I must say a few words about those eyes.

In the first place, they didn't laugh when he laughed. Have you ever noticed this strange feature in people? It's a sign either of an evil nature or of some deep and continual grief. From behind half-lowered lashes they shone with a kind of phosphorescent gleam, if one may so express it. This was not the reflection of spiritual fire or a playful

310

imagination; this was a gleam like that of polished steel, dazzling but cold. His glance, quick but penetrating and heavy, left an unpleasant impression, like an indiscreet question, and it might have seemed insolent had it not been so indifferently calm.

Thus we move another step closer to Pechorin, for the hearsay figure of *Bela,* twice removed from the reader, now has been seen by the traveling author himself. But we are to move much closer yet to Pechorin. At the end of *Maxim Maximych,* the narrator tells us that the chagrined junior captain threw out of his trunk some notebooks of Pechorin's which he had been carrying around with him since Pechorin had left the fortress five years previously, and these notebooks contain the last three stories.

Having properly motivated the possession of the notebooks, Lermontov proceeds to motivate their publication. In his *Introduction to Pechorin's Journal,* the traveling author tells us that he would not utilize the work of someone else, but that he had learned of Pechorin's death in Persia and thus felt free to publish the three stories. As for his own assessment of Pechorin, the traveling author provides an enigmatic epitaph:

> Reading over these notes, I have become convinced of the sincerity of this person who so mercilessly laid bare his own weaknesses and vices. The history of a human soul, be it even the pettiest of souls, is almost more curious and useful than the history of a whole nation, particularly when it is the result of the self-observation of a mature mind and when it is written without any vain desire to arouse sympathy or amazement. The *Confessions* of Rousseau have that very shortcoming in that he read them to his friends.

Taman [Taman'], which takes its name from a seaport town on the straits of Kerch, combines the travel tale, the military anecdote, and the tale of the supernatural. In it Pechorin relates an adventure he had while traveling under government orders on his way to the Caucasus. In Taman no housing was available except an "unclean" house on the cliffs above the shore, and there Pechorin encountered a deaf old hag, who could hear when she wanted to, a blind boy, who could easily scramble up and down the cliffs, an enticing girl, who sang enigmatic songs and refused to answer his questions, and a fearless boatman, Yanko, who miraculously could cross the straits in stormy weather. The naive Pechorin spies on the activities of these people, hints that he will report them to the authorities, and then lets himself be enticed by the girl into a boat, at which point she tries to drown him. He saves himself, but returns to his quarters to find that the blind boy has robbed him.

Pechorin's remarks which frame this anecdote show the depth of his disgust with Taman and the adventure it provided him. His story begins, "Taman is the most wretched of all Russia's maritime towns," and ends:

> What became of the old woman and the poor blind boy—I don't know. And then

311

what to me are human joys and miseries, me, an itinerant officer who has, moreover, an official travel pass!

This ire is understandable, for Pechorin, whether or not he has realized it, has been a perfect fool. Had he not been so inquisitive, he would not have provoked the smugglers to an attempt on his life. But even worse, he let himself be lured into a rowboat when he couldn't swim, and where, in any case, he could hardly have hoped to accomplish his libidinous intention. Thus, seen against the background of the two previous tales, *Taman* is the *fiasco* of the Byronic hero, for the hitherto enigmatic and dominant Pechorin is shown to be simply a fool and a dupe.

But the story has further meaning not related to Pechorin's characterization, for it is also a variant of the supernatural story. When lodging appears impossible to find in Taman, the exasperated Pechorin declares, "Take me somewhere, you cutthroat, even to the Devil, only somewhere." Thereupon it appears there *is* an available hut, but one which, he is told, is *nechisto*, which means both "evil" and "unclean." Assuming the latter, Pechorin orders himself taken there. And at this point we enter a demonic circle, which includes the hut without icons, the old witch, the blind boy with apparent supernatural ability to find his way about, and the lively girl, whom the unknowing Pechorin so aptly calls "my ondine." The suggestion of the demonic presence is continued with references to the girl as a "snake" or a "cat," and when she tries to drown Pechorin, she exhibits "supernatural strength." When Pechorin finally succeeds in throwing her into the stormy sea, she somehow survives. In the same way, the boatman Yanko has extraordinary powers. Despite the heavy seas, he is able to bring his laden boat to a safe landing, a fact which surprises the eavesdropping Pechorin.

It would appear, therefore, that unknowingly Pechorin penetrated a demonic circle, one which he never recognized and from which he escaped almost by sheer chance. Of course this interpretation of *Taman* as a variant of the supernatural tale is not necessary for understanding the novel, and, in fact, *A Hero of Our Times* cannot qualify as a novel of psychological Realism if we admit the presence of the supernatural. Still, taking *Taman* simply as a short story, out of the context of the series, it acquires this secondary significance.[3]

Once again Lermontov has worked with traditional Romantic elements—the fairy tale characters, the smuggling operation, the suspense of the quest to find the key to the puzzling behavior of the people from the hut, and the tension of his fight for life, not to mention the Romantic cliches of setting, including the remote and uncanny hut, the moonlit cliffs, the stormy sea, and the deserted beach. But when framed by Pechorin's irritable comments about Taman and its denizens, the tale links nicely with the others to serve the purpose of acquainting the reader with the psychology of Pechorin.

Having moved into Pechorin's own account in *Taman*, we have still remained more or less at a distance from him, since what we learn of him as a person is only implied in what is essentially an adventure story. With *Princess Mary [Kniazhna Meri]*, however, we enter the mind of Pechorin and at times are even able to observe his thoughts as they surface in his consciousness.

Princess Mary is a society tale, but one set in the Caucasus. In choosing the spa of Piatigorsk as his setting, Lermontov was following the advice offered by Walter Scott in his own society novel, *St. Ronan's Well,* in which he declared that the freer social manners of a watering place make it possible to bring together types who could never logically have encountered one another in the city, where codes of behavior are more strict and society more stratified. In the free atmosphere of Piatigorsk, Pechorin is able to have contact with all levels of gentry society, and, moreover, the exotic setting permits unusual adventures without sacrifice of verisimilitude.

Unlike *Taman*, this selection from Pechorin's *Journal* has the form of a diary, with dated entries of various length. In the course of several months Pechorin chronicles the events leading to a fatal duel, the cause of his exile to the fortress commanded by Maxim Maximych. Pechorin's adversary is a young cadet, Grushnitsky, a Byronic poser who is in love with Princess Mary, an eligible young lady taking the waters at the spa. Pechorin dislikes Grushnitsky, because he sees in the younger man a caricature of himself, although he does not openly recognize this. In any case, he decides to win Mary away from Grushnitsky, which is easily accomplished, but in so doing he arouses the cadet's intense enmity. Grushnitsky and some others conspire to provoke Pechorin to a duel, convinced that he will show the white feather. Their plan is to use blank charges, so that no one will be exposed to danger. However, at the dueling site, Pechorin insists that the pistols be properly loaded and that the duelists flip a coin to determine who has the first shot, the loser having to stand at the edge of a precipice. Pechorin loses, and Grushnitsky hesitates to shoot him. However, Pechorin promises to kill Grushnitsky if he himself escapes, and the cadet, goaded beyond endurance, fires. Pechorin, lightly wounded, springs from the abyss. With their roles reversed, Pechorin offers Grushnitsky his life in exchange for an admission of his base plot, but the cadet refuses and Pechorin shoots him off the cliff.

Meanwhile, Pechorin has resumed his affair with Princess Vera, a married woman who was once his mistress. Their liaison is discovered by her husband, and she is forced to abandon Piatigorsk, leaving behind a note declaring her love for the officer. Pechorin sets out in pursuit, only to founder his horse. He returns to Piatigorsk to find that the duel has been reported. Before leaving himself, he goes to Mary and tells her that he never loved her, thus ensuring her eternal hatred.

In this society tale Lermontov has used many of the techniques later utilized in canonical Realism for the delineation of character. Although this is a first-person account, with all the information originating with Pechorin, the completeness of his report makes it possible to learn the opinions of others about him. Since he delights in atagonizing people, he has no scruples about reporting their negative reactions toward himself. Pechorin is also juxtaposed to the two other major male characters, the cadet Grushnitsky and Doctor Werner, a sensitive and intelligent individual who is the only person in Piatigorsk recognized by Pechorin as an intellectual equal. Pechorin's essentially isolated existence is revealed not only by his conflicts with others but by his own statements, such as his attraction to nature, his pleasure in solitary equestrian excursions. Vera's farewell letter provides further, presumably more objective evaluation of Pechorin, joining that of Mary, Grushnitsky, and Werner to fill out the psychological portrait of the hero.

Lermontov has also used a rudimentary form of interior monologue here in those journal entries in which Pechorin seeks to explain to himself his motivation for destroying Grushnitsky's happiness, winning Mary's affections, and injuring Vera by the resumption of their affair:

> Reviewing quickly the memories of my entire past, I involuntarily ask myself why have I lived? And for what purpose was I born? But certainly there was a purpose, and certainly my assignment was an important one, for I feel the countless forces within me. But I failed to guess this assignment and was attracted by the lure of empty and thankless passions. From the forge of these passions I came out hard and cold as iron, but I have lost forever the fire of noble ardor—the best flower of life. And from that time I have already so often played the role of the axe in the hands of fate! Like an instrument of punishment I have fallen on the heads of the fated victims, often without malice, always without compassion. My love has brought happiness to no one, for I sacrificed nothing for those whom I loved; I love for myself, for my own satisfaction; I only satisfied a strange need of my heart, avidly devouring the feelings of others, their joys and sufferings—and I was never sated. . . .
>
> And, perhaps, I shall die tomorrow! And there won't remain a single being on earth who has understood me thoroughly. Some will consider me worse, others better, than I actually am. Some will say, "He was a good fellow," others, "A scoundrel." and each will be wrong. Is it worth making an effort to live after all this? And yet one lives on—from curiosity, awaiting something new. It's ludicrous and annoying!"[4]

We may also note in passing that the confessional nature of certain of Pechorin's entries, such as that quoted above, is also typical of the "psychological novel" of Romanticism, the first person *profession de foi* which often merged with the *Kuenstlernovelle*. The difference between those earlier works and that of Lermontov's is in the motivation for the confessor's behavior, which in the typical "psychological novel" was arbitrary, but in *Princess Mary* is explained by Pechorin's avowed pleasure in deceiving enemies, exposing plots, and subjecting others to his will.

The final story of the novel is *The Fatalist [Fatalist]*, which for some critics seems an unnecessary extension of Pechorin's adventures. However, the story is vital to the understanding of the personality of the hero, for in this tale we get a resolution of the clues presented in the earlier stories. By the time he comes to *The Fatalist*, the reader has a good understanding of what Pechorin is, but we do not understand why he behaves as he does. Pechorin's relationship to Fate, which is the subject of the last story, at least helps us answer the question.

The theme of Fate surfaces in all of the previous stories either directly or indirectly, being most pronounced in *Princess Mary*, where Pechorin ascribes to Fate the responsibility for his pernicious involvement with the other characters. Of course, it is Pechorin himself who goaded Grushnitsky to desperation, who toyed with Mary's affections, and who arranged an unhappy sequel to the affair with Vera. In a number of places in his *Journal*, he speaks of himself as playing a role in a drama, but at the same time he himself writes the parts of the supporting players to suit his purpose. It is not inapropos then, as Grushnitsky plunges to his death, that Pechorin declares, "Finita la commedia."

In *The Fatalist* we find that Pechorin really does not believe in Fate, yet at the same time he is unwilling to take responsibility for his actions when things turn out badly through the exercise of his will. *The Fatalist* opens with a group of officers discussing Fate and predestination, and one of them asks: "And precisely if there is such a thing as predestination, then why have we been given will, judgment? Why must we give account for our actions?" The point is made—but not by Pechorin—that one either accepts predestination and Fate or must be accountable for the acts of his free will. Pechorin eschews that responsibility. He is a man without an ethical compass, the victim of his passions and chance interests, and at the same time his personality and dynamism are so strong that inevitably he tries and succeeds in dominating others. Ultimately he tires of his victims and abandons them, as he abandons Bela, Vera, and Mary, or destroys them, as he does Grushnitsky.

Lermontov's introduction to the second edition of this work in 1841 is interesting, first because it reveals that some readers actually thought the author had intended Pechorin as a bona-fide hero of his times, and secondly because it shows that Lermontov considered his protagonist as a composite representation of the shortcomings of his generation. Note also the stress upon the reality of the type.

The Hero of Our Times, my dear sirs, is, it is true, a portrait, but not of one person: this is a portrait composed of our entire generation's vices in their full development. You again will tell me that a man can't be that bad, and I will tell you that if you believed in the possibility of the existence of all tragic and romantic villains, why then don't you believe in the reality of Pechorin? If you delighted in fictions much more terrible and monstrous, why is it that this character, even as a fiction, finds no mercy at your hands? Is it not that there is more truth in him than you would like?

But don't think. . . that the author of this book had some sort of proud dream of becoming a reformer of human vices. . . . He simply found it pleasant to sketch the contemporary man, as he understands him and, to his and your misfortune, has met too often.

And there is indeed a great deal of similarity between the way Pechorin acts and the fruitless life which Lermontov sketches in his accusatory elegy of 1838, *Meditation [Duma]* .

Much has been written about the influence of Pushkin's narrative poem, *Eugene Onegin*, on *A Hero of Our Times*. Pushkin's protagonist, Onegin, is a Russianized version of Byron's Childe Harold combined with Benjamin Constant's Adolfe, an intelligent but superficial young man from the Petersburg *jeunesse dorée*, who spurns the love of Tatiana Larina when she is a mere provincial maiden but develops a passionate desire for her after she has married and become a dominant figure in Petersburg society. Lermontov's first Pechorin, that of *Princess Ligovskaya*, is closer to Onegin than the Pechorin of *A Hero of Our Times*, for the second Grigory Pechorin possesses a dynamism and viciousness not found in either Onegin or Pechorin I. Still, there is no doubt that Pushkin's work had a significant influence upon both of Lermontov's by pointing him in the direction of psychological Realism and providing an example of the devices to utilize in achieving this end.

There are also a number of demonstrable foreign influences upon *A Hero of Our Times*, some of which it shares with *Eugene Onegin*, including Byron and Benjamin Constant. Lermontov certainly knew Charles Bernard's novel *Gerfaut* (1839), as parallel scenes indicate. One may also find Alfred de Musset's *Confession d'un enfant du siècle* (1835) as a source for the alienated and emotionally cold Pechorin. Although more difficult to establish on the basis of concrete similarities, the influence of Balzac cannot be ignored. His *Scènes de la vie privée* provided models for the treatment of character and formulae typical of the society tale, influencing other authors as well, such as I.I. Panaev.

The significance of *A Hero of Our Times* is not confined to its role as the first example in Russian prose literature of a novel of psychological Realism. The work also demonstrated that Russian literary prose had finally reached maturity, a process begun with Karamzin's reform and continued through the first four decades of the nineteenth century. Lermontov's prose is the language used by Turgenev and Tolstoy, or even by Chekhov at the end of the century.

A Hero of Our Time is a Janus figure standing between Romanticism and Realism. Its themes, its types, and its genres are all a part of its Romantic heritage, but with its dominant concern for psychological portraiture, as evidenced by its non-chronological structure and its formal devices, such as interior monologue and delineation by contiguity, it looks directly toward the new era of classic prose Realists, the greatest of whom, Tolstoy, Dostoevsky, and Turgenev, all show clearly the influence of this work on their own novelist art.

Lermontov's final prose work was unfinished, a parody of the tale of the supernatural, or the *Kuenstlernovelle*, or Pushkin, or Gogol—perhaps of all of them. The title *Shtoss [Shtoss]* is based on a three-way pun, for the word is a proper name, the name of a card game, and is phonetically equivalent to *Shto-s*, meaning "What, sir?" The story is about an artist, Lugin, who hears voices telling him to go to a specific address and find a certain Shtoss. Investigation reveals that Shtoss's apartment is vacant, so Lugin rents it. Soon an apparition appears and engages him in a game of shtoss, Lugin gambling his gold in hopes of winning some shadowy companion of the spectre, which the deranged artist perceives as the ideal of feminine beauty. The story ends with the report of Lugin's loss of his money and (here the manuscript becomes complicated by abbreviations) his death? or his suicide? or his bankruptcy?

There is some obvious play with Gogol's Petersburg cycle and Pushkin's *The Queen of Spades*, since elements of both are in Lermontov's work. Still, his purpose in incorporating these is not easy to explain, unless we see the work as a literary joke appreciated only by a knowledgeable audience. And in fact the work was first aired in 1841 when Lermontov invited a number of friends to hear a new "novel," and then treated them to a mere thirty minutes of this rather nonsensical tale. To consider *Shtoss*, as some have done, as an abortive attempt at the supernatural is nonsense, since an author capable of *A Hero of Our Times* would hardly have been likely to regress to the cliches of the mid-thirties.

Lermontov's implacable antagonism toward the court and its circle of servile sycophants had led to Caucasian exile on two occasions, in 1837 and 1840. During the latter sojourn he had taken active part in the campaign against the mountaineers and distinguished himself in battle. Rewards were specifically refused by the Tsar. In the winter of 1841 he was enjoying leave in Petersburg when orders came to report without delay to the Tengin Regiment, which at that time was being decimated by malaria and the enemy in an area along the north shore of the Black Sea. When he reached the northern Caucasus in the summer of that year, he detoured to Piatigorsk "for medical reasons." Among those at the spa was the retired Major Martynov, a poseur who became the target of Lermontov's wit and lampoons. The inevitable challenge was made, and the two met at dusk outside town at the foot of Mount Mashuk. A storm was brewing. Lermontov was shot dead when Martynov fired first.

Title page to the first edition of *Dead Souls*, from a sketch by Gogol

XXVII. Gogol's *Dead Souls.*

Lermontov brought the productive phase of Romantic fiction to a close in 1840, yet others continued to produce variations of old themes in second-hand styles. I do not intend to conclude this study with a resumé of the Romantic epigons but with the Movement's greatest fictionist, Nikolay Gogol. His *magnum opus, Dead Souls [Mertvye dushi]*, appeared in 1842, at the indefinite further edge of the Romantic period, and although he tried for the next ten years of his life to write its sequel, he was unsuccessful. *Dead Souls* remains the last major work of Russian Romantic fiction.

Even now many consider this a realistic work. However, in virtually all respects Gogol's novel reflects the norms which dominated fiction at the apogee of Romanticism. The discussion below will focus primarily on these normative Romantic features.[1]

The genre of *Dead Souls* is even older than Romanticism, a variant of the picaresque novel, with its mountebank protagonist participating in a string-of-bead adventures. Our hero, Pavel Chichikov, whose surname suggests sneezing, travels about provincial Russia buying title to deceased serfs in the hope of mortgaging them as live ones before the next census officially eliminates their names from among the living. This plot, supposedly suggested to Gogol by Pushkin, is sufficiently impossible in itself to exclude the novel from any serious consideration as a realistic work.

Gogol conceived *Dead Souls* as a *Divine Comedy* in three parts corresponding to Hell, Purgatory, and Paradise. In Part One, which is all that he was able to complete to his own satisfaction, Chichikov is depicted in a milieu of exclusively negative types embodying various moral and venal sins, with the protagonist worse than any of them. In Part Two he was to undergo amelioration of his rotten soul through contact with positive characters, and in the final volume undergo complete regeneration. Unfortunately, Gogol seems to have been successful only in the creation of negative types, and his efforts to provide Chichikov with positive companions failed. On his deathbed he ordered all the drafts subsequent to Part One destroyed.

Dead Souls, therefore, is a work which has a metaphorical basis, and, as one proceeds through the work, it becomes apparent that the title refers not to the deceased serfs but rather to Chichikov himself and those with whom he deals. All of them are morally dead, incarnations of life's *poshlust*, which the author saw as the handiwork of the Devil, the triviality of actions and goals which subvert man from his higher destiny as the creation of God.

Gogol's method of exposing the Devil was to laugh at his works, and in this respect *Dead Souls* is extremely humorous. At the same time it is a sad work, since it presents only an unrelieved picture of ubiquitous mediocrity. Gogol claimed that when Pushkin read parts of the novel written prior to his death in 1837, he commented upon what a sad story it was.

Typical of the arbitrary, one-sided characters found in much Romantic fiction, Chichikov has no redeeming qualities. He is a soft and rotund little man whose personality depends upon his circumstances, and he is invariably agreeable when he hopes to gain something from others:

In his conversations with these men of power, he very artfully knew how to flatter everyone. As if in passing he hinted to the governor that entering his province was like entering heaven, the roads were like velvet. . . . To the chief of police he said something very flattering about the town watchmen, and in his conversations with the vice-governor and the council president, who were just state councellors, he twice said by mistake: "Your excellencey," which pleased them very much. The result of all this was that the governor presented an invitation to visit him that very day at an evening gathering, and the other officials also invited him, one to dinner, one to play a bit of boston, another for a cup of tea.

At the same time this social charmer can be captious or fearful when confronted with those who want something from him. In the end his plot is exposed through his own stupidity, and he takes flight, his personality unaltered by the experience.

Gogol's method of characterization is that of stylization or conventionalization. In the course of his travels in the quest for dead souls, Chichikov encounters a number of provincial landowners, each of whom has some dominant note to which everything surrounding him conforms. The landowner Manilov, whose name suggests the Russian word for "to lure" or "to entice," is a Cheshire cat of saccharine sweetness, a vacuous man whose agreeable wife favors him with birthday surprises of her own handiwork and lingering kisses. The rough Sobakevich, or "Sonofabitch," has the appearance and personality of a bear, and with this zoological note everything around him is tuned. His voice is rough and his language coarse, he is a gourmand capable of devouring whole turkeys and saddles of lamb, his wife is clumsy, his furniture mammoth and heavy. Sobakevich is a regular bear:

When Chichikov looked sideways at Sobakevich, this time he looked quite like a medium sized bear. To complete the resemblance, his coat was of an absolutely bear-like color, long sleeves, long pantaloons, when he walked he blundered about and constantly stepped on other people's feet. The color of his face was fiery, burning, like that of a copper coin. It is known that there are many such faces on earth on whose finishing Nature didn't worry her mind too much and didn't use any finishing tools, such as files and drills and the like but simply chopped with full swings: one blow of the axe and out comes the nose, another and there are the lips, the eyes are gouged out with a large auger, and without any sanding she set him on earth, saying: "It lives!"

The miser Plyushkin is a pack rat, his house filled with useless and broken items, and, while his peasants starve along with their master, the grain from his harvests is hoarded in rotting heaps. The bully Nozdryov, who is congenitally incapable of telling the truth, reduces everything to the denominator of confusion, which prevails in his excursions to the local fairs, in his motley pack of hounds, in the strange concoctions which his cook prepares and the wines which accompany them. It is he who reveals Chichikov's queer business to the town officials, assisted by the superstitious and suspicious widow Korobochka, whose name suggests a jack-in-the-box which pops up suddenly, as indeed she does when she makes a special trip to town to ascertain the going price for dead souls.

This work is saturated with comparisons, which deepen its metaphorical essence. As Carl Proffer has shown in his study of Gogol's similes in *Dead Souls*, most of these relate man to some aspect of the zoological world, as for example those comparisons in which man is seen as a fly, a bug, or some lower form of animal or insect life. The unusual tendency of Gogol's comparisons to spin off into different dimensions has been noted by commentators. Perhaps the best known is that in which dandies dressed for a ball change into flies clustering on a sugar loaf, which conjures up a purblind old housekeeper who tries to shoo them away while they fly back for social conviviality.

Not only people but things are depicted in animal metaphors, especially in the chapter dealing with Chichikov's visit to Korobochka's estate, in which the zoological saturation is complete. The clock hisses like a snake, and even the road in her part of the country crawls off in all directions like a crab. The background action is also zoological. Chichikov, idly looking out the window, sees a sow gobble down a baby chick along with some melon rind, and a rooster wanders about, oblivious to the fact that its jealous comrades have pecked away half its brain.

Gross naturalism is typical of *Dead Souls*, in which everything is soiled, broken, cracked, stained, worn out, or misshapen. This is not the real world, which despite the plentitude of imperfect objects, is not entirely blemished.

In considering the ways in which *Dead Souls* implements the norms of Romantic fiction, one must not overlook the heterogeneity of the narrative voice. At times we listen to the author, or his mask, moralistically insisting that his characters are real:

That's the kind of person Nozdryov was! Maybe you'll call him a hackneyed character, you'll start saying that there are no Nozdryov's today. Alas, those who start saying that are unjust. Nozdryov won't be gone from the world for a long time yet. He is everywhere among us and, perhaps, is just going about in a different coat. But people are thoughtlessly gullible, and a person in a different coat seems to them to be a different person.

The narrative voice can drip with venomous irony. Speaking of the disorder that reigned in the Manilov household, our narrator explains:

But all these are low matters, and Mrs. Manilov was well educated. And a good education, as everyone knows, is accomplished in boarding schools, and in boarding schools, as everyone knows, three chief subjects constitute the basis of human virtue: the French language, necessary for the joy of family life; the piano, for providing one's spouse with pleasant moments; and finally, a purely domestic science, the knitting of little purses and other surprises.

Seldom is there neutral reportage, as in Realist fiction. The author-narrator, or some surrogate, is continually visible. Perhaps the most intrusive voice is that of the lyrical prophet, whose declamations reach the height of absurdity at the very end of the novel, when, in a scene reminiscent of the dream sequence at the conclusion of Kvitka-Osnovyanenko's *Pan Khalyavsky*, the carriage conveying the arch *poshlyak* Chichikov, his smelly lackey, and drunk coachman is transformed into a symbol of Russia's destiny, causing all other nations to gape in disbelief (along with the reader). The lyrical gymnastics of *The Overcoat* pale in comparison with the fervor of this Messianic conclusion:

Rus, whither fliest thou? Give thy answer. But no answer is given. The harness bells burst forth with wondrous sound, the air, torn to shreds, thunders and turns to wind. Everything flies past, everything on earth, and the other peoples and nations look askance, and stand aside, and give it the right of way.

Or is this the supreme irony?

Towards the end of *Dead Souls* the town worthies gather to speculate on the true identity of Chichikov, and the postmaster narrates his "Story of Captain Kopeikin," a tale of a double amputee who becomes a bandit when the government withholds assistance. This *skaz* narrative represents yet another distinctive stylistic element, and at the same time is a thoroughly non-Realistic, Sternean play with the reader. Not only is it the height of absurdity for characters in the novel to associate Chichikov with the veteran, but it is even more ridiculous for the reader to be obliged to follow the vicissitudes of the aggrieved captain.

Earlier we have seen that more than a little of Gogol's apparent originality is simply an ability to borrow creatively. While not intending to underestimate the originality of *Dead Souls*, I should note that the bizarre collection of characters he presents are descendants of other literary types. Thus the miser Plyushkin bears striking resemblance to Charles Maturin's Sir John Melmoth, or to the miser Tarakh of Narezhny's *Aristion*, while Nozdryov seems a relative of the latter author's hunter Sylvester, from the same novel. Chichikov is the nephew of Perovsky's original *poshlyak*, Klim Dyundik of *The Smolny Institute Graduate*. The very sources from which Gogol borrowed show the essence of the characters to be caricatures.

Unlike Pushkin, Marlinsky, and Lermontov, Gogol did not die a violent death. His last years were poisoned by illness and fear of loss of talent and possession by the devil. One of his last acts just before his death was to burn the manuscript of a continuation of *Dead Souls*, which represented almost ten years of his creative life.

Gogol's death in 1852 did not really diminish the creative power of Russian fiction, for during the final decade of his struggles with imaginary and real diseases new figures of importance had appeared. Fyodor Dostoevsky had already concluded the initial part of his career and was languishing in Siberian exile, Ivan Turgenev was famous for his *Sportsman's Sketches*, Ivan Goncharov was an established author, and Leo Tolstoy was publishing *Childhood*, his first work. Russian fiction was in skillful hands.

CHAPTER I

1. Those interested in theoretical aspects should read Lauren Leighton's RUSSIAN ROMANTICISM (The Hague: Mouton & Co., 1975).

2. One may see the commonly accepted literary movements as dynamic systems of norms, with certain norms in dominant positions. For more explicit explanation, consult my "Towards a Normative Definition of Russian Realism," AMERICAN CONTRIBUTIONS TO THE SEVENTH INTERNATIONAL CONGRESS OF SLAVISTS (The Hague: Mouton & Co., 1973).

3. Some commentators see Pushkin as a Janus figure, his poetry representing the summation of Neoclassicism and his prose serving as a harbinger of Realism. The critic Sipovsky credits Pushkin with creating "true romanticism," by which he means realism. Gogol has been "proved" to be a realist, naturalist, surrealist, symbolist. A good case can be made that Lermontov was a realist in so far as his prose was concerned; his poetry is another matter.

4. The existence of a Russian Romantic movement is argued at length in my "Yes, Virginia, There was a Russian Romantic Movement," RUSSIAN LITERATURE TRIQUARTERLY (Ann Arbor, Michigan: Ardis, 1972). III, 128-146.

5. Lomonosov was Russia's "Renaissance Man." In addition to work in chemistry, geology, and physical sciences, he was a grammarian and poet. He is credited with establishing the preeminence of syllabo-tonic versification with his "Ode on the Capture of Khotin," a work celebrating victory over the Turks in 1739.

6. Zhukovsky's range was inspiring. In addition to his original works, he translated idyls, ballads, fables, elegies, odes, etc. from La Fontaine, J. B. Rousseau, Gessner, Klopstock, Pope, Dryden, Southey, Byron, and still others.

7. Karamzin himself later became aware of the overly precious practice of such substitutions, and when he republished his LETTERS OF A RUSSIAN TRAVELER, which originally appeared in 1792, he replaced some of the Russified French words with Russian ones.

8. V. V. Vinogradov, OCHERKI PO ISTORII RUSSKOGO LITERATURNOGO IAZYKA XVII-XIX vv. (Leiden: Brill, 1950), 165.

9. Yuri Tynyanov dubbed this group the "younger archaists." His book on their literary views and practice is considered definitive. See Iurii Tynianov, ARKHAISTY I NOVATORY (n.p.: Priboi, 1929).

10. The pun is untranslatable: The Colloquy of Lovers of the Russian Word, *Beseda Liubitelei rossiiskogo slova. Liubitel'* means *lover, gubitel'* means *destroyer*.

11. Some of the conservatives, including the fabulist Ivan Krylov, who used vernacular in his animal fables, and Shakhovskoy, who had parodied Zhukovsky, approved Pushkin's work. Years later Wilhelm Kuechelbecker, while discounting the content of the poem as "nonsense," called the style "truly marvelous." See Tynianov, 142-143.

12. I do not insist that all these were strictly speaking part of the Pleiad; certainly they were all quite different in many respects. The Golden Age also includes Fyodor Tyutchev, but he passed virtually unnoticed during the thirties.

13. Russian readers were to learn a great deal more about Lavater, since his ideas of correlating personality and facial features became very popular with Romantic authors. Just about every one of them alludes to Lavater at one time or another.

14. Cf. A. E. Izmailov, BEDNAIA MASHA (1801), N. P. Brusilov, ISTORIIA BEDNOI MARII (1803), I. Svechnikov, OBOL'SHCHENNAIA GENRIETTA (1801).

15. Belinskii, POLNOE SOBRANIE SOCHINENII (1955), VIII, 53. I have not

translated the word *bursak*, which has no English equivalent. It is a term identifying a student of a religious seminary, who was maintained at the expense of the sponsoring monastery.

CHAPTER II

1. See Pushkin's "Freedom. An Ode" (1817), "Fables. Noel" (1818), "To Chaa-daev" (1818). His epigram of 1818 on Arakcheev, Alexander's notorious minion, pro-claimed his worthy of Sand's dagger!
2. V. G. Belinskii, POLNOE SOBRANIE SOCHINENII (1917), XI, 330.
3. SYN OTECHESTVA, 1820, No. 34, 15. "Kakaia zhe ona [poema]? Bogatyr-skaia. . . volshebnaia. . . shutochnaia. . ."
4. N. I. Mordovchenko, RUSSKAIA KRITIKA PERVOI CHETVERTI XIX-GO VEKA (Moskva-Leningrad, 1959), 162.
5. The essay was subsequently published as a separate booklet under the auspices of the society.
6. *narod* means *people, mesto* means *place;* the *-nost'* suffix is a feature of ab-stract nouns.
7. A full inventory of Pushkin's references to himself as a romantic can be found in my "Pushkin's Concept of Romanticism," STUDIES IN ROMANTICISM. Vol. III (Autumn, 1963), No. 1, 25-26.
8. Bestuzhev's theories were expressed in "A Look at Russian Literature in the Course of 1824 and the Beginning of 1825," published in POLAR STAR FOR 1825. Pushkin drafted a rebuttal, "An Objection to the Article of A. Bestuzhev," but he did not publish it.
9. Pushkin valued Goethe above Byron. In TABLE-TALK he states, "Goethe had a great influence upon Byron. Faust agitated the imagination of Childe Harold. Twice Byron tried to clash with this Giant of romantic poetry—and ended up lame, like Jacob."
10. The neglect of fiction is seen in the fact that Batteaux's BASIC RULES OF LITERATURE, published in 1807 in Moscow, mentions only oratorical, epistolary, sci-entific and historical prose, completely ignoring fictional tales and other forms of *belles-lettres.* See Jozef Smaga, ANTONI POGORIELSKI. ŻYCIE I TWÓRCZOŚĆ NA TLE EPOKI (Warsaw, 1970), p. 15. This book provides an excellent account of the back-ground of the Romantic period and merits translation into English.

CHAPTER III

1. To keep the record straight, both Bulgarin and Senkovsky were Poles whose careers had led them to Petersburg. Polish spellings: Bułharyn and Sękowski.
2. THE NEVA ALMANAC appeared yearly until 1833 and again in 1846-1847; NORTHERN FLOWERS ceased publication with its eighth issue in 1832. See my BARON ANTON DELVIG'S "NORTHERN FLOWERS," LITERARY ALMANAC OF THE PUSHKIN PLEIAD (Carbondale, Illinois: Southern Illinois University Press, 1968.
3. Livonia is the term used to designate what is now Estonia and Latvia. Revel (English spelling Reval), now known as Tallinn, is on the Gulf of Finland facing Helsinki. Lauren Leighton's useful ALEXANDER BESTUZHEV-MARLINSKY (Boston: Twayne Publishers, 1975) appeared after I had written what follows about this author.

4. ESSAI CRITIQUE SUR L'HISTOIRE DE LA LIVONIE SUIVI D'UN TA-
BLEAU DE L'ETAT ACTUAL DE CETTE PROVINCE (Dorpat, 1817), vol. 3, 108.

CHAPTER IV

1. Bestuzhev did not use his pseudonym, Marlinsky, for any of his contributions
in POLAR STAR. Still, we shall refer to him by his *nom de plume*, because it became
better known than his real name and helps to avoid confusing him with his brother.
2. In this variation of the historical tale, Marlinsky avoids authorial play with his
readers. However, in some later examples of this genre, he reverts to the narrational
whims of Karamzin in NATALIA, THE BOYAR'S DAUGHTER.
3. *Berkut* means *golden eagle*. The brigand bears this name because of his pred-
atory occupation.
4. Leighton rates this tale very highly, "perhaps, the best single piece of prose
writing in Russia prior to the 1830's." *Op. cit.,* 80. Personally, I think it one of the least
interesting of his works, although I would admit that it contains much of the typical
Marlinsky that was later to become formulaic for Romanticism.
5. "Chto budet, to budet, chto budet, to budet, a budet to, chto Bog dast."
6. Orest Somov's KIKIMORA [MONSTER], which appeared in NORTHERN
FLOWERS FOR 1830, represents a much more sophisticated development of the
skaz technique.
7. In "On the 'Livonian' Tales of the Decembrists," S.G. Isakov notes that the
historicism and ethnographic content which one might have expected of Nikolay Bestuzhev, who published historical notes on Holland and on the Russian fleet, are almost absent. See TRUDY PO RUSSKOI I SLAVIANSKOI FILOLOGII, VIII, UCHENYE ZA-
PISKI TARTUSKOGO GOSUDARSTVENNOGO UNIVERSITETA, 1965, 33-80.
8. They are also known as the Archive Youths (arkhivnye iunoshi), as several of
them had positions in the archives of the Ministery of Foreign Affairs. They were generally students of German idealistic philosophy and partisans of German Romanticism.
9. See V.T. Adams, " ' Estonskaia povest' ' V. K. Kiukhel'bekera," IZVESTIIA
AKADEMII NAUK SSSR, Otdelenie literatury i iazyka, 1956, vol. 4, no. 3258. This
study is most revealing with respect to the extent and accuracy of Kuechelbecker's
knowledge of Estonian history and customs. In the early part of his article Adams
claims that ". . . ADO proves that he [Kuechelbecker] was acquainted with the past of
the people occupying this region and with many ethnographic details of the life of the
Estonians," but much of Adam's study, and in particular his footnotes, demonstrates
clearly that at best Kuechelbecker had only a dilettante's knowledge of these matters.
10. Among others, dshcher', liko, breg, glas, dlan', veshchat', prag, deviat' na-
desiat', glagolet'. However, the syntax is post-Karamzin.
11. In 1820 in THE NEVA SPECTATOR, Kuechelbecker had published another,
considerably longer, fantastic journey. Entitled EUROPEAN LETTERS [EVROPEI-
SKIE PIS'MA], the correspondent is a 26th century American who visits Spain and
Italy. His letters concern history, philosophy, national characteristics, the pleasures
of nature, the qualities of the man of virtue, and there is a measure of allusion to contemporary events (that is, circa 1820). The theme of citizenship is strongly developed,
particularly in the one fictional character, Dobrov (Mr. Goodman), a paragon of right
thinking, proper behavior, and so forth. There is no dialogue and no plot. The piece is of
interest as an example of clarity of exposition and simplicity of expression in the treatment of historical and philosophical material.

CHAPTER V

1. See Carl Proffer, "Washington Irving in Russia," COMPARATIVE LITERATURE XX (Fall, 1968), no. 4, 330-331. There is a rich scholarship on Hoffmann's role in Russian fiction, especially his effect upon Gogol. See Stender-Petersen, "Gogol und die deutsche Romantik," EUPHORION, 1922; S. Shtein, PUSHKIN I GOFMAN (Dorpat, 1927); N. Nilsson, GOGOL ET PETERSBOURG (Stockholm, 1954); Norman Ingham, E.T.A. HOFFMANN IN RUSSIAN LITERATURE.

CHAPTER VI

1. This was first published in London by Alexander Herzen. It is reprinted in DEKABRISTY, 439-442.

CHAPTER VII

1. To satisfy the reader's curiosity, we should note the best travelogues in later issues of NORTHERN FLOWERS: EXCERPTS FROM LETTERS FROM ITALY, by P---y (1825 and 1827), A JOURNEY FROM SAINT BERNARD, by Victor Tepliakov (1831), BAIKAL, A LETTER TO O.M. SOMOV., by Nikitin Bichurin (1832). Somov's own LETTERS FROM FINLAND, three in THE NORTHERN BEE in 1829 and three in THE LITERARY GAZETTE in 1830, are the best of all of these. Very interesting also are Petr Sumarokov's LETTERS FROM THE CAUCASUS, published in THE MOSCOW TELEGRAPH in 1830.
2. ISTORIIA GOSUDARSTVA ROSSIISKOGO, IX, 261. Italics Karamzin's.
3. In this narrative poem, Wallenrod, a knight whose exploits elevate him to the position of Grand Master of the Teutonic Order, is finally exposed as a Lithuanian patriot who devoted his life to destroying the Knights of the Sword from within.

CHAPTER VIII

1. See A.G. Tseitlin, STANOVLENIE REALIZMA RUSSKOI LITERATURY (Moskva, 1965), 98. He reports that over seven hundred of these sketches were published between 1839 and 1848.
2. Tzvetan Todorov has defined this state in which the reader is uncertain whether he is faced with the supernatural or only with its appearance as an essential quality of the fantastic in literature. See INTRODUCTION A LA LITTERATURE FANTASTIQUE (Paris: Editions du Seuil, 1970), 46.
3. Josef Smaga, ANTONI POGORIELSKI. p. 49.
4. Smaga, op. cit., 74.
5. A footnote to this didactic summation appeared about a decade later in Prince V.F. Odoevsky's THE FAIRY TALE OF WHY IT IS DANGEROUS FOR YOUNG LADIES TO WALK IN A CROWD ALONG NEVSKY PROSPECT, which comically depicts how individualistic young girls become mannequins once they accept the fashions and mores of the *haut monde*.
6. ANTONII POGORELSKII. DVOINIK. MONASTYRKA (Moskva, 1960), 14.

7. VLIUBLENNYI BES, A.S. Pushkin, POLNOE SOBRANIE SOCHINENII V DESIATI TOMAKH (Moskva-Leningrad, 1949), VI, 625.

CHAPTER IX

1. Italics mine.
2. V.A. Pokrovskii, PROBLEMA VOZNIKNOVENIIA RUSSKOGO "NRAVST-VENNOSATIRICHESKOGO" ROMANA (O GENEZISE "IVANA VYZHIGINA") (Leningrad, 1933), 35 pp.
3. M.B. Finch and E. Allison Peers, THE ORIGINS OF FRENCH ROMANTICISM (London, Constable, 1920), 238.

CHAPTER X
1. See Frank Mocha, TADEUSZ BULHARYN (FADDEI V. BULGARIN) 1789-1859: A STUDY IN LITERARY MANEUVER (Antemurale XVII, Rome, 1974), 177.
2. Iz rasskazov puteshestvennika or Iz rasskazov puteshestvennikov.
3. The late Pushkinist, Prof. Waclaw Lednicki, suggested that Mickiewicz was the prototype for the improvisor in Pushkin's EGYPTIAN NIGHTS.
4. Earlier I noted that Marlinsky's EISEN CASTLE is also narrated in the individualized idiom of an army captain, encountered while the author was *en route* to Revel. However the attitude and beliefs of the captain are of no consequence to the story and, in fact, although his language is distinctly colloquial, it does not reveal his personality.

CHAPTER XI

1. Chapter IV was printed in NORTHERN FLOWERS FOR 1829 but was unsigned.
2. RUSSIA, POLAND AND THE WEST (New York, 1954), 213 ff.
3. A Soviet acquaintance of mine once attributed this act of supreme *insouciance* to Lermontov at the time of his duel with Martynov, but that is simply a case of confusing fiction with fact.
4. At Skulyani 15,000 Turkish cavalry decimated a force of some 700 Greek liberationists.
5. Purrful's given name was actually Aristarchus.
6. Pushkin's parody of POOR LIZA is also, paradoxically, a parody of Pyotr Mashkov's MARIYA, OR THE TRIBULATIONS OF THE PRODIGAL DAUGHTER, which was written three years *after* Pushkin's work.

CHAPTER XII

1. See my BARON ANTON DELVIG'S "NORTHERN FLOWERS," cited above.
2. B. Bukhshtab, "Pervye romany Vel'tmana," RUSSKAIA PROZA (Leningrad, 1926), 196.
3. See Pushkin's letter to Lazhechnikov of November 3, 1835. Pushkin also objected to Lazhechnikov's gross caricature of the poet and theoretician Vasily Trediakovsky, who is depicted as a venal toady and talentless boaster.

4. See notes to I. Lazhechnikov, LEDIANOI DOM (Moskva, 1956), 26.

CHAPTER XIII

1. His name is usually spelled Weltman or Weltmann, presumably to reflect German derivation. However, the family originally was Swedish, Weldman, and Russified its name to *Vel'tman*.
2. Acclaim did not necessarily generate large or multiple editions. THE WANDERER was originally published in 600 copies and its second edition, of the same size, appeared only in 1841. The first printing of KOSHCHEY was only 1,250 copies. See J. Gebhard, THE EARLY NOVELS OF A.F. VEL'TMAN, Indiana University Ph.D. 1968, 49.
3. B. Bukhshtab, "Pervye romany Vel'tmana," VOPROSY POETIKI (Leningrad, 1926), 192-231.

CHAPTER XIV

1. Belinsky's "Letter to Gogol" circulated in handwritten copies and was considered so dangerous that in 1849 the young Dostoevsky was sentenced to death for reading the letter to the clandestine Petrashevsky Circle.
2. NIKOLAI GOGOL (Norfolk, Connecticut: New Directions Books, 1944); Erlich's book was published in 1969 by Yale University Press, New Haven and London. Also useful is F.C. Driessen, GOGOL AS A SHORT STORY WRITER (The Hague: Mouton & Co., 1965).
3. Erlich credits his predecessors for ideas and findings; Nabokov seldom does.
4. Reviews in Polevoy's MOSCOW TELEGRAPH and Bulgarin's NORTHERN BEE must have caused poor Gogol to wince. Fortunately, he had used the pseudonym of A. Alov, and Orest Somov protected Gogol's anonymity in his brief remarks about the work in NORTHERN FLOWERS FOR 1830, where he professed to detect in it signs of talent. See my BARON DELVIG'S "NORTHERN FLOWERS," 67-68. Somov was useful to Gogol in his early career, a fact which Gogol seems to have ignored.
5. Belkin collected written versions of others' stories, whereas Panko himself transcribed the tales related at his 'evenings.'
6. See his NIKOLAI GOGOL, as cited.
7. At the end of his introduction, Rudy Panko says that this game, which is called *tesnaia baba*, is played by school boys, who crowd on a bench until one group pushes the other off.

CHAPTER XV

1. See Norman Ingham's E.T.A. HOFFMANN IN RUSSIA, 1822-1845, Harvard dissertation. This is the fullest treatment of the subject and unfortunately no published version exists.
2. In adapting his stories for inclusion in RUSSIAN NIGHTS, Odoevsky often altered them extensively. For example, the Piranesi tale has a completely different setting. A translation of RUSSIAN NIGHTS was published in 1965 by Dutton & Co., with an informative introduction by Ralph Matlaw. The most extensive study of this author, by the Russian scholar P.N. Sakulin, has never been translated into English.

CHAPTER XVI

1. My translation of this work into English can be found in RUSSIAN LITER-
ATURE TRIQUARTERLY, No. 8 (Winter, 1974) and also in RUSSIAN ROMANTIC
PROSE: AN ANTHOLOGY (Ann Arbor: Translation Press, 1979).

CHAPTER XVII

1. Begichev subsequently wrote OLGA, OR THE RUSSIAN GENTRY'S WAY
OF LIFE AT THE BEGINNING OF THE PRESENT CENTURY [OL'GA, ILI BYT
RUSSKIKH DVORIAN V NACHALE NYNESHNOGO STOLETIIA] (1840) in four
parts and PROVINCIAL SCENES [PROVINTSIAL'NYE STSENY] (1840), during the
period that interests us.
2. I have at my disposal only the 1840 edition of ABBADDONNA, which does
not contain the epilogue of the original version. Happily, E.Z. Tsybenko in "Osobennosti
pol'skoi i russkoi romanticheskoi prozy 30-40 gg. XIX veka," published by Moscow
University in 1973 and representing his contribution to the Seventh International Congress of Slavists in Warsaw, 1973, provides a summary of this epilogue: "The continuation of the novel is an accumulation of passions, crimes, abductions. Eleanora persecutes
Henrietta; Baron Hillei, in order to get hold of documents which Eleanora needs, stran-
gles the owner of these documents. Reichenbach learns that an abduction of Henrietta is
taking place, but is himself abducted; Eleanora is ready to kill him, but at the last moment, under the influence of love, helps him escape, and she herself takes poison. The
author, obviously, was not satisfied with this epilogue and therefore did not include it
in the second edition of the novel (1840)." See page 44.
3. I have treated this story at greater length than it deserves, but for a reason: in
discussions of the *Kuenstlernovelle* mention is always made of this work, usually in a
footnote, but no evaluation or description is provided. What I have to say here is intended to make other commentators confident that they may spare themselves the peni-
tential experience of reading these three volumes.

CHAPTER XVIII

1. Kaverin's book was republished in 1966 with corrections and new information.
In his introduction the author also speaks highly of the monograph by my fellow-student
and friend, Louis Pedrotti, JOZEF JULIAN SEKOWSKI, THE GENESIS OF A LITER-
ARY ALIEN (Berkley and Los Angeles: University of California Press, 1965). Pedrotti
employs the Polish spelling of the author's name.
2. The foregoing discussion relies heavily upon Pedrotti's monograph.

CHAPTER XX

1. The unexpected revelation is not, however, original, for in Narezhny's BUR-
SAK the hero, Neon, learns after his marriage to Neonila that his ideal of femininity,
Melitina, is actually his sister.
2. Eugenia's desire to fly is reiterated by Turgenev's Asya, Tolstoy's Natasha, and
Ostrovsky's Katerina (THE STORM).

CHAPTER XXI

1. The matter of the tale's narrator has caused concern among the commentators. When the work first appeared separately in the almanac HOUSEWARMING it bore the subtitle, ONE OF THE UNPUBLISHED TRUE STORIES OF BEEKEEPER RUDY PANKO, but this was not retained when the work was included in the MIRGOROD collection of 1835. Victor Erlich says that Panko narrates the tale, "only he has become a downright fool" [Erlich, 71], while Driessen says the narrator is "Gogol in a disguise of which he again and again deliberately draws back the folds" [Driessen, 175]. In "Gogol's Mockery of Romantic Taste: Varieties of Language in the Tale of the Two Ivans," Paul Debreczeny establishes with ponderous documentation the various language levels in the story, asserting that "There is no doubt, then, that Rudy Pan'ko's voice can be heard in the tale, whether addressed to a local group or to a distant reader. His voice, however, is not the only one we hear: indeed, it is sometimes drowned out by a chorus of other voices." The "chorus" of which Debreczeny speaks is a rather variegated style of narration incorporating officialese, romantic cliches, sentimental effusion, grandiloquent language, which appears to be a satire on contemporary romantic taste as exemplified by Bulgarin, Zagoskin, Polevoy and other second-raters who enjoyed public favor during the thirties. See Debreczeny's article in CANADIAN-AMERICAN SLAVIC STUDIES, Fall 1973, 327-341.

2. Erlich expands interestingly on this subject, *op. cit.,* 83 ff.

CHAPTER XXII

1. Lermontov took pride in his Scots ancestor, George Learmont, an artillerist-mercenary who served the Poles and later Muscovy in the Time of Troubles, and through him he "traced" his genealogy to Thomas the Rhymer. However, he also liked the idea of ties to the Spanish dukes of Lerma.

CHAPTER XXIV

1. Some of the ideas expressed here appeared in 1838 in Lermontov's pessimistic poem MEDITATION [DUMA], which begins, "With Sorrow I Look Upon Our Generation" [Pechal'no ia glazhu na nashe pokolenie].

2. Probably eyebrows will be raised at my translation of *bedovik*, which currently does not mean *schlemiel*. However, the word serves perfectly to describe the innocuous and hapless hero of this story, who comments upon the application of the term *bedovik* to himself: "I am simply a *bedovik*. Let anyone interpret this word as he will or may, but I understand it. And how could I not understand, if it was invented by me and, obviously, for me? Yes, with this word, one may say, I have enriched the Russian language, explaining its meaning by my very actions!"

CHAPTER XXV

1. Cf. Boris Eikhenbaum, "Kak sdelana 'Shinel' ' Gogolia," SKVOZ' LITERATURU, VOPROSY POETIKI, 4 (Leningrad, 1924), 171-195; Dmitrii Chizevskii, "O 'Shineli' Gogolia," SOVREMMENYE ZAPISKI, 67 (Paris, 1938).

2. Chizhevsky has commented upon the odd effect of the frequent appearance in this story of the word *even*, which in normal usage suggests the superlative but here leads to ludicrous betrayal of the reader's expectations. One must also watch for Gogol's gratuitous *already*.

3. Eikhenbaum sees this sentimental tirade as a deliberate stylistic contrast to the unique idiom normally employed by the narrator. Its function, then, is orchestral rather than didactic. Vasily Rozanov interprets the passage as an authorial wail: "Beyond all doubt, the lyrical excerpt quoted above is an outburst of deep sorrow on the part of the author at the sight of what he has created; it is he who 'shudders' upon completing a work of 'savage coarseness,' it is he who buries his face in his hands' . . . ." "How the Character Akaky Akakiyevich Originated," ESSAYS IN RUSSIAN LITERATURE, selected, edited, translated and with an introduction by Spencer E. Roberts (Athens: Ohio University Press, 1968), 381. Rozanov goes on to note that this type of passage occurs in those works of Gogol which are devoid of positive characters but not in the Ukrainian stories, which do have positive types.

4. The *already quite taller* [uzhe gorazdo vyshe] of the last sentence perhaps may disturb the reader's sense of balance.

5. You will recall that Pushkin's THE STATION MASTER also satirized this type of story.

CHAPTER XXVI

1. There are still in print older works in English on Lermontov: Janko Lavrin's LERMONTOV (New York: Hillary House, 1959) and my own MIKHAIL LERMONTOV (Carbondale, Southern Illinois University Press, 1963). The first focuses more on Lermontov's poetry, whereas my study is primarily concerned with his prose. More recent works include: Laurence Kelly's LERMONTOV: TRAGEDY IN THE CAUCASUS (New York: Brazillev, 1978), a biography; G.J.G. Turner's PECHORIN (Birmingham, England: University of Birmingham, 1978), concerned with A HERO OF OUR TIMES; John Garrard's MIKHAIL LERMONTOV (Boston: Twayne, 1982), which its author describes as "the first full-length English language study of his life and the entire spectrum of his works in both poetry and prose."

2. Guy Daniels has translated this work. He gives it higher marks than I would, asserting its potential superiority to A HERO OF OUR TIMES. See A LERMONTOV READER, edited, translated, with an introduction by Guy Daniels New York: Macmillan, 1965).

3. "Taman" was first published by itself in 1840 in NOTES OF THE FATHERLAND. "Bela" and "The Fatalist" had appeared the previous year in the same periodical.

4. The critic Chernyshevsky credited Lermontov with the first example of this technique which was later widely used by Tolstoy. Professor Gleb Struve has written on this subject in "*Monologue Interieur*: The Origins of the Formula and the First Statement of Its Possibilities," PUBLICATIONS OF THE MODERN LANGUAGE ASSOCIATION OF AMERICA, LXIX (December, 1954), 1101-1111.

CHAPTER XXVII

1. Those who wish more detailed analyses are advised to consult the works of Nabokov and Erlich mentioned earlier; the translation by Bernard Guilbert Guerney is recommended.

335

336